Monitoring American Federalism

Monitoring American Federalism examines some of the nation's most significant controversies in which state legislatures have attempted to be active partners in the process of constitutional decision-making. Christian G. Fritz looks at interposition, which is the practice of states opposing federal government decisions that were deemed unconstitutional. Interposition became a much-used constitutional tool to monitor the federal government and organize resistance, beginning with the Constitution's ratification and continuing through the present affecting issues including gun control, immigration, and healthcare. Though the use of interposition was largely abandoned because of its association with nullification and the Civil War, recent interest reminds us that the federal government cannot run roughshod over states, and that states lack any legitimate power to nullify federal laws. Insightful and comprehensive, this appraisal of interposition breaks new ground in American political and constitutional history, and can help us preserve our constitutional system and democracy.

Christian G. Fritz is Emeritus Professor of Law at the University of New Mexico School of Law. He is the author of *American Sovereigns: The People and America's Constitutional Tradition before the Civil War*.

STUDIES IN LEGAL HISTORY

See the Studies in Legal History series website at
http://studiesinlegalhistory.org/

Studies in Legal History

EDITORS

Lisa Ford, *University of New South Wales*
Sarah Barringer Gordon, *University of Pennsylvania*
Thomas McSweeney, *William & Mary Law School*
Reuel Schiller, *University of California, Hastings College of the Law*
Taisu Zhang, *Yale Law School*

Ada Maria Kuskowski, *Vernacular Law: Writing and the Reinvention of Customary Law in Medieval France*

E. Claire Cage, *The Science of Proof: Forensic Medicine in Modern France*

Kristin A. Olbertson, *The Dreadful Word: Speech Crime and Polite Gentlemen in Massachusetts, 1690–1776*

Edgardo Pérez Morales, *Unraveling Abolition: Legal Culture and Slave Emancipation in Colombia*

Lyndsay Campbell, *Truth and Privilege: Libel Law in Massachusetts and Nova Scotia, 1820–1840*

Sara M. Butler, *Pain, Penance, and Protest: Peine Forte et Dure in Medieval England*

Michael Lobban, *Imperial Incarceration: Detention without Trial in the Making of British Colonial Africa*

Stefan Jurasinski and Lisi Oliver, *The Laws of Alfred: The Domboc and the Making of Anglo-Saxon Law*

Sascha Auerbach, *Armed with Sword and Scales: Law, Culture, and Local Courtrooms in London, 1860–1913*

Monitoring American Federalism

The History of State Legislative Resistance

CHRISTIAN G. FRITZ

University of New Mexico

CAMBRIDGE
UNIVERSITY PRESS

CAMBRIDGE
UNIVERSITY PRESS

Shaftesbury Road, Cambridge CB2 8EA, United Kingdom

One Liberty Plaza, 20th Floor, New York, NY 10006, USA

477 Williamstown Road, Port Melbourne, VIC 3207, Australia

314–321, 3rd Floor, Plot 3, Splendor Forum, Jasola District Centre, New Delhi – 110025, India

103 Penang Road, #05–06/07, Visioncrest Commercial, Singapore 238467

Cambridge University Press is part of Cambridge University Press & Assessment, a department of the University of Cambridge.

We share the University's mission to contribute to society through the pursuit of education, learning and research at the highest international levels of excellence.

www.cambridge.org
Information on this title: www.cambridge.org/9781009325578
DOI: 10.1017/9781009325608

First published 2023

Printed in the United Kingdom by TJ Books Limited, Padstow Cornwall

A catalogue record for this publication is available from the British Library.

ISBN 978-1-009-32557-8 Hardback

To my wife Marlene and to Professor Robert Middlekauff,
dedicated scholar and teacher

Contents

Acknowledgments

No one conceptualizes, writes or struggles with a book alone. During the creation of this work, I have received much appreciated support and encouragement from many friends and hiking buddies, including Teresa Colwell, Ken Finney, David W. Greenthal, Mike Jacobs, Walter Kopp, Janet and Rob McCray, Linde Mohr, Maryann Phipps, Arthur Rypinski, and Glenn Westreich. Joe Franaszek, as ever, has been a tremendous sounding board during the countless miles we've trekked over the years and he deserves credit for pointing me towards Southern legislatures during the Civil War.

My family has also been an indispensable source of strength and I am blessed with two wonderful sisters, Marilu Reid and Diana Boyce. While seeing little of the manuscript but much of the author, their loving presence is very much a part of this book. Nana has had my back even before I could walk and her pride in the completion of this project is reciprocated by my gratitude for all that she has meant to me. Her three daughters, Jessica Solberg, Nikki Boyce, and Kaitlin Boyce (and their loved ones) have also left their mark on this book through their care and concern for the author. Alea Rae Boyce Yokom was born during the pandemic and the final stages of this work and she will never really know how much joy her arrival has brought to all of us.

Numerous colleagues and friends have also provided important help. Tony Freyer, Ron Formisano, and Mel Yazawa each gave valuable feedback on an earlier introduction to the book and Todd Estes read a version of Chapters 1 and 3 as well as the Introduction and made extremely helpful suggestions. Reid Mitchell provided a close reading of the entire manuscript late in the process, and John D. Gordan III undertook that task twice – each time saving me from egregious errors. Their commitment to the author and the project is deeply appreciated.

For thirty-five years I have had the benefit of the staff of the law library of the University of New Mexico (UNM) School of Law. With this book, as with preceding publications, I am most grateful for their assistance in locating and providing elusive source material. My colleagues and friends from my time at the law school, Barbara Bergman and April Land, have done much to lift my spirits.

Two additional friends and colleagues at UNM School of Law deserve special recognition: Michael Browde and Jim Ellis. Each brought profound knowledge of American constitutional law along with unstinting support for the author and commitment to this book. Each has read versions of this work multiple times – in Michael's case an astonishing three times –on each occasion making this a far better book than it otherwise would have been. I am humbled by their friendship and their gift of time.

I am grateful for two wonderful editors. Sally Barringer Gordon, my editor for the Studies in Legal History, expressed early enthusiasm for the book, has been a joy to work with, and has provided extraordinarily helpful guidance in facilitating the review process. I also wish to thank Cecelia Cancellaro, my editor at Cambridge University Press, who challenged me to reduce the length of the manuscript and, in so doing, helped me produce a much better book. Thanks are also due to Ken Moxham for excellent copyediting.

Teachers often impact their students in ways that go unnoticed. As a young history graduate student at Berkeley, I was fortunate to have numerous role models – although none finer than Robert Middlekauff. During a lunch more than ten years ago, Professor Middlekauff made an insightful observation that led me to a broader study of the nature of political representation in America and, in particular, changes in the relationship between representatives and their constituents as a consequence of the widespread acceptance of popular sovereignty. The present book represents a digression from that much broader study of the history of American democracy.

My greatest debt is to my wife, Marlene Keller. It has been my great fortune to have married a Berkeley-trained historian and superb editor who has courageously – and at the risk of marital harmony – *always* told me the truth about my writing. Her commitment to the editing and refinement of this book makes it as much her book as mine.

Introduction

Americans have monitored federalism from the beginning of the republic, questioning whether the newly established government was more attuned to a Jeffersonian vision of sovereign states resting on the sovereignty of the people of each state – or a Hamiltonian vision of a consolidated nation resting on the sovereignty of one national people. The answer was that it was both, but it took considerable time and effort to determine the consequences for American life and government. The Constitution created what James Madison called a "compound republic" – neither a wholly national government nor one in which states retained their entire sovereignty. This shared sovereignty inevitably tested the balance of powers between nation and states. The absence of a clear delineation between the two levels of government meant that a static equilibrium had always been an ideal, but never a fact.[1]

Instead, the Constitution's tensions generated a dynamic federalism that led to continuous struggles over the balance of power. Americans expected government officials and elected representatives to act as guardians of their rights by taking appropriate constitutional action to maintain a proper balance of federalism. At times, the constant uncertainty and debate undermined the Union, most dramatically with the Civil War and in the aftermath of the postwar Constitution during Reconstruction.

From the beginning, Americans disagreed about what the equilibrium of federalism meant. Some believed the national government only possessed those powers expressly granted in the Constitution – with states *permanently* retaining all other powers. Others believed the national government's powers could expand to accomplish what was necessary and proper to sustain the nation – and that states had already surrendered sovereignty to achieve that purpose. Finally, Madison and his allies argued that there was no bright line between national and state sovereignty. Instead, the question of divided sovereignty would be forged incrementally – in a case-by-case and collaborative nation-state process.

Most debates over divided sovereignty involved the protection of slavery. Slavery and racism have played a key role in much of American political and legal history. Americans with entrenched interests in the system of human bondage constantly calculated how shifts in national versus state powers might affect their interests. Ironically, these slaveholder interests were sometimes protected and even promoted by national power and policies – and the Constitution itself. Undoubtedly, the issue of divided sovereignty played out in sustained debates and conflicts at both state and national levels. Other policies and interests – including debt and taxation, banking, internal improvements and police powers – also helped shape American federalism, even though slavery was often the most fought-over and consequential focus of disagreement after 1830.

Monitoring American Federalism focuses on some of the most significant political controversies of the nation's history where the disequilibrium of federalism was most keenly felt. It explores the ways that states framed their dissent from actions of the national government. Some have blamed the opponents of the Constitution, who became known as Anti-Federalists, for creating a constitutional legacy characterized by a local perspective that resisted change and was rooted in paranoia about anything that challenged states' rights and slavery. Yet, this book shows that for much of the time the constitutional dialogue was more nuanced. "Tension and conflict" were central to the evolving American political tradition, as Saul Cornell has pointed out – and "dissenting voices" helped shape the broader conversation about constitutional rights and authority.[2]

Ideally, public debate over political issues should not become dissent that would frustrate and undermine the government. However, political opponents routinely accused one another of overreaching, tyrannical behavior, and unwarranted deviation from the Constitution. By examining the contours of state resistance, we can better understand the issues that fueled the rhetoric surrounding the Constitution and American government. This debate reflected the "inherent elasticity and dynamism" of federalism, arguably a strength and not a weakness of the constitutional design. Such insights invite each generation to identify constitutional issues and consider what the appropriate constitutional balance should be.[3]

Monitoring American Federalism shows that state resistance to policies and actions of the national government frequently invoked interposition. Interposition was a *constitutional* tool that, unlike judicial review, did not have an immediate constitutional effect. Designed to work through political pressure, interposition sought to maintain constitutional balance between the two levels of government. Even though the achievement of a perfect equipoise was for all intents and purposes impossible, interposition was valuable. By participating in the debate about the equilibrium between the national and state governments, state legislatures developed a tradition of using interposition to sound the alarm about overreaching. This crucial method of monitoring federalism has generally been overlooked and misunderstood.

Historians often associate interposition only with South Carolina's John C. Calhoun and the Nullification crisis of the 1830s. That is, they paint interposition as part of a sovereign states' rights tradition defending slavery that inexorably led to Southern secession and the Civil War. However, before its appropriation by nullifiers and those invested in slavery who claimed the right of individual states to defy national laws and decisions of the Supreme Court, interposition emerged in the 1790s as a response to critics who worried that the Constitution's grant of national powers would obliterate state authority. In acknowledging some degree of divided sovereignty between the national government and state governments, early uses of interposition expressed a means of preserving the equilibrium of federalism, rather than a claim for state sovereignty that could displace national authority.

A crucial difference existed between the earlier and the later invocation of interposition. Those who identified states' rights that could legitimately be defended through sounding the alarm were not following the same ideology as the later sovereign states' rights theorists who embraced nullification. The gulf between the two was underscored in the 1830s, when those who had embraced interposition rejected nullification. This study recovers the history of interposition and its practice before interposition was distorted and evolved into the device of nullification. To be sure, there was an intellectual lineage and trajectory between the earliest uses of interposition and what would become nullification. Nonetheless, there was a great divide between those who advocated for the rights of state legislatures to question the federal government on any constitutional issue through interposition – and those who supported nullification.[4]

* * * * * *

This book explores three interrelated themes: (1) the thoughts of James Madison pertaining to American federalism; (2) the ways in which states exercised a role as constitutional sentinels resisting what they perceived as constitutional overreaching by the national government through interposition; and (3) the useful purpose that state resistance has played in constitutional politics. In tracing the practice of interposition, this study does not assess whether particular actions of Congress, the executive branch, or the judiciary were unconstitutional or impermissibly altered the balance of federalism.

This focus on interposition does not include many dramatic instances of aggressive assertions of state sovereignty, particularly in the context of Native peoples, because these state responses to their Native populations were often an outright defiance of national authority far closer to nullification than interposition. Nor does this book focus on James Madison, except as his thinking is pertinent to the larger discussion of the theory and uses of the constitutional tool of interposition. Instead, the intent is to explore how and why state legislators believed they were legitimately exercising a role as one of the monitors of federalism and had a right to bring attention to potential examples of the national government acting beyond its constitutional authority. Thus, interposition is helpful in understanding how legislators insisted on their right to participate in shaping the meaning and understanding of the American Constitution.[5]

This book is not an extension of my prior work on popular sovereignty. In an earlier work, *American Sovereigns: The People and America's Constitutional Tradition before the Civil War,* I explored the profound impact that the principle of the people's sovereignty had on the course of American constitutionalism. *American Sovereigns* described how the emerging understanding of the fundamental role for the sovereignty of the people also implied a right and duty of the people to scrutinize and comment on the workings of their governments, whether at the state or national level. Contemplating what might be meant by the people's sovereignty soon led to multiple depictions of 'the people' on whose authority the national government rested. These depictions ranged from envisioning a single national American people or the sovereign people of each state or the collective people of all the states acting in their highest sovereign capacity. In short, *American Sovereigns* explored how identifying the sovereign authority represented by 'We the People' was not self-evident and produced more than one possible answer. Indeed, my research indicates a clear divide between expressions of popular sovereignty and state sovereignty.

Instead of being a continuation of my focus on popular sovereignty in *American Sovereigns*, this work deals with how state legislatures, as guardians of the people's rights, sought to play a special role in monitoring the distribution of the powers under the Constitution. Thus, this book focuses on states' rights more than on state sovereignty. The thousands of resolutions passed by state legislatures and sent to their congressional representatives beginning in 1789 displayed an early and persistent determination of the legislatures to shape national laws and policies to reflect the interests of the people they represented.[6]

A crucial subset of those "instructing and requesting" resolutions of state legislatures were resolutions protesting perceived constitutional overreaching by the national government. In declaring a state's detection of constitutional disequilibrium, those resolutions were an "interposition": *a formal state protest against actions of the national government designed to focus public attention and generate interstate political pressure in an effort to reverse the national government's alleged constitutional overreach.* Such resolutions identified the cause of the overreaching and alerted the national government to the state legislature's views by sending the resolutions to members of the state's congressional delegation. State legislatures also routinely requested the state's governor share the resolutions with the legislatures of the other states in an effort to stimulate a coordinated and more effective response.[7]

While interposition was initially described in *The Federalist*, soon after ratification it became a regular practice that was frequently used by state legislatures throughout the country, persisting into the 1870s – even if encumbered with misconceptions. A key development in this political process occurred in 1798 when James Madison authored a series of resolutions for Virginia's legislature that explicitly endorsed and invoked sounding the alarm interposition by declaring the Alien and Sedition Acts unconstitutional. In the Virginia resolutions, Madison described some of the means available to the people when they believed the national government had overstepped its constitutional bounds. These steps included interposition – along with electing different political representatives and seeking constitutional amendments.[8]

But in those resolutions Madison did something else – largely unappreciated at the time and long misunderstood thereafter – that had fateful consequences for American history. In the Third Virginia Resolution, Madison described an even broader theoretical right "to interpose in the final resort" if the federal government overreached its authority in "a deliberate, palpable and dangerous" manner. That vague and troubling statement suggested that a majority of the collective people might be entitled to invoke their authority if the national government exceeded its powers in extraordinary ways. Although Madison described that right as extra-constitutional, that is, existing outside the purview of the Constitution, he insisted that right was constitutionally justified because the right rested on the people of the states "in their highest sovereign capacity" as parties to the constitutional compact. Madison's distinction sowed enormous confusion.

Identifying a constitutional right – albeit a theoretical one – *outside* of the Constitution rested on Madison's view of the hierarchy of governmental authority in America: that while governments rested on constitutions, those constitutions rested on the sovereign power of the people. If the national government overreached in extraordinary ways, the sovereign behind the Constitution retained the right "to interpose" in the final resort.[9]

Thus, Madison's words led his contemporaries and later generations to invoke and misconstrue what they called the 'Principles of '98'. Despite this, Madison maintained his consistent adherence to the distinctions that underlay his formulation of the Virginia Resolutions. For Madison, the Third resolution's authority rested on the constitutional legitimacy of a sovereign people's *theoretical* right to take action when faced with dire circumstances. For others, Madison's words seemed to legitimate extra-constitutional means that included nullification and secession. As Madison would discover, once his own, complex ideas were in the intellectual and political marketplace, those concepts were subject to conflation and distortion. Yet, upon close examination, Madison's reiterations and elaborations of the meaning of the Virginia Resolutions toward the end of his life in the 1830s reveal how well they mirrored the carefully crafted, but complex distinctions of constitutional theory he advanced in 1798 and explained in 1800.

Nonetheless, Madison's language in the Third Virginia resolution effectively narrowed the distance between sounding the alarm interposition and nullification and encouraged the leap from interposition as originally conceived to nullification by those unconcerned with Madison's careful constitutional distinctions. Madison's incautious language might have implied an intellectual pedigree and logical connection between interposition as previously practiced and the new doctrine of nullification. But as a legal and constitutional matter, there was a huge divide between the legitimacy of states to weigh in on the equilibrium of federalism and the assumption that individual states could decide, independent of the Supreme Court, what the Constitution meant. Importantly, participating in the process of examining the balance of power between the federal and state levels of government and expressing an opinion about how that balance was struck was a far cry from states supplanting the decision-making authority of the Supreme Court.

Integral to interposition before the Civil War was the belief that scrutinizing whether governments were operating within the limits of their constitutional authority included the people's elected representatives and was not the monopoly of the Supreme Court. This monitoring was understood to involve many different eyes beyond judicial ones – including those of individual citizens, juries, the press, and most importantly, state legislatures.[10]

Moreover, long before judicial review became an established feature of American government, a concept of so-called "departmental" review held considerable sway. That view assumed each of the three federal branches possessed an equal responsibility for keeping governmental operations within constitutional bounds. Acting as separate sentinels overseeing the operation of government, these various parties and branches of government collectively participated in ensuring the Constitution operated as intended to preserve and protect the liberties and rights of the people who formed the sovereign basis of the Constitution.[11]

The prospect of others besides judges laying claim to a significant role in developing an understanding of the Constitution and helping maintain an appropriate equilibrium of federalism would be challenged by what Jefferson Powell has called "the 'lawyerizing'" of the Constitution. Led by lawyers and prominently by Chief Justice John Marshall, the movement towards 'lawyerization' declared a preeminent and exclusive role for the Supreme Court as the arbiter of disputes over the boundary that separated national from state authority. One aspect of this "legalist" conception of the Constitution believed that "the Constitution had entrusted only the federal judiciary, not the elected branches and not the sovereign people, with the final authority to determine the meaning of the Constitution."[12]

Narrowing the range of those entitled to interpret the Constitution and monitor federalism eventually led to more widespread assertions that the federal judiciary should enjoy a monopoly over the question of whether acts of the national government were within constitutional bounds. The future Chief Justice of the Supreme Court, Charles Evans Hughes, epitomized this position by remarking in 1907 that "the Constitution is what the judges say it is." Such a claim for judicial monopoly discounted an earlier tradition – as well as constitutional design – involving a much wider universe of constitutional interpreters, including state legislatures employing interposition. As interposition competed with judicial interpretation, 'lawyerization' increasingly took hold and eclipsed legislative interposition as the preferred theory and practice – at least in the minds of members of the judiciary and lawyers.[13]

The theory of interposition is part of a constitutional world that featured a role for states that we have largely forgotten, but which is reappearing in efforts today to resist federal authority – whether by blue or red states. In the beginning, America's political leaders were uncertain about what to make of the Constitution while it was being drafted, ratified, and initially debated in Congress. They wrestled over multiple and conflicting "imaginings" about the essence of the document in an effort to "fix" a meaning to the Constitution. The indeterminacy of the Constitution was predicted by James Madison, who, along with others, pointed out the inherent limits of language. For him, a written constitution inevitably introduced doubts until the meaning of the text could be clarified after a sufficient and perhaps a never-ending number of "discussions and adjudications."[14]

If Congress was one obvious place for those ongoing and necessary discussions, state legislatures – invoking the tool of interposition – served as an additional and important venue to provide constitutional meaning and an assessment of the equilibrium of federalism. The fact that state legislatures selected who would serve in the U.S. Senate was an important aspect of that world. The resultant stream of 'instructions' that state legislatures sent to their Senators, as well as 'requests' to their members of Congress, assumed the national councils should not act independently of the wishes and input of the states. Such instructions became a primary means for states to influence the behavior of U.S. Senators until the Seventeenth Amendment transferred the direct election of Senators to the people.

The early history of interposition occurred during a period when a form of state-centric governance held sway against a vision of national dominance. Despite Hamilton's hopes for a consolidated government, Jefferson's vision of a smaller national footprint prevailed for half a century after the Constitution's ratification. Before the Civil War, the national government played a minor part in the lives of most Americans. Only with the war would the national government begin to acquire more sweeping powers and a greater presence relative to the local and state influences that had traditionally bound communities.

Before the Civil War, Southern states used sounding the alarm interposition to proactively invoke states' rights as a sword to protect slavery interests while non-slave states invoked states' rights to protect the rights and liberties of their citizens from the operation of the federal Fugitive Slave Acts. After the Civil War, and particularly during and after Reconstruction, Southern states invoked states' rights as a shield to resist the implementation of the Civil War Amendments – the Thirteenth, Fourteenth, and Fifteenth Amendments that abolished slavery and protected the legal and political rights of freed Blacks. Yet often missing in much scholarship is an appreciation that invocations of states' rights could involve more than simply defending slavery and justifying secession.

In part, the declining practice of interposition can be traced to the growth of powers the federal government assumed during the war. The Civil War Amendments placed even more power in the hands of the national government. Thus, as the enhancement of national authority and power shifted the balance of federalism, what remained in the hands of the states were their reserved rights, now subject to the constraints imposed on them by the new powers granted to the national government. Concerned that the balance of federalism had shifted, it is no wonder that the mantra of states' rights became a common refrain after the war by those who resisted Reconstruction and the efforts to implement the Civil War Amendments. Enhanced federal authority carried with it a renewed insistence that the Supreme Court was the rightful and final constitutional arbiter, lending further support for the 'lawyerization' of the Constitution.

As the process of lawyerization of the Constitution increasingly took hold, the practice of interposition gradually faded from view and ultimately from memory. By the 1870s, the growing assumption that the Supreme Court was the natural arbiter of the constitutional relationship between the federal and state governments largely eclipsed the basic function of interposition to protest perceived imbalance in the equilibrium of federalism. The question that remains is whether interposition as a sounding the alarm function of the states serves any useful purpose today.

The Riddle of Federalism and the Genesis of Interposition

One key feature of the Constitution – the concept of federalism – was unclear when it was introduced, and that lack of clarity threatened the Constitution's ratification by those who feared the new government would undermine state sovereignty. In proposing an arrangement for two levels of government, the framers not only broke new ground, but were criticized for endangering the existence of the state governments. Proponents of the new governmental framework were questioned about the underlying theory of the Constitution as well as how it would operate in practice, and their explanations produced intense and extended debate over how to monitor federalism.

In their famous defense of the Constitution in *The Federalist*, Alexander Hamilton and James Madison described a monitoring role for state legislatures that anticipated the practice of interposition. Although never using the term "interposition," Hamilton and Madison responded to opponents of the Constitution by arguing that state legislatures were uniquely situated to be the voice of the people who would sound the alarm if the general government exceeded its rightful authority. What originated as a debate-like response to opponents of ratification eventually took on a life of its own, producing a settled tradition of monitoring federalism that has largely been overlooked and which laid the groundwork for future conversations about constitutional meaning and federalism's balancing of powers.

In a series of essays written under the pen name "Publius" in 1787 and 1788, Hamilton and Madison detailed the essential features of what became the constitutional tool of interposition later used by state legislatures to monitor the actions of the national government. In responding to critics of the Constitution, Hamilton and Madison described the government that would be created and addressed fears about the balance between national and state authority.[1]

*   *   *   *   *   *

The Framing of the Federal Constitution

The principle of federalism entails a deceptively simple idea that most Americans take for granted today – the division of powers between the national and state governments, each exercising a degree of constitutional authority with direct impact on individuals. This basic description of federalism, however, obscures the intellectual uncertainty that surrounded the concept during the framing of the Constitution and fails to highlight the elusive nature of federalism, both as implemented in the Constitution and as it subsequently operated after ratification. Indeed, allocating power between nation and state remains, according to Gerald Gunther, "the pervasive problem" of American federalism, although some of the arguments that were advanced in favor of ratification contained the idea that state governments might help monitor the federalism established by the Constitution.[2]

The initial confusion over federalism stemmed from its unfamiliarity in 1787. Political theory in the eighteenth century lacked a conceptual category to identify what became the defining characteristic of the Constitution – a division of sovereignty between two different levels of government. At the time, the governmental structure embodied in the Constitution seemed unprecedented and appeared to violate the accepted wisdom that sovereignty was by nature indivisible, necessarily unified and located at one level only. The concept of dividing sovereignty, creating what contemporaries called an "imperium in imperio" (sovereignty within sovereignty) was considered impossible under conventional political theory.[3]

Americans of the founders' generation, including the framers of the Constitution, did not share our modern concept of federalism. While they employed the word "federal," it did not mean then what we attribute to the term today. For them, "federalism" was synonymous with the well-understood concept of "confederalism" – one of two possible types of governmental structure. For the framers, as Martin Diamond has indicated, there were essentially two options: confederal or national. Confederal preserved "the primacy and autonomy of the states," while national provided "unimpeded primacy to the government of the whole society." Thus, the choices for governmental structure entailed either a confederate arrangement in which states each retained all of their sovereign power or a national government that retained the sovereign power "with the localities entirely dependent legally upon the will of the nation."[4]

Given what many Americans considered was the principal defect of the Articles of Confederation – the grant of primary authority to state governments while leaving the national government relatively weak – the framers tried to redress that balance. They sought to grant sufficient authority to the national government without creating a consolidated government while avoiding the problems associated with the Articles that had left the states with their sovereignty intact. The answer proposed by the Philadelphia convention was what Akhil Amar has described as a "third model that balanced centripetal and centrifugal political forces – a harmonious Newtonian solar system in which individual states were preserved as distinct spheres, each with its own mass and pull, maintained in their proper orbit by the gravitational force of a common central body." While some ratification convention delegates invoked astronomical metaphors, most frequently the Constitution was referred to as a "system" with the goal of preserving "harmony" or maintaining "equilibrium" – both of which, like the planetary imagery, entailed striking a balance.[5]

Such a middle ground between the two acknowledged forms of government was unknown at the time and only belatedly became associated with the government proposed by the Constitution. During the constitutional convention, the challenge of vertically distributing power between the two levels of government was readily acknowledged. In the letter transmitting the proposed Constitution to the Confederation Congress, George Washington noted that the convention had found it "difficult to draw with Precision the Lines between those Rights which must be surrendered and those which may be reserved."[6]

Nevertheless, the Constitution incorporated aspects of each of the established modes of government. As Martin Diamond has observed, "We now give the single word federal to the system the framers regarded as possessing both federal and national features." Madison and other framers were hardly as self-conscious, as we are today, that they had succeeded in dividing sovereignty. Nonetheless, as Gordon Wood has noted, by achieving "the remarkable division of power between central and provincial governments" in the Constitution, "Americans offered the world a new way of organizing government." This novelty has also been recognized by Allison LaCroix who credits eighteenth-century Americans with developing a "new federal ideology" resting on "a belief that multiple independent levels of government could legitimately exist within a single polity, and that such an arrangement was not a defect to be lamented but a virtue to be celebrated."[7]

Americans before the Civil War were more likely to refer to what we call the "federal government" as the "general government" or "national government." Indeed, calling the central government established under the Constitution the federal government was a misnomer in eighteenth-century terms. For clarity, what we now consider the federal government will often be referred to in this book as the national government.[8]

While historians have traced the intellectual and institutional precursors of the concept of federalism introduced in the Constitution, many of the framers struggled to describe and understand federalism. For those debating the Constitution, the idea of a confederal as well as a national government was familiar. They were far less comfortable, however, with the idea of a government structured somewhere in between the two familiar models.[9]

The compound nature of the government proposed was fully acknowledged by one of the Constitution's principal architects and defenders: James Madison. During the ratification debates, Madison explained that the convention faced the challenge of establishing a national government with sufficient "stability and energy" while still preserving republicanism, or as Madison also put it, "marking the proper line of partition, between the authority of the general, and that of the State Governments." Madison cautioned Americans not to assume that federalism could be reduced to a bright line of divided authority between the two levels of government. As LaCroix describes it: "the belief in multiplicity, in overlap and concurrence, became a foundational principle of the entire American political enterprise." Apart from the difficulty of conceptualizing federalism and determining jurisdictional boundaries, there were limitations presented by the existing political vocabulary. Collectively, these factors prevented the convention from offering a precise account of federalism. This combination, Madison noted in *Federalist* 37, produced "a certain degree of obscurity" in the balance between the two levels of government created by the Constitution. In the end, Madison mused, the wonder was not that the convention failed to develop an unambiguous theory of federalism with "regular symmetry," but that the delegates came up with something at all.[10]

Madison's warning about the conceptual difficulties and uncertainties inherent in the federalism created by the Constitution was borne out when he tried to describe that system in *Federalist* 39. In analyzing the Constitution, Madison carefully parsed its unique nature – explaining the ways in which the proposed government was "partly federal" and "partly national." In assessing the Constitution's characteristics, Madison lamented that in embarking on their novel enterprise, convention delegates only possessed negative precedents. That is, the Articles of Confederation and similar arrangements rested on incorrect principles. As such, the experience of those confederacies furnishes "no other light than that of beacons, which give warning of the course to be shunned, without pointing out that which ought to be pursued." During and after the ratification debates, Madison reiterated that the government proposed by the Constitution was a unique "compound." Moreover, he reminded observers that the absence of "technical terms or phrases" made it difficult to describe the form of government advanced by the delegates.[11]

In *Federalist* 39 Madison identified the "evident" truth that the government established by the Constitution had to be "strictly republican" to honor "the people of America" and "the fundamental principles of the revolution." In addressing the charge that delegates had created a consolidated national government, Madison responded that the proposed Constitution was neither national nor federal, but "a composition of both." Namely, the Constitution was neither national in the sense of consolidating the states nor was it federal in the sense of establishing a confederacy of sovereign states. Implicit in Madison's description of the mixed federal and national features of the Constitution was his appreciation of an inevitable and ongoing tension in the equilibrium of federalism.[12]

Because the Constitution drew from both traditional models of government, its defense by proponents of the Constitution was complicated and invited criticism from those who viewed the proposal through the lens of the traditional binary choice between confederal or national government. Proponents of the Constitution called themselves Federalists, thus labeling their opponents Anti-Federalists, a designation the latter protested since they viewed themselves as the true supporters of federalism. Indeed, one Anti-Federalist, Luther Martin, opposed ratification on the grounds that the Constitution was not sufficiently confederal. He recognized the mixture of federal and national elements, but thought the Constitution contained enough federal features to allow its proponents to pass it off as such upon "the unsuspecting multitude" while allowing its advocates, after ratification, "to strike out every part that has the appearance of being federal, and to render it wholly and entirely a national government." Martin clearly understood that the Constitution did not leave the states entirely sovereign. Moreover, many Anti-Federalists were concerned that the proposed Constitution also included open-ended phrases, such as "all means necessary and proper" that invited an expansion of national power, perhaps without limit.[13]

Other Anti-Federalists, while conceding deficiencies experienced with the confederal model embodied in the Articles of Confederation, were also concerned about features of national power in the Constitution. Herbert Storing described such Anti-Federalists as embracing a form of "new federalism." This distinguished them from advocates of traditional or pure federalism by being receptive to a combination of a federal and a national system. Storing noted yet another important shift during the ratification debates after the legitimacy of the new federalism was accepted. The Federalists began emphasizing "the primacy of the national component in the mixture, while the Anti-Federalists urged the importance of a strict division of power and even something like a divided sovereignty, the possibility of which their earlier, strictly federal argument had denied."[14]

The Constitution's division of powers between a national government and state governments produced a dynamic equilibrium in the newly established system. As Bernard Bailyn has noted, the Constitution was for its proponents "a great web of tensions, a system poised in tense equilibrium like the physical systems Newtonian mechanics had revealed." For Samuel Beer, the Constitution "established two sets of governments which would watch and control one another" with neither having unlimited authority. The importance of maintaining the constitutional equilibrium of federalism was readily acknowledged by its proponents during the ratification debates. But how that balance would be monitored was less clear, even though Madison and Hamilton would address some of the possibilities in *The Federalist*.[15]

In an ideal world, according to James Monroe, one should "mark the precise point at which the powers of the general government shall cease" and where "those of the states shall commence." Others, however, pointed out the impossibility of such precision since the "inaccuracy of language" precluded that objective. Proponents of the Constitution conceded it did not and could not provide crystal clarity in dividing authority and power between the national government and those of the states.[16]

For Alison LaCroix, sovereignty gave way to jurisdiction "as the central organizing principle – and battlefield – of American federalism." Yet, as this study will show, questions of sovereignty *and* jurisdiction were both areas of contention for American federalism. Furthermore, as Gerald Leonard and Saul Cornell have pointed out, "The distribution of power between the states and the new powerful central government created by the Constitution meant that defining and policing the boundaries of federalism would become a central problem in American law."[17]

Fear of Consolidation by Opponents of the Constitution

How Hamilton and Madison became the architects of interposition is linked to the debate over ratification in New York, which precipitated the appearance of *The Federalist*. Scholars have long agreed that a central contention of Anti-Federalists was that the proposed frame of government threatened the existence of the states. As expressed by Jackson Turner Main, Anti-Federalists believed that the Constitution had consolidated "previously independent states" into a national government, reducing sovereign states to "a shadow of their former power."[18]

That conviction represented an essential divide between supporters and opponents of the Constitution. In Jack Rakove's words, Federalists wanted to identify "a middle ground between confederation and consolidation" but Anti-Federalists denied "that such a middle ground could ever be discovered or any equilibrium long maintained" and warned that ratification of the Constitution would inevitably lead "to the 'annihilation' of the states." Opponents of the Constitution saw signs of consolidation from the moment the convention completed its work. One purportedly damning piece of evidence was the cover letter to Congress that accompanied the proposed Constitution. Written by Gouverneur Morris but signed by Washington, the letter described "the Consolidation of our Union" as the guiding principle of the convention's delegates. When Samuel Adams read the opening words, 'We, the people,' he immediately identified consolidation. As he put it, "as I enter the Building I stumble at the Threshold." If the Constitution intended the creation of a truly federal government, it should have proclaimed "a Federal Union of Sovereign States." As it was, the words 'We, the people,' signaled the intent, according to a member of Massachusetts's ratifying convention, for "an actual consolidation of the states" with the necessary consequence of "a dissolution of the state governments."[19]

Fears about consolidation and the extinction of the states were particularly acute in New York and shaped the response and argument of *The Federalist*. The issue of consolidation surfaced even before the debate over ratification. After attending the convention for six weeks, two of the three New York delegates, Robert Yates and John Lansing, Jr., left Philadelphia in disgust. They believed the convention had disregarded its instructions to revise the Articles of Confederation and was bent on establishing a "consolidated government." Nonetheless, Yates and Lansing stayed long enough to hear Hamilton advocate for a far more centralized government – one that would overshadow the states – than the proposed form of government he later celebrated in *The Federalist*. In a dramatic confrontation in the New York ratifying convention, Yates and Lansing accused Hamilton of duplicity and threw his words back at him in defiance of the informal agreement not to breach the secrecy of the constitutional convention.[20]

Before those fireworks erupted in the state's ratifying convention, Hamilton and Madison as the principal authors of "Publius" responded to a New York critic who focused on the supposedly consolidating effects of the Constitution. Nine days before Hamilton's initial *Federalist* essay appeared, the *New York Journal* published the first of a series of essays by "Brutus." James Madison, then in New York City, read the piece and took notice, writing a fellow Virginian about a "new Combatant" in the ratification debate. "Brutus" speculated if "a confederated government" was "best for the United States," but concluded that consolidation was inevitable under the proposed Constitution given the distribution of power between the two levels of government. For Brutus, the reserved powers of the states would soon dwindle "except so far as they are barely necessary to the organization of the general government." Such "power retained by individual states, small as it is, will be a clog upon the wheels of the government of the United States," encouraging that government to move it "out of the way." Although the Constitution might not have achieved complete consolidation, that prospect would become clear enough once the national government began exercising its broad grants of power.[21]

Both Madison and Hamilton denied an intent to create a consolidated government even as they conceded that the Constitution departed from a purely confederate model. Nonetheless, Hamilton's disavowal of any inclination towards consolidation was clearly a form of what Garry Wills has called "sweet talk," arguments designed to disarm and sway critics of the Constitution. The scenario of the aggrandizement of the authority and power in the national government at the expense of state governments described by "Brutus" was not an unpleasant picture for Hamilton. Indeed, during the formation of the Constitution and in the early years of its operation, Hamilton retained a national vision consistent with what "Brutus" predicted. As Jack Rakove has described, Hamilton even as he was writing essays for *The Federalist* "was already looking beyond ratification to consider what other measures and policies would be required to convert the ambiguous promise of the Constitution into the nation-state whose most ambitious architect he was intent on becoming." For Madison, the case was otherwise. On the eve of the convention, Madison shared his hopes with Washington for "a new system" that would "reform" the existing governmental structure. Madison thought that "a consolidation of the whole into one simple republic would be as inexpedient as it is unattainable." Instead, he sought a "middle ground" that could support both "a due supremacy of the national authority" and the utility of "the local authorities."[22]

Given the task at hand – securing ratification – more was needed from Madison and Hamilton than simply denying an intent to create a consolidated government or describing the Constitution as partly federal, partly national. The fact remained that two levels of government were created under the Constitution. Madison and Hamilton were forced to address what critics of the Constitution – and "Brutus" in particular – wanted to know: how the equilibrium of federalism would operate as a practical matter. Although expressed in different ways by Anti-Federalists, their central concern came down to one basic question: What assurance did those who might ratify the Constitution have that the national government under that Constitution would not exceed its rightful authority and encroach upon the rights of the state governments or the liberties of the people?

Madison and Hamilton responded by suggesting that multiple monitors of federalism existed to ensure that such potential overreaching by the national government would not occur. The first obvious and practical check against encroachment involved the courts. Both Madison and Hamilton assigned a primary role for judges, and particularly the Supreme Court, to serve as arbiters of the proper operation of federalism. Madison described the Supreme Court's function in the course of analyzing the federal as opposed to national traits of the Constitution in *Federalist* 39. The division of sovereignty between the two levels of government under the Constitution meant that in "controversies relating to the boundary between the two jurisdictions, the tribunal which is ultimately to decide, is to be established under the general Government." The Supreme Court was "clearly essential to prevent an appeal to the sword, and a dissolution of the compact." But it was left to Hamilton to offer a more complete explanation of how the judiciary might operate to monitor federalism.[23]

Like Madison, Hamilton asserted that the national government "must judge ... the proper exercise of its powers." Judicial independence was crucial for judges to fulfill their duty as "faithful guardians of the constitution." For Hamilton, legislatures could not be "the constitutional judges of their own powers." Instead, the courts were "designed to be an intermediate body between the people and the legislature, in order ... to keep the latter within the limits assigned to their authority."[24]

In *Federalist* 80, Hamilton considered the "proper extent" of federal judicial authority. He thought that federal jurisdiction extended to issues arising "out of the laws of the United States, passed in pursuance of their just and constitutional powers of legislation." Although legislative encroachment exceeding constitutional powers might come from either Congress or the state legislatures, Hamilton highlighted the Supreme Court's role by emphasizing the court as a counterweight to state legislatures. Of necessity, "an authority in the federal courts" with effective power was needed "to over-rule" state laws that might be in "manifest contravention" of the Constitution. But such judicial monitoring hardly addressed the concerns of Anti-Federalists who were focused on possible intrusions from the opposite direction. What assurance existed that the national government would not, as "Brutus" predicted, seek to move "out of the way" the powers left to the states.[25]

Initial Responses to Charges of Consolidation

A more fundamental answer to the charge that the Constitution implied consolidation was the response by Madison and Hamilton in *The Federalist*, as well as by other Federalists during the ratification debates: that the federal structure of the Constitution rested on the ultimate sovereignty of the people. This foundation ensured that states possessed greater means and legitimacy to resist encroachments by the national government than that government possessed to vindicate its own authority. They argued that the outwardly directed centrifugal forces sustaining state interests were more powerful than the inwardly directed centripetal forces supporting the national government. Thus, the federal balance under the Constitution was tipped in favor of the state governments and not towards the national government. The people, who were the basis of all authority, would naturally have greater and deeper ties, attachments, and loyalties to their local and state governments than they would to the national government. The people's vigilance of government would be accompanied by a supportive attitude towards their state governments and a wariness of the national government. In addition, the large number of state and local representatives and officials dwarfed the comparatively few federal office-holders and provided an abundance of watchful eyes on the operation of the national government. Such scrutiny coupled with the means of effecting political change and exerting pressure on wayward federal representatives formed a powerful check to keep the actions of the national government within proper constitutional bounds. And in the final resort, the existence of state militias and the natural law right of revolution gave the people in the states a clear advantage in any ultimate standoff between the two levels of government.

As Madison expressed it in *Federalist* 45, "the balance" between the two levels of government was "much more likely" to be influenced by the weight of the state governments. In addition, in *Federalist* 46, Madison argued that state governments possessed unique advantages in protecting their rights and those of the people of their states. State governments had both greater means and heightened disposition to "resist and frustrate" measures of the national government.[26]

Madison compared the influence of state as opposed to national laws. A popular state law that impinged on the national government would likely be "executed immediately," while an unpopular measure of the national government that exceeded its authority would face powerful and readily available state opposition. Such opposition might include the "refusal to co-operate with the officers of the Union" as well as the passage of legislative measures. Resistance from a large state presented "very serious impediments" which if supported by many other states would erect "obstructions" the national government would seek to avoid.[27]

Hamilton similarly suggested that in the unlikely event federal officers attempted to "usurp" their rightful powers under the Constitution, Congress, which represented the people in the states, "would controul" such a misuse of authority. Hamilton echoed Madison's reasoning: that human nature gave people deeper attachments to governmental institutions closer and more familiar to them than those at a distance. Consequently, it was clear to Hamilton that in any "contest" between the national and state governments the people would take the side of their "local government."[28]

Federalists had argued that state governments possessed an advantage over the national government even before its expression in *The Federalist*, and Federalists continued to make that argument in ratification conventions even as "Publius" began to appear. For example, in early December 1787 James Wilson in the Pennsylvania ratifying convention dismissed the idea that under the Constitution the states would be unable to defend their prerogatives. Instead, he thought that the national government "will not be able to maintain the powers given it against the encroachments and combined attacks of the state governments." In mid-January 1788 Charles Pinckney reached a similar conclusion in the South Carolina ratifying convention. An "infringement" or "invasion" of the rights of the state governments by the national government appeared to him "the most remote of all our public dangers." Instead, he feared the proposed national government would not be "sufficiently energetic" and that the state governments will "naturally slide into an opposition against the general one." Ultimately, it was argued that state governments could easily protect their rights because they derived their power from the sovereignty of the people.[29]

Both Hamilton and Madison also referred to the ultimate authority of the people to monitor the constitutional order – at least as a matter of constitutional theory. In *Federalist* 16 and 31, Hamilton suggested that overreaching by state governments under the Constitution "would always be hazardous" since "strength is always on the side of the people" in republics. In the end, the balance of federalism "must be left to the prudence and firmness of the people; who, as they will hold the scales in their own hands, it is to be hoped, will always take care to preserve the constitutional equilibrium between the General and the State Governments." Hamilton was even more explicit in *Federalist* 33 where he identified the specific role of the Supreme Court to ascertain the "proper exercise" of the national government's powers. Nonetheless, "If the Federal Government should overpass the just bounds of its authority ... the people ... must appeal ... and take such measures to redress the injury done to the constitution, as the exigency may suggest and prudence justify."[30]

Madison also devoted attention to the vital role that the people played in maintaining the equilibrium of federalism. In discussing the relationship between the national and state governments, Madison in *Federalist* 46 admonished critics of the Constitution for ignoring a crucial fact. They have "lost sight of the people altogether." He offered the reminder that the people were "the ultimate authority" that could act if either the federal or state government attempted "to enlarge its sphere of jurisdiction at the expense of the other." Because the people were the Constitution's "only legitimate fountain of power," it was consistent with republican theory to recur to the people's authority "whenever any one of the departments may commit encroachments on the chartered authorities of the others." The plenary authority of the people gave them the right "in the last resort" to decide if the national government exceeded its constitutional authority. Ultimately, the Constitution – founded on a sovereign people – made them "the primary controul on the government."[31]

Thus, in *The Federalist*, Madison and Hamilton both defined the scope of enhanced national power and deflected the charge of consolidation. In *Federalist* 39, Madison argued that the power of the national government "extends to certain enumerated objects only, and leaves to the several States a residuary and inviolable sovereignty over all other objects." In *Federalist* 40 Madison asserted that the Constitution regarded states as "distinct and independent sovereigns." In *Federalist* 9 Hamilton dismissed concerns about consolidation by insisting that instead of "implying an abolition of the State Governments," the Constitution "leaves in their possession certain exclusive and very important portions of sovereign power." And in *Federalist* 32 Hamilton maintained that the state governments "would clearly retain all the rights of sovereignty" that they previously possessed and that the Constitution had not "*exclusively* delegated to the United States."[32]

Hamilton's and Madison's Elaboration of Interposition

It was one thing to identify the theoretical role that the people might play in matters of the last resort. But "Brutus" had challenged Federalists to prove how in practice an equilibrium might be maintained between the two levels of government before matters became dire. In *The Federalist*, Hamilton and Madison described how the state legislatures in particular could and would operate as effective watchdogs of the governmental structure through the constitutional tool of interposition and thereby help maintain federalism's proper balance.

Scholars have noticed that *The Federalist* had minimal impact on the broader ratification debate because the essays received little attention outside of New York. Despite that fact and its origin as campaign rhetoric, the work importantly shaped early American constitutional thinking and behavior. The *Federalist* essays written by Hamilton and Madison deeply resonated with Americans when the essays described how state legislatures – on behalf of the people – would be able to oppose oppressive and unconstitutional measures of a national government. A few writers had speculated about the importance of state legislatures during the ratification debate, but the *Federalist* essays offered the most thoroughgoing description of what became the practice of interposition. In four essays written by Hamilton (*Federalist* 26, 28, 84, and 85) and four by Madison (*Federalist* 44, 46, 52, and 55) they identified all of the features that interposition would later assume in the hands of state legislatures that challenged actions of the national government for unduly expanding its constitutional authority.[33]

The interposition-related essays of *The Federalist* have rarely been examined collectively and without attention to the passages setting out the tool of interposition partly because neither Madison nor Hamilton used the term "interposition." Although the elements of interposition as it would be practiced were described in *The Federalist* essays, scholars assume that interposition was born of a post-ratification doctrine of states' rights. That assumption is incorrect and is the primary reason that the roots of interposition in *The Federalist* have been overlooked.

Three Principal Elements of State Legislative Interposition: Monitoring, Sounding the Alarm, and Interstate Communication

There were three principal elements of the tool of interposition that can be gleaned from the eight interposition-related *Federalist* essays. First, they identified the state legislatures as one of the monitors of the constitutional equilibrium of federalism, often described as "sentinels" or "guardians." Second, as guardians of that equilibrium, it was the function of state legislators to identify and then declare their perception of potential encroachments by the national government on the authority of the state governments or the rights of the people. Both Madison and Hamilton described that step as sounding the alarm. Third, they envisioned state legislatures launching interstate efforts to bring widespread attention to the alleged enlargement of powers by the national government.

Sounding the alarm was not simply a matter for individual states, but a means of stimulating a nationwide conversation and debate that might result in a correction or reversal of such overreaching by focusing scrutiny on the questionable action and generating political pressure. Both Madison and Hamilton described initiating correspondence with other state legislatures and formulating plans to respond to the encroachments. Neither of them suggested that sounding the alarm amounted to a nullification of the acts taken by the national government. Instead, the "alarm" was the considered judgment of a legislative body acting as a monitor of the constitutional equilibrium.

In every particular, these three elements emerged in the practice initiated by state legislatures after the Constitution's ratification when they passed instructing and requesting resolutions directed at their congressional delegations. In those resolutions, the state legislatures specified what they believed to be the unconstitutional acts of the national government and requested the state's governor to share the resolutions with other state legislatures.

Two months after the first "Brutus" essay appeared, Hamilton in *Federalist* 26 and 28 described several elements of interposition in addressing concerns raised by Anti-Federalists about standing armies as a result of the Constitution's grant of congressional authority over military appropriations. In *Federalist* 26 Hamilton analyzed the requirement (in Art. I, Sec. 8, Clause 12) that no military appropriations would exceed two years. He pointed out that even if Congress tried to "exceed the proper limits" of the Constitution, the public would learn of the danger and have "an opportunity of taking measures to guard against it." This awareness, Hamilton explained, did not rely on political parties because state legislatures would be monitoring the national government. During congressional debates over military appropriations, state legislatures would "always be not only vigilant but suspicious and jealous guardians of the rights of the citizens, against incroachments from the Federal government."[34]

Hamilton predicted that state legislatures would "constantly have their attention awake to the conduct of the national rulers and will be ready enough, if anything improper appears, to sound the alarm to the people." Hamilton's alarm imagery of the role of state legislatures to bring attention to potentially unconstitutional encroachments by the national government and thereby invite discussion and renewed consideration was echoed by Madison.[35]

In *Federalist* 28 Hamilton expanded his argument that state legislatures as "select bodies of men" would provide "complete security" against overreaching by the national government since they would see though the pretenses of unwarranted national authority that might escape the people's attention. They could then exercise their role to: "discover the danger," "adopt a regular plan of opposition," "readily communicate with each other in the different states; and unite their common forces for the protection of their common liberty." In stressing the ability of state legislatures to develop political opposition through interstate communication in order to respond to instances where the national government overstepped its authority, Hamilton advanced an idea that Madison further developed.[36]

Madison's contributions to developing the idea of interposition began in *Federalist* 44 and 46. In *Federalist* 44 Madison addressed a fierce point of contention advanced by Anti-Federalists: the supposed danger of granting Congress authority to enact all laws 'necessary and proper' in exercising the national government's delegated powers. Few other clauses of the Constitution, he correctly noted, had received more critical attention. Opponents of the Constitution worried that the clause might result in widespread, dangerous, and unchecked powers that would overawe the state governments. Madison asked: "[W]hat is to be the consequence, in case the Congress shall misconstrue this part of the Constitution, and exercise powers not warranted by its true meaning?"[37]

Madison responded that such "usurpation" was unlikely since it required connivance between the judicial and executive branches.

But should those branches of the national government collude in grabbing unauthorized power, "in the last resort, a remedy must be obtained from the people, who can by the election of more faithful representatives, annul the acts of the usurpers." The people possessed this same political check if their state governments exceeded the authority granted them under state constitutions, but this "ultimate redress" would be far more effective in the context of the federal government because the state legislatures exercised an interposing role between the national government and the people.[38]

As Madison explained, unconstitutional acts of Congress would inevitably invade the rights of the state legislatures, and thus those bodies "will be ever ready to mark the innovation, to sound the alarm to the people, and to exert their local influence in effecting a change of federal representatives." The existence and function of state legislative interposition meant that unconstitutional acts of the national government would be more likely noticed and redressed than would violations of the state constitutions. That was because, Madison explained, there was no similar "intermediate body between the State Legislatures and the people" in the event that state legislators exceeded their powers under their state constitutions whereas the state legislatures would react to constitutional overreaching by any branch of the national government. Obviously, the state's judiciary might play an intervening role between the state government and the people of a given state. But here Madison stressed the absence of a body in the state context that might assume the role of interposition like state legislatures who would always be "watching the conduct" of the national government.[39]

In *Federalist* 46, Madison described the dynamics of state legislative reaction that foreshadowed the practice of interposition. Madison predicted that "ambitious encroachments of the Federal Government, on the authority of the State governments" would not merely "excite" one or a few states, but would be "signals of general alarm." "Every Government would espouse the common cause. A correspondence would be opened. Plans of resistance would be concerted."[40]

Madison's description of interstate efforts to coordinate a response to actions of national government overreaching was prescient. Such interstate action through correspondence was exactly what happened after ratification when state legislatures passed instructing and requesting resolutions on issues of allegedly unconstitutional activity of the national government. Directing that such resolutions be shared with other state legislatures became the means of coordinating the "Plans of resistance" that Madison spoke of in *Federalist* 46. Moreover, legislative resolutions instructing and requesting the state's congressional delegation about national encroachments on the authority of the state governments served to bring the tool of interposition to the attention of Congress.

Madison's words not only echoed Hamilton's language in *Federalist* 26 but provided justification for those who employed interposition after ratification. In *Federalist* 46 Madison reiterated the monitoring function of the state legislatures and in *Federalist* 52 he reminded his readers that Congress would not only be "restrained" by the people but would also be "watched and controuled" by state legislatures. And in *Federalist* 55 Madison revisited the theme that it was unlikely that the state legislatures "would fail either to detect or to defeat a conspiracy" by Congress "against the liberties of their common constituents."[41]

Even as *The Federalist* advanced the case for ratification, Hamilton returned to the idea that state legislatures would serve as key sentinels to detect and respond to federal government overreaching. In *Federalist* 84, Hamilton addressed critics worried about giving "large powers" to a distant national government. He conceded that the distance between where most state inhabitants lived and the nation's capital meant that they could not monitor the activity of the national government in person. Yet "the vigilance of the state governments" and in particular the state legislatures would perform that monitoring function. Hamilton described the practical operation of interposition in much the same way as had Madison: "The executive and legislative bodies of each state will be so many centinels over … the national administration"; and they "can readily communicate the same knowledge to the people." Thus, both governors and state legislators, as well as citizens, would be able to "sound the alarm when necessary."[42]

Significantly, the last essay in *The Federalist* echoed the theme of state legislatures as protectors of the people's liberties and as an interposing body responding to impending encroachments by the national government. In *Federalist* 85 Hamilton addressed the concern of some Anti-Federalists about securing the supermajority requirements of state legislatures for constitutional amendments and for holding future constitutional conventions. Whatever challenges that might exist in meeting those requirements for changes affecting only "local interests," Hamilton identified no such "difficulty" when issues involved "the general liberty or security of the people." He confidently concluded with words that captured the idea of interposition that both he and Madison had formulated: "We may safely rely on the disposition of the state legislatures to erect barriers against the encroachments of the national authority."[43]

The Federalist's denial that the Constitution created or was intended to produce a single consolidated national government was coupled with the assertion that instead it called for a balance of authority between the two levels of governments and *some* measure of divided sovereignty between them. Working out the dimensions of that division and the proper equilibrium of federalism provided the context for interposition as a mechanism for monitoring the balance between the two levels of government. It also left the state legislatures – as Madison and Hamilton described in *The Federalist* – free to sound the alarm if they believed the national government overreached its constitutional bounds.

One impediment in appreciating the tool of interposition as elaborated by Madison and Hamilton is that they also alluded to a wide range of actions that state legislatures might take – some of which went well beyond the sounding the alarm function of interposition. For example, in *Federalist* 26 Hamilton wrote that state legislatures might not only give voice to perceived encroachment by the national government but potentially serve as "the ARM" of the people's discontent while Madison in *Federalist* 46 referred to the possibility of an "appeal to a trial of force" in the event of "ambitious encroachments" by the government on the authority of state governments. Both statements apparently referred to the well-known and widely accepted right of revolution. Grounded in natural law, the right of revolution always remained an option of an oppressed people as a matter of final resort.[44]

Indeed, when Madison and Hamilton wrote about state legislatures formulating plans of "opposition" and "resistance," many scholars have assumed they were talking about a resort to arms through the use of state militias or by invoking the natural law right of revolution. Madison also made a vague reference to state "legislative devices" should the federal government pass "unwarrantable" measures. If state legislative "devices" were intended to invalidate national laws or policies, such responses – along with the invocation of the right of armed resistance or other forceful opposition to the national government – definitely went well beyond the sounding the alarm function of interposition. Such language meant that the concept of interposition was somewhat muddied and potentially dangerous from the beginning.[45]

Some of those to whom Madison and Hamilton directed their argument about the benefits of interposition were openly dismissive of this supposed check against overreaching by the national government. One Anti-Federalist, who took the name the "Federal Farmer," writing after Hamilton's *Federalist* 26 and 28 but before Madison's *Federalist* 44, 46, and 52, regarded the idea of interposition as an essentially toothless constitutional tool. He had been told by Federalists that state governments "will stand between the arbitrary exercise of power and the people." The "Federal Farmer" conceded that if Congress expanded its powers, state governments could petition Congress and protest such measures. At the end of the day, however, this was "no more than individuals may do." He complained that the Constitution failed to provide the means "by which the state governments can constitutionally and regularly check the arbitrary measures of congress." In a subsequent letter, the "Federal Farmer" dismissed the value of state governments serving as the "ready advocates" and "guardians of the people" if they possessed "no kind of power" provided by the Constitution "to stop, in their passage, the laws of congress injurious to the people."[46]

A more direct challenge to the idea of interposition was directed at Hamilton in New York's ratifying convention by John Lansing, Jr. Hamilton repeated the argument that both he and Madison made in *The Federalist* that state governments possessed "natural strength and resources" that "will ever give them an important superiority over the general government." After enumerating the ways such attachments and support flowed to the state governments, Hamilton concluded that it would be "shocking to common sense" to think that the people would ever allow their state legislatures "to be reduced to a shadow and a name." Lansing dismissed Hamilton's argument, saying it "only proved that the people would be under some advantages to discern the encroachments of Congress, and to take the alarm." But, so what? What "other resource" did the people have, he asked – other than "rebellion" – which he was not encouraging. He then proceeded to answer his own question: "None but to wait patiently till the long terms of their senators were expired, and then elect other men. All the boasted advantages enjoyed by the states were finally reduced to this." Beyond the political pressure of interposition, Lansing wanted – along with the "Federal Farmer" – a check provided in the Constitution, such as a provision vesting the power of senatorial recall in the state legislatures.[47]

The Rhetorical Dimensions of Hamilton's and Madison's Discussion of Interposition

Hamilton's and Madison's description of interposition in *The Federalist* rightly makes them co-authors of the concept. However, their advocacy of a special role for state legislatures as monitors of the equilibrium of the two levels of government was in the end a rhetorical argument designed to address the objections of Anti-Federalists in general and "Brutus" in particular.[48]

During the ratification debates, Hamilton and Madison were deeply disenchanted with the behavior of state legislatures. Madison's own service as a state legislator in the Virginia assembly from 1784 to 1787 had convinced him, as Gordon Wood has put it, that "the real problem of American politics lay in the state legislatures." Madison objected to both the substance and the process by which a bewildering array of state legislative measures were passed and then as quickly altered or repealed. Even before the federal constitutional convention met, Madison cataloged his concerns in a well-known memorandum in 1787 entitled *Vices of the Political System of the United States*. After the convention adjourned, Madison assured Jefferson that the "mutability" and "injustice" of state legislation had widely been considered "a serious evil" and served as a catalyst for the constitutional convention. During the convention, Hamilton explained that his suggestion that states should be abolished rested on the fact that since "no boundary could be drawn between the National & State Legislatures; ... the former must therefore have indefinite authority." While more circumspect in public, Hamilton still criticized state legislators in *Federalist* 71 for thinking they were "the people themselves" and for not tolerating opposition from either their own states' executive branch or judiciary. Given their strong reservations about state legislatures, it is unlikely that Madison's and Hamilton's elaboration of a mechanism of interposition came with their wholehearted endorsement. After all, the power of interposition depended on the initiative, reliability, and judgment of state legislators.[49]

Despite their concerns about state legislatures, Madison and Hamilton accepted the underlying premise of interposition that state governments were more than a match for the authority of the new national government. During the ratification debate, each believed the proposed Constitution made it more likely that states would encroach on the national government instead of the other way around. Madison's and Hamilton's misgivings about the Constitution reflected their disappointment that the convention had not granted the national government greater powers. As Jack Rakove has put it, "in dispelling the specter of consolidation, Madison and Hamilton could be entirely sincere because they still doubted that the Convention had in fact solved the dilemma of divided sovereignty in a way that would give the Union the decided advantage over the states."[50]

While delegates labored to produce a draft Constitution, Hamilton wrote to Washington sharing the consensus among "thinking men" that the convention would "not go far enough" to produce an "energetic" and "efficient constitution." After the convention adjourned and before beginning work on *The Federalist*, Hamilton offered some "Conjectures about the New Constitution." Even if as expected Washington became the first President, the only hope Hamilton had for the Constitution was that over time a "good administration" might garner "the confidence and affection of the people" and eventually "triumph altogether over the state governments and reduce them to an [entire] subordination, dividing the larger states into smaller districts." In addition, "the general government may also acquire additional strength." Without this, he predicted that in a few years' time "contests" over "the boundaries of power between the particular governments and the general government" would "produce a dissolution of the Union."[51]

Madison shared Hamilton's belief that the Constitution provided insufficient power to the national government and that it lacked adequate means to control the state governments. During the convention Madison proposed and strenuously argued for a congressional veto over state legislation. Madison wanted to ensure that state legislatures could not enact laws disapproved of by the national legislature. Giving Congress such power was indispensable to "controul the centrifugal tendency of the States; which, without it, will continually fly out of their proper orbits." If anything, Madison was even more concerned about the states and the need for a veto than his notes of the convention debate indicated. He was bitterly disappointed when the convention did not incorporate the veto into the Constitution. Shortly before the convention's adjournment, Madison wrote Jefferson predicting that the proposed Constitution would "neither effectually *answer* its *national object* nor prevent the local *mischiefs* which every where *excite disgusts* agst the *state governments.*" Soon after the convention disbanded, Madison, who became one of the most indefatigable advocates for ratification, wrote a long letter to Jefferson explaining his profound disappointment with the Constitution. In Madison's view the Constitution lacked a crucial ingredient to ensure the supremacy of the national government and the protection of individual rights: "A constitutional negative on the laws of the States." Madison doubted that the judiciary alone provided an adequate check against state legislatures and he anticipated the need for "a recurrence to force" in the event states disobeyed judicial opinions supporting "the Legislative rights of the Union."[52]

During the convention Madison also supported proportional representation in both houses of Congress that provided "constitutional protections for slaveholders." However, convention delegates would not support this and agreed that only the House should reflect proportional state representation. With the three-fifths clause approved, "southern delegates coalesced around slavery" and northern delegates were willing to "compromise over slavery." Madison remained opposed to the compromise.[53]

How Americans perceived the balance of national and state power under the Constitution varied and shifted over time. Indeed, Madison's views about the equilibrium of federalism soon underwent a change from the attitudes he held in the wake of the drafting of the Constitution. But during the ratification debates, the potential effectiveness of interposition due to the great influence attributed to state legislatures did not seem farfetched to many Federalists, including Madison and Hamilton. By describing a role for state legislatures to sound the alarm about unconstitutional actions of the federal government, they expressed an idea and provided a justification for steps that some state legislatures began to take.

As much as Hamilton wished to disown his support for the tool of interposition in *The Federalist* after the ratification debate, the fact remained that he had articulated an active role for state legislatures as monitors of the constitutional order that foretold the actions later taken by legislators and governors. Once words are reduced to print, authors lose control over how their expressions and ideas are used. Thus, the language used by Hamilton and Madison in the course of the ratification debate took on a life of its own. The controversy over interposition could not be put to rest by claiming that ideas expressed in *The Federalist* no longer meant in later periods what they clearly seemed to suggest at the time. Prominent Federalists had indeed asserted that state legislatures would play an important role as sentinels to help ensure that the national government would not encroach on the authority of state governments and that they would thus serve as a vital part of the system of government contemplated by the Constitution.[54]

Misconceptions Surrounding Interposition

When the sounding the alarm function of interposition was invoked by state legislatures after ratification, some criticized that step as utterly impractical for resolving questions of constitutional overreaching by the national government or identifying an imbalance in the equilibrium of federalism. Multiple states rendering their judgments on those issues would only create confusion since a definitive resolution required a single decision-maker such as the Supreme Court. But the idea of interposition advanced as a rhetorical argument in *The Federalist* was not a challenge to the Supreme Court's *authority* to interpret the

Constitution and render judicial decisions about the boundaries of federalism.

When state legislatures sounded the alarm by highlighting potential unconstitutional overreaching by the federal government, they were not wresting away from the Supreme Court its authority to render judicial decisions. Those alarms were only designed to stimulate a wider, interstate awareness and concern about the action in question, a heightened interest that might ultimately result in a shift in public opinion helping to facilitate a reversal of the purported constitutional encroachments by the national government. Potentially, interposition could prompt a change of political representation, or stimulate Congress to enact new laws, or create a movement for constitutional amendment that might revisit the constitutional issue.

The consequence of describing state legislatures as sentinels and guardians introduced a broader vision of constitutional discourse in which other parties and groups – and not the Supreme Court alone – had a role in ensuring that the federal government stayed within its proper bounds. The Constitution called for all federal *and* state officials, including state legislators, to support the Constitution "by oath or affirmation." Many state legislators viewed that requirement as not only commanding them to obey constitutional acts of the national government, but also obligating them to identify and resist unconstitutional acts of that government.[55]

While multiple eyes might keep watch on the operation of the federal government to identify when it might be overreaching, state legislatures were best positioned for interposition. Unlike other sources of critique, such as those coming from individual citizens or the press, a legislature could claim to speak for an entire state. Resolutions passed by state legislators could legitimately be considered an expression of "the people." Moreover, that popular "voice" came in the form of a resolution capable of being shared with other state legislatures and a state's congressional delegation. Passage of a state legislative resolution gave that constitutional opinion a tangible means of transmission not enjoyed by other actors weighing in on instances of allegedly unwarranted acts of the national government. State legislatures not only possessed the logistical means for expressing concerns about constitutional boundaries, but were better suited for watching the national government. With the advantage of acquiring information through direct communication with the state's congressional delegation and with the expectation that one of their duties was to keep an eye on the operation of the national government, state legislators were arguably better informed than average citizens.

* * * * * *

Viewing interposition with historical hindsight tends to associate it with a sovereign states' rights theory linked to the defense and preservation of slavery and the doctrines of nullification and secession that led to the Civil War. Moreover, interposition bears the burden of its association with White supremacist resistance to the Civil Rights movement of the twentieth century. Viewing interposition from the opposite direction and within the context of the immediate aftermath of the Constitution offers a different picture.

Considering its roots, interposition emerges as a practice of state legislatures playing a more benign and logical role within the unfolding enterprise of balancing the newly minted federalism of the Constitution. As Madison and other Federalists repeatedly assured their opponents during the ratification debate, the Constitution did not create a consolidated government. According to Federalists, the Constitution was neither designed nor did it have the tendency to swallow up all of the authority of state governments. On the other hand, as Madison frequently pointed out, the Constitution did not create a confederated government that left the states with their state sovereignty fully intact. Instead, the Constitution created a government that was partly national and partly federal – and this key characteristic involved a continuing search for a divided, but balanced, sovereignty.[56]

From that perspective, the early concept of interposition was but one of the means to monitor the appropriate operation of the national government. Ultimately, interposition was justified if it defended the authority and power that Federalists insisted was left to the states by the Constitution and helped preserve the rights and liberties of the citizens of those states. If and when the federal government exceeded its appropriate constitutional powers or undermined the legitimate rights of the state governments or citizens of the states, the use of interposition could hardly be considered subversive. Instead, the early practice of interposition could be portrayed as protective of the constitutional order established by the Constitution.

Such views and arguments were not universally shared. From the moment the practice of interposition began, it faced criticism and condemnation from some quarters. During its initial use, Republicans justified their invocation of interposition because Hamilton's economic policies seemed to threaten the proper equilibrium of the Constitution by greatly increasing national power. On the other hand, for Hamilton and other Federalists of the 1790s, the danger to the proper equilibrium of the Constitution came from the opposite direction: the lack of sufficient national power in the face of local and state-oriented tendencies. Perceiving danger from unreasonable and parochial claims by the states, Hamilton and like-minded Federalists developed a hearty aversion to interposition resolutions issued by state legislatures. The criticism heaped on interposition when it first surfaced after ratification, coupled with additional burdens that would denigrate the word "interposition" both before and after the Civil War, complicate the recovery of the concept of interposition as a legitimate tool of American constitutionalism.[57]

2

Early State Use of Interposition: Testing the Powers of the New National Government

The new Constitution had existed for a short time before some Americans including James Madison detected troubling signs of an imbalance in the equilibrium of federalism. In particular, they believed the national government was expanding its authority over crucial issues involving debt, taxes, and the establishment of a national bank. Twenty months after the First Congress convened, Virginia legislators sounded the alarm in response to measures of Washington's administration they considered unconstitutional. While not using the term "interposition," Virginia's legislature employed the tool of state legislative intervention as described in *The Federalist*.

This inaugural use of interposition was coupled with an effort to make the operation of the national government more transparent. Virginia, along with other states, initiated a movement that gradually made the Senate's debates public, asserting that a closed-door United States Senate impeded the ability of state legislatures to serve as timely and fully knowledgeable sentinels of the work of the national government. At the same time, state legislatures also wanted to weigh in on Congress' decisions about amending the Constitution and the permanent location of the government.

Virginia's interposition occurred after Anti-Federalists there and in other states concluded that the amendments proposed by Congress – which became the Bill of Rights – did little to address structural issues of national powers that seemed to undermine the position of states in the Union. In addition, some of the earliest fiscal measures of

Washington's administration displayed troubling signs of a consolidation of national power that some Anti-Federalists had predicted during the ratification debates.

That Virginia, along with other state legislatures, claimed a right to monitor the operation of the federal government triggered significant resistance. A vigorous debate ensued over the legitimacy of state legislators passing resolutions describing the new national government's financial policies as unconstitutional. This national debate served as an early test of the tool of interposition. While members of Washington's administration castigated Virginia's interposition, the state's legislature justified its actions in terms strikingly similar to explanations given in *The Federalist*. Virginia's defense was echoed by legislators from other states. Competing and conflicting perceptions of how the equilibrium of federalism should operate eventually led to a major clash between those seeking to enhance national powers and those who resisted that effort and defended states' rights.

Several ironies accompanied the first use of interposition. Virginia defended its resolutions declaring fiscal measures designed by the Secretary of the Treasury Alexander Hamilton as unconstitutional in the same way that "Publius" and Hamilton had described the uses of interposition. Unwilling to acknowledge his fingerprints on the idea of interposition, Hamilton branded Virginia's resolutions illegitimate statements that undermined the Constitution and the Union.

Madison's position was even more ironic. During the ratification debates in 1788, Madison joined Hamilton in elaborating the mechanism of state interposition even though he remained convinced that the Constitution did not allocate enough power to the national government. During the First Congress in 1789, Madison played a crucial part in defeating the attempts of critics of the Constitution to limit the national government to expressly delegated powers and to achieve structural changes that would alter the relative powers between the two levels of government. However, only one year later in 1790, Hamilton's fiscal policies calling for the assumption of state debts gave Madison pause about the operation of the national government. Moreover, the uncompromising sectionalism during debates over where to locate the capital frustrated Madison to a degree that he questioned Virginia's ratification of the Constitution.

By 1792, Hamilton's effort to establish a national bank by broadly construing national powers further alarmed Madison who believed the plan undermined the proper equilibrium of federalism and the limited delegation of powers the Constitution granted the national government.

Thus, within only a few years, Madison's perception of the challenges and dangers to American government significantly shifted. When the constitutional convention in Philadelphia concluded, Madison thought state legislatures posed the greatest threat to a constitutional union and that the national government had not been given sufficient power. Five years later, he saw assertions of national power that seemed headed towards consolidated government destined to undermine the slaveholding states. Those concerns led Madison to wholeheartedly embrace the tool of interposition and defend its practice by drawing on the ideas he and Hamilton had advanced in *The Federalist*.

Because Madison and other Virginians became increasing fearful of the expanded power of the national government, they sought an understanding of the Constitution that would address their concerns about the distribution of powers between the two levels of governments. Thus, the early national dialogue over federalism centered on what each side viewed as undesirable disequilibrium: either forces that would weaken the relative authority of states or forces that would diminish national authority.

* * * * * *

State Interposition Efforts to Amend the Constitution and Protect States' Rights

During the constitutional convention, George Mason of Virginia and Elbridge Gerry of Massachusetts proposed that the Constitution be "prefaced with a Bill of Rights," but their idea was summarily defeated. Similarly, in the ratification debates Anti-Federalists repeatedly cited the absence of a bill of rights as a defect of the proposed constitution. But for many Anti-Federalists even more important than adding a bill of rights to protect civil liberties was the need for constitutional amendments to constrain the powers of the national government. As J. Gordon Hylton noted, for Virginians: "The principal problem was ... that a national majority, particularly a northern majority, could someday strip the citizens of Virginia of their collective rights of self-government." Those rights obviously included the state's ability to defend the institution of slavery. For Jonathan Gienapp, while Anti-Federalists regularly demanded a bill of rights, "they tended to believe that fundamental changes to the Constitution's structure – ones that altered the federal government's powers and returned many of them to the states – were more urgent."[1]

Virginia's ratifying convention that convened in June 1788 was split between supporters and opponents of the Constitution. A crucial question was whether the convention would make amendments a condition of ratification, or would ratify and then seek amendments. During the debate, Anti-Federalists led by Patrick Henry proposed a bill of rights as well as structural and substantive amendments. The possibility of a conditional ratification, as well as a second constitutional convention to consider amendments, worried Federalists like Madison who thought conditional ratifications might threaten the entire constitutional project. Federalists narrowly defeated the attempt late in Virginia's convention to make the state's ratification conditional on amendments. Instead, by another close vote, the convention ratified the Constitution but recommended amendments to Congress. Madison later described the agreement to consider amendments part of the "tacit compact" underlying the ratification vote.[2]

After the vote to ratify, a committee was appointed to propose amendments – most of which Madison opposed. They included a bill of rights and barriers to a strong national government, specifically an amendment that required a two-thirds vote of Congress to pass laws regulating navigation and commerce and another that precluded Congress from collecting direct taxes until it first made a request for such taxes from the states. After Virginia's convention adjourned, Madison described many of the proposals as "highly objectionable." He thought that "friends of the Constitution" ought to support constitutional changes that provided "additional guards for liberty, without abridging the sum of power transferred from the States to the general Government" and only if achieved by amendments instead of the unpredictability of another convention.[3]

Because of these ratification controversies, Madison faced considerable opposition in gaining a seat in the new House of Representatives. Earlier, the machinations of Patrick Henry and others who had opposed the Constitution in Virginia denied Madison a Senate seat. Later during his campaign for the House, Madison pledged to consider amendments if he was elected and he courted Virginia's Baptist vote by declaring his support for a bill of rights that included full protection of the "rights of Conscience." On February 2, 1789 Madison beat his opponent, James Monroe, in a close election.[4]

George Mason, a fellow Virginian and opponent of the Constitution, was doubtful that structural changes affecting the distribution of powers between the two levels of government would be attained given Madison's opposition to anything that diminished the powers of the national government. Mason thought that "some Milk & Water Propositions may be made" but predicted no "important & substantial Amendments," and he knew that Madison had questioned the practical importance of bills of rights, describing them as "parchment barriers."[5]

After sending the convention's draft constitution to Jefferson then in Paris, Madison responded to Jefferson's reaction that the absence of a bill of rights was a big mistake. Madison offered numerous reasons for considering such a bill unnecessary, including James Wilson's argument that all powers not granted to the national government would remain with the states or the people – including such rights that might be identified in a bill of rights. However, Madison conceded two purposes that bills of rights served in America's new constitutional order. One was that solemnly declared "political truths" might "acquire by degrees the character of fundamental maxims of free Government, and as they become incorporated with the national sentiment, counteract the impulses of interest and passion." The second purpose was that in the event of "usurped acts of the Government," a bill of rights "will be a good ground for an appeal to the sense of the community." Jefferson echoed Madison's latter point when he replied and suggested that "the subordinate governments" of the states needed a bill of rights against which they could measure "all the acts of the federal government."[6]

Madison returned to the value of declaring political truths and the utility of a bill of rights when he introduced his proposal for amendments to the Constitution on June 8, 1789. Despite the intrinsic weakness of "paper barriers" Madison argued that a bill of rights would help courts guard against the national government's encroachment of such rights. In making that argument, Madison anticipated the monitoring role that Virginia's legislature would play two years later. The additional "security" of judicial enforcement of a bill of rights, according to Madison, was that "the state legislatures will jealously and closely watch the operations of this government."[7]

One of Madison's proposals sought an opening declaration, "That all power is originally vested in, and consequently derived from the people." Even though the House failed to adopt that suggestion, the principle of popular sovereignty was not controversial and had been repeatedly invoked from the time of the Revolution. During the constitutional convention, Madison explained how popular ratification could cure any perceived procedural irregularities of the convention. As he put it, "The people were in fact, the fountain of all power, and by resorting to them, all difficulties were got over. They could alter constitutions as they pleased." The sovereignty of the people was one of the "first principles" found in the state bills of rights.[8]

Because they dominated the First Congress, Federalists could have sidestepped the issue of amendments and moved on to the business of organizing the new government. Instead, Madison's determination to fulfill his commitment to support a consideration of amendments forced Congress to engage in a three-month debate over the issue. Madison offered a series of amendments drawn from proposals emanating from the state conventions and he served on the select committee deciding which amendments should be sent to the floor of the House.[9]

Although honoring his campaign promise, Madison made it clear that he would not "injure the constitution" by supporting amendments that revisited "the whole structure of the government" or "the principles and the substance of the powers given" to the national government. Indeed, Madison helped defeat proposed amendments that might have changed the current balance of power between the two levels of government. Among the defeated structural changes suggested by ratifying conventions were proposals denying congressional authority over state electoral regulations and limitations on Congress' ability to impose direct taxes. Moreover, Madison opposed the Anti-Federalist effort to alter the text of what became the Tenth Amendment so that it would read: "The powers not *expressly* delegated to the United States by the Constitution, nor prohibited by it to the States, are reserved to the States respectively, or to the people." Madison's successful argument to delete the word "expressly" was a major setback for Anti-Federalists seeking to preserve greater retained powers in the states.[10]

The House and Senate finally agreed on twelve proposed amendments, the last ten becoming the bill of rights. The first two amendments (that were not ratified) dealt with increasing the size of the House and requiring intervening elections before congressional pay increases could go into effect. As the proposed constitutional revisions proceeded through Congress, some Anti-Federalists described the amendments as "a tub thrown out to a whale," a practice sometimes employed by sailing vessels to distract the whale and thereby protect the ship. Instead of meaningful changes addressing the balance of power between the two levels of government, Anti-Federalists had been tossed a "tub" of civil rights protections.[11]

Madison worked diligently to ensure that proposed amendments would garner the support of two-thirds of the House and three-fourths of the states. While avoiding substantive structural changes, Madison hardly got everything he wanted. He failed to see amendments integrated into the text of the Constitution instead of being appended at the end of the document. As a result, Madison anticipated that "ambiguities will be produced" because questions would arise about "how far the original text is or is not necessarily superseded, by the supplemental act." Congress approved the twelve amendments on September 25.[12]

Both Virginia's U.S. Senators, Richard Henry Lee and William Grayson, were unhappy. On September 28, 1789 Lee and Grayson sent the proposed amendments to their state's governor and Speaker of the Virginia House of Representatives with an explosive cover letter. They apologized for the lack of more wide-ranging amendments. For Virginia's Senators, if amendments went no further than the ones currently proposed, the structural relationship between the federal government and those of the states meant "the annihilation of the State Government." Senator Grayson also wrote to Virginia's Governor Patrick Henry complaining that the proposed amendments "are so mutilated & gutted that in fact they are good for nothing." Once the letters became public and widely circulated, they provoked attacks on the two Senators and the state. Madison thought the letters were intended "to keep alive the disaffection to the Government."[13]

As the House finished work on the amendments, another contentious issue arose about where to locate the permanent capital of the national government and gave Madison misgivings about the operation of Congress. Madison thought that the capital should be located near the center of the country and not in some "eccentric position" that would disadvantage any particular region, including the South. The tenor of debate suggested that Northern members intended to dictate a location to the Southern states' detriment. That attitude deeply shocked Madison. Indeed, the high-handed manner of discussion and an absence of "moderation and liberality" led Madison to speculate that had Virginia's ratifying convention foreseen the present "declarations and proceedings" of the House, "Virginia might not have been part of the union at this moment." Notwithstanding the stir caused by his comment, Madison stood his ground and repeated his concerns about Northern states acting as "an overbearing Majority." The issue of the capital's location was postponed until the second session after the House adjourned in late September.[14]

Meanwhile, in October 1789 President Washington transmitted the twelve amendments passed by Congress to the states for their ratification. When the proposed amendments reached the Virginia legislature in November, Patrick Henry failed to muster effective opposition even with Anti-Federalists disappointed with the scope of the amendments. After preliminary defeats, including a failed effort to postpone consideration of the amendments until the next legislative session, Henry went home. After he left, the House took up the amendments and voted to ratify them all, but with an application to Congress seeking an amendment that would limit Congress' powers over direct taxation. The Senate disagreed, believing that Virginians would not have ratified the Constitution but for the expectation that it would be "much more materially altered and amended." The Senate's action effectively postponed the issue until the Virginia legislature reconvened in October 1790.[15]

When Virginia returned to the ratification issue it did so in the midst of controversial actions of the national government that seemed to vindicate earlier warnings by Patrick Henry and others. In mid-January 1790 Hamilton issued his first Report on Public Credit, which included a plan to assume state debts that was opposed by Madison and other Federalist members of Virginia's congressional delegation. Only after the session in which Virginia registered its objections to the policy of the assumption of state debts would the ratification of proposed amendments resurface, by which time those who initially opposed the Constitution basically capitulated to the new frame of government. In December 1791 Virginia's House and Senate ratified the amendments.[16]

States Interposition to Open the Senate's Proceedings and Hold Senators Accountable

Since it was now important for states to monitor actions of their elected representatives in Congress, Virginia led a successful effort to open the Senate. Colonial Americans were familiar with a broad array of practices when it came to publicizing the work of legislative bodies. Since the late seventeenth century, the British Parliament had given its members unfettered freedom of speech, but only behind closed doors. Indeed, privacy of debate was one of the privileges of Parliament. That parliamentary practice of secrecy continued in early American colonial legislative bodies. Only in 1764 would the Virginia House of Burgesses open its doors to the public, followed by the Massachusetts House of Representatives in 1766. In 1770, Pennsylvania's legislature opened its proceedings as well, at least to qualified electors.[17]

Even as popular sovereignty came to define the American Revolution, the tradition of closed legislative proceedings did not easily give way. Both America's Continental Congress and the Confederation Congress generally operated in secret. Indeed, the Confederation Congress in 1783 defeated an open-door proposal. Similarly, the Convention of 1787 drafted the Constitution behind closed doors and under a pledge of secrecy.[18]

When Americans created new governments after independence, they proclaimed that the legitimacy of those governments rested solely on the authority of the people. The sovereignty of the people invoked in the self-conscious process of creating American constitutions called for greater knowledge of legislative debate, particularly at the state level. The new state constitutions increasingly emphasized transparency, such as requirements to record and publish proceedings, with some states such as Pennsylvania opening up legislative debates to the public.[19]

Despite the trend in state constitutions towards legislative openness, the Federal Constitution in Article I, Sec. 5 only directed the House and Senate to keep and occasionally publish a journal of their proceedings, "excepting such Parts as may in their Judgment require Secrecy." Although the Constitution did not require either the House or the Senate to open their doors to the public, the House normally conducted its sessions in public from the start, while the Senate only opened its doors in 1795. When Senators assembled for their first session in 1789, they assumed they would meet behind closed doors, following the practice of delegates to the Confederation Congress, and the constitutional convention. The Senate's initial secrecy, even if consistent with earlier practices of legislative bodies, prompted criticism. In 1789, George Washington heard from a fellow Virginian that the Senate was "much censured for keeping their doors shut."[20]

Virginia's opposition to the new government operating in secrecy made the state a leader in the effort to open up the debates in the Senate. On December 16, 1789 Virginia's legislature passed a resolution instructing its Senators to allow the "free admission" of people into the Senate. Virginia's Senators Richard Henry Lee and John Walker spent two full days urging their colleagues to support that position, only to see the Senate reject their plea. William Maclay of Pennsylvania was the lone Senator who voted with them. That rejection prompted one Virginian to predict that the Senate's action would prompt the Virginia legislature to seek the support of other states.[21]

Indeed, on November 22, 1790 Virginia's House of Delegates considered several resolutions dealing with the Senate's closed proceedings. One resolution asserted that hearing those debates was "among the important privileges of the people" and instructed the state's Senators to seek to open the Senate. Even before Virginia's request for interstate action reached North Carolina, that state's legislature passed a similar resolution instructing its Senators to open the Senate's doors and to send copies to the other state legislatures. The legislatures of Maryland and South Carolina responded and joined Virginia and North Carolina in instructing their Senators to pursue the same objective. Both New York's and Pennsylvania's lower Houses also passed similar resolutions that were narrowly defeated in their respective state Senates. In addition, Massachusetts' legislature appointed a committee to explore resolutions to open the Senate, but evidently never passed them.[22]

The struggle to open the Senate is sometimes described as a matter of partisan politics, but it also rested on the question of whether instructions to Senators were obligatory. Senatorial accountability to state legislatures "could not be fully effective" unless the legislatures knew about senatorial deliberations. Indeed, a closed Senate hampered the ability of state legislatures to serve as sentinels of the national government and to monitor their own Senators. By functioning largely out of sight, the Senate impeded the tool of interposition and the ability of state legislatures to identify potential overreaching by the federal government.[23]

The need to open up the Senate was touched on in a series of motions, ultimately not passed by the Senate, during the course of senatorial debate. Opponents argued that it would be too costly to publish the Senate's extensive *Journals* and, in any event, the information they contained would not adequately shed light on "the principles, motives and designs, of individual members." Proponents on the other hand, thought that conducting legislative business publicly with deliberations published in the newspapers was the best means of holding Senators accountable. While not adopted, these motions reflected an awareness that effective monitoring of the Senate relied on information gained through open debates.[24]

In the end, providing better access to the workings of the Senate merged with a republican instinct favoring greater openness of government. The desire for transparency was often expressed in terms of the need for the people to participate in the newly created national government. A widely published newspaper article argued that confidence in government could not be maintained when citizens were "kept in the dark." The danger seemed clear: "If rulers will exact obedience from the people, they must not treat them like slaves; they must convince them of the reasonableness and propriety of the laws, or they will not continue to respect and obey them."[25]

Philip Freneau, a vocal critic of the Federalist administration and editor of the *National Gazette*, insisted that all governments tried to avoid scrutiny. Therefore, "the people ... who are the fountain of government" needed "to *demand* the free circulation of political information." Increasingly frustrated at the failure of the Senate to open its doors, Freneau in 1793 posed this question to his readers: "How are you to know the just from the unjust steward when they are covered with the mantle of concealment?"[26]

Early Opposition to Hamilton's Economic Proposals to Centralize National Power

While leading the successful movement to open the Senate, Virginia was also at the forefront of other, perhaps even more substantive interpositions by state legislatures. Both the Continental Congress and individual states had incurred considerable debt during the American Revolution. The importance of dealing with the public debt was broadly understood, but how to manage that debt spawned considerable disagreement. Public debate focused on economic measures adopted by Washington's administration that were seen as overstepping proper constitutional bounds, threatening the appropriate equilibrium between the two levels of government, and imposing an excise tax to pay for the national debts.

One of Hamilton's first tasks after being appointed Secretary of the Treasury in September 1789 was to develop a financial plan for the nation. Placing American credit on a solid foundation meant addressing the problem of its large outstanding debts, incurred both by the nation and the states. Hamilton's answer was his *Report Relative to a Provision for the Support of Public Credit*, delivered to Congress in January 1790. The extensive report took hours to read aloud, after which Congress sat in stunned silence. The *Report* became controversial because it rested on Hamilton's vision for the new nation: "a monolithic nationalism" centered on a powerful federal government. Following fierce debate,

Hamilton's *Report* eventually became the basis of the so-called Funding Act that Congress adopted on August 4, 1790.[27]

Hamilton's intricate *Report* raised many questions, but what drew most attention was his plan for the national government to assume the debts of the states. Hamilton considered the military expenditures creating the state debts a common expense to obtain independence, thus making it appropriate for the new federal government to assume the bulk of the Revolutionary war debt. Hamilton also argued that consolidating the debt served the useful purpose of binding the nation together.[28]

Hamilton was surprised by Madison's opposition. Hamilton thought he had Madison's full support even though there were indications of a growing divide between the two that surfaced while Hamilton was drafting his *Report*. During that drafting process, Hamilton asked Madison what further taxes might be *"least unpopular"* to Americans. Madison offered some suggestions, but also expressly disapproved of long-term government debt. In part, he feared that wealthy foreigners would "buy out the Americans." Given Hamilton's view that the nation's debt usefully served to strengthen the national government, Madison's negative comments about long-term debt signaled their growing differences. Indeed, five months later Madison concluded that Hamilton's *Report* was "faulty in many respects" and he declared that "Public Debt is a Public curse."[29]

When Hamilton issued his *Report*, Congress was still sorting through the complex process of calculating how much each state government had contributed to support independence. Madison partly objected to assumption because Virginia had already paid off much of its debt. Thus, the policy of assumption would force Virginia to pay a disproportionate share of the total war costs. Madison instead proposed that the national government should assume the state debts as they stood at the end of the war in 1783 because assuming the state debts as they stood in 1790 unfairly benefited those states that still carried considerable debt while penalizing those states that had taken steps to fulfill their obligations.[30]

Madison's concern also surfaced in other states, such as Maryland and Georgia, that like Virginia anticipated coming out losers under assumption. On the other hand, states such as Massachusetts, Connecticut, and South Carolina having made less progress with repayment and thus with heavier debts outstanding were considerably more receptive to assumption. Indeed, some states like Massachusetts vehemently insisted on assumption. But if Hamilton's plan for assumption had states consulting their self-interest, it also generated anxiety about the equilibrium of federalism.[31]

Madison became sensitized to maintaining a balance between the concurrent governments in ways that Hamilton never did. For Madison, the federal government could rightfully exercise powers within its governmental sphere, but misuse of powers by the national government was worrisome. Thus, when Madison complained to Jefferson on March 8, 1790 about the harmful economic impact of assumption on Virginia, he underscored his objection that assumption would increase national legislative powers that were "already sufficiently great."[32]

Madison's initial impressions of the national government's operation were positive. During this early period, Madison saw little evidence of the consolidating effects that opponents of the Constitution had predicted. However, little more than a year later, Hamilton's proposed funding plan and especially the scheme for assumption of state debt caused Madison to reevaluate. In addition to its unfair financial impact on Virginia, Madison detected a distinct shift towards increasing the powers of the national government that would diminish the powers of the state governments, and that suggested further imbalances were likely.[33]

During a highly contentious House debate, Madison questioned the constitutional basis for assumption. On April 22, 1790 he responded to the argument that the nation would be strengthened if it assumed state debts. Madison was willing to support any needed changes to the national government, but he wanted such deficiencies "to be remedied by additional constitutional powers, if they should be found necessary." By insisting on formal constitutional amendment, Madison now opposed the expansion of national powers through the principle of implied powers that he had described with approval in *The Federalist*.[34]

Other Virginians besides Madison worried that assumption would threaten the balance of federalism. David Stuart, Washington's close friend and a staunch Federalist, warned the President in early June 1790 that assumption seemed "subversive of the true principles of the

Constitution" and was viewed by Virginians as a seizure of power by "unwarrantable constructions of the Constitution." Assumption played into the hands of opponents of ratification such as Patrick Henry who foresaw such encroachment by the federal government when the Constitution was proposed. Stuart warned Washington that if Henry was bold enough to aim a "blow" at the national government, "he can never meet with a more favourable opportunity" than if states were forced to accept assumption of the war debts.[35]

Other Virginians also saw in the proposed Constitution an inevitable increase in the national government's powers over those of the states. Richard Henry Lee had complained about creating a system which established "One Government founded on the ruin of State Governments." For Lee, "the friends of liberty" (who were by implication supporters of a proper federal balance) should take steps "to guard with perfect vigilance every right that belongs to the states, and to protest against every invasion of them, taking care always to procure as many protesting states as possible." Lee thought such vigilance might "prevent a consolidating effect from taking place by slow but sure degrees." Lee's suggestions were consistent with interposition: collective action by states to resist potential abuse by the national government.[36]

Madison became one of many, both in and outside of the House of Representatives, who resisted Hamilton's assumption plan. Objections ranged from the perceived impact on individual states, to the terms under which assumption would take place, and to assumption's effect on the ongoing accounting efforts to determine the existing state debts. Such congressional reservations stymied the issue. The deadlock over assumption was broken by the deal supposedly brokered by Jefferson during a June 1790 dinner he hosted with Hamilton and Madison in attendance. The bargain entailed mustering sufficient Southern votes to pass the Funding Act including assumption in return for a promise to locate the national capital on the Potomac River.[37]

States Sound the Alarm That Debt Assumption Diminishes State Sovereignty

On November 2, 1790, three months after the passage of the Funding Act, North Carolina Governor Alexander Martin sounded the alarm about the legitimacy of assumption in an address to the state legislature. Like Virginia, North Carolina had already discharged the bulk of its Revolutionary War debt. According to Martin, the congressional act that assumed state debts without the "consent, or application of their citizens for this purpose" was an "extraordinary measure" that would diminish "the independence and internal sovereignty of the state." In warning about this potential misuse of power by the national government, Martin took on the role that Hamilton had predicted both a state "executive" as well as legislatures would play, namely as sentinels "over ... the national administration."[38]

Soon after Martin's address, North Carolina's legislature responded to the Funding Act. Local newspapers reported that most state representatives were "violently opposed" to assumption and described the angry proceedings in North Carolina's House of Commons in late November, where members declared congressional assumption without a state's consent to be "an infringement" of the state's sovereignty. The House instructed the state's congressional delegation to oppose the current assumption plan and any further assumption schemes until the states consented. The House's resolutions clearly challenged the unilateral authority of Congress to assume state debts. While the language of the House resolutions did not explicitly declare assumption to be unconstitutional, it called into question the proper equilibrium of federalism given the alleged infringement of the state's sovereignty.[39]

North Carolina's House, with the state Senate's concurrence, passed a series of resolutions directed at the state's U.S. Senators, whom the legislators blamed for "the alarming measures of the late session of Congress" and for failing to correspond regularly with the legislature. The North Carolina House tried to censure the Senators, but the Senate struck that language from the final version of the resolutions that passed both houses. The state's Senators were instructed on a wide range of issues, including to oppose "every excise and direct taxation law." That instruction was aimed at assumption because Hamilton's fiscal program depended on the passage of an excise tax to pay off the interest and principal of the national debt, which included the assumption of state debts. The Governor was to send the resolutions to all other state legislatures, in addition to the state's Senators.[40]

Several months before Congress passed the Funding Act in 1790, Virginia's Governor Beverley Randolph alerted Madison about hostility toward assumption. If anything, he underestimated the strength and depth of that feeling. As state legislators gathered in Richmond in October 1790, one observer found that resistance to assumption was the only topic of conversation. Indeed, one day after the House of Delegates convened, the act was read and referred to a committee on the State of the Commonwealth. A range of views about how to respond to the policy of assumption was predictable, but when the House met on November 3 it considered a resolution declaring the assumption of state debts to be "repugnant to the constitution of the United States" because it exercised "a power not expressly granted to the General Government."[41]

Federalists and moderates in the House sought a compromise that rejected the need for specific constitutional language to authorize assumption. They denied that the national government's powers were limited to those expressly stated in the Constitution – the position unsuccessfully lobbied for by former opponents of the Constitution when the First Congress had considered amendments in 1789. Their counterproposal called assumption "highly injurious" and unjust to those states, like Virginia, that had redeemed much of their state debt. The legislators proposing this substitute, including the Federalist lawyer John Marshall, were willing to condemn the Funding Act, but not declare it unconstitutional. The Federalist substitute failed, after which the original resolution passed.[42]

The House of Delegates, however, was not finished. The following day a second resolution was adopted that objected to the Funding Act from the opposite direction. While the November 3 resolution denied the national government had express constitutional authority to act on assumption, a resolution of November 4 suggested the Funding Act undermined the implied rights and powers reserved to the states, including the right of states to redeem the public debt. Finally, although a majority had rejected the Federalist substitute resolution, the House subsequently, on November 8, passed a third resolution incorporating language from the proposed substitute describing assumption as unfair to certain states, such as Virginia. As Meriwether Smith wrote to Jefferson: "One party charges the Congress with an *unconstitutional* Act; and both parties charge it with an Act of injustice." Virginia's Senate eventually adopted a compromise version of the House's three resolutions, but even before it acted, critics focused on the language of Virginia's House resolutions.[43]

Federalists Reject State Challenges to the National Government's Authority

Hamilton was among the first to respond, largely because his network of Treasury Department agents and political friends kept him informed about resistance to his economic agenda. Hamilton wrote Chief Justice John Jay and included copies of the first two resolutions passed by Virginia's House. Hamilton dismissed the idea of state legislators questioning the constitutional authority of the national government: "This is the first symptom of a spirit which must either be killed or will kill the constitution of the United States." In seeking Jay's opinion about the resolutions Hamilton wondered if "the collective weight of the different parts of the Government" should "be employed in exploding the principles they contain." Jay responded that it was probably best for the national government to proceed with assumption and ignore the opposition. Jay's understated response still assumed that Virginia's legislators had acted illegitimately, writing that "Every indecent Interference of State assemblies will diminish their Influence."[44]

When he received Jay's letter, Hamilton was preparing notes for President Washington's impending Second Annual Address to Congress on December 8, 1790. Hamilton rejected Jay's advice and wanted the President to emphasize the "Utility and benefits of the National Government" in order to counter the "symptom of discontent" represented by Virginia's resolutions. A week after Jay's letter, Hamilton was encouraged by an account from Boston, offered by the Federalist Benjamin Lincoln who had led the private army formed to suppress the so-called Shays' Rebellion in western Massachusetts in 1787. Lincoln reported that the Virginia resolutions lacked support in Massachusetts; indeed, they were strengthening the case that greater national power was needed "to control the whole." Lincoln hoped that state resolutions on "the doings of Congress" would not become "a general practice" because they would endanger the nation and "keep the minds of the people at large in a constant state of ferment and irritation."[45]

Interposition by Maryland and Virginia Opposing Debt Assumption

While most attention was focused on Virginia's claim that the federal assumption of state debts was unconstitutional, Maryland's legislature also showed a willingness to invoke the tool of interposition. On December 15, 1790 three motions were introduced in Maryland's House of Delegates, with votes taken on them the next day. Two motions describing assumption as a dangerous measure and "particularly injurious to this state" passed, but a motion declaring assumption not "authorized by the Constitution" failed. The Maryland legislators who resisted criticizing assumption and who were unwilling to declare it unconstitutional rallied their forces, narrowly succeeding in passing a proposition to rescind the previous votes critical of assumption. After the House split 26 to 26, the Speaker broke the tie and voted in favor of rescinding. Maryland's efforts represented a failed attempt at interposition, similar to what had occurred in North Carolina where only one branch of the legislature was willing to declare assumption an infringement of the state's sovereignty.[46]

The fight over the resolutions in Virginia's House anticipated changes that were needed to pass those resolutions in Virginia's Senate and set the stage for a memorial defending them. Meriwether Smith wrote to Jefferson and anticipated a justifying "declaration" from Virginia to dispel the idea that the state was hostile to the national government. Indeed, on November 8, five days after the House passed the resolution declaring assumption unconstitutional, the Virginia House appointed a committee to prepare a memorial for Congress on the subject of its resolutions which the Virginia Senate had not yet passed. On December 16 the House passed its memorial and six days later the Senate agreed to the House's three resolutions with one amendment. The Senate deleted the word "expressly" from the first resolution of the House. Instead of being repugnant to the Constitution because the assumption of state debts exercised a power not "expressly granted" to the federal government, the final version of the first resolution of the Virginia legislature simply read that it was a power "not granted" to the national government. The Senate also agreed to a modified version of the House's memorial.[47]

One impetus for the memorial was the negative reaction to the resolutions the House had passed in November. The eleven-person committee the House appointed to draft an explanatory memorial to accompany their resolutions was chaired by the Federalist Francis Corbin. The committee included other Federalists such as Henry Lee, as well as prominent opponents of ratification, such as Patrick Henry. While Patrick Henry has been credited as the author of the memorial and the force behind the resolution declaring assumption unconstitutional, he was only one member of a large committee that wrestled with the text of the memorial as it underwent changes and amendments. Indeed, Henry was not even present when the memorial came before the legislature.[48]

The initial draft of the memorial presented to the House criticized Congress for its fiscal policy and speculated that assumption would stimulate new taxes. The memorial argued that assumption violated an express provision of the Constitution, namely Article VI's guarantee that national debts contracted prior to the Constitution would remain valid against the United States, and therefore "the consent of the State Legislatures ought to be obtained, before the said act can assume a constitutional form." The draft was amended, but the most notable change in the final version adopted by both the House and the Senate deleted the reference to requiring prior state consent to cure the supposed encroachment of the national government over matters of debt protection under the Constitution.[49]

The memorial passed by Virginia's legislature on December 23, 1790 criticized the policy of the assumption of debts in the Funding Act. The memorialists saw striking similarities between Hamilton's scheme and English systems of finance. The combination of "an enormous debt" with "an unbounded influence" of the executive threatened liberty. Such language has led scholars to identify the memorial with "prerevolutionary rhetoric" and "a classic statement of Country opposition principles." Along with the statement denying the constitutionality of assumption, the memorial is considered similar to colonial assemblies "drawing up resolutions of protest against unconstitutional activity by the British government."[50]

Finally, the memorial explained why the legislature had declared assumption unconstitutional in the resolution of November 3. "During the whole discussion of the F[e]deral] Constitution by the Convention of Virginia, your Memorialists were taught to believe, 'that every power not granted, was retained.'" They found "no clause in the Constitution, authorizing Congress to assume debts of the States!" Based on this rationale, scholars have described the memorial as an early formulation of the principle of strict construction or an assertion that the Constitution rested on a union of parties on an equal footing. Other scholars have viewed the memorial as anticipating nullification, with the Virginia legislators "taking a step toward a general constitutional principle upholding the right of the states to exercise authority in cases where the policies of the state and national governments conflicted."[51]

Aspects of the memorial certainly support some of these characterizations because they are consistent with a states' rights canon of a strict constitutional interpretation. What remains unappreciated about the memorial is its significance as a defense of state legislative interposition to remedy perceived incursions on the boundaries of state governments. After concluding that nothing in the Constitution authorized assumption, Virginia's legislators justified their actions by echoing Hamilton's and Madison's arguments and language in *The Federalist*. They identified themselves as "the Guardians . . . of the rights and Interests of their Constituents" and the "Sentinels" who could shield the people from encroachments or at least "sound the alarm."[52]

After Virginia's Legislature passed its resolutions and memorial, Federalists elsewhere responded. Anticipating the arrival of Virginia's resolutions and memorial in Washington, Hamilton sought to blunt their effect. He enlisted the help of his father-in-law, Philip Schuyler, one of New York's Senators, to head off any reconsideration of the Funding Act. Schuyler's success in passing a Senate resolution opposing any change to the funding system supported the decision to table Virginia's memorial in both houses of Congress.[53]

Pennsylvania Defends Interposition

A subsequent debate in Pennsylvania raised the propriety of state legislatures weighing in on national matters. Prompting that discussion was the passage of resolutions by the Pennsylvania House of Representatives urging their U.S. Senators to oppose an excise tax bill before Congress, which became the Whiskey Excise Tax of 1791. The resolutions had the support of two prominent, democratically inclined leaders of Pennsylvania's legislature: Albert Gallatin, future Secretary of the Treasury during Thomas Jefferson's administration, and William Findley, soon to be elected to Congress. The resolutions were opposed by Federalists in the Pennsylvania House, led by the Speaker of the House, William Bingham.[54]

During the debate, Bingham and his supporters did not defend the proposed excise tax. Instead, they argued that the House – in passing resolutions dealing with a matter before Congress – improperly interfered with national legislation. Bingham asserted that Congress possessed constitutional authority to impose excise taxes. Bingham conceded that state legislatures had a right to "constitutional opposition," but only if the national government tried "to assume authorities which the states have not granted them." As long as officials of the national government stayed "within the bounds of the powers committed to them," it was "highly imprudent, by legislative agency to interfere with their proceedings."[55]

Gallatin replied "that the state legislatures have the right, whenever the rights of the people are infringed, to remonstrate" and that legislators should speak up "not only when the government of the United States" went "beyond the powers vested with them, but upon every appearance thereof." One role of state legislators, Findley asserted, was to pay attention to "the proceedings of the general government." For his part, Gallatin considered it the duty of state legislators "to give notice to the people whenever we see the approach of danger, without waiting to receive the blow." In "blowing the trumpet" they could hardly be accused of "sedition." The House passed the resolutions on January 22, 1791, but they were narrowly rejected in the Senate.[56]

While the resolutions did not challenge the constitutional authority of Congress to pass an excise tax, they expressed the House's belief that the policy of collecting federal revenue through an excise tax could be "subversive of the peace, liberty and rights of the citizen." A defense of the House's action would vindicate interposition and the role of state legislatures as watchdogs of the operations of the national government.[57]

The issue of an excise tax had always lurked behind Hamilton's economic program given the connection between funding and the assumption of the debt. Excises – particularly on liquor – represented a historically detested tax and one that led to "the Whiskey Rebellion" uprising in western Pennsylvania. A bill for an excise tax had been introduced in Congress as early as May 1790, but was soon defeated. Hamilton renewed his request for an excise in his Report of 1790, and, despite facing considerable opposition, a whiskey excise tax was passed in 1791. Before then, North Carolina's legislature had instructed its Senators to oppose any attempt to impose an excise. North Carolina's action hardly went without adverse comment. But the passage of Pennsylvania's resolutions in the House against the excise tax attracted particular attention because they came immediately after Virginia's interposition and North Carolina's instructions and after the nation's capital had recently moved from New York to Philadelphia, a temporary site before its permanent relocation on the Potomac.[58]

Most critics of the Pennsylvania resolutions focused on the perceived inappropriateness of the state legislature expressing its views about matters before Congress. One critic facetiously suggested that Americans would soon save the cost of a federal government since the state legislatures wished to perform "the work of legislation for the *whole union.*" Fisher Ames characterized the resolutions of Pennsylvania's legislature as anarchy. Ames, along with other Federalists like Hamilton, welcomed the use of military force to suppress the resistance to the excise tax that surfaced in Pennsylvania, in order to demonstrate national authority over state governments.[59]

Legislators opposed to the resolutions published a "Protest" criticizing their passage because state legislators were elected to deal with "the particular objects of municipal jurisdiction" and not "the complicated affairs of the union." Beyond claiming that their colleagues had overstepped their role as state legislators, the dissenters opposed the resolutions as a bad precedent. Federalist legislators signing the "Protest" acknowledged that Congress might sometimes pass unconstitutional acts "by encroaching on those powers, which the states have exclusively retained." Presumably the federal judiciary and the executive would check such transgressions, but the equilibrium of federalism between the federal government and the state governments did not rest with either of them. The "ultimate appeal" was to "the people, who are their common constituents, their common superior, and their common umpire." Signers of the "Protest" explicitly rejected state legislative interposition, recently practiced by Virginia's legislature and publicized throughout the country through reprints of the Virginia resolutions and memorial.[60]

After publication of the "Protest," Pennsylvania legislators who had voted in favor of the resolutions including William Findley and Albert Gallatin responded with their own justification. They emphasized the strong opposition of their constituents to the excise tax, and while conceding congressional authority to levy an excise tax, considered that policy deeply flawed. As state legislators they had "a duty" to express themselves on any public matter that might undermine the interests of their constituents. Even with confidence in and respect for Congress, "it would be criminal in us to be silent" in the face of misguided national measures and they denied that their resolutions constituted an interference. "We know our rights, and we know the rights of Congress, and should deem ourselves unworthy of the trust reposed in us, if we neglect to pay every proper attention to both." The Pennsylvania legislators who assumed a role as guardians and sentinels watching the operations of the federal government in order to detect potential unwarrantable encroachments of power were hardly alone.[61]

Americans Become Increasingly Divided over the Proper Balance of Federalism

After the passage of the Funding Act, Madison's worry about an imbalance in the equilibrium of federalism only grew deeper, especially when more of Hamilton's economic program, including the establishment of a national bank, came to light. In February 1791 Madison believed there was no constitutional authority for a national bank and thought that the "constructions of the constitution" seeking to justify its establishment subverted "every power whatever in the several States." Madison identified the "essential characteristic" of the federal government "as composed of limited and enumerated powers" which precluded its exercise of any power "which is not evidently and necessarily involved in an express power." Madison even drafted a presidential veto hoping that Washington would declare the Bank Bill a power not "expressly delegated" by the Constitution and unwarranted by any "fair and safe rules of implication."[62]

By December 1791 Madison saw signs of a dangerous disequilibrium between the two levels of government, a troubling shift that he captured in his anonymous newspaper article in the *National Gazette*, entitled, "Consolidation." In the article Madison identified a worrisome trend toward "a consolidation of the states into one government." Madison championed a different type of consolidation – one that promoted "uniformity" and "the mutual confidence and affection of all parts of the Union." He concluded the article with advice both for those who were "attached to the separate authority reserved to the states" as well as those "who may be more inclined to contemplate the people of America in the light of one nation." "Let the former," he counseled in terms that implicitly endorsed interposition, "continue to watch against every encroachment, which might lead to gradual consolidation of the states into one government." But, he continued, "Let the latter employ their utmost zeal ... to consolidate the affairs of the states into one harmonious interest." In contrast to Madison's concern in 1787 "to shift power to the center," Madison now "believed the greatest threat to liberty came from Hamiltonian consolidation."[63]

Madison's change in perspective might have prompted him to alter the notes he had taken during the constitutional convention to de-emphasize the powers of the national government. After the convention he "may have wanted to minimize his initial conviction that it was impossible to partition state and national powers. In particular, he may have thought it advisable to soften the degree to which he had repeatedly tilted in favor of national power." However, Madison's concept of interposition did not rest on his notes of the convention at all, but instead on his essays in *The Federalist* and his later explanations of his Virginia Resolutions of 1798.[64]

By early 1792, Madison vented to close friends in Virginia about Hamilton's Report on Manufactures which "broaches a new constitutional doctrine of vast consequence" and demanded "the serious attention of the public." The report proposed that the national government encourage the growth of manufacturing instead of agriculture by national subsidies from tariffs on imports. Hamilton promoted the plan as expanding productivity and technology while using immigration to supply a workforce, but denied that this would harm the South with an economy based on agriculture and slavery. Madison predicted that if such a "usurpation of power" prevailed, it would alter the essential character of the national government under the Constitution. For Madison, Hamilton's expansive interpretation of the powers of the federal government undercut the Constitution itself. As he put it, "If not only the *means*, but the *objects* are unlimited, the parchment had better be thrown into the fire at once."[65]

Similar fears influenced those who saw things from the opposite direction. For Hamilton and others, the localism and state initiatives that meddled with the operation of the nation's government equally threatened the Constitution. Even as Madison saw ominous signs of excessive national power in the advocacy for a national bank, other Federalists seized upon the behavior of state legislators who made a motion not to take an oath to support the Constitution. Radically different perceptions of the state of federalism under the new Constitution divided Americans and the two former allies, Madison and Hamilton. Conflicting views about whether the balance of federalism was being properly struck became even more strident with disputes over the legitimacy of political opposition amidst heightened partisan rhetoric.[66]

Unlike Madison, Hamilton after ratification remained focused on increasing the authority of the national government in the face of state governments' inclination to restrain that power. Hamilton believed that state governments were predisposed to encroach upon the authority of the national government, much as he had predicted in *The Federalist*. In the aftermath of the assumption fight, Hamilton redoubled efforts to check the power of state governments while increasing the nation's power. That concern shaped his understanding of the appropriate equilibrium of federalism. His stated preference was for a "liberal construction of the powers of the National Government." With that outlook Hamilton felt betrayed by Madison's opposition to assumption of the debt, complaining – without a sense of irony – that Madison had "lost no opportunity of *sounding the alarm* ... at encroachments mediated on the rights of the States."[67]

During the effort to frame and ratify the Constitution, Madison and Hamilton agreed that "the equilibrium" between the states and the federal government "stood in far greater danger of being upset by the states than by the general government." But Madison's emerging misgivings about the sweep and broad implications of Hamilton's national financial programs during the First Congress eventually placed them at odds. From that point on, as Gordon Wood has put it, Madison was no longer "Hamilton's kind of nationalist."[68]

Hamilton, however, sought to reconcile his and Madison's constitutional views in a letter that criticized Madison's legislative behavior in the First Congress. Hamilton claimed a "similarity of thinking" with Madison when it came to understanding the proper balance of federalism under the Constitution. Hamilton's claim assumed that politically, he and Madison started from "the *same point.*" However, scholars have observed that Hamilton and Madison did not approach the Constitution similarly and that Madison never became a nationalist in the same way that Hamilton did. Drew McCoy suggests that because the source of Hamilton's and Madison's support for the Constitution differed, "they brought very different attitudes and expectations to bear on their incipient careers as national political leaders." In contrast with Madison's preoccupation with federalism, Gerald Stourzh suggests that "the unitary state" remained "the ideal of Hamilton's statesmanship" and that Hamilton simply lacked a "commitment to the theory of federalism."[69]

* * * * * *

For Hamilton and others who considered the national government vulnerable to encroachments by state governments, Virginia's interposition resolutions inappropriately and illegitimately intruded into the sphere of the federal government. In contrast, for those who regarded assumption and other national measures as an inappropriate expansion of the constitutional authority of the national government, the fact that Virginia's legislature had sounded the alarm and brought attention to that matter was perfectly legitimate. The contrasting reactions to the resolutions and memorial adopted by Virginia's legislature in 1790 underscored that the proper equilibrium of federalism was, and would continue to be, in the eye of the beholder. The defense of Virginia's interposition would soon be followed by a second wave of state interposition, this time focused on a decision of the Supreme Court that seemed to threaten state sovereignty.

3

State Interposition and Debates over the Meaning of the Constitution

Two constitutional issues dominating the 1790s illustrate the increasing interest in the tool of interposition and the fluid nature of constitutional interpretation in the early republic. One issue involved whether the Constitution permitted individuals to sue states in federal court. The Supreme Court's decision in *Chisholm v. Georgia* (1793) generated widespread state interposition to resist the Court's seemingly broad interpretation of a constitutional clause and ultimately resulted in the Eleventh Amendment. A second issue was whether President Washington had exceeded his authority by allowing the proposed Jay Treaty to be signed and submitted for ratification by the Senate. Federalists argued that the Constitution's text clearly provided presidential authority, while Republicans believed that Congress should speak for the sovereign people by assessing the treaty's constitutionality. In both instances, states considered it their duty to sound the alarm when the national government intruded on state sovereignty. Without that resistance and protest, states believed that federalism would slip into disequilibrium, unduly expanding the powers of the national government at the expense of the reserved rights of the states. Interposition on these occasions illustrated that states would jealously guard their sovereignty and that citizens throughout the country would take a more active role in political life.

The larger framework for these state interpositions was the opposing constitutional viewpoints regarding equilibrium between Federalists and Republicans. Federalists embraced an interpretation of the federal system that emphasized a broad construction of national power – both actual and implied – while Republicans emphasized a narrow construction, with most governmental powers reserved to the states. Moreover, the controversy over the Jay Treaty encouraged both Federalists and Republicans to resolve questions of constitutional meaning through an historical examination of the intent of the founding generation. That process ultimately led to the idea of a more or less "fixed" Constitution with discoverable, original intentions of the framers and ratifiers – with all of the challenges that such an "excavation" implied.[1]

A dramatic and successful wave of interposition began in 1792 directed at the Supreme Court with respect to a series of cases culminating in *Chisholm* which ruled that states could be sued under Article III, section 2 of the Constitution that extended federal judicial power "to controversies ... between a State and Citizens of another State." This reading of the clause posed a serious and recognized problem for states.

In the wake of those lawsuits, interposition resolutions were passed by Massachusetts and Virginia and shared with other state legislatures that produced additional opposition to *Chisholm*. Although states were economically motivated to avoid suits compelling them to pay debts to noncitizens and other individual creditors, opposition to state suability went beyond self-interest. Resistance also rested on the belief that the national jurisdiction over states asserted in *Chisholm* undermined the sovereignty retained by the states under the Constitution. Moreover, states feared that the decision established a precedent that would lead to further incursions on state sovereignty and facilitate the absorption of states into a consolidated national government. Governors and state legislatures warned of those possibilities and contributed to a movement that led to the swift passage of a constitutional amendment that reversed *Chisholm*.

The disapproval of *Chisholm* is well known and much attention has been paid to the Eleventh Amendment passed in response to the decision and the significance of the amendment for the scope of federal court jurisdiction. Largely overlooked is how interposition and attempts at interposition contributed to the Eleventh Amendment's overturning of *Chisholm*. As with Virginia's response to perceived constitutional overreaching when the national government assumed state debts, reactions to the detected imbalance of federalism caused by *Chisholm* occurred without the explicit use of the term interposition. Scholars have noticed state legislative responses to summonses issued to states in cases filed before federal courts. Missing, however, is an appreciation that the governors and state legislatures who objected to their state being sued were using the tool of interposition. Indeed, they used that tool in the manner described by Hamilton and Madison in *The Federalist* to encourage widespread state resistance to the expanding power of the national government. *Chisholm* was part of what Jonathan Gienapp has called the project of "fixing" the Constitution after its ratification – grappling with the nature and meaning of constitutional powers.

Constitutional interpretation could also involve matters on which the Constitution was silent and therefore language was unavailable to help settle an issue. One of the first important debates in Congress involving constitutional interpretation raised the question of how executive officers could be removed and by whom – an issue that lacked constitutional text for guidance. During that debate over the removal power, Madison argued that "the meaning of the constitution" could be "ascertained" by Congress as well as the Supreme Court. *Chisholm* presented the opposite situation: an interpretation of constitutional text granting the federal courts jurisdictional authority that, if sustained, might dramatically alter the nation's understanding of the Constitution.[2]

* * * * * *

The Doctrine of Sovereign Immunity

Opposition to the suability of states invoked the idea of sovereign immunity, a doctrine with ancient roots traceable to the concept that the king could not be sued without his consent. Nonetheless, over time English common law developed procedures that undermined this obstacle to lawsuits and provided a few avenues for seeking remedies against the crown. In the American colonies, the remote distance of the king rendered such English precedents largely irrelevant. Legal claims against the king as the sovereign were more likely to be directed toward the colonial governments before the

Revolution. The charters of several colonies, including Massachusetts, Connecticut, and Rhode Island, expressly allowed suits to be filed against the government. A few other colonies recognized common law actions permitting individuals to sue governmental authorities. After the Declaration of Independence, Connecticut and Rhode Island adopted their charters as their new state constitutions and thus preserved the possibility of lawsuits against the state. The state constitutions of Delaware and Pennsylvania contained provisions permitting the legislature to regulate suits against the state. Other state constitutions were silent on the issue and none prohibited lawsuits against their state government. As such, lawsuits against governments by individuals were not entirely unknown. Such knowledge, however, did not avoid the adverse reaction to *Chisholm*, particularly given the potential implications that decision might have on the authority of states.[3]

While some cast the issue of suability as simply a matter of fairness in providing a remedy for legitimate debts a state might owe to individuals, lawsuits that forced states into court were often depicted as undermining a state's sovereign rights. This reaction was particularly acute after the Constitution created a system of divided sovereignty between the national government and state governments. The prospect of a state being hauled before a federal court by a citizen of another state undercut the idea of residual sovereignty that states supposedly possessed. As one observer put it, if a private citizen could force an unwilling state into federal court, the states would "have relinquished all their SOVEREIGNTIES, and have become mere *corporations.*"[4]

Nonetheless, suability did not create apprehension during the federal constitutional convention. That was somewhat surprising since the heavy debts incurred by colonies and later states were likely to result in lawsuits against the states. Potential litigants included holders of public securities issued during the war including Loyalists whose property had been confiscated by states during wartime, and British creditors who held prewar debts. Despite that looming threat of litigation, Article III that dealt with the judiciary, expressly extended federal jurisdiction to such controversies. Article III also granted the Supreme Court original jurisdiction in all suits "in which a State shall be [a] party." While these provisions apparently provoked no debate in the convention, they received considerable attention during the ratification process.[5]

In New York, the "Federal Farmer" questioned if individuals should be allowed "to humble a state" by dragging it into federal court. Moreover, "Brutus" asserted that the clause granting federal court jurisdiction over suits "between a state and citizens of another state" was "improper" and would "prove most pernicious and destructive." Alexander Hamilton responded in *Federalist* 81 by insisting that it was "inherent in the nature of sovereignty" for a state "not to be amenable to the suit of an individual *without its consent*." Hamilton maintained that the Constitution did not intend to "surrender" the principle of immunity and that "it will remain with the states."[6]

One extended debate over whether states could be sued under the Constitution occurred in Virginia's ratifying convention. Anti-Federalist George Mason called the state suability provisions of Article III "disgraceful" because they would allow "the sovereignty of the State" to "be arraigned like a culprit, or private offender." Madison dismissed Mason's warning by asserting that the clause authorizing jurisdiction over controversies between a state and citizens of another state was meant to apply only when the state was the plaintiff and not a defendant. As he put it, "It is not in the power of Individuals to call any State into Court." John Marshall agreed with Madison and hoped that no delegate "will think that a State will be called to the bar of the Federal Court" since it was "not rational to suppose, that the sovereign power shall be dragged before a Court." The "intent" of Article III was "to enable States to recover claims" against "individuals residing in other States." Marshall asserted "this construction" was "warranted by the words." Patrick Henry rejected Marshall's reasoning because the "clear" language of the clause apparently gave the federal courts "cognizance of controversies between a State, and citizens of another State, without discriminating between plaintiff or defendant."[7]

Such different understandings of Article III's language prompted a number of state ratifying conventions, including those in Virginia, North Carolina, and New York, to propose amendments that would have eliminated the apparent grant of federal jurisdiction over suits brought by an individual against a state. However, the First Congress failed to adopt such an amendment. Instead, Congress enacted section 13 of the Judiciary Act of 1789 which gave the Supreme Court original but not exclusive jurisdiction over controversies "between a state and citizens of other states, or aliens."[8]

Despite Federalists' assurances to the contrary, the post-ratification period saw individuals suing states in the Supreme Court. Before then, many individuals with claims against states evidently received financial compensation after petitioning and memorializing state legislatures. A failure in that system of state legislative adjustment led to the Supreme Court lawsuits. In all of the documented suits brought by individuals against states, "the plaintiffs had petitioned or memorialized the legislature before filing suit – in some cases more than once – but had received little or no satisfaction."[9]

Reaction to the First Suit against a State: *Van Staphorst v. Maryland* (1790)

Van Staphorst v. Maryland was the first of a series of eight lawsuits brought against states in the Supreme Court. The case involved the Van Staphorst brothers seeking the repayment of funds they loaned to the state of Maryland during the Revolutionary War. Although the state eventually settled the case, the filing of the lawsuit raised concerns that went to the heart of how the federalism established by the Constitution was understood. The case seemed an example of how the operation of the Constitution might undermine state powers.

Republican Massachusetts Attorney General James Sullivan advanced an argument against lawsuits against states. In *Observations Upon the Government of the United States of America*, Sullivan reminded his readers that during the ratification debates, "there were great difficulties, in the minds of many" because the Constitution seemingly granted federal judicial jurisdiction over suits brought by individuals against states. Sullivan recalled that "men of learning and ingenuity" – perhaps referring to Hamilton, Madison, and Marshall – gave Article III "a construction which made many easy with it." Sullivan joined them in concluding that Article III only anticipated states as plaintiffs, but not as defendants.[10]

Sullivan considered the Supreme Court's assumption of jurisdiction in *Van Staphorst* a dangerous step toward national governmental control. He argued that the Constitution established "two sovereign powers, independent of each other in their political capacities, exercising legislative, judicial and executive authority over the same persons, at the same time, and in the same place." To subject the sovereignty retained by state governments to lawsuits such as that brought against Maryland violated the federal structure and was "inconsistent" with "any kind of sovereignty." If the federal government had the judicial power implied by *Van Staphorst*, it converted "sovereign states" into "districts" under the "subordination" of the national government. *Van Staphorst* had crossed the line dividing the two sovereigns and put state jurisdictional rights in jeopardy.[11]

Chisholm v. Georgia (1793)

Despite the legal action against Maryland by the Van Staphorsts, it was the lawsuit filed in the U.S. Circuit Court by South Carolina citizen Alexander Chisholm against Georgia on February 24, 1791, concerning a debt contracted by the state during the revolutionary war, that proved to be the national lightning rod for the issue of suability. After receiving the summons, Georgia Governor Edward Telfair consulted his Solicitor General and Attorney General, both of whom urged the governor not to recognize the jurisdiction of the federal courts in the case. Accordingly, the state challenged the jurisdiction of the U.S. Circuit Court for the District of Georgia, the initial venue for the lawsuit brought by Chisholm. James Iredell, the Supreme Court justice presiding over the Circuit Court, ruled for the state of Georgia. Undeterred, Chisholm then filed suit in the Supreme Court and a summons was issued ordering the state to appear on the first day of the August term of the Supreme Court to answer Chisholm's plea. When Georgia's legislature met, Telfair asked the legislators to consider if the lawsuit represented an encroachment by the federal judiciary on the legitimate sphere of state authority.[12]

Georgia's House of Representatives responded with a draft interposition resolution stating that this claim of federal jurisdiction would "destroy the retained sovereignty of the states" and "annihilate" state government. Until a constitutional amendment settled the matter, the House thought that any judgment in the lawsuit would be "unconstitutional and extrajudicial" and "*ipso facto* void" and wanted to share its views with the Supreme Court and the state's congressional delegation. Although the Senate failed to act on this proposed interposition, Governor Telfair sent the House's resolution to Philadelphia where it was read to the Supreme Court justices hearing arguments in *Chisholm*.[13]

Georgia protested that by not consenting to the lawsuit, the state was immune from suit and therefore declined to make an appearance. The Attorney General of the United States, Edmund Randolph, argued for the plaintiff, and described the Constitution as originating "immediately from the people" who subjected themselves to the authority granted to the national government. Moreover, states had relinquished sovereignty to the extent they agreed to limits on "their powers." As "the letter of the Constitution" was clear, Randolph saw "nothing in the nature of sovereignties, combined as those of America are, to prevent the words of the Constitution" from receiving their "usual construction." Thus, individuals could sue states and Randolph asserted that there was "no degradation of sovereignty, in the States, to submit to the Supreme Judiciary of the *United States*." He was not seeking the "prostration of State-rights" and was confident that "the power, which the people and the Legislatures of the States indirectly hold over almost every movement of the National Government" would preserve those rights.[14]

In a four to one decision, the court upheld its jurisdiction under Article III, with Chief Justice John Jay along with associate Justices John Blair, James Wilson, and William Cushing forming the majority. Justice James Iredell issued the lone dissent, rejecting Randolph's suggestion that the Constitution vested all the judicial power in the Supreme Court whether or not Congress had acted. Instead, Iredell concluded that the Supreme Court could only exercise the jurisdiction conferred by Congress that was consistent with grants of power allocated to the national government under the Constitution. As Iredell put it, "A state is altogether exempt" from federal court jurisdiction except for "the special instances where the general government has power derived from the Constitution." Iredell viewed the formation of the Constitution differently than did the other Justices.[15]

Iredell's opinion recognized a fundamental division of sovereignty between the two levels of government and asserted that the national government's sovereignty derived solely from the "powers surrendered" by the states. Iredell did not assert that states retained *all the sovereignty they possessed prior to the ratification* of the Constitution. Instead, he considered them "completely sovereign" only so far as they had not delegated sovereignty to the federal government. Iredell's understanding of "divided sovereignty" at the time of his dissent was an unremarkable expression of "middle-of-the-road Federalism." Only later would Iredell be considered to have protected absolute state sovereignty, a view that would "endear him" to sovereign states' rights advocates.[16]

In contrast to Iredell, the majority of the *Chisholm* court, led by Wilson and Jay, offered a more nationalist interpretation of the federal system. They downplayed the concept of the creation of the Constitution as a delegation of powers by states that retained residual sovereignty. Wilson set the tone by stating that the issue of Georgia's claim "to be *sovereign*" came down to the question: "do the people of the *United States* form a NATION?" For Wilson, the people of the United States, a national people, had framed the Constitution. He traced much of the "confusion and perplexity" about America's political system to the misguided focus and attention on "the *states,* rather than the PEOPLE." It was not the states but "the 'people of the United States'" that brought the constitutional union "into Existence." The structure of the Constitution established "that the people of the United States intended to form themselves into a nation for national purposes," including a judiciary with powers "extending over the whole nation." That objective made it incongruous, if not "repugnant" to America's national existence, if the state of Georgia "should be permitted to claim successfully an entire exemption from the jurisdiction of the national government." Moreover, Justices Wilson, Blair, and Cushing argued that Georgia's amenability to suit could simply rest on the clear language of Article III.[17]

Chief Justice Jay asked "in what sense" Georgia could be considered "a sovereign State" and "whether suability is incompatible with such sovereignty." Although he conceded the "residuary sovereignty" of states, Jay focused on "the sovereignty of the nation." For Jay, the Constitution was established by "the people, in their collective and national capacity" who in "acting as sovereigns of the whole people" had created a constitution "by which it was their will, that State Governments should be bound." During the creation of "this great compact," numerous "prerogatives were transferred to the national Government," including states' immunity from suit. According to Jefferson Powell, if the views of Wilson and Jay had prevailed, "reference to the states as sovereigns would play no role in constitutional argument."[18]

Georgia's Response to Chisholm

After the Supreme Court's opinion in *Chisholm*, Georgia's Governor Telfair again prodded his legislature to act. In a November 1793 address, Telfair urged the legislature to recommend a constitutional amendment to reverse the decision. For Telfair, *Chisholm* threatened the state's political existence. The House of Representatives referred Telfair's Address to a committee that recommended an act memorializing the state's retained sovereignty and seeking the support of other state legislatures for a constitutional amendment to overturn *Chisholm*. In the end, Georgia's legislature never acted on the House committee's report because the legislators were diverted by a more draconian response to *Chisholm*. After the committee reported a bill proclaiming the state's retained sovereignty, the House wanted to subject anyone executing a judgment in a lawsuit against the state of Georgia to capital punishment. After the death penalty provision passed the House, it was sent to the Senate where it died, evidently because the Senate found the bill "too rigid."[19]

Other Reactions to Chisholm

Chisholm is often considered the first important case to be decided by the Supreme Court with its "significance ... quickly grasped by all of the states." The ruling was seen as an "unacceptable interpretation of Article III" that prompted Americans to "reject the decision." As David Currie has put it, "just about everybody in Congress agreed the Supreme Court had misread the Constitution."[20]

By the time the Supreme Court rendered its decision in *Chisholm* on February 18, 1793, two more states, New York and Virginia, had been sued in the Supreme Court by individuals. New York contested the Court's jurisdiction by hiring the lawyer Jared Ingersoll who challenged the suit on the grounds that New York was "a free, sovereign, and independent State." Virginia's legislature concluded that the Court's assertion of jurisdiction represented "a dangerous and unconstitutional assumption of power" interfering with the "unimpaired sovereignty" left to the states in "all matters of internal Government." It was hardly lost on the legislators that such "internal" state matters included the regulation and protection of slavery. The legislature passed resolutions denying the Supreme Court any jurisdiction over suits brought by individuals against Virginia or any other state.[21]

While *Chisholm* clearly increased the vulnerability of states to lawsuits that might compel them to pay debts to non-state citizens and other foreign creditors, scholars differ over how much that economic motive prompted opposition to the decision and influenced the ratification of the Eleventh Amendment. For some, according to Clyde Jacobs, *Chisholm* cried out "for repudiation, perhaps not so much because it subjected the states to federal judicial process as because the principal opinions in the case expounded Federalist constitutional philosophy and all but denied the sovereignty of the states."[22]

What scholars have overlooked is how effectively the tool of interposition was employed during the movement to overturn the decision through the Eleventh Amendment. State use of interposition involved resolutions that the legislatures of Virginia and Massachusetts passed and shared with other states, which in turn prompted complementary resolutions by Connecticut, North Carolina, and New Hampshire. But the practice of interposition also included the failed attempts made by Republicans in New York and the initial efforts in the Georgia House of Representatives, as well as subsequent attempts to pass interposition resolutions in South Carolina, Maryland, and Pennsylvania.[23]

Massachusetts' Leadership in Reversing Chisholm

Massachusetts was the first state legislature to pass interposition resolutions questioning the principle established by *Chisholm*, and in doing so led the way in securing the Eleventh Amendment. In Congress, on February 19, 1793, Representative Theodore Sedgwick of Massachusetts proposed a constitutional amendment in response to *Chisholm*. After Sedgwick's motion was tabled, his colleague from Massachusetts, Caleb Strong, made a similar motion that Congress also failed to act upon. In Boston, within a month of the *Chisholm* decision, the Massachusetts House of Representatives appointed a committee to address the Court's decision.[24]

In June 1793, after a copy of the *Chisholm* proceedings arrived, a new joint committee of the Massachusetts legislature analyzed the opinion and issued a report. Legislators thought that allowing individual citizens to sue state governments violated state sovereignty and was "repugnant to every idea of a *Federal Government*." The report resolved that the state's congressional delegation be instructed and requested to use their utmost influence to either expunge the language in Article III relating to controversies between a state and the citizens of other states or modify the article. This joint report of June 20, 1793 was referred to the next session of the Massachusetts legislature scheduled for January 1794, but in the meantime the state learned that it was also being sued in the Supreme Court.[25]

On July 9, 1793 both Governor John Hancock and Attorney General James Sullivan were subpoenaed in the case of *Vassall v. Massachusetts*. William Vassall was a seventy-seven-year-old Loyalist refugee living in England who was suing the state for mortgaging his Boston mansion and auctioning off his furniture during the war. Notice of the lawsuit prompted Hancock to issue a proclamation for a special session of the legislature to meet in September 1793 to respond to the lawsuit. The proclamation effectively merged the steps the legislature had begun to take in responding to *Chisholm* with the response to the immediate threat posed to the state by *Vassall*. The issue of suability had long been on the minds of some state officials like Attorney General Sullivan, who two years earlier had criticized the case of *Van Staphorst*.[26]

The *Vassall* case also renewed debate in Massachusetts over whether states could be sued. Those who saw suits against states as a usurpation by federal courts remembered that supporters of the Constitution had dismissed foreboding about consolidation during the ratification debates, particularly in Massachusetts' ratifying convention. It seemed to critics of *Chisholm* that suability formed part of a longstanding plan to absorb state governments. If *Chisholm* "aimed a blow at the sovereignty of the individual States," some observers anticipated legislative interposition in response.[27]

While Governor Hancock brought attention to the *Vassall* lawsuit in his Proclamation calling for a special session of the legislature, it was his Address at the start of that session on August 18, 1793 that explicitly sounded the alarm about overreaching by the national government. Hancock wanted the federal government supported with "force and efficacy," but without undermining the powers that "the People intended to vest and to reserve in the State Governments." Failing to maintain that proper balance might lead to a "consolidation of all the States" and "endanger the Nation."[28]

Within days of the Address, a joint committee of the legislature concluded that the result in *Chisholm* was "not *expedient*" and instructed and requested their congressional delegation to seek a constitutional amendment to protect states against such suits. The committee's report asked the governor to share resolutions the legislature might adopt with the other state governors and their legislatures. Although approved by the Senate, the report prompted a discussion in the House about the propriety of raising the question of lawsuits against states.[29]

Four speeches in the House illustrated a consensus that the legislature was entitled to comment on *Chisholm* and that a constitutional amendment was needed to restore a proper national–state balance. One legislator considered it "high time" to amend the Constitution. Even a legislator who believed that Article III supported the decision in *Chisholm* thought an "expression of the sense of the Commonwealth" in favor of constitutional revision was the "most proper and efficient" approach. Two other legislators agreed with the Court even as they asserted their right as state legislators to question the *Chisholm* decision.[30]

After debate, the original joint committee report went to a new House committee that produced the version of Massachusetts' interposition resolution that Governor Hancock signed on September 27, 1793. While the original report described suability as inexpedient, the final resolution objected to such jurisdiction because it was "dangerous to the peace, safety and independence of the several States, and repugnant to the first principles of a Federal Government."

Like the original report, the final resolution also instructed and requested the state's congressional delegation to seek a federal constitutional amendment to reverse *Chisholm*. The legislature's resolution requested the governor to share the resolves with the governors of other states and their legislatures.[31]

The importance of interstate communication and action on the matter of the vulnerability of states to lawsuits by individuals was emphasized in the transmittal letter of Massachusetts' interposition resolution. After John Hancock died, Samuel Adams, the state's Lieutenant Governor, became Governor and immediately wrote to all of the other state governors and included the recent proceedings of the Massachusetts legislature "upon a principle of national Government, in which each State in the Union is equally interested." While it was important to support the national government, permitting states to be sued would totally undermine "the federal principle, and procure a consolidation of all the Governments." He endorsed interstate consultation by means of an interposition resolution in order to invigorate discussion about an action of the national government that potentially disrupted the federal balance under the Constitution.[32]

In calling for other states to consider the matter of lawsuits against states, the Massachusetts legislature and its governor stimulated interposition efforts from other legislatures, including Virginia – the state that had first utilized the tool of interposition after the ratification of the Constitution. Virginia's legislature had earlier passed interposition resolutions of its own rejecting the Supreme Court's jurisdiction in a suit filed against the state. Now, however, it followed Massachusetts' lead in formulating interposition resolutions among the states directed at *Chisholm*, all of which formed an important catalyst in the movement leading to the Eleventh Amendment.[33]

Response to Massachusetts' Interposition

Connecticut was the first state to respond to Massachusetts' interposition resolution. Within a week of receiving Samuel Adams' communication to the state governors, Connecticut's General Assembly formed a joint committee on October 18, 1793 to consider the issue of a constitutional amendment. The House of Representatives accepted a version of a resolution from the Governor and Council of the state, passing it on October 29. That resolution urged the state's congressional delegation to support an amendment reversing *Chisholm*.[34]

Georgia's legislature was the next to act, although the record is unclear if Georgia was responding to the actions of the Massachusetts legislature. Governor Telfair addressed the Georgia legislature on November 4, arguably in time for Adams' circular letter of October 9 to have reached him. But neither Telfair's address, nor the subsequent House report calling for a similar amendment to respond to *Chisholm*, nor an interstate address on the issue, explicitly referred to Massachusetts' September interposition resolution.[35]

Whatever the situation with Georgia, Virginia's response to *Chisholm* was clearly influenced by the Massachusetts legislature. In addressing Virginia's House on November 13, 1793 Henry Lee attached Adams' circular letter and the proceedings of the Massachusetts legislature. He had earlier written to Adams' predecessor, John Hancock, as soon as he learned that Massachusetts was considering the constitutional question. Lee asked to be informed about what actions Massachusetts was taking. Thus, when Lee shared his thoughts about the broader implications of suability and how Virginia's legislature might wish to respond, he was fully aware of Massachusetts' interposition resolution.[36]

Lee asserted that Article III rested on the "fundamental principle" that the Constitution created two levels of government. This divided sovereignty demanded maintaining an appropriate balance between those two levels of government. "They are then both Sovereign, derive their Sovereignty from the Same Source, and are intended to produce in their respective Spheres the Same object, to wit, the common felicity." The notion of two spheres of government with "respective Sovereignties" made the possibility of overlap between the two levels inevitable. In *Chisholm*, the federal judiciary had exceeded its legitimate authority.[37]

Lee knew exactly what the legislature should do. He urged "a disavowal of the right of the Judiciary to call a State into Court" and urged the legislature to draft a memorial on the subject, a suggestion that harkened back to the memorial Virginia's legislature had sent to Congress a few years earlier about the assumption of state debts. Lee did not specifically recommend a constitutional amendment to reverse

Chisholm, but thought the state's Senators could be instructed to support the passage of a law that would "forever crush the doctrine" asserted by the Supreme Court relative to the suability of states.[38]

Virginia's legislature quickly responded to Lee, with the Massachusetts resolutions before them. The legislature passed two resolutions in late November 1793. The first rejected *Chisholm* as "incompatible with, and dangerous to the sovereignty and independence of the individual states" since the decision "tends to a general consolidation of these confederated republics." A second resolution instructed and requested the state's congressional delegation to seek a constitutional amendment to overturn *Chisholm*. The resolution also requested, as had Massachusetts' resolution, that the governor communicate the resolve to the governors and legislatures of the other states. Governor Lee forwarded Virginia's interposition resolutions to state governors on December 5, 1793.[39]

Julius Goebel has contrasted the supposedly aggressive tone of Virginia's resolutions of November 28, 1793 – the legislature being "addicted to the tactic of defiant resolutions" – with the reputedly more "sedate" response by Massachusetts' resolutions of September 27, 1793. Yet both legislatures were engaged in interposition and considered *Chisholm* an intrusion by the national government. Virginia called the decision unconstitutional and Massachusetts considered it incompatible with the federalism established by the Constitution. Both states instructed and requested their congressional delegations to seek a constitutional amendment to reverse *Chisholm*. And finally, both Massachusetts and Virginia pointedly sought interstate communication and action by requesting that their governors share their resolutions with their fellow governors for review by their legislatures. In every meaningful way, the resolutions of the two states functioned as comparable examples of interposition.[40]

Even scholars writing much closer to the events in question alluded to interposition in the passage of the Eleventh Amendment while not identifying it as such. One example is St. George Tucker, the author of the much-celebrated American edition of Blackstone's *Commentaries*. In Tucker's Appendix to his *Commentaries*, first published in 1803, entitled "View of the Constitution of the United States," Tucker rhetorically asked what should happen if the federal government exercised powers not "warranted" by the Constitution. In answering that question – which went to the heart of interposition – Tucker replied that "where the act of usurpation may immediately affect an individual, the remedy is to be sought by recourse" to the "judiciary." However, a different response was called for should such an act of usurpation "affect a state." In such a case the state legislature, "whose rights will be invaded by every such act, will be ready to mark the innovation and sound the alarm to the people."[41]

Tucker's question and answer were not original; he knew he was paraphrasing James Madison in *Federalist* 44, one of the interposition-related essays. Tucker cited Madison's essay that had posed a similar hypothetical: "[W]hat is to be the consequence, in case the Congress shall misconstrue this part of the Constitution, and exercise powers not warranted by its true meaning?" Madison answered that the executive branch and the judiciary formed the first line of defense since they existed "to expound and give effect to the legislative acts." "[I]n the last resort," however, "a remedy must be obtained from the people, who can by the election of more faithful representatives, annul the acts of the usurpers." Tucker echoed Madison's point that state legislatures were particularly well suited to check the enlargement or encroachment of powers by the national government since such action "will be an invasion of the rights of the [state legislatures]" who "will be ever ready to mark the innovation, to sound the alarm to the people, and to exert their local influence in effecting a change of federal representatives." Thus, the consequence of legislatively sounding of the alarm would be either to seek new representatives or a constitutional amendment.[42]

Interposition Leads to Calls for a Constitutional Amendment

With the interposition resolutions of Massachusetts and Virginia in interstate circulation, the pace of legislative response to *Chisholm* sped up. After Virginia's resolutions, the state legislatures of North Carolina and New Hampshire passed resolutions of their own. In addition, within a month of Virginia's resolutions being circulated to other state governors, the legislatures of three other states, South Carolina, Maryland, and Pennsylvania, each took steps towards toward passing interposition resolutions, sometimes with one, but not both houses of the legislature approving them.[43]

Although Pennsylvania's legislators did not pass an interposition resolution protesting state suability, they were reminded of their right to do so. In September 1794 manufacturers of snuff and refined sugar in Philadelphia sent a memorial to the legislature opposing an impending congressional excise tax on those products. The memorialists had "in vain petitioned and remonstrated" Congress against such a tax and wanted the legislature to interpose "as the most immediate guardians of the rights and liberties of the citizens of Pennsylvania." Such support could resemble how the legislature had acted when Pennsylvania's House passed resolutions opposing the whiskey excise tax and defended its right to question national policies that seemed wrongheaded. The manufacturers hoped that "a seasonable interposition" by Pennsylvania's legislature would help convince "the general government" not to "persevere in the pernicious and oppressive course which it has unhappily commenced by the imposition of an odious excise."[44]

Eventually, other state legislatures, including those in North Carolina and New Hampshire, passed resolutions calling for a constitutional amendment to reverse *Chisholm*. In January 1794, North Carolina concluded that the idea of individuals suing states was not contemplated when the state ratified the Constitution and that the Supreme Court's exercise of such jurisdiction was "derogatory of the reserved rights and sovereignty of this State." The resolution instructed and requested the congressional delegation to support an amendment and "secure the Sovereignty of the Several States." New Hampshire also approved a joint resolution calling for an amendment after considering both Massachusetts' and Virginia's resolutions.[45]

In the end, of the five state legislatures that passed resolutions seeking a constitutional amendment to reverse *Chisholm* – Massachusetts, Virginia, Connecticut, North Carolina, and New Hampshire – only the first two had lawsuits filed against their states. The other legislatures, Connecticut, North Carolina, and New Hampshire, along with individual state legislators in South Carolina, Maryland, Pennsylvania, and New York who took steps to draft interposition resolutions, obviously agreed with Samuel Adams' statement in his circular letter that suability concerned every state.

Within weeks of the final judgment entered in *Chisholm*, both houses of Congress considered the proposed Eleventh Amendment and it received quick and overwhelming support. Although Federalists and Republicans backed the Amendment, each side viewed its passage through a distinct lens. Federalists could regard the Amendment as simply an adjustment and extension of the principle of sovereign immunity: now a citizen of another state – and not merely a state's own citizens – was precluded from bringing suit against the state in federal court. For Republicans, however, the Eleventh Amendment could be seen as a vindication of their understanding of the federalism established by the Constitution: that a state's sovereignty precluded it from being sued in national courts. Both views were plausible, but the competing ideas about the foundation of the Constitution raised by individuals suing states in federal court demonstrated that struggles over the equilibrium of federalism would persist.[46]

Constitutional Concerns about the Jay Treaty

During this period of agitation against *Chisholm*, Americans engaged in a national debate over the Jay Treaty with Great Britain. That discussion had particular relevance for interposition because it marked a transition towards a democratization of American political culture by elevating the importance of public opinion in ways that broke the mold of an older, more deferential model of politics. Even those who subscribed to that traditional model of politics employed tactics and arguments designed to shape public opinion. As Todd Estes has observed about the treaty debate, "Because *both* sides had appealed directly to the people in an open effort to shape and mobilize public opinion, it helped to legitimize popular politics."[47]

Negotiated by Chief Justice John Jay of the Supreme Court in the unusual capacity as a special envoy who nonetheless did not resign his seat on the Court, the treaty was signed in November 1794, but only reached the United States in March of the following year. Upon its arrival, President Washington called a special session of Congress in June 1795 during which the Senate considered the treaty behind closed doors. That secrecy prompted attacks on the treaty ratification process as being contrary to the legacy of the American Revolution and akin to discredited British practices. The closed proceedings of the Senate contributed to rumors and speculations about the terms of the treaty and gave further impetus to the longstanding calls to open up Senate debates.[48]

Federalists dominated the Senate, but Republican opponents of the treaty raised political objections as well as constitutional challenges. One of Virginia's senators, Henry Tazewell, urged the Senate to withhold its consent because the treaty "unconstitutionally invaded" the "rights of individual States" and threatened to destroy Congress' constitutional authority over foreign relations. The Senate rejected the constitutional challenges along party lines and approved the treaty on June 24, 1795. After the Senate vote, President Washington sought the opinion of Alexander Hamilton, his former Treasury Secretary. Hamilton offered a detailed analysis that expressly rejected Tazewell's assertion that one of the provisions of the treaty impinged on state authority.[49]

Soon after the Senate's vote, the treaty was leaked to a Republican newspaper by Virginia's other Senator, Stevens T. Mason, and its publication produced a fierce political struggle that pitted Federalists supporting Washington's foreign policy against Republican detractors of the treaty. The struggle largely split along sectional lines, with Federalist strongholds in Northeastern states supporting the treaty and much of the opposition coming from Southern states. An enormous number of public meetings produced a stream of memorials, petitions, addresses, resolutions, and remonstrances against the treaty.[50]

Some Americans were angry that Britain refused to honor important provisions of the 1783 Treaty of Paris. Moreover, fresh memories of the Revolutionary War's violence and continued British tyranny demanded opposition. By 1793, Britain had effectively blockaded the French West Indies, seized American ships, and was trying to foment hostility against the United States among Native Americans along the American–Canadian border. Additionally, the treaty created worrisome ties with monarchical Britain. According to Madison, Federalists who supported the treaty formed "a British party, systematically aiming at an exclusive connection with the British Governt." Thomas Jefferson and other Republicans wanted economic independence from Britain and feared that Hamilton and other Federalists were modeling the national government "on the underlying principles of the British nation-state – a large national debt and national bank, a standing army, and expansive executive patronage."[51]

The public debate also echoed the theme first raised in the Senate that the treaty was unconstitutional, both because it violated the separation of powers and intruded upon states' rights. In that respect, the public discussion prefigured the debate in Congress. The core dispute entailed determining the respective powers of the President and Congress over diplomatic matters and treaties. For Hamilton and other Federalists, "foreign affairs were inherently executive in nature and the Constitution vested all executive authority in the president." A few exceptions were the Senate's enumerated role in approving treaties and Congress' right to declare war. For Madison and other Republicans, Congress' crucial role was to make laws on behalf of the people, and thus treaty-making could not be the exclusive province of the executive. Between July 1795 and January 1796 Hamilton authored over thirty essays as "Camillus" and "Philo Camillus" to defend the merits of the treaty as well as its constitutionality.[52]

Despite the public outcry following the Senate's vote to ratify and strong opposition to the treaty expressed in petitions directed to the President, Washington signaled that he would ignore public opinion in making his decision. While struggling over the issue, Washington finally took Hamilton's counsel and signed the treaty. Jefferson predicted that the House of Representatives would oppose the treaty "as constitutionally void." After ratification, Republicans shifted tactics and sought to convince state legislatures to amend the Constitution to reverse the precedent established by the Jay Treaty. Action by the state legislatures might also encourage Republicans in the House of Representatives to scrutinize the treaty. Madison's constituents instructed him to oppose the treaty "in every point where it infringes the constitution." Madison not only took a leading role in the debate in the House of Representatives, but behind the scenes helped organize Virginia's interposition to the treaty.[53]

State Interposition Efforts Regarding the Jay Treaty

Madison drafted documents that formed the basis for a petition to Virginia's legislature urging it to weigh in on the treaty. The petition disapproved of the President's refusal to regard "representations of the people as ... worthy of his consideration." It also asserted the legislature's "constitutional right" to appoint the state's United States Senators as a reason for those legislators to make "a declaration of the public sentiment" about the treaty. The petition urged legislators to take "such measures towards a remedy" that were "consistent with constitutional principles."[54]

Even as Madison sought to provoke a response from Virginia, a member of the state's legislature, Joseph Jones, was thinking along similar lines. Jones wrote Madison hoping to speak to him about "what course [should] be taken by the legislature." Jones saw nothing wrong with the legislators "declaring their opinions generally of the late Treaty" or in proposing "an amendment in the constitution to prevent a similar inconvenience in [the] future." Ten days later, on his way to join Congress at Philadelphia, Madison stopped at Fredericksburg to confer with Jones, who thought the treaty should to be the first order of business after the state legislature met.[55]

Within a week of the Virginia legislature's convening, a resolution was introduced in the House of Delegates congratulating the state's two Senators for opposing the treaty on constitutional grounds. Federalist legislators rejected the constitutional challenge to the treaty, and questioned whether it was appropriate to congratulate the Senators for their votes, but agreed that legislators had a right to express constitutional objections to the treaty.

Charles Lee, soon the Attorney General of the United States, offered a substitute resolution to the one congratulating the state's Senators. Lee's resolution acknowledged that the powers granted to the national government and those of the states "are and should remain separate and distinct, so that neither exercise what is granted to the other." Nevertheless, his resolution considered the discussion of the treaty by Virginia's House "unnecessary" since foreign relations "belonged to the constituted authorities of the Genl. Govt," and thus for Lee, the state legislature "had no controul or right of censure."[56]

For three days Virginia's House debated the original resolution and the constitutionality of the treaty. John Marshall spoke at length in favor of the treaty and argued the resolution was improper because it "indirectly" disparaged the treaty. Federalists offered another substitute motion that conceded the right of the state legislature to examine the treaty's constitutionality, but concluded that a judgment on that issue was premature. The resolution proposed that no discussion of the treaty should occur in the House since that body could not offer a "mature opinion" without fully understanding the treaty's constitutional issues.[57]

Virginia's resolution congratulated its Senators for opposing the treaty, but that resolution did not bring the issue of the treaty before the House of Representatives. Serving that purpose were four resolutions seeking amendments to the Constitution that passed the House of Delegates on December 12, 1795 and agreed to by the Senate. One proposal required treaties that affected congressional powers to be submitted to the House of Representatives and to receive approval by a majority of that body before becoming law. Madison complimented Virginia's legislature for setting "a firm example" even if other states failed to follow Virginia's lead and instead expressed approval of the treaty. Little more than three months later, Madison, while serving in the House of Representatives, would reject Washington's claim that the intent of the Constitution with respect to the treaty-making power was best derived from the journals of the constitutional convention. No, argued Madison, "the sense of that body could never be regarded as the oracular guide in expounding the Constitution" since the draft the convention produced was but "a dead letter" until life was "breathed into it by the voice of the people." Thus, far more compelling in the search for "the meaning of the instrument" were "the State Conventions, which accepted and ratified the Constitution."[58]

If Virginia's resolutions received little support from other states, they did prompt one governor to endorse interposition. After Governor Samuel Adams of Massachusetts received Virginia's resolutions, he shared them with the legislature. In addressing the General Court on January 19, 1796 Adams stressed the role of the legislature as a monitor of the balance of federalism. For Adams, the operation of two levels of government underscored the importance of determining if "the Constitutional rights of our federal and local Governments should on either side be infringed." The persistence of such encroachments threatened to change the Constitution and produce political unrest. He thought the Jay Treaty might be such a circumstance and he wanted legislators to consider the need for a constitutional amendment.[59]

The Massachusetts legislature rejected the Governor's position. The House urged "a respectful submission on the part of the people to constituted authority," and the Senate claimed it would be "an interference with the power entrusted" to the federal government "for the state Legislatures to decide on the British treaty." Madison's collaborator, the Virginia legislator Joseph Jones, was "astonished" by Massachusetts' response. Indeed, he could not imagine there was anything "unconstitutional in a state legislature speaking its opinion of any public measure" or "improper" in "proposing to the other States objects of amendment for their consideration." Even as Virginia's legislature weighed in on the treaty, Kentucky's Governor Isaac Shelby offered the reminder of "the indispensable duty" of the state legislature to express their sentiments of such parts of the treaty as are unconstitutional.[60]

Although Virginia's resolutions were not adopted by other states, they were not exactly a failure. As Robert Farnham has observed, "They accomplished all that could be expected of them; they had assured Republicans that the treaty struggle would be renewed in the United States House of Representatives."[61]

* * * * * *

The two issues of suability and the Jay Treaty prompted states to sound the alarm about questionable assertions of constitutional authority advanced respectively by the Supreme Court and the Executive branch. Perceived threats to state sovereignty fueled interposition efforts directed at the *Chisholm* decision and formed part of the movement to pass the Eleventh Amendment. For its part, the negotiation of the Jay Treaty triggered an important debate over the constitutional scope of presidential treaty authority and potential congressional involvement. Both issues entailed discerning the intent of provisions of the new Constitution.

During Congress' debate over the Jay Treaty during most of March and April, 1796, legislators struggled "over the Constitution's essential character and what it meant to be subject to its authority." Federalists, wanting a strong executive, insisted that the text of the Constitution and the treaty provided all the clarity that was needed. Republicans, seeking congressional checks on the executive, emphasized the House's "unique capacity to speak for the sovereign people," which was of particular importance since the Constitution's text was susceptible to more than one meaning. Federalists conceded that if the treaty was unconstitutional – which they denied – it should not be implemented and that Congress played a role in that assessment. As Samuel Lyman of Massachusetts explained, members of the House were "sent here as the guardians of the rights of our fellow-citizens, and for that purpose are sworn to support their Constitution." If the treaty was unconstitutional "it is a nullity" and was "not binding upon the nation." But, along with Hamilton, Federalists in the House did not doubt the treaty's constitutionality.[62]

The Jay Treaty convinced Congress and others that there was a value to an "archival Constitution" – understanding the intent of those who drafted and ratified it – and then using that history in interpreting the document. Inevitably such historical excavation was troubled. As Jonathan Gienapp indicates: "In appealing to history, Republicans, like Federalists, could be vague and speculative, relying on personal knowledge, experience, and memory or just general inferences drawn from the text of the Constitution or the perceived expectations that must have accompanied its construction."[63]

Even with their differing views, however, the historical search did allow for political resolution and ratification of the treaty. The nation was able to close that political chapter and move on to other issues. Indeed, not long after the struggles over *Chisholm* and the Jay Treaty were concluded, the country focused on another interposition movement, this time over the Virginia and Kentucky Resolutions that challenged the constitutionality of the Alien and Sedition Acts. Once again, there would be a vigorous debate over the Constitution's meaning and the intent of the framers.

4

The Virginia and Kentucky Resolutions and Madison's Report of 1800

The Virginia and Kentucky Resolutions of 1798 were authored respectively by James Madison and Thomas Jefferson as interposition resolutions to repudiate the Federalist-backed Alien and Sedition Acts of 1798. The Acts demonized political opposition and attacked free speech and freedom of the press. The Alien Act empowered the President to deport any aliens he deemed "dangerous to the peace and safety" of the nation or suspected of "treasonable or secret machinations." The Sedition Act was aimed at American citizens deemed to be subversive. It criminalized any combination or conspiracy "to oppose any measure" of the government of the United States and prohibited the "writing, printing, uttering or publishing" of any "false, slanderous, and malicious writing" tending to bring the national government, Congress, or the President, at the time, Federalist John Adams, into "contempt or disrepute."[1]

The Alien and Sedition Acts of 1798

The Virginia and Kentucky Resolutions were a response to the Alien and Sedition Acts that had been passed during the presidency of John Adams as part of a Federalist agenda intended to prepare the country for an impending war with France. As Jeff Broadwater has observed, "Because Federalists did not recognize the idea of a loyal opposition, the law did not extend to criticism of the vice president, the Republican Jefferson, and it was set to expire on 3 March 1801, when Adams's term would end."[2]

91

The acts drew widespread opposition from Republicans, both on policy grounds and because of their alleged unconstitutionality. Republicans felt that the Alien Act exceeded Congress' constitutional powers while the Sedition Act violated the First Amendment. Both acts were considered a deplorable overreaching by the Federalist administration. Jefferson complained to Madison that the legislation showed "no respect" for the Constitution and thought they were a Federalist "experiment" to see whether Americans would tolerate violations of the Constitution. For Madison, the Sedition Act denied citizens the "right of freely examining public characters and measures" and some Federalists, at least privately, questioned the broad sweep of the acts. Few were more anxious than Alexander Hamilton to neutralize perceived Republican threats, but even he, after reading the bill that became the Sedition Act, thought that some of its provisions were "highly exceptionable" and "may endanger civil War."[3]

For Republicans, the acts perpetuated a pattern of legislation and constitutional interpretation that threatened federalism with an ongoing enlargement of national powers. Jefferson called for a greater commitment toward state governments in order to maintain the "beautiful equilibrium on which our constitution is founded." As Brian Steele has observed, "Jefferson's protest in 1798, and throughout the 1790s, was that the 'equilibrium' was unbalanced by the preponderance of power in the federal government." In addition, a groundswell of grassroots opposition to the acts reflected popular distrust of a national government that would seek such extreme powers.[4]

Since opponents of Federalist policy were the primary targets of the acts, Republicans considered the measures politically inspired, with the Sedition Act being particularly partisan. The Federalist bias of the American press began declining during the 1790s as more newspapers emerged with a Republican slant. Thus, the political objective of the Sedition Act seemed clear to Jefferson as Republican editors started being indicted during his presidential bid. The attack on the press under the act was designed to "cripple & suppress" Republican campaign efforts.[5]

Background on the Virginia and Kentucky Resolutions

Misconceptions surrounding the Virginia and Kentucky Resolutions stem from thinking that they were independent creations of Madison and Jefferson and not part of an earlier pattern of interposition that traced its roots to *The Federalist* and became the touchstone of all future discussions of federalism. Thus, the resolutions are incorrectly viewed as originating the idea that John C. Calhoun would develop into his theory of nullification or an individual state veto. In Virginia's Resolutions, Madison neither described what became the theory of nullification nor did he allude to the natural law right of revolution. Instead, he described *two distinct types of interposition, each resting on a different basis and calling for vastly different political action.* Failing to appreciate that distinction misled Madison's contemporaries as well as later generations who continued to invoke what they called the 'Principles of '98'.[6]

When Madison described a right to "interpose" in Virginia's Third resolution, he referred to the theoretical right of the collective people who were the sovereign foundation of the Constitution to serve as the ultimate arbiter of the existence of egregious constitutional overreaching by the national government in the final resort. When Madison wrote that the people as the parties to the constitutional compact retained a theoretical right to "interpose," he was not talking about the preexisting practice of sounding the alarm interposition. This theoretical right contained in the Third resolution was different from what he described in Virginia's Seventh resolution as the right of state legislatures to interpose by sounding the alarm when faced with what they believed were ordinary, unconstitutional acts of the national government.[7]

On the other hand, Federalist opponents of the Virginia and Kentucky Resolutions rejected the practice of state legislatures sounding the alarm even as they and others failed to appreciate the theoretical right Madison described in the Third resolution. They maintained that the resolutions were novel and dangerous departures from the appropriate relationship between the national and state governments. Moreover, many Federalists claimed that the judiciary had exclusive competence to assess matters of constitutionality. Such divergent views underscored how Americans had drifted apart in their understanding of federalism. In overlooking the early history of interposition, scholars have too readily accepted the assertion of Federalists that the legislatures of Kentucky and Virginia were operating in ways unintended by the framers of the Constitution.[8]

Locating the resolutions within a preexisting practice of interposition is complicated because both Madison and Jefferson were sometimes ambiguous and because Madison repeatedly restated his complex views. Indeed, the debate over Madison's language in the Virginia Resolutions prompted Madison to produce an elaborate explanation in his Report of 1800. As for Jefferson, the wording of his draft of the Kentucky Resolutions prompted ominous speculation. While neither "nullification" nor "null" appeared in Kentucky's 1798 Resolutions, the fact that Jefferson included those words in his draft has led many scholars to assume that he, and by association Madison, anticipated and provided support for the nullification doctrine later advanced by Calhoun. Indeed, Jefferson's formulations eventually resonated with a sovereign states' rights tradition that merged the two sets of resolutions under the slogan, the 'Principles of '98'. Jefferson's compact theory of the Constitution served, as Mark Neely has noted, as "the ultimate basis for secession doctrine."[9]

Without distinguishing Madison's dual purposes in the Virginia Resolutions and his distinctive view of the compact nature of the Constitution, advocates of states' rights who asserted that sovereign states were the parties to the compact claimed the Virginia and Kentucky Resolutions for their own purposes, much as Calhoun tried to use them to justify nullification. Ironically, associating the term "interposition" with the resolutions merely obscured the constitutional tool and practice of interposition. The confusion reflected in the debate over the resolutions further muddied the practice of interposition after 1800 and eventually provided fodder for would-be nullifiers.

* * * * * *

Jefferson and Madison Mount an Opposition to the Alien and Sedition Acts

Given their reaction to the acts, it was not surprising that Madison and Jefferson helped mount an opposition to them, even if out of public sight since, as Adams' Vice President, Jefferson's opposition was a delicate matter. Jefferson and Madison consulted about how to respond and each of them anonymously drafted petitions seeking redress from Virginia's legislature and protested the use of Federalist-appointed federal grand juries to intimidate Republicans. Their collaboration also led them to draft separate resolutions protesting the acts that formed the basis of what the legislatures of Kentucky and Virginia adopted in 1798. While both Jefferson and Madison initially acted behind the scenes, Madison's role became public with his election to Virginia's House of Delegates in 1799.[10]

Jefferson's draft was adopted with some modification by Kentucky, while Virginia adopted Madison's resolutions virtually as he wrote them. Both sets of resolutions served to sound the alarm about the Alien and Sedition Acts. Virginia's legislature declared the acts "unconstitutional" while Kentucky's described them as "not law" but "altogether void" and "of no force" and "effect." Despite the different wording, both sets of resolutions offered the same judgment: that the acts exceeded the constitutional authority of the federal government. Virginia's and Kentucky's legislatures, like previous legislatures invoking interposition, asked the state's governor to share the resolutions with other state governors and with the state's congressional delegation. Kentucky's Resolutions urged its congressional delegation to seek a repeal of the "unconstitutional" acts.[11]

Jefferson's Draft of the Kentucky Resolutions of 1798

After public protests, some Kentuckians anticipated legislative interposition and wanted the governor to convene the legislature to pass resolutions urging the repeal of the unconstitutional acts. Jefferson drafted resolutions meant to be shared with other states that would hopefully produce similar resolutions to be sent to the President and Congress. Although aware of the opposition toward the acts in Kentucky, Jefferson evidently drafted his initial resolutions with Virginia's legislature in mind.[12]

In September, a large number of Virginians gathered at Charlottesville to adopt resolutions condemning the acts as unconstitutional and urged state legislators to seek their repeal. Some Virginia legislators thought they might be convened earlier than the normally scheduled meeting in December. When that prospect fell through, plans for how to use Jefferson's draft shifted from Virginia to other states, including North Carolina. Eventually, Jefferson's resolutions were sent to Kentucky's legislature which met before Virginia's December session. That decision paved the way for Madison's resolutions, written shortly after Jefferson's, to be adopted by Virginia's legislature. Apart from the delicacy of Jefferson's opposition as a member of the administration, in drafting the Kentucky Resolutions he technically violated the Sedition Act.[13]

Jefferson's draft described the Constitution as having delegated "certain definite powers" to "a general government for special purposes" while "reserving" to each state "the residuary mass of right to their own self-government." Jefferson's First resolution of nine concluded that whenever the national government assumes undelegated powers, its acts are "unauthoritative, void, & of no force." Jefferson reasoned that by virtue of the compact nature of the Constitution, formed by the "co-states," the national government created by the Constitution was not "the exclusive or final judge of the extent of the powers delegated to itself; since that would have made it's discretion, & not the constitution the measure of it's powers."[14]

Jefferson's description suggested a compact between independent sovereign states that had delegated certain powers to the federal government, leaving the states with their reserved sovereign authority. That view fostered the idea that the national government served as an agent acting on behalf of certain co-partners, essentially exercising a power of attorney. For Jefferson, the national government created by that compact could neither be the exclusive nor final judge of the extent of its powers. Instead, "as in all other cases of compact among powers having no common judge, each party has an equal right to judge for itself, as well of infractions, as of the mode & measure of redress."[15]

Crucially, while Madison also spoke of the compact nature of the Federal Constitution, Jefferson and Madison identified the parties to that compact differently. Jefferson's understanding of the constitutional compact emphasized sovereign states as the parties to the compact. The most significant implication of Jefferson's formulation was that individual states, or even the people of a single state – and by extension state legislatures – could challenge the role of the Supreme Court.[16]

Jefferson's compact theory of the Constitution encouraged challenges to the Supreme Court as the rightful monitor of issues of federalism. By identifying the "co-states" as the parties to the Constitution, with each state "an integral party," Jefferson provided the basis for challenging the Court's role. In disputes that pitted states' rights against national powers, the Supreme Court could be denied an exclusive or final right to judge the extent of powers granted to the federal government.[17]

Jefferson's Second and Third resolutions asserted that the Sedition Act was unconstitutional and violated the First Amendment's protection of freedom of speech and press. Those resolutions declared the Sedition Act "not law" and therefore "void and of no force." The Fourth through Sixth resolutions detailed the unconstitutionality of the Alien Act. For those reasons, the resolutions declared that act, like the Sedition Act, similarly "void & of no force." Jefferson's Seventh resolution criticized broad interpretations of the Constitution that effectively conferred "unlimited powers" on the national government. While the trend towards expansive constitutional interpretation was worrisome, the threats to personal liberties posed by the acts demanded "immediate redress."[18]

In the concluding Eighth and Ninth resolutions Jefferson anticipated interstate legislative communication to focus attention on alleged constitutional overreaching. Those resolutions created "a committee of conference & correspondence" to share the resolutions with other state legislatures and maintain a communication with representatives of other states.[19]

Problematic Language in Jefferson's Draft

In his draft of the Kentucky Resolutions, the most problematic wording was Jefferson's assertion in the Eighth resolution that:

in cases of an abuse of the delegated powers, the members of the general government being chosen by the people, a change by the people would be the constitutional remedy; but where powers are assumed which have not been delegated a nullification of the act is the rightful remedy: that every state has a natural right, in cases not within the compact ... to nullify of their own authority all assumptions of power by others within their limits.

The words "nullification" and "nullify" in this passage were omitted in the version of the resolutions passed by Kentucky's legislature in 1798. Yet Jefferson's language has generated much speculation about his views as well as considerable misunderstanding about interposition and its relationship to the doctrine of nullification that Calhoun advanced three decades later. Many scholars simply assume that Jefferson was advocating nullification. While his resolution is open to that interpretation, several distinctions made by Jefferson in this passage as well as his allusion to different bases that could justify actions by state legislatures have often been overlooked. When Madison later defended Jefferson from the charge of advocating nullification, he focused on those distinctions.[20]

Jefferson contrasted the situation of the federal government abusing powers that were delegated to it under the Constitution with its exercise of undelegated powers. In the case of an abuse of delegated powers, the people – who elected members of Congress – could choose different representatives. Electoral change, Jefferson wrote, constituted a "constitutional remedy." But if the national government exercised undelegated powers, Jefferson thought "a nullification of the act" was "the rightful remedy." Immediately after using the word "nullification," Jefferson alluded to the *natural law basis* of responding to governmental actions deemed beyond the constitutional pale. Every individual state possessed "a natural right" – not a constitutional right – "to nullify" all assumptions of undelegated power. A natural law right was always retained by individuals and the people, just as all states retained a natural law right of revolution even after they ratified the Constitution.[21]

Immediately after describing this natural law option Jefferson wrote "that nevertheless this commonwealth" sought "to communicate" with other states to determine if there was collective agreement about the illegitimacy of the acts. Jefferson warned that unless such acts were repealed, they would "necessarily drive these states into revolution and blood." Although Jefferson recognized the possibility of forceful resistance, he reiterated the purpose of the resolutions: Kentucky only sought to ascertain if its "co-states" also believed the acts were unconstitutional.[22]

In soliciting the views of other states, Jefferson returned to the theme of the natural law right of states to protect themselves from a potential "surrender" of the Constitution imperiled by the acts. Other states might see the acts as "seizing the rights of the states & consolidating them in the hands" of the federal government. Jefferson concluded the

Eighth resolution by anticipating that "the costates, recurring to their natural right in cases not made federal, will concur in declaring these acts void & of no force" and would "each take measures of it's own" to ensure that no actions of the national government "not plainly & intentionally authorized by the [Constitution] shall be exercised within their respective territories."[23]

To the extent that Jefferson was describing or endorsing the ability *of individual states* to challenge *by force* any laws passed by the federal government, even if the laws were deemed to be unconstitutional, he was suggesting action outside of the Constitution. That language came closest to the meaning of nullification that later nullifiers would adopt. But by linking the word "nullification" with "a natural right" and speaking of "the costates, recurring to their natural right" it was possible that Jefferson – as Madison would later insist – was only thinking of the right of revolution.[24]

The sense in which Jefferson used the words "nullification" and "nullify" in his draft was consistent with the objective of both sets of resolutions to bring attention to the unconstitutional acts. Thus, while Jefferson recognized the natural law right of individual states to act outside of the Constitution, his draft distinguished such extralegal action from the constitutional remedy of voting out representatives complicit in the exercise of unconstitutional powers. Equally constitutional and legitimate was the role of state legislatures to monitor federalism and sound the alarm when they believed the national government was overstepping its bounds.

Jefferson's draft resolutions thus called for an interstate judgment about constitutional overreaching. To reinforce the point that unconstitutional laws were always void and of no authority, Jefferson repeatedly described the Alien and Sedition Acts as "void," and of "no force." He consistently described such unconstitutional measures as "altogether void and of no force" not because the state legislature had nullified them, but because they were unconstitutional acts in the first place. John Marshall used the same terminology a few years later in *Marbury v. Madison*, when he reached the same conclusion that "an act of the legislature, repugnant to the constitution, is void."[25]

Both before and after the Virginia and Kentucky Resolutions, Jefferson repeatedly described unconstitutional acts as being null and void. In Jefferson's *Notes on the State of Virginia,* written in the 1780s, he lamented that the state's 1776 constitution had not been framed by a constitutional convention and then popularly ratified. That constitutional process would "bind up the several branches" of the state government "by certain laws, which when they transgress their acts shall become nullities." What was true of state constitutions was also true of the Federal Constitution.[26]

After his election, Jefferson described the Sedition law as "a nullity" and "void" because it transgressed the Constitution. Jefferson explicitly made this point in a draft of his First Annual Message to Congress when he described the consequences of Congress passing unconstitutional acts and in a draft message to the Senate in 1801. Madison, along with other commentators, drew the same conclusion. Such usage, as Brian Steele has observed, suggests that Jefferson's "use of the word 'nullification' was closer to a statement of fact, a truism, than an incitement to any particular action." Yet in time, Jefferson's language would be invoked for a more troubling interpretation in the hands of sovereign states' rights theorists.[27]

Kentucky's Legislature Considers Jefferson's Draft

When Kentucky's legislature assembled for its November 1798 session, Governor James Garrard declared his willingness to support the national government in all constitutional measures. Nonetheless, Garrard questioned the validity of the Alien and Sedition Acts and urged legislators to "protest against all unconstitutional laws." He described the Alien law as an "evasion" of the Constitution. Secretary of State Timothy Pickering thought Garrard's "inflammatory speech" deserved prosecution.[28]

Kentucky's legislature responded. John Breckinridge, a member of the House of Representatives who had received a copy of Jefferson's draft resolutions a month earlier, introduced them. Breckinridge's version of the resolutions and what Kentucky's legislature eventually adopted closely followed the first seven resolutions of Jefferson's draft, with several significant departures in the last two resolutions. In the Eighth and Ninth resolutions, Breckinridge omitted Jefferson's reference to "nullification" and the suggestion that each state "take measures" to ensure that unconstitutional acts would not be exercised within their state. Instead, Breckinridge substituted more traditional language of interposition, including sending the resolutions to the state's congressional delegation to ask for their support in repealing the "unconstitutional and obnoxious" acts. The final resolution called for the state's governor to share the resolutions with the other state legislatures. While the Ninth resolution retained the reference to a recurrence to "natural right," it did not call for the acts to be nullified within the states. Instead, the Kentucky Resolutions ended with an appeal to other state legislatures for "an expression of their sentiments" and the hope they would "concur in declaring these acts void and of no force" and join with Kentucky "in requesting their repeal at the next session of Congress." As such, Kentucky's legislature followed in the footsteps of earlier interposition efforts and its resolutions represented nothing extraordinary. Despite changes to his draft, Jefferson was satisfied with the Kentucky Resolutions when he sent a copy of them to Madison.[29]

Breckinridge's version of the resolutions prompted a three-day debate in the House. Federalist William Murray questioned the propriety of adopting interposition resolutions. He found no constitutional authority for Kentucky's legislature "to repeal or to declare void the laws of the United States" or to exercise "censorship" over Congress. Expressing such a critical judgment, he insisted, rested with "the people at large." Murray concluded that only the people had the right to question if Congress exceeded its powers and then to appeal for redress.[30]

Breckinridge defended legislative interposition – embodied in the proposed resolutions – and identified "the right and duty of the several States to nullify" unconstitutional acts of the national government in matters of "the last resort." For Breckinridge, Jefferson's draft justified the right of every state to "nullify" undelegated assumptions of power by the national government on the grounds of a "natural right" by taking "measures of it's own" – even though this was language that Breckinridge had omitted from the resolutions. Instead, Breckinridge asserted that nullification was legitimate if it was exercised by a majority of the co-States who formed the underlying sovereign of the Constitution, but not by an individual state and he endorsed a theoretical right of the people to act in the last resort.[31]

Breckinridge rejected the idea that the general government's own assessment about whether it had exceeded its authority was the only check on the national government. State legislatures served as additional bodies to "censure" Congress and bring attention to actions that possibly exceeded congressional authority. Contrary to Murray's view, Breckinridge considered "the co-States to be alone parties to the Federal compact, and *solely* authorized to judge in the last resort of the power exercised under that compact." Thus, Congress was not "a party in the Federal compact." Members of Congress were "agents intrusted with a limited authority" from the people, which, if they exceeded those limits, subjected them "to the authority by which they were constituted."[32]

Breckinridge described a number of possible responses. When Congress acted within its authority, but with bad judgment, the only recourse was to seek a repeal of such acts. When Congress passed laws beyond its authority, the response of interposition was appropriate. Ideally, Congress would change course if state legislatures concluded that the national legislature had acted unconstitutionally. However, persistent attempts by Congress to enforce unconstitutional acts despite the protests of states might warrant nullification. Under those circumstances it was "the right and duty of the several States to nullify those acts, *and to protect their citizens from their operation.*" At present, however, Kentucky's legislature was only addressing the other states, simply sharing its "opinions" about the acts and soliciting the views of other states. After Breckinridge's resolutions were passed overwhelmingly, copies were sent to the governors of the other states as well as Kentucky's congressional delegation.[33]

Madison's Draft of the Virginia Resolutions of 1798

A week after Kentucky's legislature acted, Jefferson shared a copy of the draft of "the Kentucky resolves" with Madison, noting that "we should distinctly affirm all the important principles they contain, so as to hold to that ground in future." A week later, Jefferson endorsed the interposition of Kentucky's legislature in a letter to John Taylor of Caroline, who would soon introduce Madison's resolutions in the Virginia legislature.[34]

Madison's draft, which he began composing in the last two weeks of November, reflected his tendency to draw fine constitutional and theoretical distinctions. If Jefferson's resolutions were written with verve, passion, and rhetorical flourish, Madison's effort was far more studied. Jefferson exhibited a "habit," Madison later recalled, "of expressing in strong and round terms impressions of the moment." Jefferson's draft channeled his visceral reaction to the acts and included a veiled threat of disunion made in response to what he saw as the Federalists' contempt for constitutional limits. Madison's draft took a less rhetorical tone, avoided Jefferson's language about the possibility of being driven into revolution and sought to distinguish the right of the parties of the constitutional compact from the right of state legislatures to sound the alarm.[35]

Jefferson's draft did not clearly distinguish the ordinary constitutional tool of interposition from the natural law right of any state to respond to perceived oppression as a matter of final resort. Mingling these two different types of potential responses produced a document that failed to differentiate the foundations on which those separate actions rested. Jefferson's neglect influenced Madison's approach.[36]

If Jefferson's language lacked analytical precision, Madison's attempt to identify the Virginia legislature's interposition while also stating a constitutional principle introduced its own confusion. Madison's Virginia Resolutions embodied a legislature's normal process of interposition by passing resolutions declaring certain acts of the national government unconstitutional. In addition, however, his resolutions affirmed the theoretical right that the parties to the Constitution might invoke in matters of the final resort, *resting that constitutional right on America's principle of the sovereignty of the people and not on natural law.* This created a troubling uncertainty about how the sovereign people could invoke that right, a process that Madison never explained.

Otherwise, Madison's eight Virginia Resolutions broke no new ground by claiming the role of state legislatures as monitors of the Constitution's divided sovereignty who were entitled, if not obliged, to identify when the national government might have overstepped its constitutional authority. The First resolution declared that the legislature would defend both the Federal Constitution and Virginia's constitution and support the national government in all measures "warranted" by the Constitution. Nonetheless, interposition was alluded to in the Second resolution when it asserted the legislature's "duty, to watch over and oppose every infraction" of constitutional authority.[37]

The much-misunderstood Third resolution identified constraints on the federal government imposed by the Constitution, or, as Madison phrased it, by "the compact to which the states are parties." The powers of the national government were limited by "the plain sense and intention" of the compact and by the Constitution's enumeration of grants of powers. *Crucially, and distinct from Jefferson, for Madison "the States" collectively – and not each state individually – formed the parties to the compact.* This distinction was not a matter of semantics. As Jefferson Powell has observed, "This seemingly esoteric disagreement in fact created an extremely important practical difference between Madison's and Jefferson's views."[38]

Madison's concept of the compact informed what role he thought the Supreme Court played in normal circumstances in monitoring federalism, what role state legislatures could play in that process, and finally, who in matters of the last resort was the ultimate decision-maker of whether the national government had exceeded its constitutional authority. In the Third resolution, Madison expounded on the theoretical implications of the compact established by the Constitution. Madison wrote that "in case of a deliberate, palpable and dangerous exercise of other powers not granted" to the federal government, "the states alone who are parties thereto have the right, and are in duty bound, to interpose for arresting the pro[gress] of the evil, and for maintaining within their respective limits, the authorities, rights and liberties appertaining to them."[39]

Madison's Fourth resolution criticized the Adams administration for expanding its powers through "forced constructions" of the Constitution that would inevitably convert the divided sovereignty of two levels of government into a consolidated government. The Fifth and Sixth resolutions explained why the Alien and Sedition Acts were "palpable and alarming infractions of the constitution." The Seventh resolution not only declared the acts unconstitutional, but appealed to the other states to make similar declarations and take "necessary and proper measures" with Virginia "in maintaining unimpaired the authorities, rights, and liberties, reserved to the States respectively, or to the people." The Eighth resolution arranged to share the resolutions with other state legislatures in hopes of encouraging interstate cooperation and resistance to the unconstitutional acts, as well as furnishing copies to the state's congressional delegation.[40]

Madison's resolutions, like Jefferson's draft, contained language that prompted debate and confusion. Especially puzzling was what Madison meant by "the states" and his use of the phrase "the states alone" in his original draft of the Third resolution. Madison's contemporaries parsed the meaning of those words when they passed a slightly amended version of his original resolutions in 1798 and Madison attempted to explain what he meant in person when he joined Virginia's legislature a year later.

Virginia's Legislature Considers Madison's Draft

Madison completed his draft resolutions before the December 1798 session of Virginia's House of Delegates. Madison left the resolutions with Wilson Cary Nicholas who passed them on to John Taylor for introduction, but first Nicholas shared them with Jefferson. Jefferson suggested revising Madison's Seventh resolution so as to describe Virginia's "invitation" to other states "to cooperate in the annulment of the acts" and Jefferson wanted the other states to join Virginia in declaring that the acts "are, and were ab initio – null, void and of no force, or effect."[41]

Jefferson's proposed changes reflected his understanding that neither Kentucky's nor Virginia's legislatures were nullifying the Alien and Sedition Acts, but were instead acknowledging that those acts were never law because they were unconstitutional. In other words, Jefferson sought to emphasize that the acts – at their inception – were nullities because they sought to exercise undelegated constitutional powers. Indeed, three days before he used the word "annulment" to describe Madison's Seventh resolution, Jefferson clarified that Kentucky's Resolutions, which he hoped the Virginia Resolutions would emulate, only represented "declarations" that the acts were "against the constitution & merely void."[42]

Nicholas responded to Jefferson's recommendation by adding words to Madison's resolution, going beyond Madison's description of the acts as unconstitutional, to read: "unconstitutional and not law, but utterly null, void and of no force or effect." Eventually, those added words were deleted from the resolutions and Madison's original language was restored in the final version.

Thirty years later, Madison asserted that the words Jefferson sought to add only gave "emphasis to the *declaration*" by Virginia's legislature that the Alien and Sedition Acts were unconstitutional "and not that the addition of them could annul the acts or sanction a resistance of them." Moreover, Madison explained that those words were "synonymous with 'unconstitutional'" and had been deleted out of an abundance of caution "to guard against a misunderstanding of this phrase as more than declaratory of opinion."[43]

Madison's resolutions prompted a week-long debate, much of which featured Republicans and Federalists disputing the constitutionality of the acts and the legitimacy of interposition. Republicans, including John Taylor, focused on the oath of office legislators took to uphold the Constitution. That oath made state legislators responsible for monitoring a government with limited constitutional powers. The crucial question was whether Congress had "overleaped their bounds" in passing the acts. Taylor believed that Virginia's legislature had the right, if not the duty – through interposition – to weigh in on such potential constitutional abuse. That position echoed what he had written four years earlier: that the people of the nation "must watch over the constitution" and "preserve it from violation." Taylor depicted state legislatures as "the people themselves" who had "at least as good a right to judge of every infraction of the constitution, as Congress itself." Indeed, the summer before Jefferson drafted the Kentucky Resolutions, Taylor corresponded with Jefferson and described the "right of the State governments to expound the constitution." That letter and Taylor's earlier tract has led some scholars to attribute the genesis of the Virginia and Kentucky Resolutions to Taylor, or at least speculate that he was their inspiration. That view overlooks the roots of interposition in *The Federalist* and its practice in the early 1790s.[44]

During the debate, Taylor specifically referred to legislative interposition, arguing that in the event of "a clashing of opinion ... between Congress and the states, respecting the true limits of their constitutional territories" an appropriate "remedy" was to invoke the provisions in Article V to alter the Constitution. Taylor hoped Congress would rescind the acts and thus avoid the need for constitutional revision. Virginia Republican William Branch Giles agreed that legislators had both a duty to support the Constitution and to "speak their opinions." Since state House and Senate members took the same oath to support the Constitution as did Congress and federal judges, if state legislators identified constitutional overreaching "they were bound to say so, otherwise it would be a dereliction of the oath."[45]

In contrast, some Federalists in Virginia's legislature insisted that the judiciary alone possessed the competence to assess matters of constitutionality. Others were inclined to regard the people in general, through elections or petitions, as the appropriate body to raise the alarm about whether Congress was acting constitutionally. The "proper arbiter" of potential overreaching, according to Henry Lee, was the "people themselves" acting through elections. The judiciary, too, was a "source of correction" in case Congress exceeded its constitutional authority and even the state legislatures had a role – but one limited to proposing constitutional amendments. Indeed, before the House passed the resolutions, Federalists unsuccessfully tried to substitute the resolutions with a statement that the people had the right to assemble and petition the government for a redress of grievances. Federalists also objected to the tone of the resolutions. George Keith Taylor, soon to become John Marshall's brother-in-law, wanted them couched in "different language." Edmund Brooke considered the resolutions extremely "dangerous and improper" because they would "inflame the public mind," diminish confidence in the government, and encourage resistance to its laws.[46]

Problematic Language and the Defense of Interposition

During the debate over Virginia's Resolutions, the House paid considerable attention to the words added at Jefferson's behest declaring the acts not only unconstitutional, but "utterly null, void and of no force or effect." For Federalist George Keith Taylor, that language implied that the legislature was not declaring the acts unconstitutional "as an *opinion*," but as "a certain and incontrovertible fact; in consequence of which the people of the state owe no submission to the laws." In effect, Taylor claimed that Virginia's proposed resolutions amounted to nullification. According to him, if Congress passed laws believing them to be "constitutional" and Virginia's legislature had "a right to annul those laws by declaring them to be unconstitutional," the principle of majoritarianism enshrined in the Constitution would be lost. Moreover, he worried that if a single state such as "Virginia could repeal and annul the alien and sedition laws, she could repeal and annul any other acts of Congress," a right every other state also possessed.[47]

Republicans responded that the proposed language merely stated the logical consequence of the acts being unconstitutional. The legislature did not render them so, but if the acts were unconstitutional, they lacked legitimacy. According to the Republican lawyer Peter Johnston, objection to the "style" of the resolution declaring the acts null and void was irrelevant. "For, if they were unconstitutional, they of course were null and void." In the end, Jefferson's proposed language was deleted and Madison's original text restored, a change accepted by the Republicans with the understanding that it did not undercut the principle that if the acts were unconstitutional, they lacked authority.[48]

Another word choice in Madison's draft resolutions that prompted considerable discussion was his reference, in the Third resolution, that "the states *alone* are parties" instead of "the states are parties" to the constitutional compact. That proposed word change raised the question of who were the parties to the compact, and underscored the elusiveness of the word "states" in the Third resolution – an issue that Madison would revisit in his Report of 1800.[49]

Some Federalist legislators denied that "the existing constitution was a compact of states," declaring it instead to be "a compact among the people" and objected to the phrase states alone because it effectively excluded the people. Likewise, George Keith Taylor considered the proposed wording "unfounded and false" since "the *states* are not the only parties to the federal compact." The Constitution did not emanate from states "as particular sovereignties" or state legislatures; instead, it "was the creature of *the people* of united America."[50]

Republican legislators emphasized the role of the states and considered the Constitution "a deputation of power from the several states." Likewise, Republican Peter Johnston disputed Henry Lee's claim that the people and not the states were the parties to the compact. He noted that under the Articles of Confederation the states – and not the people – called for a constitutional convention. Those convention delegates represented "the people of America," but the Constitution had been submitted to conventions of the people of the several states. In his view, because the ratifying conventions assembled under the auspices of the different legislatures, the states were the parties. He thought "the words, 'we the people'" did not change the nature of the compact.[51]

Still other legislators, like the Republican James Barbour, described both "the people and the states" as the parties that formed the compact. Given that mixed basis, Barbour identified a special role for the state legislatures as "the immediate representatives of the people, and consequently the immediate guardians of their rights" to "sound the tocsin of alarm, at the approach of danger" and to identify potential overreaching by the federal government. John Taylor took a similar position, rejecting the idea that "the people alone are parties to the compact." The Constitution – particularly in its provisions dealing with constitutional revision and the admission of new states – "recognizes the states as parties to the contract." Still, he acknowledged that the Ninth and Tenth Amendments spoke of rights and powers retained and reserved to the people. While not denying that the people were "parties to the contract" it was equally true "that the states are parties also." Dispute over what it meant to describe the states as the only parties to the Constitution led the legislature to delete the adjective "alone."[52]

In the end, despite wrangling over specific wording and the broader question of whether the legislature should weigh in on the constitutionality of congressional actions, the resolutions were generally understood as calling for interposition. During the debate, legislators were reminded of the legitimacy of interposition and its origins in *The Federalist*. The Republican lawyer John Mercer insisted on the right of the legislature to monitor the operation of "the respective powers of the state and general government" to preserve the powers and independence of each. The purpose of such scrutiny was simply "to produce a temper in Congress for a repeal." Mercer thought the best means of changing political attitudes lay in "a declaration similar to the one before the committee, made by a majority of states or by several of them."[53]

Mercer then responded to the argument of Federalist George Keith Taylor that sharing the resolutions violated Article I, Section 10 of the Constitution, which prohibited interstate agreements or compacts without congressional approval. Mercer replied, as would John Taylor, that consulting other states about potential constitutional amendment or revision necessarily required interstate communication. Mercer pointed out that the authors of *The Federalist* embraced the interposition now being proposed in the resolutions and he quoted extensively from *Federalist* 26 and 28. Indeed, Mercer noted that "Publius" used much stronger language than Virginia's Resolutions. The House and then the Senate passed the resolutions with wide margins.[54]

After the legislature acted, but before Madison learned of the Richmond debates, he wrote to Jefferson worried that in their "zeal" Virginia's legislators "may forget some considerations which ought to temper their proceedings." Madison asked Jefferson if, with respect to the formation of the Constitution, he had considered "the distinction between the power of the *State*, & that of *the Legislature*." That question may well have been rhetorical since Madison knew that Jefferson had not labored over that distinction in his draft of the Kentucky Resolutions. Largely for that reason, Madison's draft resolutions differentiated and discussed separately actions that the states as opposed to state legislatures might take in monitoring whether the national government was acting within constitutional bounds. In identifying different potential actors, Madison dealt with the states in his Third resolution and state legislatures in the Seventh resolution and sensed that some of Virginia's legislators, along with Jefferson, failed to appreciate the difference. Madison insisted on distinguishing between the tool of interposition that state legislatures could use to bring attention to perceived overreaching by the national government and the steps the states might take as the parties who ratified the Constitution. For Madison, the people of Virginia, along with those of the other states were "clearly the ultimate Judge of infractions" of the Constitution. While the legislature played a role in "protesting agst the usurpations of Congress" it remained for the states, not state legislatures, to take such ultimate, if as yet unspecified, additional steps.[55]

State Reactions to the 1798 Resolutions

Before adjourning, Virginia's legislators drafted a public address describing the resolutions as a product of their "representative responsibility" inherent in their oath to support the Constitution and their duty to identify instances of "usurped power." State legislatures detecting "encroachments" by the federal government were obligated "to preserve unimpaired the line of partition." Acquiescing in such unwarranted assumptions of power would either lead to consolidated government, or, risk the possibility of "a revolution" if such infractions persisted.[56]

After failing to block the address, Federalists submitted a Minority Report deploring the resolutions as a "deviation from our legislative usage." While Federalists could reject the resolutions as ill-advised and dangerous, they were hard-pressed to maintain they represented a departure from established practice given the legislature's passage of similar resolutions as early as 1790. Even so, the Minority Report conceded the inherent challenges of monitoring a system of divided governmental sovereignty. The report suggested that constitutional issues were best left to others and not to state legislators. Specifically, it was the duty of the federal judiciary to construe the Constitution. In taking this position the report anticipated the reaction of many of the Federalist-dominated legislatures that rejected Virginia's Resolutions. Republicans in the House handily rejected the Minority Report.[57]

Instead of rallying other legislatures to protest the acts, the Virginia and Kentucky Resolutions elicited more Federalist repudiation. George Washington dismissed criticism of the acts as simply party politics. For Washington, Virginia's Resolutions tended to "dissolve the Union." The President's fears were echoed by other Federalists who considered the resolutions "a declaration of war" or that they implied "a right to disobey" national laws.[58]

Two states, Tennessee and Georgia, did support the Virginia and Kentucky Resolutions. Governor John Sevier forwarded the Kentucky Resolutions to the Tennessee legislature in early December 1798. In January, Tennessee's legislature passed a resolution instructing its congressional delegation to seek a repeal of the acts because they were in several respects "opposed to the constitution, and are impolitic, oppressive, and unnecessary." Georgia's Governor James Jackson transmitted both Kentucky's and Virginia's Resolutions to the state's legislature in January 1799. When the Georgia legislature considered them the following session, it withheld approval of the Alien and Sedition Acts and stated that it hoped the acts might be repealed without the need for the state legislature to interpose.[59]

Many negative responses to Virginia's Resolutions quickly surfaced, particularly from New England states with Federalist-dominated legislatures. Delaware's legislature responded on February 1, 1799 declaring Virginia's Resolutions an "unjustifiable interference with the general government" that had a "dangerous tendency." That same month, Rhode Island's legislature charged Virginia's legislature with usurping the authority of the federal courts to decide issues of constitutionality. Unwilling to evaluate the acts in their public capacity, Rhode Island's legislators nonetheless offered their "private opinions" that the acts were constitutional.[60]

On February 9, 1799 the Massachusetts Senate echoed but expanded on the Rhode Island legislature's accusation that Virginia's resolutions represented an unwarranted assumption of authority. The Massachusetts legislature declared that matters of constitutionality were "exclusively vested by the people in the judicial courts of the United States." The Constitution gave state legislatures the authority to propose constitutional amendments when appropriate, but did not make them "judges of the acts or measures" of the national government. Massachusetts considered Virginia's action a threat to the Constitution and the Union. But to avoid their silence about the resolutions being misunderstood, the Massachusetts legislature declared the Alien and Sedition Acts both constitutional and necessary.[61]

After Massachusetts' response, a Boston newspaper editor, Thomas Adams, accused the legislators of violating their oaths of office by denying the right of state legislatures *"to decide on the constitutionality of any acts of Congress."* That statement prompted a state prosecution for libeling members of the legislature. On February 28, 1799, Thomas and his brother Abijah, who served as the newspaper's bookkeeper, were indicted by the Suffolk grand jury after being charged by Chief Justice Francis Dana who described supporters of Virginia's Resolutions as abettors of "a traitorous enterprise" aimed at the national government. Illness precluded the prosecution of Thomas Adams, but the state's Attorney General proceeded against Abijah.[62]

During the trial, Abijah's attorneys, Benjamin Whitman and George Blake, sought to vindicate the charge by Thomas Adams that the Massachusetts legislators had abdicated their responsibility. The attorneys argued that state legislatures were guardians who could sound the alarm if Congress enacted laws undermining the sovereignty of states. They described state legislatures as a type of *"political Telegraphs,* so arranged and connected as to reflect the will of the people." Under the Constitution, they acted as "vigils" of the federal system in order to "protect the *freedom,* the *sovereignty,* and *independence* of the states." Whitman and Blake succinctly described the way interposition ideally worked: "If the federal compact be defective, they speak and it is amended; if the laws be *oppressive* or *unconstitutional,* though they cannot indeed command a repeal, yet a seasonable remonstrance from so respectable an authority can seldom fail to correct and remove the inequity." In the end, the jury found Abijah Adams guilty and he was sentenced to thirty days in the county jail.[63]

The Massachusetts legislature's response – that Virginia's and Kentucky's legislatures had no business considering the constitutionality of acts of the national government – drew similar reactions from other Federalists. Yet, claims for a judicial monopoly of constitutional interpretation remained contested and the arguments of those who disputed the legitimacy of what the legislatures in Kentucky and Virginia had done hardly settled the matter. Thus, even as a tradition of judicial review developed and grew stronger, it operated within a context that saw continued assertions for the right of the people as well as state legislatures to monitor America's constitutional order. What remained a matter of debate was what actions could be taken if the national government enacted unconstitutional laws.

In early March 1799, New York's Senate branded the Virginia and Kentucky Resolutions "inflamatory and pernicious." Like the legislatures of Rhode Island and Massachusetts, New York's Senate assigned responsibility for construing the Constitution to the federal judiciary and Senators proclaimed "their incompetency as a branch of the legislature of this state, to supervise the acts of the general government." Three additional New England state legislatures, Connecticut, New Hampshire, and Vermont, also disapproved of the resolutions between May and October 1799. New Hampshire's and Vermont's legislatures joined in denying the right of state legislatures to decide on the constitutionality of acts of the national government, each of them vesting that authority exclusively in the federal courts. Even so, New Hampshire's legislature offered its opinion that the Alien and Sedition Acts were both constitutional and "highly expedient."[64]

The negative responses by state legislatures to the Virginia and Kentucky Resolutions convey a false sense of consensus. Those responses reflected Federalist dominance in many of the legislatures that replied, but frequently obscured a sizable Republican dissent. For example, in New York a motion in the House to declare the Sedition Act unconstitutional lost by a small margin. In Vermont, the legislature rejected the Virginia Resolutions, but those on the losing side entered a protest defending the right of every state to decide on the constitutionality of national laws and the ability of legislators to communicate with other states. In some cases, outnumbered Republicans boycotted proceedings and their views were often not memorialized. In other instances, the existence of a Republican minority served to mute the response to the resolutions. For example, in Pennsylvania and New Jersey only one body of each legislature responded to the resolutions.[65]

There were unsuccessful efforts in other legislatures to support the Virginia and Kentucky Resolutions. For example, after North Carolina's legislature received Kentucky's Resolutions in December 1798, its House passed a resolution condemning the acts for violating "the principles of the Constitution" and directing the state's congressional delegation to support their repeal. The state's Senate, however, dominated by Federalists, handily defeated that resolution. And in South Carolina, other matters prevented the legislature from considering the resolutions. Because the legislature had a Republican majority and both the state's governor and the state's leading Federalist Charles Cotesworth Pinckney considered the Sedition Act unconstitutional, it seems likely that South Carolina's legislature would have responded favorably. Indeed, three months after the Kentucky and Virginia Resolutions, a leading Federalist, Theodore Sedgwick, concluded that state legislators in the country showed no unanimity about the resolutions. In the end, half of the states, eight in all, did not oppose one or both of the sets of resolutions from Virginia and Kentucky.[66]

After Virginia's legislature passed its resolutions, but before he joined that body, Madison anonymously underscored the essential role of interposition in America in an essay entitled "Political Reflections." Madison argued that federalism provided America with an advantage over consolidated European governments. "Our state governments" by forming "so many bodies of observation" on the federal government "must always be a powerful barrier against dangerous encroachments." The need for the people to act in order to restrain the excesses of their governments was the lesson Madison could draw from his involvement with how Virginia's and Kentucky's legislatures called attention to the national government's "encroachments" with the Alien and Sedition Acts.[67]

Even as Kentucky's and Virginia's Resolutions were being drafted and circulated, a grassroots campaign flooded Congress with petitions and remonstrances seeking the repeal of the Alien and Sedition Acts. Thomas Jefferson marveled at the number of appeals coming from New York, New Jersey, Pennsylvania, and Vermont. When the House of Representatives referred those petitions at the end of January 1799 to a committee composed of four Federalists and one Republican, it effectively postponed a response until the end of the session.[68]

When the House committee submitted its report on February 21, it found most petitions concluded the acts were "unconstitutional, oppressive and impolitic," but the committee dismissed that judgment. Having disposed of the substance of the petitions, the report considered their tone. It concluded that some petitions reflected "innocent misconceptions" that posed little danger, but that other petitions displayed a "vehement and acrimonious" style that were "the bane of public as well as private tranquility and order."[69]

The House report captured the attitude of the Federalist majority in rejecting a repeal of the Acts. Jefferson described for Madison the "scandalous scene" that accompanied the report. In caucus,

Federalists had decided "that not a word would be spoken on their side in answer to any thing which should be said on the other." Republicans Albert Gallatin from Pennsylvania and John Nicholas of Virginia urged a repeal of the acts. Their effort was soon interrupted by Federalists who made it impossible for the Republicans to be heard. By a slim margin the House voted to keep the acts in force.[70]

Defending the Virginia and Kentucky Resolutions

The reactions to their resolutions of 1798 prompted Kentucky's and Virginia's legislatures to draft replies, once again with Jefferson's and Madison's assistance. The two collaborated about how to respond: Jefferson would correspond with Kentucky legislators while Madison would eventually stand for election to Virginia's legislature in order to defend his resolutions.

In the decade following the Constitution's ratification, Madison experienced increasing qualms about the centralizing financial schemes, many successfully engineered by Hamilton, as well as aggressively nationalistic interpretations of the federal government's authority. By the time of the Alien and Sedition Acts, both Madison and Jefferson believed that the equilibrium of federalism had tipped too far toward the national government. That conviction led Madison to give a heartfelt defense of interposition in the wake of negative reactions to the Virginia and Kentucky Resolutions.

In early February 1799, Virginia's congressional delegation urged Madison to seek election in Virginia's legislature, reminding him of the need for "*wise* and *firm* State Measures" to keep "the general Government within the just Limits of the Constitution." A month later Madison received a letter from John Taylor, claiming that all of Madison's friends wanted him to run for office. Reluctantly, Madison agreed and he was elected to Virginia's House of Delegates in April 1799.[71]

In late August, Jefferson invited Madison to Monticello to discuss how the legislatures of Virginia and Kentucky should respond to the negative reactions to their resolutions. Beyond reiterating the unconstitutionality of the acts, and the right of Virginia's and Kentucky's legislatures in declaring them so, Jefferson hoped to "rally" the "American people" around "the true principles of our federal compact." While replying in conciliatory language that showed an attachment to the Union, Jefferson entertained issuing a threat that Virginia and Kentucky might secede due to a denial of their constitutional rights. Madison visited Jefferson in September and they evidently reached an agreement about how to proceed. Madison's visit also had a calming effect on Jefferson because after their meeting, "in deference" to Madison's judgment, Jefferson dropped the language about potential secession.[72]

Jefferson's position as Vice President hampered his direct involvement in crafting a response for Virginia and it was agreed that Madison, as a member of the legislature, would take the leading role in drafting that state's response. Jefferson was invited to prepare a response for Kentucky's legislature, but he declined, in part "to avoid suspicions" about his role in opposing the acts. Instead, Jefferson urged Wilson Cary Nicholas, a Virginia legislator who was heading to Kentucky, to write something that might become the basis of Kentucky's response. Whether or not Nicholas drafted the resolution that John Breckinridge introduced in the Kentucky legislature is uncertain, but Nicholas undoubtedly shared Jefferson's idea that both states should respond in concert. When Kentucky's legislature convened in November 1799, some were inclined to ignore the negative responses of other states to the resolutions. But John Breckinridge successfully urged Kentucky's legislature to vindicate its actions of 1798 lest "improper conclusions" were "drawn from our silence."[73]

Kentucky's 1799 Resolution

The preamble and resolution introduced by Breckinridge that Kentucky's legislature adopted in 1799 affirmed the state's unequivocal attachment to the Union and the Constitution. Still, it warned that if the national government continued to "transgress the limits fixed by that compact" the result would be "an annihilation of the State governments" and the creation of one "general consolidated government." Moreover, the doctrine embraced by some state legislatures that "the general government is the exclusive judge of the extent of the powers delegated to it" amounted to "despotism." The resolution asserted, employing the word "nullification" omitted in 1798, that "the several states" not only possessed "the unquestionable right to judge" infractions of the Constitution but that "a nullification by those sovereignties of all unauthorized acts done under color of that instrument, is the rightful remedy."[74]

Significantly, such a drastic step was not described as a remedy for an individual state but one collectively exercised by "the several states" and the "sovereignties" that formed the Constitution. As such, the resolution was not an act of nullification. Kentucky's legislators were simply reiterating "their opinion" that the Alien and Sedition Acts were unconstitutional by entering their "SOLEMN PROTEST." Despite that opinion, the legislature was willing to "bow to the laws of the Union" while reserving the right to oppose the acts "in a constitutional manner." Jefferson was pleased with Kentucky's 1799 Resolutions and congratulated Breckinridge for having "the subject taken up, and done with so much temper, firmness and propriety."[75]

After Kentucky's House passed its resolution on November 14, 1799, but before the Virginia legislature convened in early December, Jefferson wanted to strategize with Madison about Virginia's response. According to James Monroe, Jefferson planned to pay Madison a visit, but Monroe warned that with Madison's "present public engagement" and Jefferson's "public station," the meeting would compromise them both. Jefferson stayed away and instead sent Madison letters with recommendations for Virginia's response, including a protest against "violations of the true principles of our constitution." Jefferson wanted nothing to "be said or done which shall look or lead to force, and give any pretext for keeping up the army."[76]

Madison's Report of 1800

Madison apparently started drafting the Report of 1800, what he later referred to as "the justifying Report," soon after he moved to Richmond to prepare for the legislative session that convened in early December 1799. On the day Virginia's legislature met, an essay by "Agricola" appeared in the Richmond *Examiner* recalling that in 1787 proponents of the Constitution had predicted that state governments "would prove so many checks upon ... the federal government." In urging ratification, proponents argued that state legislatures would become sentinels of the operation of the national government and sound the alarm if need be.[77]

Given how other states had reacted, Madison was determined to offer a thorough clarification of the constitutional and theoretical basis for the Virginia Resolutions. On December 23 in the House of Delegates, Madison moved to create a committee to report on any communications received from other states about Virginia's 1798 Resolutions. The House appointed Madison to a seven-person committee that included John Taylor who had introduced Madison's resolutions the year before, as well as John Mercer who had defended them at the time by invoking the authority of "Publius" and the earlier practice of interposition. Although Republicans dominated the committee, it included a key Federalist critic of the resolutions, George Keith Taylor. Given his advance work, Madison submitted the committee's report the next day. The report was debated for five days by the Committee of the Whole before being returned to the House with an amendment which passed both the House and the Senate.[78]

In addition to adopting Madison's Report, the legislature, upon the motion of William Branch Giles, a member of Madison's committee, passed a series of instructions directed at Virginia's United States Senators that included seeking the repeal of the Alien and Sedition Acts on grounds of their unconstitutionality. Madison's Report elaborated and clarified the language used in each of the eight resolutions. Madison's defense of the first two resolutions was perfunctory because he believed they were unobjectionable truisms: that it was the duty of state legislatures to be engaged in "watching over and opposing" every constitutional "infraction" by the national government and that a "faithful observance" of the Constitution's principles was indispensable to "secure its existence." The crucial analysis of Madison's Report differentiated sounding the alarm interposition – the action taken by Virginia's legislature in the Seventh resolution while never using the words "interpose" or "interposition" – from the statement of constitutional principle in the Third resolution.[79]

Madison explained that in the Third resolution he had described "the states" as the "parties" to the Constitution or "compact" that granted the federal government its powers. As such, "the states" were entitled to act when the national government overstepped constitutional bounds. "[I]n case of a deliberate, palpable and dangerous exercise of other powers, not granted by the said compact" it was "the right" and "duty" of "the states ... to interpose, for arresting the progress of the evil, and for maintaining within their respective limits, the authorities, rights and liberties appertaining to them."[80]

Although Madison used the word "interpose" in the Third resolution, his explanation of that resolution clearly indicated that he was not referring to a state legislature's declaration that in its judgment an act of the national government exceeded its constitutional authority and was thus unconstitutional. Instead of considering what actions a state legislature might take, the Third resolution focused on what authority *as a matter of constitutional theory* resided in the parties who represented the underlying sovereignty of the Constitution and what action they might take.

The fact that Madison contemplated two different contexts within which action might be taken eluded many of his colleagues at the time of the 1798 resolutions and continued to confuse many of them during the debate over the Report of 1800. The confusion that surrounded, and continues to surround, Madison's resolutions stems from two sources. For one, Madison was not talking about legislative interposition in the Third resolution despite the fact he used the word "interposition" in the course of analyzing that resolution in the report. Secondly, uncertainty surrounded his use of the term "the states" in the Third resolution. In the report, Madison took great pains to demonstrate that the phrase "the states are parties to the Constitution or compact" was "free from objection," even as he conceded the potential ambiguity of that phrase. Madison explained that when the Virginia Resolution said "the states," it meant the people "in their highest sovereign capacity" as the "States" who ratified the Constitution and were "parties to the compact from which the powers of the Federal Government result." Madison then addressed the proposition in the Third resolution that the federal government had limited powers, namely only those powers that were granted under the Constitution. Powers not granted to the national government were necessarily left to the state governments, or left to the people. Madison reiterated the concept of divided sovereignty under the Constitution.[81]

Given that federal structure, there might be occasions to resolve "a deliberate, palpable and dangerous" overreaching of constitutional authority by the national government. For Madison it was "a plain principle" inherent in the nature of compacts "that where resort can be had to no tribunal superior to the authority of the parties, the parties themselves must be the rightful judges in the last resort" to determine if constitutional authority had been exceeded. But crucially, Madison was describing the step that the underlying sovereigns of the Constitution could take, but only as a matter of "the last resort." Madison emphasized that the Third resolution articulated nothing more than a "theoretically true" declaration of the rights of the parties to the Constitution or compact.[82]

The Report explained that the Third resolution stated when, but not how the sovereign source of the Constitution might exercise its authority. According to Madison, the people in the states constituted the parties to the Constitution and thus represented the true meaning of the term "the states." Therefore:

The states then being the parties to the constitutional compact, and in their sovereign capacity, it follows of necessity, that there can be no tribunal above their authority, to decide in the last resort, whether the compact made by them be violated; and consequently that as the parties to it, they must themselves decide in the last resort, such questions as may be of sufficient magnitude to require their interposition.

Madison used the word "interposition" in describing how the people in the states who formed the parties to the Constitution could theoretically serve as judges in the final resort. Madison was clearly not talking about an action to be taken by individual states or state legislatures. Instead, he was referring to the people of the states "in their highest sovereign capacity."[83]

Madison also identified *preconditions* for this theoretical right of the people to interpose. For Madison, it was "evident that the interposition of the parties, in their sovereign capacity, can be called for by occasions only, deeply and essentially affecting the vital principles of their political system." This explained why the Third resolution had spoken of cases of "deliberate, palpable and dangerous" constitutional breaches. The step of "the interposition of the parties" was thus coupled with the existence of dire circumstances of constitutional overreaching beyond situations when a state legislature sought to sound the alarm about allegedly unconstitutional acts of the national government. All that Virginia's legislature had done in the Third resolution was to announce the right and the circumstances under which the people "in their highest sovereign capacity" might act in matters of the "last resort." This important right allowed others besides the Supreme Court to monitor the Constitution.[84]

Madison rejected the idea that the Court was "the sole expositor of the constitution, in the last resort." Madison's position hinged on the overly complex distinction he drew between the *theoretical right of the parties to the Constitution to decide in the last resort* and the Supreme Court's role in *rendering decisions in the last resort as to questions coming before it* under "the forms of the constitution." When the Court heard cases arising under the Constitution that raised issues of constitutionality, the Court exercised final judgment with respect to the other branches of government. But this was a matter of relative finality. Even though Madison was differentiating between two different types of decisions in the last resort, sovereign states' rights theorists would invoke his Virginia resolutions as authority for challenging the role of the Supreme Court and claiming for state courts an equal and competing right to adjudicate the constitutional boundaries between the two levels of government.[85]

For Madison, even the Court's decisions in the last resort in cases over which it had jurisdiction were not necessarily truly final since the people of the states might have the last word through constitutional amendment, as had occurred with *Chisholm* and the Eleventh Amendment. The Supreme Court's right to decide in the last resort meant they did so "in relation to the authorities of the other departments of the government; not in relation to the rights of the parties to the constitutional compact."[86]

Action by the sovereign people served as a check beyond judicial review. The people's agents – public officials, representatives, and judges – could not exercise sovereign authority. Madison was suggesting that if the people ever chose to act in the last resort in their highest sovereign capacity, they would be justified in doing so as a matter of constitutional theory – and that there was great value in formally announcing such "fundamental principles." Madison concluded with a statement that summarized the theoretical right of the sovereign people to act in the last resort: "The authority of constitutions over governments, and of the sovereignty of the people over constitutions, are truths which are at all times necessary to be kept in mind; and at no time perhaps more necessary than at the present."[87]

Madison then analyzed various formal procedures available for constitutional change including amendment and senatorial instructions, all of which were "strictly within the limits of the constitution." When Madison wrote that the state legislatures could have appealed directly to Congress to rescind "the two offensive acts" he was referring to instruction since that was how state legislatures traditionally communicated with Congress. Likewise, if state legislatures wanted to react to an unconstitutional act of Congress by amending the Constitution, that approach would also have entailed instructions to their congressional delegation, including their Senators. However, "the first and most obvious" step was declaring the unconstitutionality of the acts by passing interposition resolutions. That step still allowed other states to choose "among the farther measures that might become necessary and proper."[88]

In concluding his report, Madison identified the historical roots and justification for interposition. He recalled the discussion of legislative interposition in *The Federalist* without identifying himself or Hamilton as authors. He pointed out that one of the arguments addressed to critics of the Constitution was that vigilant state governments would identify "the first symptoms of usurpation" and then "sound the alarm to the public." According to Madison those descriptions of interposition in *The Federalist* helped to secure the Constitution's ratification and he suggested that if the argument for interposition "was a proper one, then, to recommend the establishment of the constitution; it must be a proper one now, to assist in its interpretation." Madison ended his report by declaring that it was "only by maintaining the different governments and departments within their respective limits, that the blessings of either can be perpetuated." Madison thus underscored the continuing, vital role for state legislatures to monitor federalism and help maintain the Constitution.[89]

Reactions to Madison's Report

Although Madison tried to clarify his resolutions in the Report of 1800, fellow Virginia legislators – including a member of his own drafting committee – continued to overlook distinctions Madison insisted were at the heart of the resolutions. As Jack Rakove has noted, "Madison's effort was too detailed and studied to command close attention."[90]

After the legislature debated the report for several days, Madison wrote Jefferson that interposition, or, as he put it, "the right of the Legislature to interfere by declarations of opinion" would become "a material point" in the discussion. Indeed, the issue of legislative protest raised questions about what states might do when the national government palpably overreached its powers given Madison's statements in the Third resolution.[91]

Madison's complex phrasing of the theoretical right in the Third resolution drew the first opposition. Madison largely succeeded in getting his fellow legislators, even Federalists, to agree that the word "states" meant the parties to the Constitution in the sense of "the people ... in their highest sovereign capacity." But he failed to convey the idea that the Third resolution only referred to the *theoretical right* of how that sovereign might interpose in the last resort. During the debate some wondered about Madison's felt necessity "to announce that the people of the states were parties to the constitution" who had the right to "abrogate it." That statement seemed unnecessary and invited charges that the legislature was engaged in "subterfuge." Madison replied that the arguments used to defend the Alien and Sedition Acts made it appropriate for his report to "go to the foundation of the Constitution, [which] rested on certain truisms."[92]

The importance of reaffirming constitutional truths was nothing new for Madison: he had expressed that idea when accepting the value of a federal Bill of Rights. Although initially skeptical about its benefits, Madison embraced the federal Bill of Rights as statements of principle that might promote civic understandings. Memorializing "fundamental maxims of free Government" helped them "become incorporated with the national sentiment." Madison seemed to be motivated by a similar desire to spell out such fundamental maxims when drafting the Virginia Resolutions. Nonetheless, Madison's need to articulate the theoretical implications of the formation of the Constitution in the Third resolution had the unintended consequence of diverting attention away from the actual employment of interposition as described in the Seventh resolution.[93]

George Keith Taylor, a Federalist member of Madison's committee, exemplified how Madison's penchant to maintain theoretical distinctions introduced misconceptions about the resolutions and raised questions about his subsequent report. After the debate over the report, Taylor introduced a substitute resolution that failed to recognize or accept Madison's most crucial distinction. Focusing on the Third resolution, Taylor moved that Virginia's Resolutions were "irregular and improper." Taylor agreed that the states "or the people in their highest sovereign capacity" were "the parties to the constitutional compact," meaning "that there can be no tribunal above their authority, to decide whether the compact made by them be violated." Consequently, it was up to the parties to "decide in the last resort, such questions as may be of sufficient magnitude to require their interposition." "But," Taylor's motion continued, "the General Assembly of Virginia" did not represent the people of Virginia in their highest sovereign capacity and therefore could not "interpose for the purpose of arresting the operation of particular measures of the General Government of which it may disapprove." Therefore, any state legislative protests "against particular acts of Congress as unconstitutional, accompanied with invitations to other states to join in such protests, are improper and unauthorized assumptions of a power not permitted or intended to be permitted to the state Legislatures."[94]

Taylor's motion rejected the legitimacy of Virginia's interposition as well as the preexisting practice of interposition by other state legislatures. Crucially, Taylor failed to see that the Third resolution only represented Madison's assertion of the theoretical right of the people as the parties to the Constitution to act in the last resort. Moreover, Taylor did not appreciate that the interposition of Virginia's legislature did not rest on those grounds, but was justified by the Seventh resolution which described sounding the alarm about purportedly unconstitutional acts of the national government and calling on other state legislatures for their concurrence. Distinguishing between the two resolutions was needlessly rendered more difficult because the words "interposition" and "interpose" were used in the context of the Third resolution but not in the Seventh resolution. In the end, Taylor's substitute resolution failed before the House voted to accept Madison's Report.[95]

After vindicating the 1798 resolutions, Virginia's legislature renewed its protest against the acts as "palpable and alarming infractions of the constitution." In so characterizing the acts, the legislature stated the preconditions for the potential interposition of the people in their highest sovereign capacity articulated in the Third resolution – a step not yet taken, but which left the legislature free to offer its opinion and judgment that the acts were unconstitutional.[96]

The Success of the "Failed" Resolutions

The Virginia and Kentucky Resolutions heightened scrutiny of the Alien and Sedition Acts. For Richard Buel, the condemnation of the resolutions "clearly drew more attention to them than silence would have done." Indeed, when American voters went to the polls in 1800, they faced a choice between two political parties taking opposing positions on the acts and Jefferson made "violations of the true principles" of the Constitution a central campaign issue for the Republican Party. His election to the presidency and those of his followers to Congress reflected strong public opinion about the unconstitutionality of the acts. Indeed, Jefferson attributed his election to the "mighty wave of public opinion" that had "rolled over" America and marked a "recovery from delusion" that included the Alien and Sedition Acts. Madison later described the acts as a "usurping experiment" that was finally "crushed" and he concluded that the resolutions achieved "a triumph over the obnoxious acts, and an apparent abandonment of them forever."[97]

* * * * * *

Despite their political success, what Madison and Jefferson said they meant by the language they used in the Virginia and Kentucky Resolutions burdened the future efforts of states seeking to monitor governmental equilibrium and resulted in a deeply troubling political legacy. Madison might have been "America's most incisive constitutional thinker," but his occasional inability to express himself clearly produced an enormous toll, no more so than in the language he used in Virginia's Third resolution. Often Madison drew subtle, but crucial constitutional distinctions, yet failed to explain clearly what he meant. Madison particularly confused contemporaries with his language about the theoretical right of the sovereign people to interpose in the last resort, expressed in the Virginia Resolutions and in his Report of 1800. That confusion resulted in his convoluted words being employed later to support more direct resistance to the powers of the national government.[98]

Ironically, Madison's troublesome language in the Third resolution was unnecessary for the task at hand: sounding the alarm about the unconstitutionality of the Alien and Sedition Acts. Instead, Madison's formulation of the Third resolution indulged his need to declare a principle of constitutional theory, but in doing so he unwittingly provided the raw materials for future constitutional catastrophe and planted the seeds for dangerous ideas that would be taken up later by nullifiers and secessionists. Initially, the resolutions would be used to assert the right of state courts to determine matters of constitutionality independent of the Supreme Court, then to advance the theory of nullification, and finally to justify secession from the Union. The distortion of Madison's views, in particular, and the uses to which the 'Principles of '98' would be applied would cause severe damage to the nation.

The legacy of the resolutions propelled interposition into dangerous political territory. Jefferson's statements, as he drafted the Kentucky Resolutions, seemingly foreshadowed the extra-constitutional remedy of nullification when he stated that unconstitutional laws were null and void, suggesting nullification as a possible remedy in some undetermined circumstances.

The debate over the Virginia and Kentucky Resolutions reveals significant differences in how Americans understood divided sovereignty ten years after the Constitution's ratification. Resistance to the resolutions by Hamilton and others focused on maintaining that only the federal courts were responsible for monitoring federalism and that it was illegitimate for state legislatures to assert a monitoring role. Hamilton's repudiation in 1790 of his description and defense of interposition in *The Federalist* was part of a broader theme of resistance to sounding the alarm interposition: a desire to confine the interpretation and meaning of the Constitution to the federal courts and, particularly, to the Supreme Court. No one doubted that the Supreme Court played a role in interpreting the Constitution and resolving disputes over the boundaries of authority between the two levels of government. However, even if one conceded the Court's right to render final decisions to resolve constitutional conflicts in cases coming before it, the question remained: Were state legislatures legitimate sentinels to point out constitutional overreaching by the national government? And what were legitimate actions that aggrieved states might take as remedies to overreaching?

5

State Interposition during the Jefferson and Madison Presidencies

The interposition directed at the Alien and Sedition Acts galvanized political support that helped elect Thomas Jefferson President. His election ushered in the so-called 'Revolution of 1800' that displaced Federalist control of the presidency with the first of several Republican administrations. Given Jefferson's and Madison's role in drafting the Virginia and Kentucky Resolutions, it might seem ironic that their administrations confronted interposition during their presidencies as well. However, given the inherent fluidity of federalism, interposition inevitably came to be used by all parties to resist policies of the national government whenever it might be said that the party in power had thrown the federal system out of constitutional balance.

In Jefferson's second term, his embargo policy, beginning with the Embargo Act of 1807, prompted an interposition movement by Federalist state legislatures in New England. Although the embargo was repealed by the time of James Madison's inauguration in March 1809, other decisions of Madison's administration – many related to the War of 1812 – stimulated additional instances of interposition as state legislatures challenged the constitutionality of various acts of his administration.

Many New England legislatures continued to be dominated by Federalists who previously had condemned as illegitimate earlier state legislative protests against federal laws passed by the Washington and Adams administrations, but now supported interposition resolutions similar to the Virginia and Kentucky Resolutions. This inverted state of affairs meant that those who now invoked interposition often ignored the previous use of sounding the alarm interposition and expanded the possible actions that legislatures might take, even as the term interposition came into common use.

Complications in understanding interposition during the Jefferson and Madison presidencies occurred on at least two occasions when state legislatures said they were willing to go beyond merely declaring acts of the national government unconstitutional, intimating that they might be prepared to nullify acts of the national government. That posture went well beyond protests and efforts to muster interstate cooperation, leading others to brand as illegitimate all efforts by state legislatures that disagreed with Jefferson's and Madison's administrations. Indeed, during the early stages of Federalist opposition to Jefferson's policies, some Republicans questioned the right of Federalists to criticize those policies and the propriety of state legislatures commenting on national affairs at all, mirroring previous Federalist denunciations of Republican criticisms of the Alien and Sedition Acts.

Rebuking state legislatures for expressing views on national issues or for passing resolutions challenging the national government's constitutional authority ignored what state legislatures had been doing from the start of the republic. For example, when interposition surfaced during Jefferson's and Madison's administrations, Federalist Chief Justice John Marshall asserted that sounding the alarm interposition was illegitimate and undermined the rightful function of the federal courts. His position was part of the effort to 'lawyerize' the Constitution by excluding state legislatures from a role in monitoring federalism. But now Federalist state legislatures ignored Marshall's warning and passed interposition resolutions protesting: Jefferson's and Madison's embargo policies, *United States v. Peters* (1809) emphasizing the Supreme Court's final say over constitutionality, the recharter of the Bank of the United States, and Madison's efforts to mobilize state militias prior to the War of 1812.

After the controversy over the Alien and Sedition Acts and Jefferson's election in 1800, most Americans expected Republicans to follow the principle of 'strict construction' when it came to identifying national powers under the Constitution. However, both Jefferson and Madison occasionally construed the national government's power broadly, much to the chagrin of Federalists who now began to argue for strict construction, as well as Republicans who did not want to endorse a vigorous exercise of federal power. Thus, as Gerald Leonard and Saul Cornell have pointed out, "defenses of states' rights were never exclusively the province of Republicans any more than defenses of federal power were the exclusive preserve of Federalists."[1]

* * * * *

Jefferson's Embargo Acts (1807–1809)

Jefferson's embargo policy evolved as he tried to steer clear of a European conflict – the war between France and Britain that started in 1803. Early in that war, American merchants profited handsomely from trade with both sides, but those opportunities dwindled when Britain and France started blockading the ports of their adversaries. The United States claimed the right to trade freely as a neutral party, but this neutrality was rejected by both Britain and France. In addition, the British navy began boarding American vessels, seizing cargo without compensation and engaging in the practice of impressment – forcing merchant sailors to serve in the British navy. Instead of declaring war, Jefferson employed economic coercion, hoping to force the belligerents to respect America's neutrality.

Between December 1807 and January 1809, Republicans in Congress passed five embargo acts of increasing severity that reflected Jefferson's determination to enforce his policy. The first embargo act prohibited shipping to foreign ports and received the strong backing of Jefferson's Secretary of State James Madison. The embargo strategy proved to be a colossal failure and was enormously unpopular in the maritime states of New England and in many seaport towns throughout the nation.[2]

Early Reaction in Massachusetts

Notwithstanding its severe economic impact, the embargo was initially endorsed by Massachusetts with the election of Republican Governor James Sullivan and with a Republican majority in the legislature. Like earlier Federalists, Republicans equated criticism of the policies of their party, including the embargo, as illegitimate, undermining the national government, and bordering on sedition. They questioned whether state legislatures should comment on national policies and were entitled to question a law's constitutionality. Republicans ignored the earlier practice of state legislatures, including the resolutions Republicans had directed at the Federalist administrations of George Washington and John Adams.

In January 1808 Republican Governor Sullivan raised the embargo issue with Massachusetts' legislature. He conceded that the policy adversely affected shipping, but argued it was necessary to reestablish American rights to neutrality on the seas. He denounced "sedition," but urged "ready obedience" to laws of the national government enacted "within the authority given them by the constitution." The House and the Senate also defended the embargo, with the Senate agreeing that opposition constituted sedition. Those views prompted an open letter to Governor Sullivan from one of the state's U.S. Senators, Federalist Timothy Pickering. Paranoid, impulsive and something of a loose cannon within his party, Pickering believed that Jefferson was plotting to undermine New England's political influence. With Republicans controlling Congress, Pickering thought it imperative that the state legislature express its opposition and pass an interposition resolution declaring the embargo unconstitutional.[3]

Pickering's letter prompted Governor Sullivan to respond with his own open letter stating that the embargo was a congressional matter and none of the legislature's business. Sullivan considered the embargo "a constitutional act" beyond the right of state legislatures to question. For Sullivan, America's "first principle" was majority rule and since a congressional majority had spoken, Pickering's agitation promoted "rebellion and sedition." In a second open letter, Pickering replied that legislators should respond because the embargo was harmful to Massachusetts and he wondered if the legislature could only express approval of national measures, but never dissent.[4]

Interposition and Legal Challenges against the Embargo in Massachusetts

After Federalists gained control of the Massachusetts legislature in 1808 with a small majority despite Governor Sullivan's reelection, the House immediately passed resolutions that sounded the alarm about the embargo's unconstitutionality. While the national government might have the authority to create a temporary embargo, a permanent embargo "which a majority of Congress cannot repeal against the consent of the President" was not "contemplated by the framers of the Constitution." Moreover, the provisions requiring special permission from the President before any ship could leave American ports and giving him discretion over the coastal trade surrendered "the LEGISLATIVE POWER into a single hand."[5]

After the resolutions passed, Sullivan ignored the legislature's allegations of unconstitutionality and only spoke of the embargo's "expediency and propriety." Federalists in both the House and Senate quickly reminded Sullivan that they considered the embargo unconstitutional and would not shy away from saying so. The legislature then adjourned until its next session in November 1808.[6]

Before the next legislative session, Massachusetts Federalists mounted a judicial attack in the fall of 1808 hoping the U.S. District Court of Massachusetts would declare the embargo unconstitutional. However, Judge John Davis, a Federalist appointee, upheld the embargo as an act regulating commerce within the power of Congress. Despite that decision, the embargo's enforcement was severely hampered when juries were involved. Although some convictions were obtained in non-jury cases coming before Judge Davis, federal juries in Massachusetts seldom convicted alleged violators, acquitting four out of five such defendants.[7]

Federalists remained preoccupied with the embargo. When the Massachusetts legislature met in November 1808, it passed two resolutions, the first instructing the state's congressional delegation to seek an immediate repeal of the embargo and the second expressing the legislature's disagreement that the only alternative to the embargo was war. The legislature then adjourned until January 1809.[8]

Before the January session, Harrison Gray Otis, President of the Senate, wrote to Boston's congressman Josiah Quincy. Since the legislature had already declared the embargo unconstitutional, Otis wondered if the legislature should wait until more states were willing to interpose and if other New England states might support Massachusetts in a more dramatic form of interposition. Specifically, were those states ready to appoint delegates to meet "for the purpose of providing some mode of relief that may not be *inconsistent with the union of these States?*"⁹

Christopher Gore, a member of Massachusetts' House and soon-to-be Governor of the state, also asked Senator Pickering on "what measures and to what extent" the other New England states might cooperate with Massachusetts. Gore and Pickering agreed that effective opposition to the embargo required New England to unite behind "whatever great measure shall be adopted." Pickering thought a regional convention "obviously proper and necessary" and suggested the legislature draft an address identifying the objectionable measures of Jefferson's administration. But Pickering also anticipated a step towards nullification when he wondered how states could maintain their reserved powers except by *"judging for themselves and putting their negative on the usurpations of the general government?"*¹⁰

Reaction to Embargo Enforcement

Despite growing calls for the repeal of Jefferson's economic policy, congressional Republicans passed a federal Enforcement Act on January 9, 1809 to strengthen implementation of the embargo. The so-called "Force Act" also stimulated great resistance in New England and prompted further interposition because the act was seen as an egregiously unconstitutional step by the national government. The Force Act gave federal officers authority to make warrantless seizures of goods suspected of being shipped abroad, prohibited ships from being loaded without official permission, and allowed the national government to use state militias to enforce its provisions.¹¹

In a headline announcing the act, the Boston *New England Palladium* proclaimed, *"The CONSTITUTION gone!!"* while another Massachusetts newspaper called it "the DEATH WARRANT of New-England Liberty." A massive public meeting at Newburyport on January 12, 1809 drafted resolutions and a memorial to the Massachusetts legislature that expressed outrage at giving federal officers "powers unknown to the constitution" that undermined the liberties of citizens and threatened to convert America into a "military despotism." As the "immediate guardians of our rights," the memorialists wanted the state legislators "to interpose, as a constitutional shield." They considered the extraordinary powers granted by the Force Act patently unconstitutional and they sought "an interposition" from the state legislature to avert economic destruction and war – and to preserve the Constitution.[12]

While some scholars consider the Newburyport memorial a veiled call for nullification, its language was perfectly consistent with sounding the alarm interposition. The Newburyport meeting simply wanted the Massachusetts legislature to take a public stand against the unconstitutional aspects of the embargo when it convened for its January session. Just before the legislature met, over 4,000 people gathered at Faneuil Hall in Boston to protest the Force Act. The "Boston Constitutional Meeting," as one newspaper described it, met to address the disturbing situation. The meeting passed a series of resolutions claiming that the national government had adopted commercial restrictions in conflict with the "true intent and design of the Constitution." Moreover, the "unprecedented, arbitrary and unconstitutional" enforcement measures justified petitioning the state legislature for its "interposition, to save the people" of Massachusetts from the destructive consequences of the embargo.[13]

When Massachusetts' legislature convened on January 26, 1809, Republican Lieutenant Governor Levi Lincoln – who became acting Governor upon the death of James Sullivan in December – defended the embargo's constitutionality while criticizing its opponents. He doubted if the "citizens in the streets" who gathered at Newburyport and Boston were "capable of deciding on great, complicated constitutional questions," and wanted an end to the debate.[14]

Both houses of Massachusetts' legislature replied, with the Senate asserting that it was always legitimate to question actions of the national government and rejecting the idea that such scrutiny undermined the Constitution. The Senate also thought the Governor was wrong in doubting "the capacity of the people to decide on questions involving their unalienable rights." The House dismissed the idea that in "a free country there is any stage at which the *constitutionality* of an act may no longer be open to discussion and debate." The House asked: if laws became "stamped with the seal of infallibility" and constitutionality once they were enacted, to what "lengths might not an arbitrary and tyrannical administration carry its power?"[15]

A joint committee considered the complaints about the embargo laws in general and the Force Act in particular. While no "adequate and satisfactory remedy" seemed "within the power of this present legislature," the committee drafted resolutions that constituted the legislature's interposition. The first resolution declared the Force Act "unjust, oppressive and unconstitutional, and not legally binding on the citizens of this state." However, the committee wanted citizens "to abstain from forcible resistance, and to apply for their remedy in a peaceable manner." A second resolution called for a remonstrance to be sent to Congress urging a repeal of the Force Act. A third resolution declared the legislature's willingness to "co-operate with any of the other states, in all legal and constitutional measures" seeking constitutional amendments to provide relief from the embargo. The committee asked the President of the Senate and the Speaker of the House (and not acting Governor Lincoln) to transmit the report and resolutions to those legislatures negatively impacted by the embargo laws.[16]

Although these resolutions resembled the interposition described by Hamilton and Madison in *The Federalist* and were not threats of "disunion" or "forcible resistance," some legislators questioned their legitimacy. Given Massachusetts' disapproval of the Virginia and Kentucky Resolutions, one Republican considered the committee's report "inconsistent." Federalists defended their use of interposition even as they drew dubious contrasts with Virginia's 1798 Resolutions. One Federalist claimed that Virginia's legislature had declared certain laws of the national government unconstitutional while "we merely express *an opinion* with respect to this law." The Federalist majority in the legislature not only approved the report and resolutions, but also drafted a remonstrance to Congress and an address to the people of the state that were widely distributed. The remonstrance urged Congress to repeal the embargo laws because they violated the Constitution's "spirit and intention." The crisis warranted the legislature's interposition to alert citizens about the national government's unconstitutional acts and its call for an interstate movement to restore the proper balance of federalism.[17]

Criticism of Massachusetts' Interposition Resolutions

Seventeen Republican Senators in Massachusetts' legislature protested the report and resolutions and rejected the claim of unconstitutionality because the U.S. District Court of Massachusetts had upheld the Force Act. Moreover, even if they disagreed with the District Court, the Senators believed it was not "within the constitutional authority of a branch of a state legislature to decide the question." They regarded the first resolution's statement that the Force Act was not "legally binding" an incitement to insurrection, disunion, and anarchy. The *Boston Patriot*, a Republican newspaper, called Federalists hypocrites for doing what they had condemned in the Virginia and Kentucky Resolutions by giving *"their judgments, or if they please, opinions"* on the unconstitutionality of the embargo laws.[18]

Thomas Ritchie, the Republican editor of the *Richmond Enquirer*, accused Massachusetts' Federalists of taking a position "utterly inconsistent with the doctrine, which your party maintained, during *their* political ascendancy." Federalists had denounced the Virginia and Kentucky Resolutions as a "daring encroachment upon the rights of the General Government." At the time, Massachusetts' and other New England legislatures claimed it was a great transgression for any other body than "a *judicial court* of the U.S. to examine the constitutionality of a law."[19]

Ritchie did not dispute the principle and practice of interposition, but claimed that Massachusetts was improperly using the constitutional tool. Ritchie distinguished the Virginia legislature's 1798 dissent from what he thought were the obviously unconstitutional Alien and Sedition laws from the Massachusetts legislature's objections to the embargo. For Ritchie, the precondition of a palpable and dangerous encroachment of the national government was not met since a federal judge had upheld the embargo's constitutionality. According to Ritchie, Massachusetts' position that the eastern states could unilaterally declare the conditions for the preservation of the Union meant they could accomplish "dissolution at the point of the bayonet." In contrast, noted Ritchie, during the Alien and Sedition crisis, Virginia only wanted interstate cooperation for any *"necessary and proper means"* to maintain the "rights and liberties, reserved in the states respectively, or to the people."[20]

Interposition Efforts in Other States

Even before Massachusetts' legislature passed its interposition resolutions, a similar effort had been made in Delaware in late January 1809. Federalists in that state's House of Representatives passed resolutions calling the embargo an invasion of "the constitutional sovereignty of the State governments." The state's Senate refused to approve the resolutions and they became a failed attempt at interposition. However, two other New England states, Connecticut and Rhode Island, responded to Massachusetts' call for interstate efforts to repeal the embargo by passing their own interposition resolutions. While they have been described as "tepid responses," the steps taken in Connecticut and Rhode Island clearly adhered to the sounding the alarm function of interposition.[21]

When Federalist Governor Jonathan Trumbull, Jr., of Connecticut convened a special session of the legislature in January 1809, he highlighted what he believed were the unconstitutional features of the Force Act and encouraged the legislators to "cast a watchful eye" on the embargo. If Congress should "overleap the prescribed bounds of their constitutional powers" it was the right and duty of state legislatures "to interpose their protecting shield between the rights and liberties of the people, and the assumed power of the General Government."[22]

Connecticut's legislators believed the federal government had exceeded its delegated powers through "encroachments made on the powers reserved to the States respectively, and the people." Republicans ridiculed that view, with the Hartford *American Mercury* recalling that Connecticut legislators in the past had taken the position that state legislatures had "no right to interfere in the affairs of the general government."[23]

Despite the criticism, Connecticut's legislature passed several resolutions, including one explaining that state legislatures as "guardians" of rights were obliged to monitor and "to maintain, the powers not delegated to the United States." The legislature directed state officials not to cooperate in executing the Force Act and to support Massachusetts and other states in seeking constitutional amendments. The address distinguished the legislature's interposition from overt opposition to the national government.[24]

When Rhode Island's legislature convened in February 1809, it was flooded, as was Massachusetts' legislature, with memorials and petitions from towns angry about the embargo and the Force Act. The legislature passed a series of resolutions, including one that declared the Force Act "unjust, oppressive, tyrannical and unconstitutional." While mindful of the "rights of the general government," the legislature had a duty under the Constitution "to be vigilant in guarding" the state's reserved powers and rights. The Governor was to share the resolutions with Massachusetts, Connecticut, and other state legislatures inclined to support constitutional measures to preserve the Union.[25]

In the end, the interposition resolutions of the legislatures of Massachusetts, Connecticut, and Rhode Island contributed to a growing but politically polarized campaign against the embargo, which was eventually repealed and replaced by the Non-Intercourse Act of 1809 in the final days of Jefferson's presidency. Those interposition resolutions influenced the national debate over the constitutionality of the embargo and particularly the Force Act. Sixteen months after the 1809 repeal of the Embargo Act, Jefferson described the Federalists as having forced "us from the embargo" and in later years he remembered that at the time he felt "the government shaken under my feet by the New England townships." The conclusion that New England resistance deserved credit for having "protested, threatened, defied, and aroused" until the national government repealed the law, further demonstrated the crucial role that interposition played in ending Jefferson's embargo policy.[26]

Pennsylvania and *United States v. Peters* (1809)

On the eve of the repeal of the embargo, a different controversy arose at the beginning of the Madison administration, involving a jurisdictional dispute between a Republican-led state and the federal courts. Pennsylvania's claim that the federal government had overstepped its constitutional bounds originated during the Revolutionary War with the seizure of the British sloop *Active* in 1778. After a Connecticut born sea captain and privateer, Gideon Olmstead, along with several other American sailors who had been impressed in the Royal Navy succeeded in overpowering the crew of

the *Active*, they sailed to America to assert their claim to the ship as
a prize under maritime law, that is, a vessel captured in armed conflict.
They were soon joined by two other ships, one an American privateer
and the other a Pennsylvania state brigantine, each of which also
claimed the *Active* as a prize. A Pennsylvania court of admiralty
sitting in Philadelphia – acting on a jury's finding that Olmstead had
not established sufficient control over the *Active* – divided the prize
money into four parts and awarded a quarter each to Olmstead, the
captains of the two other vessels, and the Pennsylvania government as
owner of the brigantine. Olmstead appealed to the Continental
Congress and won a judgment from the Committee of Appeals for
Cases of Capture for the entirety of the proceeds. Pennsylvania
challenged the jurisdiction asserted by the congressional committee
and refused to distribute the proceeds retained by the state. After
fifteen years, Olmstead brought suit in the U.S. District Court in
Pennsylvania and won another decree for the entire funds in question
from Judge Richard Peters in *Olmstead v. The Active* (1803).[27]

Legally speaking, this should have ended the matter given an earlier
precedent arising out of New Hampshire. In 1795 the U.S. Supreme
Court, in *Penhallow v. Doane's Administrators*, held that the
Continental Congress's admiralty appellate court had "full authority
to revise and correct the sentences of the courts of admiralty of the
several states, in prize causes." Some scholars view the ruling in
Penhallow as "an early step" in the Supreme Court's "development
as an arbiter of the federal–state balance."[28]

Despite *Penhallow*, the aftermath of Judge Peters' ruling in
Olmstead saw both Pennsylvania's Governor and the state's
legislature questioning if the federal courts were the only monitors of
federalism. They claimed that Judge Peters had assumed
unconstitutional powers by overturning the state's initial admiralty
court decision in the Olmstead matter. Pennsylvania's legislature
criticized the U.S. District Court's ruling, but its reaction went well
beyond interposition by broaching forceful resistance to federal
authorities. Pennsylvania's Governor, Thomas McKean, sent Judge
Peters' opinion to the legislature in January, complaining about the
federal court's "strained construction" that undermined the state's
rightful jurisdiction. McKean sought the legislature's advice.
A committee of Pennsylvania's House reviewed the matter and

reported a bill that became law on April 2, 1803. The report concluded that Judge Peters' assumption of jurisdiction and decree violated the newly enacted Eleventh Amendment because Olmstead was suing the state of Pennsylvania. Such a finding might have become the basis of an interposition resolution, but instead it was incorporated in a state law that went well beyond the traditional step of sounding the alarm. Apart from its assessment of *Olmstead*, the legislature declared that Judge Peters' decision should not be "supported or obeyed" and "authorized and required" the Governor to use "any further means and measures that he may deem necessary" to protect the state's claim against federal judicial process.[29]

According to legislators present at the 1803 session, despite the language used, the law was not intended to "call out an armed force" or "make war against the union," but just to intimidate Judge Peters. That tactic was apparently successful, since the judge failed to issue an order implementing his decree. The effort to stall proceedings worked, at least until 1808, when the eighty-two-year-old Olmstead secured a writ of mandamus from the U.S. Supreme Court commanding Judge Peters to enforce his decree.[30]

Marshall's Opinion in United States v. Peters

Chief Justice John Marshall delivered the Court's opinion in *United States v. Peters* on February 20, 1809. While not citing *Penhallow*, his *Peters* decision held: that Pennsylvania had no constitutional right to resist the legal process in the case; that an admiralty appellate court created by Congress had authority over state admiralty matters; and rejected the argument that the Eleventh Amendment barred the lawsuit because private parties, not the state, were involved in the suit. In resolving the case, Marshall's opinion also asserted the Court's monopoly over questions of constitutionality and denied the state's attempt at interposition.[31]

Pennsylvania's 1803 law undermined Judge Peters' decree and Marshall warned that if state legislatures could "at will, annul" the judgments of federal courts, the nation loses "the means of enforcing its laws." But in rejecting such a nullifying authority for state legislatures, Marshall simultaneously repudiated any role for those legislatures to sound the alarm about perceived constitutional overreaching by the national government, including the federal judiciary.[32]

Marshall noted that the Pennsylvania legislature was not asserting the "right of the state to interpose in every case whatever," but instead justified this particular "interposition" on the ground that the federal court lacked jurisdiction. Marshall's use of the words "interpose" and "interposition" suggested he was referring to the Seventh Virginia resolution of 1798 since he focused on actions that a state legislature might take. Believing that state legislatures were not parties to the constitutional compact, Marshall tried to discredit their passing sounding the alarm resolutions at the same time that he advanced the argument for the Supreme Court's monopoly over matters of constitutionality.[33]

According to Marshall, if the Constitution gave "the ultimate right to determine the jurisdiction" of federal courts to "the several state legislatures," then Pennsylvania's 1803 law ended the matter. On the other hand, if "that power necessarily resides in the supreme judicial tribunal of the nation," then only the Supreme Court could decide the question of the District Court's jurisdiction. Marshall implied that even questioning the constitutional authority of the federal courts, especially after the Supreme Court had spoken, was unseemly at best and at worst subversive. That federal courts might exceed their constitutional authority and thus become the subject of legislative resolutions questioning their actions was apparently unthinkable even though only a few years earlier the Supreme Court's decision in *Chisholm* was reversed in large part in response to the movement that included interposition resolutions. As a result, Marshall's assertion that only the Supreme Court determined the constitutional limits of the Court's jurisdiction was less than convincing.[34]

A week after Marshall's decision in *Peters*, Pennsylvania's Republican Governor Simon Snyder alerted the legislature about anticipated "serious difficulties" with the case and he ordered General Michael Bright to activate the state's militia to prevent service of process from the U.S. District Court. Federalists, recently criticized for opposing the embargo, greeted Snyder's message with smug satisfaction. A Federalist newspaper claimed that "cries of Treason and Rebellion would have filled every democratic paper in the Union" if Snyder was a New England Governor. The headline reporting Snyder's message in the *Salem Gazette* read: "CIVIL WAR! Pennsylvania against U. States."[35]

Pennsylvania's Response to Federal Court Overreaching

United States v. Peters helped establish the Supreme Court's jurisdiction, but the controversy still presented a conundrum of federalism. The question was how might states legitimately respond to acts of perceived constitutional overreaching by the national government, in this case by its judiciary? Pennsylvania's legislature passed six resolutions in early April 1809 to be shared with other state legislatures on the subject of the "balance between the general and state governments as guaranteed by the constitution."[36]

Before those resolutions were adopted, state and federal authorities confronted one another after Judge Peters issued a judicial writ on March 14 for the arrest of parties sued by Olmstead. The U.S. Marshal was prevented from making arrests by a detachment of the state militia under the orders of General Bright. The Marshal wanted to charge the militiamen with treason and was prepared to form a *posse comitatus* to help him summon locals to enforce the Court's decree. The image of state militia – with bayonets drawn – interfering with a federal court's order captured the imagination of contemporaries and subsequent scholars alike and has largely overshadowed the importance of the interposition resolutions issued by the Pennsylvania legislature in 1809.[37]

In the resolutions, Pennsylvania's legislators acknowledged the supremacy of "the authority of the general government, as far as that authority is delegated" by the Constitution, yet "as *guardians of the State Rights*, they cannot permit an infringement of those rights, by an unconstitutional exercise of power" by federal courts. In the view of the members of the state legislature, because of "the imperfection of language," it had been impossible for the federal framers "to define the limits" of the general and state governments to avoid occasional difficulties and "a collision of powers." Thus, to preserve the proper balance between the national and state governments, Pennsylvania's legislators proposed a constitutional amendment establishing "an impartial tribunal" to resolve disputes arising between the two levels of government. They asked the Governor to send the resolutions to

Congress and consult with the President to settle the controversy, while also appropriating money for a potential settlement of Olmstead's claim.[38]

Contemporaries mainly focused on the possibility of forcible resistance to federal judicial process. Even a Republican newspaper assumed that Pennsylvania's legislature took the position that if the national government encroached on a state's sovereignty, it was "the duty of the offended State to resist with arms." Pennsylvania's Republican-dominated legislature was accused of resisting federal laws and "precipitating the dissolution of the Union." Given this perception, no other state supported Pennsylvania's idea for a new tribunal. Indeed, eleven states passed resolutions of disapproval, including Virginia's legislature, which replied that the Constitution already provided for an "eminently qualified" body to decide such disputes, namely, the Supreme Court.[39]

After Madison's inauguration, Governor Snyder wrote the President, included the legislature's resolutions, and hoped to prevent an "unhappy collision" between "the two governments." Madison's contributions to *The Federalist* and authorship of the Virginia Resolutions led Snyder to believe that Madison would be sympathetic to Pennsylvania's position. After all, Madison's Report of 1800 had identified situations that might require a review *other than by the Supreme Court* if the judiciary ever exercised powers "beyond the grant of the constitution." Snyder thought Madison would not insist that the Supreme Court was in all circumstances the only body entitled to weigh in on matters of constitutionality and to decide if the balance of federalism was being struck appropriately.[40]

As he reviewed the appeal from Pennsylvania, Madison understood that the finality of the Court's decisions was relative, being subject to revision through constitutional amendment, as in the *Chisholm* decision, and that theoretically, in extraordinary circumstances, the people – as the underlying sovereigns of the Constitution – had the final say. However, none of those possibilities were relevant. Pennsylvania's legislature could not invoke the ultimate authority of the collective people of the states to act in the final resort. Moreover, interposition *did not* include military resistance to a federal judicial decree even if that order seemed unconstitutional. Governor Snyder's actions brought the state and federal authorities to the brink of violence and

Madison could not support Pennsylvania. He tersely replied to Snyder that it was "unnecessary, if not improper" for him to interfere in the matter. As President he was not only "unauthorized to prevent the execution of a Decree sanctioned by the Supreme Court" but "expressly enjoined by Statute, to carry into effect any such decree." Madison suggested a monetary settlement.[41]

Even as the parties sought a compromise, the potential for confrontation between the federal and state authorities remained. On April 12, 1809, a federal grand jury indicted General Bright and eight of his militiamen for resisting federal law. Madison's Attorney General favored prosecuting "the principal offenders," while the U.S. Marshal prepared to summon a posse. The crisis was averted when Pennsylvania settled the lawsuit. Madison was relieved that the Olmstead affair had ended peacefully. Although General Bright and his militiamen were convicted and fined on May 2, 1809, all received presidential pardons since the offenders acted from "a mistaken sense of duty" instead of "a spirit of disobedience to the authority and laws of the United States." Madison also wanted to lessen public sympathy for Bright and his men.[42]

After Madison forwarded Pennsylvania's resolutions to Congress, John Porter, one of Pennsylvania's Republican representatives, moved to have them printed in accordance with the practice of responding to official state communications. Porter's Federalist colleague from Pennsylvania, William Milnor, opposed the motion and denied the right of legislators to play a role in monitoring federalism even as he acknowledged that Pennsylvania's legislature had reached the conclusion that the federal court had assumed "a power not delegated by the Constitution." The House chose not to print the resolutions.[43]

Pennsylvania's effort to generate public, political pressure to reverse an allegedly unconstitutional exercise of federal judicial power failed. Although Pennsylvania employed interposition in opposition to the *Peters* case, the advocacy of forceful resistance by the legislature and Governor stigmatized their actions as illegitimate and subversive.

Rechartering the Bank of the United States

Originally established in 1791 with a twenty-year charter, the Bank of the United States was crucial to Hamilton's fiscal program. Like the response to Hamilton's plan for the assumption of state debts, opponents of the first charter of the bank alleged that the recharter exceeded Congress's authority. Leaders of the opposition included Jefferson and Madison. As Washington's Secretary of State, Jefferson argued that, strictly construed, the Constitution did not authorize the federal government to charter a national bank and while a bank might be considered convenient, it was not necessary. In the House of Representatives, Madison contended that a national bank stood "condemned" by many factors including the absence of constitutional text, the statements of proponents during the ratification debate, and the Tenth Amendment.[44]

Hamilton, as Washington's Secretary of the Treasury, responded with a broad construction of national power. The delegation of general powers to Congress, Hamilton argued, necessarily implied the right to pass laws appropriate for exercising them. The Necessary and Proper Clause in the last paragraph of the enumerated powers of Congress, found in Article I, section 8 of the Constitution, provided power "to make all laws which shall be necessary and proper for carrying into execution the foregoing [list of seventeen enumerated] powers." Despite the doubts raised about the bank's constitutionality, Washington sided with Hamilton and signed the bank into law.[45]

Interposition would be used by state legislatures to challenge the constitutionality of the bank twenty years later during the struggle over its recharter. Before the bank's charter expired in 1811, stockholders of the bank lobbied Congress for its renewal in 1808. In March 1809 President Jefferson's Secretary of the Treasury, Albert Gallatin, issued a report supporting the bank's recharter and by 1810 the constitutionality of the bank was hotly debated in Congress. Constitutional concerns were echoed by numerous state legislatures that instructed and requested their congressional delegations to oppose rechartering. This interstate effort succeeded in temporarily delaying the bank's recharter when the House indefinitely postponed consideration of Secretary Gallatin's report in January 1811. The bank's advocates eventually succeeded in establishing the Second Bank of the United States in 1816, with the Supreme Court upholding the bank's constitutionality in *McCulloch v. Maryland* (1819).[46]

Opposition to the recharter of the First Bank of the United States partly rested on the desire to protect state banks from competition with a national bank. That motive has led some to characterize claims about the bank's unconstitutionality as "insincere." Nonetheless, from the standpoint of interposition, the recharter fight in 1811 found numerous state legislatures declaring their opposition on constitutional grounds. Those efforts supported an initially successful campaign to deny the bank's recharter by the narrowest of margins. As Eric Lomazoff describes it, the debate over the bank from 1791 to 1832 was "dynamic" and reshaped understandings about the bank's purposes. Forces driving this debate included monetary and economic stress during and after the War of 1812 and the "ordinary politics" of Congress wanting the bank to better control state banks without endorsing either a broad or a strict interpretation of the Necessary and Proper Clause.[47]

Pennsylvania's Interposition against the Bank

On December 13, 1810, Republican Jacob Holgate of Pennsylvania's House introduced two resolutions justifying the legislature's interposition and asserting that the bank, and therefore its recharter, was unconstitutional. One resolution instructed and requested the state's congressional delegation to oppose recharter and a second directed the Governor to send copies to the state's congressional delegation and to the Governors of the other states, for distribution to their legislatures.[48]

Holgate relied on a compact theory of the Constitution that drew from the Kentucky Resolutions of 1798 and he offered an explicit defense of interposition that echoed Madison's Report of 1800. Going beyond Jefferson's general statement that each party to that compact had a right to judge "infractions" of the compact and the means of "redress," Holgate asserted that each state had "at all times ... an indubitable right to express its opinions and use its influence in national councils and with its sister states, to prevent any apprehended infraction of the general compact." Indeed, "Should the general government, in any of its departments violate any of the provisions of the constitution, it rests with the states to apply constitutional remedies." Consistent with these principles, Pennsylvania's legislators considered it their duty to make their opinions known that Congress lacked constitutional authority for the bank charter.[49]

The House passed Holgate's preamble and resolutions by wide margins, while the Senate sought significant changes. Instead of identifying "the states" as adopting the Constitution, the Senate substituted "the people of the United States." Moreover, the compact was described as one between each state and the "United States" and not the "other states." The Senate endorsed the position that the national government was not the exclusive or final judge of its powers, but rather than leaving redress of perceived infractions up to the states alone, its version declared: "Should the general government in any of its departments, violate the provisions of the constitution, it rests with the states, and with the people, to apply suitable remedies."[50]

The House accepted most of the Senate's amendments, but reintroduced the description of the compact as being between each state and "other states" in place of the "United States." When the Senate balked, the House relented and the bill as amended by the Senate passed on January 11, 1811. The final version of the bill expressed the traditional iteration of legislative interposition: the right and the duty of a state legislature to express its views when it appeared the national government was overstepping its constitutional authority and undermining the "true spirit" of how the "respective constitutions" of the two levels of government should operate.[51]

Interposition by Additional States

Virginia's legislature also passed an interposition resolution two weeks later directed at the bank's recharter, believing the bank to be "not only unconstitutional, but a dangerous encroachment on the sovereignty of the States." The legislature instructed and requested its congressional delegation to oppose the recharter. The day after Virginia's legislature acted, Massachusetts' legislature convened and immediately approved a similar resolution.[52]

Kentucky's legislature acted next when its Senate passed resolutions on January 25, 1811 requesting its congressional delegation to oppose the bank's recharter. When the resolutions came to the House, an effort was made to amend them by elaborating on the unconstitutional features of the bank and instructing the state's U.S. Senators to act. The proposed amendment resolved that the national government lacked the power to establish the bank and characterized Congress's action as encroaching on rights and powers retained by the states. Although the amendment failed, the Senate's original resolution passed overwhelmingly, displaying a shared opposition to the bank despite disagreement over senatorial instruction.[53]

New Jersey's legislature introduced a similar instructing and requesting resolution. On January 19, 1811 a preamble and resolution were drafted declaring the bank unconstitutional. After approval by the House on February 8, 1811, the resolution went to the state's Executive Council for concurrence, but before the Council could act, the bill in Congress to renew the bank's charter was defeated in the U.S. Senate on February 20.[54]

Maryland nearly became the sixth state legislature to call the bank's constitutionality into question. After the legislature convened, House Representative Theodorick Bland introduced a preamble and resolution instructing and requesting the state's congressional delegation to oppose the recharter. Dubbed "Mr. Bland's Protest," the preamble criticized the bank as both unconstitutional and bad policy and justified interposition when threats existed to the Union and people's liberties, even as it was wary of instructing the state's congressional delegation.[55]

The debate over Bland's resolutions revealed a split in the House over the bank's recharter. After several changes were passed by a close vote, a member moved a substitute declaring it "highly impolitic and inexpedient" to instruct and request the congressional delegation to oppose the bank's renewal without more information and a better sense of public opinion. Absent such knowledge, it was best to withhold "an interposition which must necessarily tend to embarrass the national administration." Bland's resolution then failed by a single vote.[56]

An Underlying Controversy over the Right of Instruction

The central question during the bank recharter debate was not whether legislatures *could* instruct their Senators, but *if* those instructions were binding and mandatory. The conduct of Virginia's Senators during the recharter controversy, however, sparked a debate that vindicated interposition while misconstruing its use in Virginia's Resolutions of

1798. After the state legislature instructed its Senators and requested its House representatives to vote against rechartering the bank, Virginia's Republican Senator Richard Brent disregarded his instructions and voted in favor of renewal, while his Republican colleague, William Giles, although voting against recharter, explicitly rejected the binding nature of instructions. The actions of Brent and the arguments of Giles prompted a response from Virginia's legislature which in 1812 passed a preamble and resolutions formally censuring the two Senators and defending the right of state legislatures to issue them binding instructions.[57]

The Virginia legislature asserted that "the people composing each state in their sovereign capacity" were entitled to instruct their Senators. But it was hard to see "how the *people* can give such instructions, otherwise than thro[ugh] their *state legislatures*." The legislature linked its defense of instruction with its right "to interpose on questions of deep political interest, in the affairs of the general government." Some Virginia legislators relied on "the Letters of *Publius*" to support the argument for mandatory senatorial instruction because of the explicit case made for interposition in *The Federalist*. Those supporting mandatory instruction quoted Hamilton's *Federalist* 26 describing state legislatures as vigilant "guardians" who could "sound the alarm" and Hamilton's *Federalist* 28 asserting that those legislatures were best positioned to detect and oppose usurpation by the national government. They noted that *The Federalist* agreed that "state legislatures may interpose to prevent danger, or to resist usurpation," a position supporting mandatory senatorial instructions.[58]

The Virginia legislature also relied on Madison's authority, but in doing so demonstrated how the Virginia Resolutions and Madison's defense of them continued to be misread. In 1811, Virginia's legislators cited Madison's Report of 1800 for the proposition of "the state right of interposition in the affairs of the general government." The quote they offered, however, came from Madison's defense of the Third resolution and his elaboration of the theoretical right of the people to serve as the ultimate arbiters of the Constitution in the last resort. As such, Virginia's legislators confused legislative interposition with an action that – in Madison's view – no state legislature could invoke.[59]

The debate over the binding nature of senatorial instruction that surfaced during the bank recharter debate would continue for many decades. But even as the right of instruction remained a contested subject, state legislatures never stopped passing interposition resolutions sounding the alarm about apparently unconstitutional actions of the national government.[60]

The War of 1812 and the Militia Dispute

The War of 1812 prompted yet another wave of sounding the alarm interposition from New England legislatures. On June 18, 1812 President Madison initiated what Federalists called "Mr. Madison's War" by signing a declaration of war against Great Britain. Yet America only had a small standing army and a weak navy, necessitating a reliance on volunteers and the state militias. Four days later, under instructions from the President, U.S. Army General Henry Dearborn requested state militia detachments from the Governors of Connecticut, Massachusetts, and Rhode Island. Those Governors, supported by their legislatures, refused to comply on grounds that the federal requisition lacked constitutional authority and that each Governor retained the right to decide when to call out the militia.[61]

Many scholars have suggested their objections were a feeble excuse to oppose the war and Madison's administration, a position consistent with Madison's complaint that New England's constitutional interpretation was both "novel and unfortunate." Antiwar sentiment was clearly deep-seated, but the issue of constitutionality was not merely a figment of Federalist imagination or limited to New England. Even Madison's Secretary of State, Albert Gallatin, gave credence to the argument that presidential power over the militia did not arise until a state Governor called it into federal service. The showdown between President Madison and the New England Governors raised the question of the constitutional limits on federal use of the state militias. Only with its decision in *Martin v. Mott* (1827) would the Supreme Court decide that a president possessed the authority that Madison claimed in 1812.[62]

The partisanship surrounding the deployment of the militia has obscured the use of the interposition it triggered. The Governors of

Connecticut, Massachusetts, and Rhode Island alerted their
legislatures after receiving what they considered constitutionally
dubious requests from federal officials. Those legislatures passed
resolutions identifying actions of the federal government they
deemed unconstitutional. In this wave of interposition, Governors
and state legislatures accused the executive branch – President
Madison and his administration, instead of Congress or the
judiciary – of exceeding its constitutional authority.

Connecticut on Federal Use of the State Militia

Upon receiving General Dearborn's letter, Connecticut's Federalist
Governor Roger Griswold convened his Executive Council to ask
"whether the militia can be constitutionally and legally demanded"
without an official determination of the existence of one of the
federal powers specified in Article I, section 8 of the Constitution.
The   Council   concluded   that   Dearborn's   request   was
unconstitutional because the President had not declared "that the
militia are required *to execute the laws of the Union, suppress
insurrections, or repel invasions, or that the United States are in
imminent danger of invasion.*" The Council concluded that
command over Connecticut's militia remained with the Governor
and in early July 1812, Governor Griswold refused Dearborn's
request.[63]

Governor Griswold called a special session of Connecticut's
legislature for August 25, 1812 to allow the legislature to weigh
in on the constitutional issue. The legislature produced a report
and passed a resolution approving the Governor's decision, noting
that the Constitution prohibited the exercise of powers not
delegated to the federal government, but reserved to the states.
This divided authority was particularly relevant in the present
instance since the Constitution granted the national government
authority to use the militia only in clearly specified cases, while all
other power over the militia was left to the states. The legislators
concluded that the constitutionally required circumstances were
absent, but promised that in the event of an actual or even
a threatened invasion, Connecticut's militia would promptly
defend the country.[64]

Massachusetts and Its Militia

Connecticut's legislature was not alone in refusing to comply on constitutional grounds. A similar request had been made to Massachusetts' Federalist Governor Caleb Strong who responded to Secretary of War William Eustis on August 5, 1812. In his letter, Strong stated his belief that Massachusetts was not in apparent danger of invasion, one of the constitutional grounds for calling the militia into service. Acting on the prevailing opinion that a Governor had no authority to make such a call unless one of the urgent circumstances specified in the Constitution existed, he had convened the Executive Council which concurred with his judgment. The Council also recommended obtaining an advisory opinion from the state's Supreme Judicial Court on two questions: Whether Governors had to make the determination that the constitutionally specified circumstances existed, and if so, whether the militia called into the service of the United States could be commanded by anyone but the President.[65]

The Court agreed with Strong and the Council, holding that the Governor was entitled to determine the existence of the circumstances specified in the Constitution. The Court noted that the Constitution neither gave the President nor Congress the power to make that determination. But since the Constitution did not delegate such a power to the federal government, nor prohibit it to the states, it was reserved to the states, and thus Governors must assess the circumstances in their capacity as commanders of their state militia.[66]

Moreover, Massachusetts' Supreme Judicial Court held that even if one of the specified circumstances existed, the Constitution only explicitly authorized the President to command the militia. The Constitution plainly made the President the Commander in Chief of the militia of the several states when called into actual service. Less clear was who other than the President could take command, and the Supreme Judicial Court refused to extend such authority to subordinate officers such as General Dearborn. Armed with the judicial opinion and the support of his Executive Council, Governor Strong refused to comply with Dearborn's requisition or the Secretary of War's request.[67]

After Massachusetts' legislature convened in October and with the advisory opinion in hand, Governor Strong justified his position as preserving the equilibrium of federalism and the rights reserved to the states. If General Dearborn's constitutional interpretation prevailed, the President and Congress could "at any time, by declaring War, ... call the whole Militia of the United States into actual service, and march them to such places as they may think fit ... as long as the War shall continue." Strong argued that a crucial right retained by the states was their control of the militia subject to the Constitution's requirements. Suspending that right created "a consolidation of the military force of the States" and transferred entire control to the national government.[68]

The House applauded the Governor's resistance to "unconstitutional encroachments" and his determination "to maintain the rights of the State." The Senate, however, dismissed what it considered Strong's finely wrought constitutional distinctions and defense of states' rights during a time of war. The Governor's "jealousy" of national authority endangered the Union. Even if the constitutional language was ambiguous, the "hour of danger is not the fit time for abstract speculation." President Madison responded to the Governors of Massachusetts and Connecticut in his Fourth Annual Message by stating that if federal authority could not call out the militia even under threat of invasion, America was "not one nation" during a critical time.[69]

Reactions from Rhode Island and Vermont

Before addressing Congress, Madison was assured by Rhode Island's Governor William Jones that his state's militia would act in the service of the United States as soon as he believed the specified circumstances described in the Constitution existed. However, Governor Jones reached the same conclusion as had the Governors of Massachusetts and Connecticut: the grounds for calling up the militia had not yet been established.

When Federalist Martin Chittenden became Vermont's Governor in 1813, he too criticized "Mr. Madison's War" and the President's militia policy. He encouraged the legislature to consider militias as primarily for the protection of the states and accused Madison's administration of improperly construing Article I, section 8 of the Constitution. Moreover, since the Constitution also protected freedom of speech, it was not only the right but the duty of state officials to express their views about how the national government might be exceeding its constitutional authority.[70]

Chittenden sought to recall a contingent of Vermont's militia previously dispatched to New York under orders from someone other than the President. Although unsuccessful, Chittenden's effort was denounced by several state legislatures and prompted calls for the Governor to be tried for treason. That threat led Harrison Gray Otis in Massachusetts' legislature to introduce a resolution condemning any potential prosecution of Chittenden and promising the support of Massachusetts' legislature should Vermont need help in defending its constitutional rights against "infringement" by the national government. Although tabled, Otis's gesture did not go unnoticed: Pennsylvania's legislature viewed Otis' resolution with the same "astonishment and high disapprobation" as it did the actions of Vermont's Governor.[71]

Madison's Embargo (1813)

The war became even more unpopular in New England after Congress enacted a new embargo during Madison's administration on December 17, 1813. The law prohibited all American ships and goods from leaving port, a provision with devastating impact on maritime commerce, Southern states exporting tobacco and cotton, and the intrastate coasting trade. Although that embargo would soon be repealed, it triggered further interposition resolutions, particularly from Massachusetts. In addition, opposition to the embargo and the war pressed the limits of what interposition might entail beyond sounding the alarm resolutions.[72]

Massachusetts' legislature led efforts for a regional interstate convention with the objective of amending the Constitution. Specific invocations of "interposition" sought to draw parallels to the Virginia Resolutions of 1798, but without acknowledging some of Madison's crucial distinctions. Massachusetts' Governor Caleb Strong addressed the 1813 embargo when the legislature convened for its January 1814 session. Strong stressed the importance of "investigating political subjects and of freely expressing our sentiments." But even during an "unjust or unnecessary" war, the people still needed "to submit" to laws constitutionally enacted. However, given certain provisions in the embargo, the Governor encouraged the legislature to urge Congress to repeal or amend the most troubling provisions. The House concluded that prohibiting the coasting trade was unconstitutional and ominously suggested it might be time for "the people of this state, to decide whether these burdens are not too grievous to be borne" and to prepare to protect "their unalienable rights." The Senate agreed with the House that some provisions were unconstitutional, deserving censure, and might "demand legislative interposition." Like the House, the Senate hinted at more serious responses.[73]

Despite the threatening allusions, the legislature chose a moderate response. A joint committee responding to the flood of memorials and petitions from Massachusetts towns issued what became known as "Lloyd's Report." The report proposed resolutions sounding the alarm about unconstitutional measures, but also explained how legislative interposition might entail something more than simply declaring actions of the national government unconstitutional. The report invoked Madison's Virginia Resolutions and his Report of 1800, but confused Madison's statement of the theoretical right of the states as parties to the compact with interposition by state legislatures. Even so, adopters of Lloyd's Report did not contemplate nullification, but instead urged an interstate convention to propose constitutional amendments.[74]

The report accused Jefferson and Madison of supporting policies that were intended to impair, if not to destroy New England's commerce and had significantly altered the sectional balance of the Union. Evidence for such a scheme existed in the commercial programs of the Republican administrations, the prosecution of the war with Britain, and most recently the new embargo, which the report called "a gross and palpable violation of the principles of the constitution." The report insisted that the Massachusetts legislature could rightfully "interpose its power" in response to abuses of power and usurpations by the federal government. Connecting this idea with Madison, the report accused the President of hypocrisy. Interposition had "been explained by the very man, who now sets at defiance all the principles of his early political life."[75]

The report considered three forms of relief suggested by those who objected to the embargo: a legislative protest to Congress opposing the embargo, passage of laws to protect the property rights of the state's citizens, and finally, appointing delegates to an interstate convention to propose constitutional amendments. The protest option was rejected as having repeatedly been tried without effect; existing constitutional provisions and the common law already protected property, thus making new laws unnecessary; but the third option might return the Constitution to its "true spirit." Lloyd's Report claimed that Madison had blessed this third option in his Report of 1800. The committee recommended a delay to let the next election serve as a referendum on the embargo and the war, and give peace negotiations time to succeed.[76]

The resolutions adopted by the legislature declared that the embargo of 1813 contained unconstitutional provisions, that power over the intrastate coastal trade was never delegated to the national government and thus a congressional act claiming that right was "unconstitutional and void." Massachusetts' legislators, like Jefferson in Kentucky's Resolutions of 1798, were suggesting that the unconstitutionality of the embargo rendered it void. Indeed, if Massachusetts' legislators thought they were nullifying the embargo, it would have been pointless to call a convention to propose a constitutional amendment restricting congressional embargo authority.[77]

Congress Repeals the Embargo of 1813

Prior to the next session of Massachusetts' legislature, Congress repealed the embargo, which Governor Strong noted when he addressed the legislature in May 1814. The legislature replied to the Governor and described the adoption of Lloyd's Report and resolutions of the previous session as a successful interposition. The House noted demands for the legislature's "interposition" in the memorials of Massachusetts' citizens. Both the House and Senate condemned the war, but adjourned in mid-June before the course of the war dramatically affected Massachusetts.[78]

Although Massachusetts' legislature was due to reconvene in early 1815, Governor Strong called a special session in October 1814 to deal with Britain's invasion of the state which Strong blamed on Madison's administration. A motion in the House soon after it convened expressed a similar view. One member urged a delegation of New England states to call on the President and demand that he either resign or remove those "Officers of the General Government, who have by their nefarious plans ruined the nation."[79]

The Hartford Convention (1814)

After Governor Strong's address, a joint committee issued a report on October 15, 1814 reviving the previously discussed step of additional "interposition," namely, a call for a New England convention. Significantly, however, this self-described step of interposition did not entail identifying supposedly unconstitutional acts of the national government, but asserted that the Constitution itself was in disequilibrium and required rebalancing – perhaps through another constitutional convention. The alleged imbalance involved a regional and sectional shift since the ratification of the Constitution, with the South gaining disproportionate political power relative to New England. Dealing with the state's military vulnerability was of immediate concern, but the report also sought to address the underlying cause of New England's plight through "a radical reform in the national compact."[80]

While acknowledging that Article V of the Constitution governed constitutional revision, the report concluded that the normal amending process would take too long to provide the relief desperately needed by Massachusetts and New England. In justifying a circumvention of the revision process, the report concluded that the framers had included Article V because they recognized imperfections in the Constitution. Indeed, Article V itself was just as "liable to be found defective" over time as were other constitutional provisions. As such, the joint committee envisioned a convention of delegates from New England states that might propose constitutional revisions for consideration by a national constitutional convention. The report recommended numerous resolutions, but included one that foreshadowed the Hartford Convention. The stated purpose of a convention was to propose constitutional changes to ensure "fair representation" and influence for the New England states. After adopting the report and resolutions, the legislature sent a circular letter to the Governors of New Hampshire, Rhode Island, Connecticut, and Vermont inviting their state's participation in a regional convention in New England.[81]

The letter examined how amendments might be offered to restore equal advantages to New England states. It suggested "an experiment" of a convention drawn from those states that were interested in amendments to meet and thus bypass the Constitution's requirement that two-thirds of the state legislatures apply for such a convention. Ultimately, twenty-six delegates from five Federalist-dominated New England states assembled in Hartford, Connecticut on December 15, 1814. After meeting behind closed doors, the convention adopted a report probably authored by Harrison Gray Otis that endorsed a series of resolutions.[82]

The Hartford Convention's Report

The report focused on the inadequate national military defense of New England, but also accused Madison's administration of misconstruing the Constitution and exceeding its constitutional authority. Rejecting Madison's assertion that he had discretion to decide when the Constitution warranted calling out the militia, the report stressed the monitoring role of state legislatures. Given "a total disregard for the Constitution," it was appropriate for individual states to offer their "decided opposition." In justification, the report paraphrased Madison's Third Virginia resolution, but in a manner that allowed state legislatures to act in ways that Madison had limited to "the states," by which he meant the people of the states in their highest sovereign capacity.[83]

In declaring that unconstitutional acts of Congress were "absolutely void," the report did not mean that states should resist "every infraction" of the Constitution. The report described the preconditions that Madison identified in his Third resolution and explained in his Report of 1800. Nonetheless, in words that largely tracked to Madison's Third resolution, the report asserted that "in cases of deliberate, dangerous, and palpable infractions of the Constitution, affecting the sovereignty of a State, and liberties of the people; it is not only the right but the duty of such a State to interpose its authority for their protection." Despite the report's claims, nullifying national laws deemed unconstitutional far exceeded the role of state legislatures to sound the alarm about the constitutionality of laws that Madison had endorsed in Virginia's Seventh resolution. Moreover, nullifying acts of the federal government and assuming the authority to decide in the last resort was not up to individual state legislatures.[84]

Federalist newspapers also claimed that Madison had endorsed resistance by individual states. In essays directed to "The President of the United States," a writer in the *Boston Daily Advertiser* in November 1814 attributed "axioms" and "principles" to Madison, including that "a State Legislature has a right to interfere, and oppose the Government of the United States, whenever it is dissatisfied with the *policy* which that Government may pursue." The writer in the *Boston Daily Advertiser* claimed that Madison's *Federalist* 46, dealing with "the authority of the State governments" to resist "ambitious encroachments of the Federal Government," proved that Madison had repudiated the principles of his earlier political life. His views "*then* and *now*," the writer asserted, "are wonderfully different!" But New England Federalists misunderstood how Madison explained interposition.[85]

After describing an interposition that amounted to nullification, the Hartford Report turned to seven specific constitutional amendments designed to address New England's grievances. The proposals included the abolition of the Three-Fifths Clause, so as to base political representation on each state's free population and hence eliminate the advantage of Southern states being able to add three-fifths of their enslaved population into the calculation of its eligible number of House members. Other proposals included a requirement that new states be admitted only by a vote of two-thirds of both Houses, and that Presidents be limited to a single term and could not come from the same state two terms in succession. Those changes were aimed at curbing Southern political dominance, particularly that of Virginia.[86]

Responses to the Hartford Convention

Publicly, Madison did not acknowledge the convention, even as he sent a military observer to Hartford to report to him confidentially about the proceedings. Nor did he comment on how his authority was being used to justify the convention's claims. However, Madison did question the loyalty of convention delegates and those they represented and he blamed New England as "the source of our greatest difficulties in carrying on the war." Their antiwar stance explained why Britain continued to fight. New England's leaders simply sought power and invited "revolt and separation." In retirement at Monticello, Jefferson dismissed the convention and called its delegates "venal traitors" for trying to "anarchize" the nation by threatening secession. He thought the convention demonstrated Massachusetts' political "degradation."[87]

After the convention adjourned, Massachusetts' legislature dispatched a three-person delegation, including Harrison Gray Otis, to Washington with the convention's resolutions. Their arrival coincided with news of Andrew Jackson's victory over the British at the Battle of New Orleans and word that a peace treaty was nearing completion at Ghent, thus making their mission futile and condemned as treasonable. Eventually, only the Massachusetts and Connecticut legislatures endorsed the convention's proposed constitutional amendments. Although submitted to the House of Representatives in early March 1815, they were tabled without debate while nine other state legislatures passed resolutions of disapproval.[88]

The Hartford delegates were labeled traitors and disunionists, yet neither they nor most Federalists seriously endorsed secession. Murmurs and threats of secession had long percolated among more extreme New England Federalists and were often associated with the Hartford Convention. However, the convention displayed a more moderate approach. In suggesting that the Union might be "destined" for "dissolution," the convention's report rejected that step for the time being. Nonetheless, Hartford's delegates were tainted with the enduring stigma of disloyalty and disunion. More than a quarter-century later, Otis was still defending the convention as "constitutional & peaceable." He insisted that the convention had merely addressed a "question of *constitutional law*" over the respective powers of "the General and State governments."[89]

Otis could reasonably refute charges of secession, but he was hard-pressed to demonstrate that the Hartford Report – which he likely wrote – only reflected a traditional form of interposition. In defending the convention in the 1820s, Otis glossed over the implications of some of the report's recommendations by asserting that only two measures were contemplated: federal funding for state militias and constitutional amendments. He did not discuss the report's call for individual state legislatures to pass laws that would effectively negate the operation and effects of allegedly unconstitutional acts of the national government. As the author of the report, he could hardly say he had never believed in *"nullification."* He seemed unaware that the Hartford Report could have been used to buttress the claims of Southern nullifiers had not the convention's delegates been discredited as disloyal secessionists. Indeed, the Hartford Report provided a far better precedent for South Carolina's nullification than the authority Southern nullifiers of the 1830s would invoke: the Virginia and Kentucky Resolutions.[90]

Had they only known, later nullifiers could have cited a speech of Daniel Webster in the House of Representatives on the eve of the Hartford Convention – a speech he withheld from publication and which only appeared in print during the twentieth century. Webster opposed a bill establishing a military draft, calling it an "unconstitutional and illegal" measure whose operation "ought not to be carried into effect." According to Webster, should Congress pass the law, "It will be the solemn duty of the State Governments to protect their own authority over their own militia, and to interpose between their citizens and arbitrary power."[91]

* * * * * *

Webster's and Otis' versions of interposition eventually found their champions in the Southern nullifiers of the 1830s. Before then, however, state legislatures would continue to practice conventional sounding the alarm interposition, but in doing so further perpetuate misunderstandings about Madison's reference to interposition in his Virginia Resolutions. The fact that those resolutions dealt with two different types of interposition that Madison failed to clearly articulate continued to elude Americans who invoked the 'Principles of '98'. Importantly, those 'Principles of '98' would soon be invoked to support a compact theory of the Constitution that Madison did not endorse and that challenged the authority of the Supreme Court and the stability of the Union.

6

State Challenges to the Supreme Court's Control over Constitutional Interpretation

From the beginning of the enterprise to create the American nation, the debate over federalism rested on fundamentally different views of the foundation and formation of the Constitution. For John Marshall and other nationally minded Americans, the Constitution had been established as the act of one national people, forming a national government with considerable powers. For Judge Spencer Roane of Virginia and other sovereign states' rights advocates, the Constitution was a compact of sovereign states, leaving state sovereignty largely intact except for limited and express grants of power to the national government. Moreover, advocates of sovereign states' rights often implied that the Constitution had not dissolved the early Articles of Confederation, emphasizing that the Constitution was intended to prevent consolidation of power in the national government and to preserve the sovereignty of states.

These competing views also shaped how each side viewed the role and authority of the Supreme Court, and rhetoric became more extreme as nationalists feared disunion and states' rights advocates feared the disintegration of state authority during the inevitable and intractable struggle over slavery. Marshall believed the Constitution intended and required that the Court serve as the final monitor of federalism and, therefore, the Supreme Court rightly exercised appellate jurisdiction over state courts. However, for sovereign states' rights advocates, conflicts between the national government and the states could only be resolved by the states themselves, since they were the crucial parties to the constitutional compact, and should not be resolved by the Supreme Court. Jefferson also denied the Supreme Court's right to settle such disputes, though for him resolution required recourse to the people in constitutional conventions. Thus, Americans became increasingly and deeply divided in the 1820s – as they had been in the 1790s – over the state versus federal balance under the Constitution. A series of lawsuits represented an increasingly stark division in American thinking about the Constitution and the role and authority of the Supreme Court: *Hunter v. Martin, Devisee of Fairfax* (1814), *Martin v. Hunter's Lessee* (1816), *McCulloch v. Maryland* (1819), and *Cohens v. Virginia* (1821).

* * * * * *

Virginia and the Fairfax Litigation

A crucial challenge to the Supreme Court's appellate review over state court decisions involved the litigation over millions of acres in northern Virginia once held by Thomas Fairfax, sixth Lord Fairfax of Cameron, under a royal grant. The death of Fairfax in 1781 initiated a long controversy that pitted the successors and heirs of Fairfax against the state of Virginia. Future Chief Justice John Marshall became involved, both as a buyer of Fairfax lands and as an attorney for the Fairfax interests. In *Hunter v. Fairfax's Devisee* (1809), Virginia's Court of Appeals ruled against the Fairfax side. In 1813 the Supreme Court reversed the decision of Virginia's Court of Appeals in *Fairfax's Devisee v. Hunter's Lessee*, with an opinion by Joseph Story, Marshall having recused himself due to his personal involvement. The Supreme Court's mandate that the state follow the federal court's decision prompted Virginia's Court of Appeals to review the constitutionality of the federal statute authorizing the Supreme Court to review decisions of a state's highest court. In *Hunter v. Martin, Devisee of Fairfax* (1814), Virginia's Court of Appeals unanimously held that the Supreme Court lacked appellate authority over Virginia's court and that the purported grant of that authority was unconstitutional. Thus, a land dispute led to a constitutional crisis over the Supreme Court's appellate jurisdiction.[1]

Scholars have explored how this constitutional crisis produced a strong statement of states' rights by Virginia's Court of Appeals. Far less appreciated is how that crisis helped instill a description of the Constitution's foundation as either the product of a national people or of sovereign states. That dichotomy persisted in constitutional debates and effectively obscured Madison's views even as both sides claimed his authority. Additionally, scholars overlook the Virginia court's mangling of Madison's sounding the alarm interposition.[2]

Virginia's Court of Appeals delivered its unanimous decision in *Hunter v. Martin, Devisee of Fairfax* after a week of oral argument from leaders of the state's bar. The first opinion, that of Judge William Cabell, concluded, as would his fellow judges Francis Brooke, Spencer Roane, and Chief Judge William Fleming, that Congress in enacting the Judiciary Act of 1789 lacked constitutional authority to give the Supreme Court final review over decisions of Virginia's Court of Appeals.

For Judge Cabell, the Constitution created two levels of government, each possessing "its portion of the divided sovereignty." His description of federalism rested on Madison's *Federalist* 39 while not explicitly citing that essay. "The constitution of the United States," wrote Cabell, "contemplates the independence of both governments, and regards the *residuary* sovereignty of the states, as not less inviolable, than the *delegated* sovereignty of the United States." According to Cabell, the Supremacy Clause did not give federal courts the final authority over the supreme law of the land; instead, he asserted that state judges also had a right to determine the meaning of the Constitution in cases that came before their courts.[3]

Judge Brooke also cited Madison to reach a similar conclusion. Brooke saw "state authorities" as "the guardians of the people's and their own rights" with the "right to resist" any infractions of the Constitution by the "general government." Perceived overreaching by the national government invited a range of responses that fell short of forceful opposition. Brooke's assertion of a right to resist infractions of the Constitution also implied that state authorities – instead of "the states" – had an ultimate right to judge infractions in the last resort. Like Cabell, Judge Brooke invoked Madison's *Federalist* 39 to support Virginia's decision to rule on the constitutionality of the statute giving the Supreme Court appellate review over state courts. Brooke quoted Madison's discussion of the "respective spheres" of the two levels of government with the national government having supremacy within its lawful authority while leaving "a residuary and inviolable sovereignty" in the states. Brooke did not accept the Supreme Court as the ultimate decider in disputes between the two jurisdictions. Instead, he focused on Article VI's requirement that state judges – along with other officers of state and national governments – take an oath to support the Constitution. For Brooke, that article did not give the Supreme Court "power to enforce the responsibility of state judges," but entitled state judges to ask whether laws and treaties were constitutional. Therefore, Virginia's Court of Appeals could examine, and even refuse compliance with, the Supreme Court's mandate if the state court deemed the laws were unconstitutional.[4]

Judge Roane questioned the authority of *The Federalist* since it originated as "a mere newspaper publication, written in the heat and hurry" of the ratification debate and because one of its main authors, Hamilton, was "an active partizan" favoring consolidated government. Instead, Roane relied on the principles of the Virginia Resolutions and Madison's "celebrated report." Roane's description of federalism stressed the independence and sovereignty of individual states joined in "a perpetual Confederacy," but which still remained independent under both the Articles and the Constitution. Roane quoted from Virginia's Third resolution that the federal government's powers came from "the compact to which the *states* are parties" (emphasis supplied by Roane) and were valid to the extent they were "authorized by the grants enumerated in the compact." In case of "a deliberate, palpable, and dangerous exercise of powers," states must "arrest the progress of the evil." Roane drew his own conclusion: that the states, whether through their legislatures or courts, were "authorized to interfere" in the case of a palpable exercise of ungranted power by the national government. Roane distorted Madison's position in several key respects: by thinking that the Third resolution authorized state legislatures and state courts to take action; overlooking the specific role for state legislatures to sound the alarm; and assuming that state courts were as entitled as the Supreme Court to decide controversies over the boundaries between the two levels of government.[5]

Chief Judge Fleming's short opinion relied on Madison's description of state governments in *Federalist* 39 and the Tenth Amendment. Fleming's reading of those two sources induced him to join the court's unanimous decision to ignore the federal court mandate on the ground that the Judiciary Act granting the Supreme Court appellate authority over Virginia's court was unconstitutional.

The Supreme Court Responds: *Martin v. Hunter's Lessee* (1816)

After Virginia's ruling, John Marshall appealed to the Supreme Court. In *Martin v. Hunter's Lessee*, the Supreme Court reversed the state court's ruling in *Hunter v. Martin, Devisee of Fairfax* and upheld both its earlier decision in *Fairfax's Devisee v. Hunter's Lessee* and the constitutionality of the Judiciary Act. With Marshall formally disqualified, Justice Joseph Story wrote the majority opinion, but later recalled that Marshall "concurred in every word of it." Story rejected the compact theory advanced by the Virginia judges, stressed the difference between the Constitution and the Articles, and stated that unlike the earlier "compact between states," the Constitution was established "by 'the people of the United States'" who produced a government with "new substantive powers." One new power was the Supreme Court's right to review state court decisions. Story emphasized the need for one ultimate appellate court. It made no sense for the nation's judicial system to render independent and conflicting interpretations of the Constitution. As Story put it, "the absolute right of decision, in the last resort, must rest somewhere."[6]

While Story's explanation made sense to many observers then and now, his description of the Court deciding in the last resort implied greater finality for the Supreme Court than some, including Madison, acknowledged at the time. Conceding Story's point that the Court could resolve controversies involving the boundaries between the two levels of government in cases coming before the Court was one thing. But in doing so, the Supreme Court was not truly acting in the last resort since its decisions were always subject to revision through constitutional amendment. Story's preoccupation with the role of the Court, which Marshall shared, was part of a wider effort to make constitutional matters the exclusive domain of lawyers and judges. By downplaying the role that others besides the Supreme Court might have in construing the Constitution and monitoring federalism, the Court also undermined sounding the alarm interposition by state legislatures.

While *Martin v. Hunters Lessee* upheld the Supreme Court's appellate jurisdiction, Story declined to say whether the Court had the authority to issue a writ of mandamus to Virginia's Court of Appeals to enforce the Supreme Court's decision. Story merely rendered an opinion reversing the Court of Appeal's judgment, and avoided any further difficulty with that court, by remanding the case directly to the state district court. If *Martin v. Hunter's Lessee* left unsettled whether appellate supervision of state courts by the Supreme Court would become a permanent feature of the American constitutional system, that question was answered after the Supreme Court under Marshall's leadership championed a uniform law of the land through a completely national interpretation of the Constitution.[7]

Movement for a Second Bank of the United States

After the First Bank of the United States failed to be rechartered in 1811 because of opposition from legislative interpositions involving Pennsylvania, Virginia, Massachusetts, Kentucky, and New Jersey, supporters of a national bank sought its resurrection. In 1816 a Second Bank of the United States was established, partly due to the grudging acknowledgment by former opponents that the bank had proven beneficial during the economic dislocations surrounding the War of 1812. Bank advocates argued that the question of the bank's constitutionality was now "settled." Even President Madison, who initially opposed the First Bank on constitutional grounds, no longer doubted its constitutionality. Madison vetoed a bill for a new national bank in 1815, but only because the bill failed to serve its fiscal purposes. During the congressional debates preceding the reestablishment of a national bank, questions of constitutionality were largely ignored.[8]

If some thought the bank issue settled, others continued to believe the Constitution neither authorized the establishment of a national bank nor permitted state branches of such an entity. In addition, the Second Bank engendered hostility because of its perceived role in contributing to the financial Panic of 1819 and because it impinged on the authority of state banks. Ultimately, the Second Bank became much more controversial than the First Bank, emerging as a primary target of Andrew Jackson and his supporters. But a decade before Jackson's election in 1828, state legislatures focused on the bank's alleged unconstitutionality and distortion of federalism.

Initial State Reactions to the Second Bank

Between 1818 and 1819, six legislatures (Tennessee, Maryland, Georgia, North Carolina, Kentucky, and Ohio) imposed taxes on state branches of the Second Bank of the United States, while several other states made similar efforts. Such taxes and opposition to the Second Bank's existence also reflected a desire to protect state or private banks that existed in virtually all of the states.[9]

In September 1817 Tennessee's legislature introduced a bill to prevent non-state banks, namely the Second Bank of the United States, from establishing state branches even as the legislature created another state bank. In November 1817 the House passed a resolution inviting legislators to use "all lawful means in their power to prevent and prohibit" the establishment of banks unchartered by the state. The legislature imposed a $50,000 annual tax on the Second Bank. One legislator dissented, believing the federal government had not exceeded its powers in creating a national bank. He considered the tax "a bold and dangerous stretch of state sovereignty" that created "a precedent of resistance" for other states. After the session, the bank's officers described Tennessee's law as "inoperative." To correct the "ignorance" of Tennessee's legislature, the *Connecticut Herald* suggested sending "500 copies of the U. States Constitution" to the state legislators.[10]

But Congress' constitutional authority to create a national bank with state branches was hardly self-evident and those who wanted to drive the bank out of their state began to levy punitive taxes on the bank, leading to John Marshall's observation that the power to tax was the power to destroy. Often overlooked is that such taxation was part of a powerful interposition effort directed at the supposed unconstitutionality of the bank and its establishment of branches outside of the District of Columbia.[11]

State Interposition against the Second Bank

Kentucky ultimately led an interstate interposition effort to repeal the bank because of its unconstitutionality. In 1817 the state's legislators welcomed national bank branches in Lexington and Louisville thinking they "would promote the prosperity and commercial interest" of Kentuckians and "the western country generally." But that attitude toward the Second Bank did not last. One year later, the legislature imposed an annual tax of $10,000 on all of the bank's state branches.[12]

Kentucky's Governor Gabriel Slaughter convened the legislature in December 1818 and posed questions about the bank, including its failure to pay the imposed taxes. "Whether congress can erect an immense monied corporation, with power to locate branches in the different states without their consent" was, for Slaughter, a vital question. If the bank tax was appropriate, it should be enforced, but if not, it should be repealed. However, given the interstate operation of the bank's branches, Kentucky could not act alone. Slaughter suggested cooperating with other states to pass a constitutional amendment prohibiting a national bank.[13]

After the Governor's address, the Kentucky Senate adopted resolutions favoring the removal of the bank's branches in the state and instructed and requested the congressional delegation to repeal the bank's charter. The House passed a bill, accepted by the Senate, that imposed a $60,000 annual tax on all of the bank's branches. The purpose of the tax was "to drive the United States banks out of the state." Eventually, the U.S. Circuit Court struck down the tax as unconstitutional, a decision that the Kentucky courts eventually honored, but before then the Supreme Court heard a case from Maryland raising the question of state taxation of the bank.[14]

John Marshall and *McCulloch v. Maryland* (1819)

The case of *McCulloch v. Maryland* arose after the cashier of the Baltimore branch of the Second Bank issued a series of notes without paying the tax imposed by the state of Maryland. State officials brought suit for the unpaid tax and a lower court found the bank owed the tax. That judgment was affirmed by the Maryland Court of Appeals and the case was appealed to the U.S. Supreme Court.[15]

John Marshall's opinion in *McCulloch v. Maryland* has been called "the most important case" dealing with the central problem of American federalism: the allocation of power between nation and state. *McCulloch* presented two issues: whether Congress possessed the constitutional authority to charter the bank and what, if any, authority states had over a national bank. Marshall held that Congress could establish the bank and that state legislatures could not interfere by taxing its branches. In upholding the bank's constitutionality, Marshall's opinion identified broad, implied national powers in the Constitution which necessarily stoked the debate over the principles of constitutional interpretation between those who supported states' rights and wanted limited national powers and nationalists who favored a broad construction of federal authority. *McCulloch* also triggered what Saul Cornell has called "the most intense scrutiny" of "the status of the Supreme Court as the final arbiter on questions of federalism."[16]

Marshall's opinion framed the debate by describing a role for the Supreme Court that sought to preclude other monitors of federalism. For Marshall the Court was the only tribunal to decide whether a conflict existed between the constitutional "powers of the government of the Union" and "its members." This duty was "devolved" on the Court by the Constitution, but the open question – that Marshall sidestepped – was whether other parties might also play a role in monitoring the balance between the two levels of government. Although Marshall thought *The Federalist* was "entitled to great respect in expounding the constitution," he said nothing about the role for state legislatures identified in those essays.[17]

As for potential congressional overreaching, Marshall concluded that Congress had discretion over how it executed its powers under the Constitution. Only if Congress passed laws prohibited by the Constitution or for "objects not entrusted to the government" might the Court need to strike down such laws. Absent those two situations, the Court would not question the necessity of laws passed by Congress. With this construction of the Necessary and Proper Clause, Marshall justified the bank and stressed the Court's role as the primary guardian of the Constitution.[18]

After *McCulloch*, Hezekiah Niles, the Baltimore editor of *Niles'
Weekly Register*, called the decision a "deadly blow" to state
sovereignty and the "first grand step towards a *consolidation of
the states.*" When the *Richmond Enquirer*'s editor Thomas Ritchie
reported the case, he called for "firm Republicans of the Old
School" to "rally round the banners of the constitution" to defend
"the rights of the states against federal usurpation" and reminded
them of the state's role in denouncing the Alien and Sedition Acts.
Not surprisingly, the Federalist press applauded *McCulloch*, hoping
it had taught a lesson to state legislators that they had no "right to
infringe upon the National Constitution or the laws of Congress."
Marshall, however, believed that *McCulloch* had "roused the
sleeping spirit of Virginia." He predicted the opinion would be
attacked as *"damnably heretical"* and worried that without
defenders he and the Court would be "condemned as a pack of
consolidating aristocratics."[19]

The attack Marshall anticipated began with commentaries in the
Richmond Enquirer authored by Judge Roane of Virginia's Court of
Appeals and Roane's cousin William Brockenbrough, a circuit judge in
Richmond. Brockenbrough wrote two essays as *Amphictyon*, and
Roane followed with four more as *Hampden*. Alarmed by their
critiques, Marshall took the extraordinary step of anonymously
defending his opinion in two essays responding to Brockenbrough as
A Friend to the Union and nine additional essays responding to Roane
as *A Friend of the Constitution*. Marshall wanted to vindicate the
Court's decision and discourage interposition resolutions. He
believed that criticism of *McCulloch* degraded the Court and that
interposition interfered with the Court's exclusive right to interpret
the Constitution and monitor the balance of federalism. For Marshall,
interposition rested on a sovereign states' rights compact theory at
odds with his belief that the American people as a whole had created
the Constitution.[20]

Brockenbrough and Roane challenged the Court's monopoly on
interpreting the Constitution and resolving controversies between the
two levels of government, the position Roane had taken in *Hunter
v. Martin, Devisee of Fairfax*. Both Roane and Brockenbrough
assumed that the right of states to challenge the Court's monopolistic
interpretative role rested on a compact theory of the Constitution.

They both endorsed sounding the alarm interposition, but conflated Madison's Third and Seventh resolutions.

In *Amphictyon*, Brockenbrough identified two principles in Marshall's opinion that endangered states' rights and encouraged national consolidation. One was Marshall's denial that the powers of the federal government were delegated by the states and the second was that the Necessary and Proper Clause should be construed "in a liberal, rather than a restricted sense." Brockenbrough regarded Virginia's 1798 resolutions as the definitive statement of the compact theory of the Constitution and alleged that Marshall's denial of that compact theory undercut the right of states to serve as umpires of potential overreaching by the federal government. If the states were not "parties to the compact," the state legislatures "would not have a right to ... remonstrate against the encroachment of power, nor to resist the advances of usurpation, tyranny and oppression."[21]

Brockenbrough relied on Virginia's Third resolution to defend "the right of the state governments to ... resist encroachments on their authority" and to reject Marshall's contention that the Supreme Court is "the umpire" on all contested "questions touching the constitutionality of laws." As a result, Brockenbrough mistakenly equated what state legislatures could do (and what Virginia's legislature had done in the Seventh resolution) with what the people of the states as parties to the compact might do in extraordinary circumstances as a matter of last resort.[22]

In *A Friend to the Union*, Marshall replied to Brockenbrough, but mistakenly assumed that he and Madison shared the same view of the foundation of the Constitution. According to Marshall, Madison's Report of 1800 "concurs exactly with the Supreme court, in the opinion that the constitution is the act of the people." However, when Madison described the Constitution as an act of the people, he did not mean a national people as did Marshall. Madison identified the people of the states in their highest sovereign capacity – a foundation also different from sovereign states' rights theorists who thought the Constitution rested on autonomous and independent states. Madison was neither in the nationalist nor the sovereign states' rights camps.[23]

Marshall expected a "very serious" response to *McCulloch* from Virginia's legislature with resolutions not "unlike those which were called forth by the alien & sedition laws." Marshall also learned that further critiques of *McCulloch* written by a "great man" would soon be published, referring to Judge Roane, whose *Hampden* essays began appearing in the *Richmond Enquirer* in June, 1819.[24]

Roane's Hampden *Essays*

Roane rejected Marshall's assertion of congressional authority for the bank and his conclusion that the Court was the only arbiter to settle disputes between the national government and the state governments. Roane believed Marshall's views struck an illegitimate balance of power between the federal and state governments that would lead to a substantial increase in national authority at the expense of the states. Although conceding the Court's right to decide controversies "between two or more states," Roane relied on *The Federalist* as well as Virginia's Resolutions and Madison's Report in denying the Court's "jurisdiction over its own controversies, with a state or states."[25]

For Roane, since the Constitution established a confederal government, the question was whether a state was bound by acts of the national government that violated a state's rights. Roane claimed that the framers had not provided an "impartial tribunal" to decide disputes between state and federal governments and thought *The Federalist* denied either party's supremacy in the matter. He paraphrased Madison's interposition-related essay in *Federalist* 44 and suggested that "the ultimate redress against unconstitutional acts of the general government" that invaded "the rights of the people" rested on "their *state legislatures*" who "will be ready to sound the alarm to the people, and effect a change." These state legislatures could be trusted "to erect barriers against the encroachments of the national authority." In describing Madison's defense of sounding the alarm interposition, Roane noted its effective use after the *Chisholm* decision. Nonetheless, Roane, like Brockenbrough, failed to distinguish legislative interposition from the theoretical right of the parties to the compact to judge violations of the Constitution.[26]

Despite that conflation, Roane said he only wanted state legislatures to direct attention to the decision in *McCulloch*. While Marshall's Court illegitimately made itself "the *exclusive* judge in this controversy" and ignored state legislatures, Roane sought to reclaim their role as one of the monitors of federalism. "*They* might serve, at least, to concentrate public opinion" and continue to oppose "federal usurpation." Roane considered the opposition to the Sedition Act in Virginia's Resolutions an effort to harness the "force of public opinion" without seeking "revolutionary or insurrectionary measures."[27]

Marshall's Response to Roane: A Friend of the Constitution

Roane's *Hampden* essays spurred Marshall's extended reply as *A Friend of the Constitution.* Marshall's motive in joining the debate went beyond self-vindication; he also wanted to deflect Virginia's interposition resolutions. Marshall appreciated the "considerable influence" of Roane's essays and wanted Supreme Court Justice Bushrod Washington to ensure that Marshall's refutation reached "the hands of some respectable members of the legislature" to prevent some "silly & wicked" act of the assembly. Marshall asked Washington to share copies of *A Friend of the Constitution* with Virginia's legislators "should an attempt be made to move the subject" in that body.[28]

Marshall addressed Roane's concern about the equilibrium of federalism, suggesting the danger was less a tilt towards a national consolidation than state encroachment on the national government's powers. "The equipoise thus established is as much disturbed by taking weights out of the scale containing the powers of the [national] government, as by putting weights into it." He warned that interposition was "a new mode of amendment, by way of reports of committees of a state legislature and resolutions thereon" seeking to take from the national government "power after power" and potentially shrinking it to the point that its few "acknowledged powers" could only be exercised by the means that "the states shall prescribe." He thought legislative interposition endangered the proper operation of the national government.[29]

Marshall also responded to Roane's denial of the Court's jurisdiction in *McCulloch.* That position rested on the fundamental error of thinking the Constitution was "a mere league, or a compact, between several state governments, and the general government." Marshall insisted that instead of creating a league between "independent sovereigns," the

Constitution established a government, created for the nation "by the whole American people."[30]

Marshall quoted *Federalist* 80 in support of his view that the Supreme Court must be the ultimate decider of all national questions. The prospect of thirteen "independent courts" having "final jurisdiction over the same causes," Hamilton had written, created "a hydra in government from which nothing but contradiction and confusion can proceed." That prospect prompted a counterpoint to Roane's assertion in *Hunter v. Fairfax's Devisee* that state courts should have concurrent jurisdiction with federal courts on constitutional matters. But the practical benefit of a single Supreme Court rendering *decisions* resolving conflicts between the two levels of government begged the question of whether the Court was the only body to monitor federalism and to express its views about the operation of the national government. Marshall simply ignored those portions of *The Federalist* describing a role for state legislatures to sound the alarm.[31]

Madison and Jefferson Respond to Hampden

Roane sent copies of his *Hampden* essays to Madison and Jefferson. Madison thought the essays "combated" *McCulloch*'s expansive "mode of expounding the Constitution," while for Jefferson they expressed "the true principles of the revolution of 1800." Madison focused on what he shared with Roane, namely, that Marshall's opinion unnecessarily advanced "general and abstract doctrine." Madison refrained from mentioning Roane's misreading of Virginia's Third and Seventh resolutions or their different views about the nature of the constitutional compact and the role of the Supreme Court. Instead, Madison argued that Marshall's "broad and pliant" interpretation of the Necessary and Proper Clause eroded "landmarks" in the Constitution concerning congressional powers. Marshall's "rule of construction" allowing Congress to determine the means for carrying out its constitutional powers seemed to abdicate the Court's "guardianship of the Constitution against legislative encroachments." Madison considered *McCulloch* "a constructive assumption of powers never meant to be granted." If Congress needed more power, the legitimate way to correct that deficiency of authority was with a constitutional amendment and not by "expounding" the Constitution in an overly broad manner.[32]

Jefferson congratulated Roane for identifying Marshall's decision as part of a plot he had detected for more than two decades. "[W]e find the judiciary on every occasion, still driving us into consolidation." Independence for federal judges without meaningful checks on their behavior made the Constitution "wax in the hands of the judiciary, which they may twist, and shape into any form they please." But in denying the Supreme Court's claim for "exclusively explaining the constitution," Jefferson wanted to go further than Roane. Jefferson considered it a mistake for the Court's interpretation to bind the "coordinate and independent" branches that were intended to check and balance one another. In Jefferson's view, each branch of government was "truly independent of the others, and has an equal right to decide for itself what is the meaning of the constitution in the cases submitted to its action; and especially, where it is to act ultimately and without appeal."[33]

Jefferson's theory thus imposed horizontal limitations on the Court's power of judicial review in addition to the vertical limitations advanced by Roane. Moreover, Jefferson's contention to Roane in 1819 that states could *independently* decide what was constitutional provided a critical foundation for states in the future to declare federal laws unconstitutional and to proceed to take what they deemed to be all necessary action to oppose such laws. Thus, Jefferson's constitutional views encouraged strict construction interposition in the service of unlimited resistance to national authority.[34]

Virginia's Response to McCulloch

The interposition Marshall tried to prevent occurred when Virginia's legislature convened in December 1819. Governor Thomas Mann Randolph wanted the legislature to halt the decline of the state's constitutional rights. He also shared a resolution of Pennsylvania's legislature seeking a constitutional amendment to confine national banks to the District of Columbia, in effect reversing *McCulloch*.[35]

Virginia's House of Delegates responded by introducing proposed instructions and requests for the state's congressional delegation as well as interposition resolutions to be shared with other Governors and state legislatures – all of them protesting Marshall's doctrine of implied powers as subverting the Constitution. The instructions drafted by the House sought a constitutional amendment to establish a tribunal to resolve all questions presenting a conflict between the powers and authorities of the federal government and those of the states. Virginia's congressional delegation was also to "resist" all legislation exercising any power not expressly granted to Congress. Virginia's legislators thought that Marshall's construction of the Necessary and Proper Clause would "change the whole character of the government" and "convert it from a limited and defined constitution ... into one great consolidated government, of *undefined* and *unlimited* powers." The legislators also disputed that the Supreme Court's opinions were "conclusively binding on the states, in questions relating to the extent of the powers delegated to the general government, or retained to the states." They thought that each of the parties to the compact could judge infractions. Their description of "the parties to the federal compact" as "sovereign states" implied that states under the Constitution retained the sovereignty they enjoyed under the Articles of Confederation.[36]

Virginia's House wanted Americans to "re-trace *their* steps, and rally around the constitution" because the Court had undermined it in *McCulloch*. Had Virginia's Senate acted in concert with the House's instructions, it would have explicitly rejected *McCulloch*. Ultimately, the House made one substantive change: limiting any national bank to the District of Columbia as opposed to proposing a constitutional amendment for a new tribunal. In February 1819 Virginia's House passed the instructions as amended as well as the interposition resolutions by overwhelming margins. Nonetheless, the Senate tabled the bills, according to one newspaper, because it ran out of time. As it was, five other states – Pennsylvania, Ohio, Indiana, Illinois, and Tennessee – passed resolutions seeking the constitutional amendment that Virginia's House supported.[37]

Ohio's Responses to McCulloch

Prior to the *McCulloch* decision in March 1819, Ohio's legislature imposed a $50,000 annual tax on the bank's branches in the state due for collection later in the year. After the decision, Ohio's state's auditor Ralph Osborn sent a deputy to serve a warrant on bank officials at the Chillicothe branch. According to the branch cashier, the deputy seized enough money from the vault to satisfy the disputed tax. Bank officials subsequently sued Osborn in federal court and claimed immunity from taxation under *McCulloch*.[38]

When Ohio's legislature convened in early December 1819, Governor Ethan Brown observed that other states had also imposed taxes on the bank. Brown wishfully thought the Supreme Court might be inclined to reexamine its decision given the opposition to *McCulloch*. Brown believed the legislature had two choices: concede the bank's position or pursue a lawsuit. He advised against abdicating the state's power of taxation over "monied corporations" and endorsed the path of litigation.[39]

The federal courts showed no sign of rethinking *McCulloch*. Instead, after the Chillicothe branch incident, the U.S. Circuit Court held Osborn in contempt of court and ruled that Ohio lacked authority to tax the bank. Additionally, as Ohio's legislature assembled in December 1820, an action of trespass brought against Osborn and other state officials by the bank was pending in the U.S. Circuit Court. Governor Brown's address to the legislature stressed the importance of determining the merits of the state's position.[40]

A report of the Ohio legislature concluded that the trespass action constituted a suit against the state and was thus precluded by the Eleventh Amendment. The federal court had exercised unwarranted and unconstitutional jurisdiction encroaching on state authority. Ohio's legislators along with Virginia critics of *McCulloch* rejected "the doctrine that the federal courts are exclusively vested with jurisdiction to declare, in the last resort, the true interpretation of the constitution of the United States."[41]

The report's challenge of the Court's monopoly to resolve conflicts between federal and state authority relied on the Virginia and Kentucky Resolutions and Madison's Report – what it called "the true text book of republican principles." Ohio understood that it was flaunting *McCulloch* by taxing the bank. Accusing the Supreme Court of acting unconstitutionally should not occur "lightly and unadvisedly." The report analyzed *McCulloch* and separated the issue of the power of Congress to establish the bank (which it was willing to concede) from the issue of Ohio's right to tax branches of the bank within the state. The report concluded that the bank was "a mere private corporation of trade" and thus its Ohio operations were subject to state taxation. Most troubling to the legislators was Chief Justice Marshall's reasoning that the "rights, powers and authorities of the States are not immutably established by constitutional provisions; but are subject to modification" in order to give the national government wider scope for action. Such an interpretation demanded state protest because otherwise the national government would "progressively draw all the powers of government into the vortex of its own authority."[42]

The report proposed a compromise: the return of the tax collected if the bank dropped its lawsuits against state officials and ceased operating in Ohio. Otherwise, the bank would not have access to the state's legal system, leaving its protection exclusively up to the federal government. The legislature accepted the report and passed resolutions that incorporated its findings as well as the bills suggested in the report, proposing a conditional compromise with the bank and depriving it of state legal protection.[43]

Before adjourning in early February, several legislators objected. They agreed that states could alert other states about unconstitutional measures of the federal government. But the "gross injustice" of the legislature's action went beyond acceptable sounding the alarm interposition. The editor Hezekiah Niles, a longtime opponent of the bank, announced that it was "not for any of the States, much less individuals," to oppose with force "the operations of the law."[44]

Other State Responses to Virginia's and Ohio's Resistance to the Bank

Although Ohio's report and resolutions were favorably received in Virginia and Kentucky, legislatures in other states, including Massachusetts and New Hampshire, rejected them. Nonetheless, both New England legislatures affirmed their right to monitor the governmental equilibrium. New Hampshire's legislature pledged "its full support to the general government, so long as it confines itself within its prescribed limits," but would defend any other state whose rights were encroached by the federal government. Similarly, Massachusetts' legislature backed all departments of the national government, "so long as they continue in the rightful exercise of their constitutional powers" while "ever ready to afford its aid to any state, against manifest usurpation, or real encroachments upon its rights."[45]

Ohio's defiance of *McCulloch* ended after the Supreme Court rendered *Osborn v. Bank of the United States* in 1824. Marshall's opinion in *Osborn* reaffirmed the holding of *McCulloch* in a manner that both expanded federal jurisdiction and narrowed the reach of the Eleventh Amendment. Before then, however, Marshall returned to his defense of the Supreme Court as the sole expositor of the Constitution and monitor of federalism.[46]

Although the Supreme Court upheld the bank's constitutionality in *McCulloch*, the issue was hardly settled. Presidents Andrew Jackson and John Tyler, among others, refused to accept the Court's decision. Jackson's first annual message to Congress in 1829 observed that many Americans questioned the constitutionality of a national bank, and when vetoing a bill to reestablish the bank in 1832 he challenged the idea that its constitutionality was necessarily settled by the Court's decision. As Jackson put it, "Mere precedent is a dangerous source of authority, and should not be regarded as deciding questions of constitutional power except where the acquiescence of the people and the States can be considered as well settled." As Eric Lomazoff indicates, Jackson believed that "the Court had (in his eyes) confirmed" that the meaning of the Necessary and Proper Clause "was a political question." Nine years later, President Tyler vetoed a bill to create a national bank, its constitutionality remaining an "unsettled question" notwithstanding *McCulloch*. Ultimately, Jackson's war against the bank ended in its destruction, demonstrating that *McCulloch* was not the final word on the bank.[47]

Cohens v. Virginia (1821): Virginia Challenges the Supreme Court's Role

Marshall's anonymous essays defending *McCulloch* touched on the Court's authority to decide conflicts over the respective powers between the national and state governments. Only with *Cohens v. Virginia* was Marshall presented with the judicial opportunity to answer Judge Roane and others who questioned the Supreme Court's adjudicatory role in monitoring federalism.

The case arose out of the sale in Virginia of national lottery tickets, which were a common means of raising state revenue. Congress authorized the sale of lottery tickets in the District of Columbia, but Virginia prohibited sales of tickets unauthorized by the state. Philip and Mendes Cohen argued that the congressional authorization entitled them to sell national tickets in Virginia notwithstanding the state law. After Virginia prosecuted and fined the brothers for sales in the state, the Cohens appealed to the Supreme Court, claiming the Virginia statute was unconstitutional. On October 17, 1820, Marshall accepted the case with a summons for the state of Virginia to appear at the February 1821 term of the Court.[48]

In January 1821 a committee of the Virginia House issued a report challenging Congress' power to override Virginia's lottery statute and denying the Supreme Court appellate jurisdiction over state courts. The report proposed a resolution that was adopted by the Virginia Senate refuting the Court's constitutional right "to examine and correct" the Virginia Court of Appeals judgment and entering the legislature's protest against such jurisdiction. The report described the natural tension in federalism when "two legislative bodies revolve within specified orbits circumscribed by the charter of the union; and neither can push the other from its sphere." Supposedly, the framers had not provided for the "occasional conflict of authority" between the two levels of government – overlooking Madison's description in *Federalist* 39 of the role the Court would play. According to the report, the framers accepted such clashes from time to time instead of giving the national government "absolute supremacy" to resolve disputes affecting "the existence of the state governments" and "the balance of the constitution." The report concluded that the federal government lacked constitutional authority "to make the state tribunals subordinate to, and controlable by the supreme court of the United States." Virginia's legislators saw their report as part of a long tradition of interposition. The report recounted that Federalists had defended the creation of the national government by describing the "sleepless vigilance" of state governments that would warn against misgovernment and promptly communicate such dangers to the public.[49]

Two months after Virginia responded to the summons, Marshall delivered the Supreme Court's unanimous decision on March 3, 1821.

While upholding the state's prohibition of sales of lottery tickets unauthorized by the state, of greater importance was the Court's assumption of jurisdiction which allowed it to provide an expansive reading of the Court's authority under Article III of the Constitution. Marshall asserted that the federal judiciary formed the department that was "capable of restraining peaceably, and by authority of law" any encroachments by states against legitimate powers of the national government whereas accepting Virginia's position would mean the Constitution could receive "as many constructions as there are states."[50]

Story had argued against multiple interpretations of the Constitution in *Martin v. Hunter's Lessee*, but Marshall's opinion also invoked essays from *The Federalist* – that "great authority" and "complete commentary on our constitution" – on the role and power of the federal judiciary. Marshall questioned the legitimacy of state legislators monitoring the federal government despite his endorsement of *The Federalist*. States, he observed, may differ about "the true construction of the constitutional powers of Congress" and those opinions might change over time. Potential conflict with state authorities led Marshall to emphasize "self-preservation" by the national government. Indeed, during the struggle over the Court's claim for a monopoly over constitutional interpretation, even expressions of disagreement with opinions of the Court provoked hostility and were cast as illegitimate, further undermining the role of state legislatures as monitors of federalism.[51]

Madison's Reaction to Cohens

Although Marshall's opinion drew many critics, Roane emerged once again to offer one of the most pointed rebuttals in a series of essays in the *Richmond Enquirer* as *Algernon Sydney*. Before Roane's essays were published, Madison shared his thoughts about *Cohens* with Roane. As with *McCulloch*, Madison regretted that Marshall's court habitually made "comments and reasonings" that went well beyond the scope of their judgments. Particularly troubling was further evidence of bias in how Marshall's Court was monitoring the equilibrium of federalism. The Court's decisions often reflected "an apparent disposition to amplify the authorities of the Union at the expense of those of the States." For Madison, the great "experiment" of federalism was whether the Constitution established "a just equilibrium" or would degenerate by allowing either the national government or the state governments to dominate the other. It was vital that the Court maintain "the constitutional boundary" between them impartially.[52]

Madison thought that Congress posed a greater danger for disequilibrium than did the federal courts. Despite the extensive jurisdiction claimed by the Supreme Court, it was "the latitude of power" the Court had given Congress that most worried Madison. He believed that "encroachments" by the national legislature would more likely occur with states lobbying for "expected advantages." Nonetheless, Madison was confident that Congress would not long persist in violating the rights of states even with help of the federal judiciary unless there was a dramatic shift in "the character of the nation." Thus far in America's history, the accountability of the House to the people and the Senate to the state legislatures seemed "an adequate barrier," as the Virginia and Kentucky Resolutions demonstrated. "In the case of the alien and sedition laws, which violated the general *sense* as well as the *rights* of the States, the usurping experiment was crushed at once" despite the effort of federal judges trying to sustain national power.[53]

Madison considered the authority of federal courts over cases arising under the Constitution crucial to the federal system. Nonetheless, there were limitations and exceptions to that power, including the Eleventh Amendment. That amendment, stimulated by the interposition precipitated by *Chisholm v. Georgia*, addressed the judicial equilibrium between the federal government and those of the states. Apart from constitutional limits on federal jurisdiction, it was important for the Court to limit its proceedings to "individuals only." This admonition reflected Madison's concern that many of Marshall's opinions ventured well beyond what was strictly necessary to resolve the case at hand and unnecessarily expanded federal jurisdiction.[54]

Roane's Critique of Cohens *and Madison's Response*

In criticizing *Cohens* in his *Sydney* essays, Roane went much further than Madison. Roane disputed Marshall's interpretation of Article III, but also claimed that the Article itself precluded the Court from assuming jurisdiction. Roane's argument rested on his repeated insistence that the Constitution was a compact between the state governments and the federal government – and he accused the Supreme Court of forgetting that states did not "cease to be sovereign states" even though they had given up "some of their rights" when they became "members of a federal republic." In a conflict between the two parties, neither could "bind the other" since that would make either one of them a "judge in its own cause." This addressed Marshall's claim that the Supreme Court was the tribunal to resolve such conflicts. As Roane put it, "A compact between two parties is a nullity, as to one of them, if the other by itself, or its agents, has the power of expounding it as it pleases."[55]

Roane's solution to a "contest for rights between the two parties to the federal compact" was an appeal to "their common superior," or, "the people." Under a system of government featuring "sovereign and independent states" there was "no common arbiter" of the rights of the parties but the people. Roane thus adopted Jefferson's constitutional convention solution for resolving disputes between the two levels of government. While cumbersome, Roane argued that such a process was needed to maintain "the equilibrium established by the constitution" and which would be jeopardized if either party claimed the exclusive right to make the final decision, citing both the Virginia and Kentucky Resolutions and Madison's Report.[56]

In a letter to Roane, Madison congratulated him on the *Sydney* essays, but told Roane that he had misstated Madison's position on the nature of the constitutional compact and the role of the Supreme Court. Madison insisted the Constitution was not a compact between the national government and the state governments. Instead, it was a compact "between the States as sovereign communities" surrendering "certain portions of their respective authorities to be exercised by a common government, and a reservation, for their own exercise, of all their other authorities." This division of constitutional authority presented the "problem of collision between the federal and State powers." But contrary to Roane's assertion, Madison contended that the framers did indeed understand the "possibility of disagreements concerning the line of division between" the two levels of government. Their solution was making the Supreme Court the deciding tribunal. Madison rejected the idea of sovereign states' rights advocates that maintaining a constitutional balance was a "trust to be vested" in individual states. Instead, having the Supreme Court as the decider ensured uniformity.[57]

Although accepting the practical need for the Court to resolve disputes over the powers of the federal and state governments, Madison still favored an adjustment of the tensions of federalism that differed radically from Marshall's approach. Madison preferred an incremental, case-by-case process that involved state judges even though they did not make the ultimate decision. When Madison responded to Roane's critique of *McCulloch*, he noted that it "was foreseen at the birth of the Constitution, that difficulties and differences of opinion might occasionally arise in expounding terms and phrases necessarily used in such a charter," especially the language of federalism that "divide[d] legislation between the general and local governments." Madison hoped that "jarring opinions between the national and State tribunals will be narrowed by successive decisions, sanctioned by the public concurrence" and eventually reduced to "a regular course of practice." Moreover, as the caliber of both the federal and state bench improved, those judges might "mutually contribute to the clearer and firmer establishment of the true boundaries of power" between the two levels of government.[58]

Madison had embraced the same approach in *Federalist* 37 when he identified the challenge of "marking the proper line of partition, between the authority of the general, and that of the State Governments." Judging the proper division between the two levels of government, much like grasping a full understanding of any new law however well drafted, would necessarily remain somewhat "obscure and equivocal" until meaning could be "ascertained by a series of particular discussions and adjudications." For Madison, the "Gordian" knots of federalism were meant to be resolved through a patient study of the text of the Constitution and not by a decisive "cut by any political Alexander."[59]

Divergent Views of the Equilibrium of Federalism after *McCulloch* and *Cohens*

Both the criticism and defense of *Cohens v. Virginia* illustrated divergent perceptions of the balance of federalism. Americans in the 1820s – as they had since the ratification of the Constitution – viewed that equilibrium differently. Madison saw *Cohens* as one in a series of decisions by which the Court unduly strained to find greater powers and authority for the national government than the framers intended. Instead of being a neutral umpire of the balance of federalism, Madison thought the Court placed a weight on the scales on the side of the national government, demonstrating a bias that violated its duty to ensure that the constitutional boundary between the two levels of government was "impartially maintained." Madison thought the Court's interpretation required an adjustment.[60]

For other critics of the Court, however, like Spencer Roane and Thomas Jefferson, something far more sinister was at play. Roane and Jefferson believed that the federal judiciary – and particularly Marshall's Court – was plotting to establish a consolidated national government destined to eviscerate the state governments. For them, nothing less than the preservation of the Constitution was at stake, which required more than merely readjusting the current federal and state balance.

Not surprisingly, John Marshall and Joseph Story saw matters differently from Jefferson and Roane. Marshall wrote Story about the tremendous "virulence" directed at *Cohens* and the "coarseness and malignity" of Roane's *Sydney* essays. Instead of defending states' rights under the Constitution, Marshall considered Roane "the champion of dismemberment." Story assured Marshall that the best lawyers in Massachusetts approved of *Cohens* and proclaimed it one of the Chief Justice's greatest judgments. For Story, "the whole doctrine of Virginia [in the *Cohens* case] on the subject of the constitution appears to me so fundamentally erroneous, not to say absurd, that I have a good deal of difficulty in reading with patience the elaborate attempts of her political leaders to mislead & deceive us." Story thought Jefferson wanted "to prostrate" the federal judiciary and annihilate its powers, evidenced by Jefferson's claim that it was a "very dangerous doctrine" to view federal judges as "the ultimate arbiters of all constitutional questions." Moreover, Jefferson had stated that the Constitution did not create a single tribunal to resolve all constitutional questions, but intended each branch of government, "co-equal and co-sovereign," to determine the constitutionality of actions of their own department leaving it to the people to correct any potentially unconstitutional acts.[61]

Marshall was not surprised by Jefferson's views, but worried that his wide reputation meant that "very many will adopt his opinions however unsound they may be." Marshall believed that Jefferson's hostility to the Court and an independent judiciary reflected Jefferson's concern that the courts might temper the popular support Jefferson needed. Six months after *Cohens*, Marshall detected Jefferson behind attacks on the Court as part of a "deep design to convert our government into a me[re] league of States." For Marshall, every limitation of the Court's jurisdiction undermined the national government and the "attack, if not originating with Mr. Jefferson, is obviously approved & guided by him."[62]

From Jefferson's perspective, judicial independence was problematic because the federal courts – unlike Congress and the Presidency – were not electorally accountable if they overreached their authority. In correspondence with Supreme Court Justice William Johnson, Jefferson responded to Marshall's assertion that "there must be an ultimate arbiter somewhere." Jefferson generally agreed, but denied that such an ultimate decision necessarily rested with the courts either at the national or state level. Instead, he identified the ultimate arbiter as "the people of the Union, assembled by their deputies in convention, at the call of Congress, or [at the call] of two-thirds of the States." Thus, Jefferson thought constitutional conventions should resolve conflicts over the distribution of the authority between the two levels of government.[63]

Madison continued to disagree with Jefferson about the wisdom of using conventions and reiterated his observation in *The Federalist* about the difficulty of precisely "tracing the boundary between the General and State governments." How courts might be involved in maintaining the equilibrium of federalism remained a problem, but referring "every new point of disagreement to the people in Conventions" as Jefferson proposed, was "too tardy, too troublesome, and too expensive." Besides, frequent conventions would undermine respect for the Constitution. Madison then turned to the assertion of sovereign states' rights theorists such as Roane that the states themselves were entitled to resolve conflicts between the two levels of government. That approach was inadvisable not only for its lack of uniformity, but because of the potential for violent confrontations.[64]

Having dismissed both Jefferson's and Roane's solutions, Madison addressed the question presented in *Cohens*: "whether the Judicial authority of the United States be the Constitutional resort for determining the line between the federal and State jurisdictions." Madison agreed that the framers' intended the Supreme Court to play that role. He had said so in *Federalist* 39 and never varied from that opinion. Madison knew that sovereign states' rights theorists claimed that his Virginia Resolutions and Report supported them, but in that respect, they followed a long-established pattern of misunderstanding him or misusing what he had written.[65]

Madison conceded that federal courts had not always functioned well. He thought partisanship afflicted the early federal bench and that "extra-judicial reasonings and *dicta*" in recent Supreme Court decisions "manifested a propensity to enlarge the general in derogation of the local, and to amplify its own jurisdiction." While agreeing that the Court had exceeded its constitutional authority, Madison remained unpersuaded by Jefferson's approach. Madison still preferred that any "abuse" by the Supreme Court be addressed by constitutional amendments instead of holding constitutional conventions to resolve the Court's supposedly mistaken decisions.[66]

For Madison, interposition remained the basic, initial response to abuses of power by any branch of the national government, including the Court. That approach was implicit in Madison's suggestion that there might be a "remedy of the abuse ... under the forms of the Constitution." For Madison, a state legislative resolution sounding the alarm was a means of bringing political pressure to bear on the federal government should it act beyond its constitutional authority. Indeed, after the *Cohens* decision, Madison reminded Roane that the Virginia and Kentucky Resolutions helped overturn the Alien and Sedition Acts even though those laws had received the support of federal judges.[67]

Opposition to Federal Funding for Internal Improvements

After John Quincy Adams' contentious presidential election in 1824, elements of his economic policy involving national government funding for internal improvements – part of what Henry Clay called the 'American System' – came under increasing constitutional scrutiny.

The plan for investing in public transportation infrastructure included support for dredging harbors and rivers as well as building roads and canals. Along with a national bank, congressional subsidies for internal improvements were measures designed to stimulate commercial and industrial growth. While such programs did not originate with the Adams administration, they became a focal point for opposition by those who saw them not only as misguided policies, but actions that exceeded congressional authority. Without express delegated powers to accomplish such objectives, the issue once again became a matter of whether the Necessary and Proper Clause should be construed to justify internal improvements.[68]

State and regional economic benefits from federally funded internal improvement projects led many states to acquiesce in a broad construction of constitutional authority to justify such funding. In early 1825 Madison took note of "politicians who reject the general heresies of Federalism," including "the terms 'General welfare', who yet admit the authority of Congress as to roads and canals, which they squeeze out of the enumerated articles." Constitutional orthodoxy was no match for the grassroots popularity for such projects and the pressure voters placed on their representatives. Pragmatically, Madison considered the question of internal improvements settled given how many Americans embraced them. If Madison was willing to concede the inevitability of internal improvements, others were not.[69]

South Carolina's Legislature Responds

When South Carolina's legislature assembled for its November session in 1824, Governor John Wilson identified a recent congressional appropriation for surveys of roads and canals that the President might deem of national importance. Wilson considered that act "an entering wedge" for ambitious schemes of internal improvements. It rested on a dubious construction of implied congressional powers that might one day see South Carolina "grievously assessed to pay for the cutting a canal across Cape Cod." Wilson thought the doctrine of implied powers departed from the framers' intent for a limited national government, and was one that undermined states' rights and inevitably led to a consolidation of power in the federal government.

The Governor invited the legislature, as "public sentinels," to address the matter.[70]

South Carolina's Senate quickly appointed a committee to consider the Governor's message and passed resolutions declaring that Congress lacked constitutional authority to create a national system of internal improvements. One observer criticized the Senators for expressing their views on the matter and denying "rights to Congress, which Congress have not yet assumed." The Senate proceeded with resolutions opposing nationally funded internal improvements even as the critic predicted they would be tabled in the House.[71]

The House not only tabled the Senate's resolutions, but formed its own special committee that objected both to the substance and form of the Senate's action. The House accused Senators of forgetting their duty of "double allegiance" to both levels of government that required giving neither an undue preference. In terms of that federal balance, they thought the Senators were undercutting the constitutional authority of Congress. The House also questioned the Senate's sounding the alarm interposition resolutions and declared that South Carolinians had not authorized their state legislature "to impugn the acts of the Federal Government or the decisions of the Supreme Court." The rightful monitors were "the People themselves" who could oversee their state and congressional representatives. One year later, however, South Carolina's House reversed itself and belatedly emphasized the "right of remonstrating against any encroachments" on the Constitution by Congress or any other federal officers. With that change of heart, South Carolina's legislature declared that nationally funded internal improvements were unconstitutional.[72]

Virginia's Legislature Responds

When Virginia's legislature assembled in early December 1825, Governor James Pleasants surveyed a number of national policies and raised doubts about the constitutional authority for Congress to fund roads and canals. After Governor Pleasants' message, but before the legislature acted, Jefferson and Madison considered how Virginia might respond. On Christmas Eve 1825, Jefferson shared with Madison a draft "declaration and protest" for Virginia's legislature. If Madison agreed, Jefferson invited him to make any changes and Jefferson would forward them to legislative allies with "the most sacred injunctions" that "not a shadow of suspicion shall fall on you or myself that it has come from either of us."[73]

Jefferson's draft described the Constitution as a compact dividing authority and power between two levels of government in a manner that required Virginia to oppose equally "the usurpation of either ... on the rightful powers of the other." Presently, the federal government was "enlarging its own powers by constructions, inferences, and indefinite deductions" that wrongfully eroded the powers of state governments. Those doubtful reasonings included congressional authority for internal improvements as well as permission for congressional leaders to do "whatever *they* may think" would promote the general welfare. The protest hoped that Virginia's "watchfulness" of the national government's actions might "reform its aberrations, recall it to original and legitimate principles, and restrain it within the rightful limits of self government." If national power over internal improvements was desired, the protest hoped it would be granted through formal constitutional amendment instead of constitutional interpretation. In the meantime, Jefferson proposed that the legislature declare the federal government's actions null-and-void usurpations.[74]

Madison's approach towards internal improvements was nuanced and he drew constitutional distinctions that others did not. Complicating the issue for Madison was that internal improvement schemes that might exceed the constitutional authority of the national government were supported and even lobbied for by voters. In addition, an undercurrent of jealousy and resentment was directed at Virginia due to the prominent role the state had long played in national affairs. Therefore, Madison had doubts about Virginia taking a leadership role until more states offered support. Still, he thought Jefferson's draft would be "a valuable resort" should Virginia's legislature undertake "any strong interposition" against internal improvements."[75]

Jefferson agreed with Madison's assessment and requested his contacts in Virginia's legislature to hold off for the moment. The final correspondence between the two old friends took place in late February after the legislature had assembled but not yet acted. Madison believed that the legislators were contemplating resolutions instructing the state's Senators to share Virginia's view of the constitutional limits to congressional authority over internal improvements. He thought that might be an effective interposition. Ultimately, the legislature acted far beyond what Madison imagined.[76]

A legislative committee report only belatedly responded to Governor Pleasants' allegations that Congress had exceeded its constitutional authority after reviewing Virginia's Resolutions of 1798 and Madison's Report – which it called "a commentary" on the Constitution. The report identified the duty of the legislature "to watch over and oppose every infraction" of the Constitution by the national government and concluded that internal improvements amounted to dangerous constitutional overreaching.[77]

The debate over the report in the House focused on whether the policy of internal improvements justified the same legislative response that Virginia had given twenty-eight years earlier to the Alien and Sedition Acts. Some legislators (including a few with service in the 1798 legislature) assumed that Madison's Report and the 'Principles of '98' did not warrant the proposed resolutions, "except in cases of *plain and palpable violations of the principles of the constitution*." Internal improvements, while constitutionally suspect, did not match the circumstances of 1798.[78]

The chairman of the committee, House member George Drumgoole, denied that the present situation was less deserving of interposition than "the crisis of '98" and commented that Madison had identified the duty of the legislature "to watch over and oppose" each and "every infraction" of the Constitution. The failure of Virginia's congressional delegation to block unconstitutional policies left the legislature the option of proclaiming its opinion in the same way that Virginia legislators had identified the danger of the Alien and Sedition Acts. Resolutions sounding the alarm about the unconstitutionality of internal improvements passed the House with wide margins and were approved by the Senate on March 4, 1826. One newspaper called them "a second '98."[79]

Reaction to Virginia's Response

Reactions to Virginia's resolutions varied according to attitudes toward internal improvements as well as conflicting views of interposition. The editor of *Niles' Weekly Register*, Thomas Ritchie,

saw nothing but discord in Virginia's resolutions. Making the
Constitution "dependent" on Virginia's or other states' resolutions
rendered the meaning of the Constitution anyone's guess. Ritchie
failed to appreciate that Virginia's resolutions did not make the
Constitution's interpretation dependent on them, but merely invited
a reexamination of constitutional interpretation. Even so, Ritchie
welcomed Virginia's efforts for interstate cooperation to bring the
government back to "the true principles of the Constitution."[80]

Despite declaring internal improvements unconstitutional,
Virginia's legislature returned to the subject after reconvening in
December 1826. Revisiting that issue stemmed from yet another
alarming message of an incoming Governor, John Tyler, who
considered the congressional initiatives dealing with internal
improvements as outside "the letter and the true meaning" of
national powers. He reminded legislators of their duty and role in
guarding "against the encroachment of the Federal Government."
Tyler conceded that Virginia's position was at odds with other states
but hoped that reasoning through interstate communication might
persuade those states.[81]

From Montpelier, Madison followed the proceedings at Richmond.
He began to think that legislators were endangering Virginia's standing
in the Union by moving too swiftly on the issue of internal
improvements. The state seemed intent on entering a "labyrinth"
without appreciating appropriate constitutional landmarks. He
reiterated the difference "between the exercise of unconstitutional
powers and the *abuse* of constitutional powers." Madison had little
hope that his distinction would be appreciated given the tumultuous
state of political affairs.[82]

Eventually, under the leadership of William Giles, the state's next
Governor, the House appointed a committee to examine the alleged
constitutional overreaching by the national government. That
committee issued a report and proposed resolutions similar to those
of the previous legislature protesting "the usurpations of the general
government." On March 6, 1827 Virginia's legislature passed the
resolutions of the Giles committee by wide margins. Before then, the
legislature heard objections from Robert B. Taylor, who unsuccessfully
proposed a substitute that avoided calling the national government's
measures unconstitutional. While conceding that some of the powers

used by the federal government were questionable, Taylor did not think they amounted to "such 'deliberate, palpable and dangerous breach of the constitution' as to require the interposition of the legislature." Thus, Taylor identified Madison's preconditions drawn from the Third resolution describing the theoretical right of "the parties" to act and incorrectly argued they were needed before a legislature could sound the alarm.[83]

* * * * * *

The misreading of the 1798 Virginia resolutions and Madison's defense of them perpetuated a long pattern of innocent as well as intentional misunderstandings dating back to the initial formulation of the Virginia and Kentucky Resolutions. The legacy of misperceptions and deliberate distortions about interposition set the stage for its later transformation by the end of the 1820s. In the hands of John C. Calhoun, interposition was converted into a justification for the doctrine of nullification and the individual state veto. Moreover, as the justification for interposition as part of the monitoring role of state legislatures increasingly faded and became subsumed in the debates over nullification, it became even more difficult to defend interposition as a legitimate practice sanctioned as far back as *The Federalist*. Indeed, interposition's routine association with nullification in the aftermath of the Nullification crisis soon placed a stigma on interposition from which it never fully recovered.

But, in addition to the conflicting views about interposition, also in play was the constitutional theory espoused by Jefferson, Roane, and others that states could *independently* of the national government and its courts determine the constitutionality of federal laws as well as decide what measures of resistance they would embrace. As both sides fought over a broad versus a narrow view of the power of the federal government, the rhetoric became increasingly ominous.

7

The Transformation of Interposition: The Theory of Nullification Emerges

The dispute over protective tariffs, particularly after the passage of the so-called Tariff of Abominations in 1828, marked an important turning point in the use of interposition. Some legislatures responded – as they had to the Second Bank and internal improvements – by passing resolutions declaring the measure unconstitutional, but increasingly with language threatening more forceful action. Eventually, South Carolina's legislature, in resisting the tariff, advanced a theory of nullification asserting the right of an individual state to veto acts of the national government it perceived to be unconstitutional. This theory was enunciated in a document called the South Carolina Exposition of 1828 written by John C. Calhoun. Crucially, the Exposition supposedly invoked the 'Principles of '98' embodied in the Virginia and Kentucky Resolutions, but in doing so distorted Madison's views. The arguments of would-be nullifiers effectively transformed interposition by converting Madison's theoretical statement of the collective right of the parties to the constitutional compact into an option for every individual state to negate acts of the national government. That misinterpretation – purposeful or not – has led many scholars to treat nullification and interposition interchangeably despite their conceptual differences.[1]

South Carolina's nullification doctrine prompted a national debate – including a famous one in the U.S. Senate featuring Daniel Webster and Robert Y. Hayne – over the nature of the Union. Hayne's argument rested on Calhoun's Exposition and identified the dispute over the Constitution as a matter of two opposing views, namely, whether a "consolidated" or a "federal" government had been established by the Constitution. For Calhoun, the Constitution was a compact resting on "the sovereignty of the States." Webster, however, rejected Calhoun's theory of the Constitution and insisted that the American people "in the aggregate" were the sovereign source of the Constitution.[2]

Nullifiers quoted the Virginia and Kentucky Resolutions and Madison's Report to justify their theory. Madison, aging and ailing in retirement, sought to defend himself and his now deceased friend Jefferson from the charge of originating the concept of nullification. Madison waged an uphill battle to clarify what he had written in opposition to the Alien and Sedition Acts. Accused of senility and inconsistency, few of his contemporaries appreciated his constitutional distinctions or his nuanced understanding of federalism. For Madison, the Constitution was a compact whose parties were the people of the states acting collectively with each other. That conception placed him at odds with sovereign states' rights theorists as well as with those who believed the Constitution rested on a national people.

Madison rejected the binary choice between the positions advanced by Calhoun and Webster. For Madison, what he called "a middle ground" represented the truth about the founding. Madison's defense of his position was complicated because he insisted on simultaneously maintaining a number of propositions – none of which provided a constitutional justification for Calhoun's individual state veto. Specifically, Madison differentiated three rights: an ultimate interposition retained by the parties to the constitutional compact as a matter of theoretical principle; the ordinary right of state legislatures to sound the alarm for perceived constitutional overreaching by the national government; and the natural law right of revolution that any state in dire circumstances might invoke against oppressive acts of the federal government.[3]

During the nullification debate, few of Madison's contemporaries appreciated his distinctions and like earlier Americans, most of them dismissed his efforts as a rationalization of his prior political views and a strained attempt to distinguish his thinking from that of sovereign states' rights advocates. Even sympathetic biographers have questioned Madison's claim that his views were being misinterpreted. Madison's case for consistency, however, was stronger than either his contemporaries or subsequent scholars appreciated. Reviewing Madison's explanations of the meaning of the Virginia Resolutions toward the end of his life reveals how closely they tracked with the carefully crafted distinctions of constitutional theory he advanced in 1798 and 1800.[4]

Although Madison believed that the Constitution had been created by neither a compact of sovereign states nor by a national people, many scholars continue to characterize the debate as presenting only two choices. Despite that tendency, careful studies of the Nullification crisis identify a middle ground between nationalists such as Webster and nullifiers such as Calhoun. That position was occupied by Madison and others who defended states' rights but rejected nullification and believed that because the states retained some, but not complete sovereignty, they could not act unilaterally.[5]

* * * * * *

Tariff of 1828

The dispute over protective tariffs rested on the perception that as a national policy it imposed discriminatory and unconstitutional burdens on one section of the country for the benefit of other sections. During Madison's presidency, New England states complained that a federal embargo unfairly and unconstitutionally impacted their region. In the context of protective tariffs, Southern states now argued that the tariffs were unconstitutional because they primarily aided Northern manufacturers instead of advancing a constitutional purpose in raising national revenue. Despite their protectionist purpose, tariffs – and particularly the Tariff of 1828 – significantly affected the South, which was heavily dependent on manufactured goods and needed revenue from exporting slave-harvested cotton to England. At issue was whether congressional power to raise revenue and regulate commerce included the ability to impose tariffs to protect emerging domestic industries, or whether the tariff power was limited to collecting revenue. Tariff opponents joined South Carolina in challenging the purpose for imposing the tariff and claimed one section was using its influence to transfer the earnings of Southern agriculture to Northern manufacturers.[6]

Southern Governors Sound the Alarm

One aspect of the debate over protective tariffs was an effort in 1827 to place a tariff on imported woolen goods that passed the House but was narrowly defeated in the Senate. Its defeat prompted a convention of Northern pro-tariff supporters in Harrisburg, Pennsylvania in July 1827. Memorials from that convention urged Congress to reconsider passing a tariff on wool as well as on other goods and caught the attention of several Southern Governors. Georgia's Governor George M. Troup warned his legislature early in November 1827 about violations of the Constitution, including the imposition of tariffs and other federal taxes. Troup suggested that the legislature request interstate cooperation for measures "to bring back" the national government to the "true principles of the constitution." North Carolina's Governor Hutchins G. Burton also thought the wool tariff warranted action from his legislature.[7]

Three weeks after Governor Troup's message, South Carolina's Governor John Taylor addressed his legislature. Taylor called the Harrisburg convention a "mischievous project" to support unconstitutional tariffs and he reminded legislators of earlier resolutions they had passed disapproving of the federal government's exercise of powers not granted by the Constitution. He urged legislators to identify congressional action outside the letter and spirit of the Constitution and thereby return "the general government" to "sound decisions and safe constructions."[8]

South Carolina's legislature appointed a committee to examine Congress' constitutional authority over a host of issues, including tariffs, internal improvements, general welfare appropriations, as well as slavery. The committee also addressed the question of whether the federal government rested on the people of the United States or if it was a compact of sovereign states. The committee concluded that the Constitution was "purely the act of the people of the different States, as STATES, and not of the people at large," notwithstanding what John Marshall said in *McCulloch v. Maryland*. As to remedies if Congress exceeded its rightful authority, the report distinguished between an abuse of constitutional powers and the usurpation of powers not allocated to Congress. When Congress assumes "a power unknown to the Constitution, and thus encroaches upon what is reserved to the States" it was "an interference which goes to *the destruction of the compact itself.*" With usurped powers, it was the duty of state legislators "to interfere" on behalf of "the people of each different State" who comprised "the parties" to the constitutional compact and insist on compliance with the compact. Since the Supreme Court had not been "impartial," each state could "judge for itself whether the compact has been broken or not." This challenge to the Court's authority rested on a sovereign states' rights theory of the Constitution that Spencer Roane had previously advanced.[9]

However, the committee stopped short of nullification and South Carolina's legislators only invoked traditional interposition for the constitutional transgression it identified. The report concluded that Congress lacked the authority to enact protective tariffs and recommended resolutions to that effect. The approach South Carolina's legislators endorsed for the moment was for legislatures "to be watchful, and to remonstrate with Congress." In the end, the legislature instructed its congressional delegation to oppose the tariff on constitutional grounds and requested Governor Taylor to share its proceedings with other state Governors.[10]

The legislatures of Georgia and North Carolina passed interposition resolutions similar to those enacted by South Carolina. A committee of Georgia's legislature defended interposition and claimed "a right to remonstrate" with the federal government "on all measures which they may conceive violative" of "fundamental principles." Since the people could only act through their elected officials, state legislators "have the right to protect the States from the usurpations of the General Government, and to remonstrate against any act that shall *encroach* upon the *powers* reserved by the people and *granted* to their *own Government.*" Georgia's legislature passed its resolutions in December 1827 protesting tariffs as unconstitutional.[11]

For the time being, the Georgia committee did not advocate "the mode of OPPOSITION," but only expressed resistance to the tariff by all legal means. Since Congress paid attention to "the memorials of *manufacturing companies,*" it was felt that listening to "the voice of State Legislatures" could hardly undermine Congress' authority.

Georgia's legislature also resolved that the Governor should present the state's remonstrance to Congress and send copies to the other state legislatures for their concurrence.[12]

While Georgia was sounding the alarm, Governor Burton of North Carolina was warning his state legislature about the wool tariff. North Carolina's legislature recognized congressional authority over protective tariffs, but considered the proposed woolens bill to violate the spirit of the Constitution. Consequently, the legislature sent resolutions to Congress opposing an increase of duties on imports. Soon thereafter, Alabama's legislature joined South Carolina, Georgia, and North Carolina in drafting a remonstrance declaring that a protective tariff imposed by Congress that went "beyond the fair demands of the revenue" constituted "a palpable usurpation of a power not given by the Constitution."[13]

Other Responses against Interposition

In response to these anti-tariff interposition resolutions, other state legislatures, including Indiana, Ohio, and New Jersey, passed resolutions supporting the tariffs. Ohio's legislature asserted the national government possessed constitutional authority to impose taxes on imports for purposes other than revenue. New Jersey's legislature took a similar position, finding that the "successive decisions of the General Government" upholding protective tariffs amounted to a definitive construction of the Constitution.[14]

Madison believed Congress had the authority to impose a tariff to encourage manufactures. However, he did not think Georgia's and South Carolina's resolutions were attacks on the Union, but rather the product of "electioneering zeal." Madison regretted mistaken interpretations of the Constitution that either threw "an undue weight into the scale of the General Government" or gave "a preponderance to that of the State Governments." With respect to the tariff, he hoped for "a permanent equilibrium of powers" by either a "harmonious construction, or an authoritative amendment" of the Constitution.[15]

On May 19, 1828, Congress passed the tariff that became a major issue in that year's presidential election and triggered renewed responses from state legislatures. Ironically, it emerged out of a failed

political strategy in which Southerners supported a sweeping
protective tariff designed to fail because it included goods that
heavily burdened imports to New England. When enough New
England representatives voted for the tariff because they believed it
would strengthen the manufacturing industry nationally, the plan
backfired. The resulting tariff imposed nearly a 40 percent tax on
almost all imported goods. President John Quincy Adams, signed the
tariff into law, but lost the presidential election of 1828 to Andrew
Jackson.[16]

In early November, Georgia's Governor John Forsyth declared that
the new tariff exemplified how economic harm to the South in national
policies was routinely ignored. In urging its repeal, Forsyth recalled
earlier attempts to check constitutional overreaching by the national
government through state legislative protests seeking to apply political
pressure. Given widespread resentment against the tariff, he believed it
would eventually "perish." While Forsyth described traditional
interposition, other Southerners were beginning to ponder more
radical assertions of state legislative power. Among them was the
South Carolinian, John Calhoun, Vice President to both Adams and
Jackson.[17]

Calhoun's Draft of the South Carolina Exposition

Before South Carolina's legislature convened in late November 1828,
one of its members asked Calhoun's opinion about how the state
should respond to the new tariff. Calhoun recommended that the
legislature set forth "our wrongs" and "our remedies." Calhoun
consulted the Virginia and Kentucky Resolutions and Madison's
Report. Initially, he thought "little aid can be derived from them"
given "the dissimilarity between the character of the encroachments
of the General Government then and now." Before long, however,
Calhoun changed his mind about the relevance of Virginia's response
in 1798 to the present controversy over the tariff. Calhoun completed
a draft of what became the "South Carolina Exposition" before the
state's Governor addressed the legislature on November 25, 1828.[18]

Calhoun began the Exposition by declaring the tariff of 1828
"unconstitutional, unequal and oppressive, and calculated to ...
destroy the liberty of the Country." He then detailed the oppressive

nature of the tariff and its discriminating impact on the South. The litany of grievances attributed to a protective tariff was a familiar narrative. Calhoun broke new ground, however, when he turned to the nature of federalism under the Constitution and the practical mechanisms for maintaining a proper equilibrium between the national government and the state governments.[19]

According to Calhoun, "the great difficulty" faced by the framers was how to distribute power between the two levels of government. Despite that challenge, most agreed that they had correctly drawn "the line between the powers of the ... General and State government[s]." Calhoun considered the basic formulation uncontroversial: "The powers of the General Government are particularly enumerated and specifickly [sic] delegated; and all powers, not expressly delegated, or which are not necessary and proper to execute those that are granted, are expressly reserved to the States and the people." Appreciating "this beautiful theory" of federalism was fine, but it required a practical means to maintain the proper balance between the two levels of government.[20]

Calhoun described how the federal government could prevent the states from encroaching on its powers. The Supreme Court's authority to construe the Constitution gave those judges the power "of nullifying the acts of the State Legislatures whenever in their opinion they may conflict with the power delegated to the General Government." While this protected the national government, it did little to safeguard the reserved rights of states. By "a strange misconception" the Court had come to be regarded as the only means for "restraining all the powers of the system to their proper co[nstitutiona]l spheres, and consequently of deciding on the limits belonging to each." Calhoun invoked Madison's authority to refute the Court's singular authority over monitoring federalism and claimed that Madison supported the right of an individual state to nullify acts of the national government it deemed unconstitutional.[21]

Although Calhoun's argument primarily relied on Madison's Report, he began by invoking *The Federalist*. Calhoun focused on the discussion of the separation of powers and distribution of authority between two levels of government in *Federalist* 51. As Madison summarized it: "The different governments will controul each other; at the same time that each will be controuled by itself." According to

Calhoun that essay "clearly affirms the control of the States over the General Government."[22]

Supposedly, Madison was even more explicit in his Report of 1800. Calhoun offered a mangled quotation from the Report's justification "that in cases of a deliberate, palpable and dangerous exercise of other powers, not granted by the said compact, the State[s], who are parties thereto have the right and are in duty bound to interpose to arrest the act and for maintaining within their respective limits, the authorities[,] rights and liberties appertaining to them." Calhoun also cited Madison's explanation that the "States" in "their sovereign capacity" as the "parties to the constitutional compact" were authorized "to decide in the last resort whether the compact made by them be violated; and consequently as parties to it, they must themselves decide in the last resort, each question as may be of sufficient magnitude to require their interposition."[23]

Calhoun ignored Madison's reference to the states in the plural – as parties to the compact acting in this last resort – and instead argued that *each state was entitled to act by itself* against encroachments by the national government. This allowed Calhoun to fashion a new tool of interposition for individual states. In Calhoun's hands, interposition became the right of each state to veto national laws at any time that it perceived a deliberate, palpable, and dangerous encroachment by the federal government. With interposition identified as a remedy for every state seeking to restore the equilibrium of federalism, Calhoun explored how it might be used.

Although Calhoun's version of interposition identified sovereign states as parties to the constitutional compact, he questioned if "the State can interpose its sovereignty through the ordinary legislature." Whatever doubts there might be about the legislature, Calhoun thought a convention "fully represents" such sovereignty. Calhoun described how individual state constitutional conventions could respond to the tariff by determining whether particular acts of the national government were unconstitutional; "and if so, whether they constitute a violation so deliberate, palpable and dangerous as to justify the interposition of the State to protect its rights." Assuming a convention found such a violation, it could then determine how the offending acts should be declared void within the state.[24]

Calhoun also anticipated an argument critics of his theory would raise, namely that if the Constitution intended states to exercise a power of nullification, the framers would have explicitly said so. Calhoun replied that the power of judicial review was likewise not expressly granted in the Constitution. In that respect, both judicial review *and* his theory of nullification "rests on mere inference" from the design of the Constitution.[25]

For Calhoun, every state had a right to veto (what he called an interposition) when the national government acted unconstitutionally. If the veto or interposition of a single state was warranted, the national government would likely abandon its unconstitutional action. If the issue was less clear, the federal government could invoke the amending power of three-fourths of the states. That underlying authority could "modify the whole system." If enough states supported a constitutional amendment, "a disputed power will be converted into an express grant of power," but *the lack* of such support stopped the national government's exercise of the disputed power and validated the interposition. Calhoun thus saw a role for three-fourths of states to settle the issue of what he was now calling an individual state's interposition.[26]

Calhoun suggested that interposition and judicial review worked together to maintain a proper balance of federalism with three-fourths of the states serving as the final arbiters through constitutional amendment. Despite describing interposition (or nullification) as an available remedy, Calhoun ended the Exposition on a conciliatory note. With Jackson's election, Calhoun counseled patience since an improved political prospect of repealing the tariff might render the "interposition of the State" unnecessary.[27]

South Carolina and Georgia Respond to the Tariff of 1828

When South Carolina's Governor John Taylor addressed the legislature, he had evidently seen Calhoun's draft of the Exposition. Taylor urged legislators to identify the unconstitutionality of protective tariffs. They should not shrink from their duty to declare that Congress had engaged in "*a deliberate, palpable, and dangerous exercise of other powers not granted by the Compact.*" Such a determination focused attention on the tariff, invited declarations from other states, and encouraged Congress to reverse course. Although hopeful that the national government would forgo unconstitutional powers, Taylor left open the possibility for Calhoun's interposition. At some point, the legislators needed to decide if the situation warranted invoking "the sovereign power of the people of the State of South Carolina ... to judge in the last resort, if the *'bargain made in the formation of the Constitution, has been pursued or disregarded.'*"[28]

After Taylor's address, resolutions were introduced in South Carolina's legislature calling for "interposition" because of "dangerous and palpable" encroachments by the national government on the reserved rights of the state. The Senate passed a resolution seeking interstate cooperation for "resistance" against "unconstitutional" protective tariffs. From Virginia, Madison assessed the mood of South Carolina's legislators. He thought they agreed about the oppressive nature of the tariff and its unconstitutionality, but differed over how to affect "its repeal or its nullification." Madison was largely correct: South Carolina's House proved unwilling to take the step of nullification proposed by the state's Senate but supported a "Protest" to the U.S. Senate declaring the tariff unconstitutional. The legislators agreed to publish Calhoun's Exposition and distribute it nationally. For the time being, South Carolina's legislature was content to publicize, but not invoke, the theory of nullification.[29]

Indeed, despite the provocation of the newly passed tariff, South Carolina's initial response – notwithstanding its endorsement of nullification – only reiterated earlier interposition resolutions declaring protective tariffs unconstitutional along with a call for interstate cooperation seeking their repeal. In a resolution passed in the December 1828 session the legislature reprinted resolutions it had passed in 1825 and 1827. Its 1827 resolution asserted the right of state legislatures "to remonstrate against violations of the fundamental compact." In 1828 South Carolina's legislature explained that it invoked the sovereign rights of the state in the hopes that the nation would abandon a tariff system that was "partial in its nature, unjust in its operation, and not within the powers delegated to Congress." These new resolutions of South Carolina's legislature, along with its earlier ones, were sent to other states with the ominous hint to consider what "ulterior measures" might be necessary if the tariff remained in place.[30]

Even as South Carolina acted, Georgia's legislature passed four separate measures. The first entered a protest against the tariff of 1828 to be sent to the U.S. Senate. The second agreed with South Carolina's declaration of the tariff's unconstitutionality. The third asked states favoring the tariff to abandon the policy and the last was a memorial to states opposing the tariff urging Congress to "restore Federal Legislation to the standard of Constitutional correctness." The memorial ended with a veiled threat (similar to South Carolina's) should Congress do nothing: "Future measures will be dictated by expediency; the nature and tendency of injury will suggest the mode and measure of future resistance."[31]

Virginia Responds to South Carolina and Georgia

Even before news of the legislative proceedings of South Carolina and Georgia reached Virginia, the state was suffering from what Madison called "the Tariff fever." Virginia's legislature concluded – wrongly, Madison thought – that Congress lacked constitutional authority to impose a protective tariff. Madison's stand on the tariff put him at odds with many of his state's legislators and with voters who had supported his bid to serve in public office. Now, as citizens gathered to protest the tariff within five miles of Montpelier, their action demonstrated for Madison "how little" the Constitution was understood. Opponents of the tariff questioned Madison's consistency and eventually challenged his fidelity to doctrines he supposedly endorsed during Virginia's opposition to the Alien and Sedition Acts.[32]

Madison found the public controversy over his views deeply distasteful. In the heated debate over the tariff, he concluded that whatever he said would be misinterpreted or fall on deaf ears. Nonetheless, he permitted the publication of some of his personal letters dealing with the tariff. Madison's aversion "to go into the newspapers" was vindicated when he saw his correspondence savagely criticized. In a series of essays entitled "The Letters of Mr. Madison," one writer, identified as "One of the People," accused him of changing his "constitutional costume" since the formation of the Constitution and repudiating opinions he had expressed in 1798. Madison's views became integral to the Virginia legislature's debate over the South Carolina and Georgia resolutions and eventually he was drawn into the dispute over nullification. Until his death in 1836, Madison persistently denied that Virginia's Resolutions and his Report supported nullification.[33]

When Virginia's legislature convened in 1829, Governor William Giles shared the South Carolina and Georgia resolutions. Madison anticipated that Virginia's House might support them since many members opposed the tariff, but he thought that the Senate would not. The committee reporting on the resolutions and the ensuing debate described a different compact theory of the Constitution than the one Madison embraced. Moreover, the legislature denied that the Supreme Court served as arbiter of the constitutional boundary between the national and state governments. As a result, the Virginia legislators suggested that state legislatures could check overreaching by the national government in ways that went well beyond traditional interposition. Virginia's committee thought that South Carolina's and Georgia's resolutions had merit because the federal government only possessed enumerated powers, with state governments retaining those that remained. After reviewing the text, drafting, and ratification of the Constitution, the committee concluded that the absence of an express delegation of power to create a protective tariff rendered Congress' action unconstitutional. The committee's position relied on Virginia's 1798 Resolutions and Madison's Report of 1800 that formed an "exposition of the true principles" of the Constitution. The committee viewed the Constitution as the creation of sovereign states and not of "a majority of the people of America." Both the national and state governments had supreme authority when exercising their legitimate functions, but the authority of either is "wholly void, when exerted over a subject withheld from its jurisdiction."[34]

The committee believed that state legislatures were intended to serve "as the guardians of our political institutions" and whenever federalism went out of balance it became "the duty of the several Legislatures ... to attempt" its "restoration." Instead of acting on that restorative duty, the committee recommended traditional interposition through state legislative resolutions that would be shared with other states. However, they endorsed South Carolina's doctrine of an individual state veto by declaring that since the Constitution was a compact between sovereign states without a common arbiter it followed that each state had "the right to construe the Compact for itself."[35]

Debate over the report in Virginia's House recognized that the committee rejected the Supreme Court as the arbiter for disputes over federalism. House member William Henry Fitzhugh opposed the report for that reason. He denied that an individual state could resolve the constitutionality of actions of the national government or had the right to use "forcible resistance to any law of the general government" that it considered unconstitutional.[36]

The debate in Virginia's Senate reflected confusion over Virginia's 1798 Resolutions and their supposed connection with nullification. Senators focused on the report's proposed resolution describing the Constitution as a compact of sovereign states giving each state the right to construe the compact in the absence of a common arbiter. Virginia Senator Joseph Cabell sought a substitute incorporating language about the plural "states" that Madison had used in Virginia's Third resolution. Cabell objected to the proposed resolution's endorsement that "any one state" could declare a national law unconstitutional. While Madison would not have described the Constitution as a compact between sovereign states, he would have been gratified by Cabell's effort to reintroduce his theoretical statement of the right of the parties to the constitutional compact to judge infractions. The problem remained that Virginia's legislators, including the Senators who debated Cabell's substitute, ignored the two different types of interposition embraced in the Virginia Resolutions. Perhaps because they were talking past one another, Virginia's Senators narrowly rejected Cabell's substitute and adopted the select committee's original resolution by a two to one margin.[37]

Although Virginia and other Southern states did not support South Carolina when that state invoked nullification, the passage of resolutions by Virginia in the wake of Calhoun's Exposition was significant. Virginians had moved far from Madison's constitutional understanding by adopting a compact theory of sovereign states that entitled *each state* to construe the Constitution while denying that role for the Supreme Court.[38]

Madison's Initial Response

After Virginia passed its anti-tariff interposition resolutions, Madison complained to Cabell that his views had been grossly misconstrued. Madison drafted notes for a response but predicted that whatever he said would "produce fresh torrents of deceptive and declamatory" polemics. Madison concluded that a "silent appeal to a cool and candid judgment of the public" might best "serve the cause of truth." When Cabell shared a draft essay on the "arbiter or umpire" of constitutionality, Madison reminded Cabell that in *Federalist* 39 he had identified the Court as the authority for deciding disputes over the distribution of powers between the two levels of government, a fact Virginia legislators ignored when they claimed that every state had the right to construe the compact for itself. Madison recalled parting ways with Judge Roane a decade earlier when Madison insisted on "the necessity of a definitive power" in the Supreme Court to decide "questions between the U. States and the individual States."[39]

Even as Madison agreed with Cabell about the Court's role, he wanted Cabell to clarify the existence and basis for an *ultimate* authority to resolve constitutional disputes that resided in the people of the collective states. The "Virginia doctrine" of 1798, observed Madison, identified "a *Constitutional Union*" under which the collective right "to judge *in the last resort*, concerning usurpations of power, affecting the validity of the Union" belonged to the parties to the compact. Thus, claiming that the Third resolution justified the theory of an individual state veto was simply incorrect.[40]

Madison did agree that one state might try to nullify purported encroachments by the national government, but that action could only rest on the natural law right of revolution. That *extra-constitutional* theory contemplated the possibility that in "extreme cases, a single State might indeed be so oppressed as to be justified in shaking off the yoke." Until then, "the compact is obligatory," rendering invalid "the disorganizing doctrine" that asserted "a right in every State to withdraw itself from the Union." Unfortunately, Madison's fine-tuned clarifications tended to reinforce the mistaken idea that he supported nullification and even secession.[41]

Madison's Thoughts on Constitutional Government

During his correspondence with Cabell, Madison produced his unpublished "Outline" in 1829 describing the unique compact nature of the Constitution and how usurpations by the federal government might be resisted. It was a "fundamental error" to think that state governments were parties to the constitutional compact or that the national government and the state governments were the parties. As he stated in his Virginia Resolutions and explained in his Report, it was the people of the states "in their sovereign character, and they *alone*," who were the true parties to the Constitution, not the mistaken notion that the Constitution was a compact between the governments of the states and the government of the United States. Madison's distinction – as Drew McCoy has observed – "might appear subtle, but the implications were momentous."[42]

Madison emphasized that with the Revolution, American government expressly rested on the sovereignty of the people, resulting in a constitution created "by the people composing the respective States." Dividing sovereignty between the national government and the state governments to be exercised "by each within limited spheres" produced inevitable conflicts between the boundaries of power, but the Constitution gave the Supreme Court a deciding role.[43]

The Court's deciding role did not answer the question of that how to address "usurpations" of the national government should those unconstitutional acts gain the support of the Court. Madison listed some "constitutional remedies" available to states: remonstrances and instructions; elections and impeachments; and constitutional amendments. Madison also identified some of the successful outcomes of sounding the alarm interposition – including the Virginia and Kentucky Resolutions and the resolutions preceding the reversal of *Chisholm v. Georgia*.[44]

Madison's "Outline" omitted the right of the sovereign people to judge infractions that he had articulated in the Third resolution, but Madison reiterated that right in his August 1829 letter to Joseph Cabell. The "Outline," however, did allude to the natural law option *if all the constitutional remedies failed*. If usurpations of the national government proved intolerable, individual states could avail themselves of "original rights" and shake off "the yoke" *by way of revolution*. Little wonder that contemporaries conflated Madison's discussion of the people's theoretical rights in the last resort with the people's possible resort to a natural law right of revolution when faced with what they believed was extreme oppression.[45]

Kentucky Weighs in on the Tariff

Even as Madison was absorbing Virginia's response to the South Carolina and Georgia resolutions, Kentucky entered the debate. Unlike Virginia, Kentucky's legislature supported the tariff even as it defended traditional interposition. That defense came as interposition was transforming under the guise of Calhoun's depiction of nullification. In December 1829, Kentucky's Governor Thomas Metcalf shared with his legislature resolutions from other states including those from South Carolina and Georgia. He regretted their strident tone even as he acknowledged the role Governors and state legislatures played in calling out unconstitutional acts of the national government. But Metcalf insisted that a state could not proceed one "step further and obstruct the execution of the acts of the Union, by acts of its own." Metcalf insisted that such limits were understood during the controversy over the Alien and Sedition Acts and reflected in 'the Principles of '98.'[46]

In response, a committee of Kentucky's House of Representatives agreed that state legislatures had an undeniable right to object to perceived constitutional violations, but disagreed with the language in South Carolina's resolutions claiming the right to use more obstructive measures if the tariff policy persisted. Such a position went beyond sounding the alarm and involved dire consequences involving every state. Although rejecting an individual state veto, the committee acknowledged a natural law right of revolution: "an appeal to arms" justified on grounds of extreme oppression by government.[47]

Kentucky's legislators denied interposing in 1798 even though they had engaged in sounding the alarm interposition. The committee believed that Kentucky's legislators in 1798 had strongly disapproved of the Alien and Sedition Acts, considered them unconstitutional and therefore void. It was "the incontestable right" of every state to express "its opinion of any and of every act of the federal government" and appeal to the people to "change federal rulers or federal measures." In describing the acceptable parameters of legislative declarations of unconstitutionality, the report distinguished its position from that of South Carolina. The House and Senate accepted the committee's report.[48]

The Webster–Hayne Debate (1830)

Although Calhoun's Exposition and the resolutions of South Carolina and Georgia received attention at the state level, they soon became a national issue after the Twenty-First Congress met in December 1829. During a wide-ranging debate, the Senate came to address the nature of the Union. In what became known as the Webster–Hayne debate, extending from January to May 1830, the Senate considered the propositions advanced by the legislatures of South Carolina and Georgia.

The discussion of the individual state veto (that is, Calhoun's concept of nullification) began on January 25, 1830 when Senator Robert Y. Hayne of South Carolina praised what he called "The South Carolina doctrine." According to Hayne, South Carolina's Exposition embodied "the good old Republican doctrine of '98, the doctrine of the celebrated 'Virginia Resolutions'" and "'Madison's Report.'" According to Hayne, the South Carolina doctrine was "first promulgated by the Fathers of the Faith" and later used by Virginia and Kentucky in opposing the Alien and Sedition Acts as well as used by New England to oppose the embargo during the War of 1812. New Englanders, Hayne gloated, were not shy about adopting South Carolina's principles "when they believed themselves to be the victims of unconstitutional legislation!"[49]

Hayne's comment about New England predictably brought Daniel Webster of Massachusetts to his feet and prompted a two-day speech in which he disputed that Madison's Third Virginia resolution justified nullification. He analyzed words that Americans had wrestled with for thirty years, namely Madison's statement that "the States may interpose to arrest the progress of the evil." If Madison meant the right of revolution, Webster did not object since that right was widely acknowledged and supported by legal authority, including the venerable Sir William Blackstone.[50]

But Webster correctly guessed that Hayne's description of "a direct appeal to the interference of the State Governments" envisioned a remedy that did not rest on the natural law right of revolution. Hayne confirmed that he was indeed asserting a "right of constitutional resistance." This made no sense to Webster who saw no "middle course, between submission to the laws, when regularly pronounced constitutional, on the one hand, and open resistance, which is revolution, or rebellion, on the other." By insisting on a choice between lawful submission and revolution, Webster denied a possibility between those two options that Madison had described in Virginia's Third resolution. And Hayne, by claiming a right of constitutional nullification for each state, ignored Madison's argument that only the collective people of the *states* in their highest sovereign capacity might act in the final resort.[51]

While Hayne claimed to know Madison's meaning, Webster complained that the language of the resolutions was more than "a little indefinite." In particular, the phrase alluding to a state's right "to interfere" was "susceptible of more than one interpretation." It might mean nothing more than states protesting through remonstrance or seeking constitutional amendments or alternatively it might simply be an assertion of the right of revolution. Any of these possibilities were entirely "unobjectionable." Indeed, Webster thought that was all that Madison could have meant.[52]

When Hayne responded to Webster on January 27, he too overlooked the collective, theoretical right alluded to in the Third resolution. In addition, Hayne invoked Madison's description of the states as parties to the constitutional compact and insisted that Madison agreed with him that the Constitution was "a compact between sovereigns."[53]

Madison's Private Concerns about the Debate

While Madison wanted to repudiate nullification and his supposed authority for that doctrine, he mainly vented privately to friends about the debate. In mid-February Madison reflected that as the author of the Virginia Resolutions he never intended to assert a right for the parties to the Constitution "*individually* to annul within themselves acts of the Federal Government, or to withdraw from the Union." Likewise, the Resolutions had not contemplated the extreme cases that might justify the right of revolution. The Third resolution simply described in theory how "the joint constituents of the parties" were entitled to interpose in the last resort based on the unique status of the sovereign people who formed the foundation of the Constitution. In creating the "unprecedented" federalism achieved by the Constitution, Madison asserted that the framers had not ignored inevitable controversies over "the partition line between the powers belonging to the Federal and to the State governments."[54]

Madison explained the framers' approach to that issue and noted numerous ways of redressing a perceived imbalance in the equilibrium of federalism. The Constitution clearly gave the Court a role to resolve such controversies. The Court was "immediately and ordinarily relied on" to resolve questions over the "line" between the powers of the two levels of government. In addition to the Court's role, however, other "ulterior resorts" remained to adjust the relationship between the national and state governments. Some of those means of adjustment included the elective process; "the hands of the people themselves" (presumably including interposition resolutions passed by their state representatives); "the joint constituents of the parties" (which was how Madison identified "the States" in the Third resolution); and constitutional amendments. Beyond all this lay the "extra and ultra constitutional" right of revolution.[55]

Madison resisted defending himself in the public arena. He mused that being nearly eighty years old, every argument he made would "be answered by allusions to the date of his birth." Eventually Madison did enter the public controversy over nullification. But poignantly, he was right that his efforts prompted skepticism and snide remarks that "the Last of the Fathers" had gone senile. For the time being he followed the debates in Congress where few speeches seemed to understand his Virginia Resolutions and his Report.[56]

A Rare Appreciation of Madison's Position

One of the few Senators who Madison thought grasped his thinking was Edward Livingston of Louisiana. After Livingston shared his speech of March 9, Madison congratulated him for analyzing what

Virginia's legislature had done in 1798. Livingston described the government as neither leaving the parties with "full sovereignty" nor depriving them of all "sovereign power." Instead, the Constitution was "a compact by which the people of each State have consented to take from their own Legislatures some of the powers they have conferred upon them, and to transfer them, with other enumerated powers, to the Government of the United States, created by that compact."[57]

In identifying the centrality of the principle of the sovereignty of the people, Livingston recognized the underlying basis of the right Madison described in the Third resolution even if Livingston failed to appreciate the nature of that right. Livingston thought Madison's Third resolution expressed traditional sounding the alarm interposition, yet he understood that the Third resolution did not justify an individual state veto nor was it an allusion to the right of revolution. Like others, including Webster, Livingston readily conceded the existence of the natural law right of revolution. However, he rejected the idea that every state had "a constitutional right, whenever, in the opinion of the Legislature, (or as some think, of a convention of the people of any one State) a law of Congress is palpably unconstitutional ... not only to declare the act void, but to prevent its execution within the State." This result followed from the fact that each state had ratified the Constitution which provided that the Supreme Court "shall finally decide" whether such laws were constitutional or not. If Livingston failed to grasp the full meaning of the Virginia Resolutions, in Madison's eyes he understood more than most, including the nature of the compact, the division of sovereignty, the existence of theoretical rights based on the sovereignty of the people, and the function and legitimacy of sounding the alarm interposition.[58]

Madison Responds to the Nullifiers: His Open Letter of 1830

One month after the debate, Robert Hayne sent Madison copies of his speeches replying to Webster, assuring Madison that nullification marked "the restoration of the principles of '98" as embodied in the Virginia Resolutions and "your admirable Report." He sought Madison's "present views, in relation to the great principles involved in these questions." Truly astonished, Madison thanked Hayne for sending the speeches, but in a lengthy reply rejected the constitutionality of nullification and set Hayne straight about the true meaning of the Virginia Resolutions. Equally stunned, Hayne remained silent for several months before writing back. He insisted that his speeches had captured "the true doctrines of the Constitution" and were not inconsistent with the "true spirit and meaning" of the Resolutions and Madison's Report. Although Hayne promised to amplify his views in a future letter, none was apparently sent.[59]

Although making no secret of his opinions about how nullifiers were misrepresenting him, Madison was "unwilling" to challenge them publicly. He overcame that reluctance after receiving Hayne's two letters, realizing that any private correction would not stop Hayne and others from invoking his authority. Consequently, in late August 1830, Madison wrote a long letter to Massachusetts congressman Edward Everett clearly intended for publication. The letter offered Madison's thoughts about nullification, the subject of an article Everett was writing for the *North American Review*. The open letter to Everett marked the first of several additional efforts by Madison to set the record straight.[60]

Madison stressed – as he had since 1787 – the uniqueness of the Constitution. Fully understanding its operation required avoiding the frequent mistake of "viewing it through the medium either of a consolidated Government or of a confederated Government." It was "neither the one nor the other, but a mixture of both." A fundamental characteristic of the compound nature of the Constitution lay in its formation. It was not established, as were the Articles of Confederation, "by the governments of the component States" nor was it founded "by a majority of the people of the United States, as a single community, in the manner of a consolidated Government." Instead, the Constitution was formed "by the States – that is, by the people in each of the States, acting in their highest sovereign capacity," and thus established "by the same authority which formed the State Constitutions."[61]

For Madison, the Constitution's foundation precluded the theory of nullification. Although the Constitution rested on the same sovereign source as state constitutions, there was one crucial difference. Since the Constitution was "a compact among the States in their highest sovereign capacity, and constituting the people thereof one people for certain purposes," it could not be altered or annulled by individual states – as the people of a given state were free to do with respect to their own state constitution. Changing the Constitution required collective action by the parties – the states, and not a single state.[62]

Madison insisted that the framers knew that resolving controversies over the boundaries of jurisdiction presented the great challenge of federalism. Giving each state a final decision in such conflicts necessarily undermined national uniformity. Such a diversity of independent decisions would have doomed the Union. The expedient adopted, as he explained in *Federalist* 39, was making the Supreme Court the ultimate decider of controversies over which level of government held what power. Madison conceded that federal judicial power was not always properly exercised, but "the course of the judiciary" had by and large received public approval. If the Court failed to protect states against usurpations and abuses of the national government, "the final resort within the purview of the Constitution" was a constitutional amendment. And should every constitutional resort fail, there remained the natural law right of revolution, "the 'ultima ratio' under all Governments" available even to "a single member of the Union."[63]

Madison believed his views were misconstrued because people had failed to pay attention to his precise language and the intent of the Virginia legislature in 1798. One of Madison's distinctions established the natural law right of revolution as an action *outside* the purview of the Constitution. But in a characterization that was apt to elude even close readers of his language, Madison indicated that the right of the collective people of the states acting in their highest sovereign capacity that he described in Virginia's Third resolution was also an action outside of the purview of the Constitution *even as it was constitutionally justified by the sovereignty of the people*. Thus, Madison referred to *both* the right of revolution and the collective right of the parties to the Constitution to interpose as being "ultra-constitutional." In any event, Calhoun's theory of nullification could not rest on the people's collective right alluded to in Virginia's Third resolution. Regrettably, Madison's strange logic suggested a future, dangerous path that a sovereign people might wish to take in the belief that it was constitutionally justified – that of nullification.[64]

Madison denied that Virginia's legislators in 1798 established a precedent for nullification and he insisted they had only engaged in traditional interposition. Their proceedings revealed no claim for a constitutional right of an individual state to prevent by force the operation of a national law. The objective in 1798 was to invite other states "to *concur*" with Virginia's legislature in "declaring the acts to be unconstitutional, and to *co-operate* by the necessary and proper measures" to seek a redress against the acts. Those measures were ones "known to the Constitution," which obviously included sounding the alarm interposition and senatorial instructions. Given the repudiation of the Alien and Sedition Acts, "the interposition" proved "equal to the occasion." As Bradley Hays has observed, Madison's open letter emphasized how those resolutions were part of a process through which states "were participants in a wider dialogue" appropriately expressing opposition to the acts. Madison's rejection of nullification rested on the belief that "States were not supreme but rather participants in a process of constructing constitutional consensus."[65]

In his Report of 1800 Madison described interposition without using the term. By the time of his 1830 open letter to Everett, however, Madison explicitly described "several modes and objects of interposition" – including state legislative declarations identifying unconstitutional acts of the national government. Because Virginia's Third resolution used the word "interpose" and had often been associated with the term "interposition" over the years, Madison now focused on the significance of the Seventh resolution.[66]

To establish that Virginia's legislature had only sounded the alarm, Madison drew on the drafting history of the resolutions and the legislature's address to the people of the state. Madison recounted the fate of the language that had been added to his draft of the Seventh resolution at Jefferson's suggestion. Whereas Madison's original draft simply declared the Alien and Sedition Acts unconstitutional, Jefferson wanted to add "not law, but utterly null, void, and of no force or effect" immediately thereafter. Madison insisted that Jefferson's suggested language had been deleted simply to clarify the intent of the legislature. Jefferson's words were "synonymous with 'unconstitutional,' yet, to guard against a misunderstanding of this phrase as more than declaratory of opinion, the word 'unconstitutional' alone was retained." Virginia's legislators, as they stated in their address to the citizens of the state, claimed no rights "beyond the regular ones within the forms of the Constitution."[67]

Since both he and Jefferson allegedly supported "the nullifying doctrine," Madison wanted to vindicate himself and his old friend, who had died in 1826. Madison initially defended Jefferson by saying that of Kentucky's two sets of resolutions, Jefferson's participation was limited to those of 1798 which (unlike those of 1799) did not contain the word nullification "or any equivalent word." That line of defense proved untenable after Madison subsequently acknowledged that Jefferson, in his draft of the 1798 resolutions, had written that when the national government assumed undelegated powers "a nullification of the act is the rightful remedy." Even so, Madison insisted that Jefferson was not thinking of "the idea of a constitutional right" of nullification, but of "a natural one in cases justly appealing to it." That interpretation relied on the fact that in the passage where Jefferson used the term nullification, he described the natural law right of revolution. Nonetheless, even if the Kentucky Resolutions were only sounding the alarm interposition, Jefferson was more vulnerable than Madison to the charge that he had flirted with the idea of nullification by virtue of expressions used in his draft.[68]

Madison noted that Kentucky's Resolutions (including those of 1798) were drafted primarily by Jefferson without the same care he had given Virginia's Resolutions and his Report. Madison remembered his deliberate use of "the *plural* number, States" in "*every* instance" when referring "to the authority which presided over the Government." That usage was consistent with the Third resolution's focus on the ultimate right of the parties to the constitutional compact. In contrast, Kentucky's Resolutions "being less guarded" were "more easily perverted" in part because they were not scrupulous in referring to the states as the parties to the compact. Even so, Madison's words and constitutional distinctions produced their own challenges and potential confusion that Madison continued to address after the Webster–Hayne debate.[69]

Madison's Further Explanations

When South Carolina's legislature tried to implement nullification in December 1830, Madison saw the need for further clarifications, particularly about Virginia's Third resolution. South Carolina's legislature passed six resolutions, the first five of which heavily drew on the Virginia and Kentucky Resolutions, including the verbatim text of Madison's Third resolution. The sixth resolution declared tariff provisions violations of the Constitution entitling any state to exercise its "right and duty to interpose in its sovereign capacity, for the purpose of arresting the progress of the evil occasioned by the said unconstitutional acts." While a call for a constitutional convention passed both the House and the Senate, it lacked the two-thirds vote required by the state's constitution.[70]

Two years later, when South Carolina successfully called a constitutional convention, the legislature's address to the public illustrated how nullification had subsumed the idea of interposition. Citizens of South Carolina were told that it did not matter "by what name this counter-legislation shall be designated – call it Nullification, State interposition, State veto" or any "other name." However described, the address insisted that Virginia's Resolutions endorsed nullification. The gulf between Madison and the nullifiers was not merely a matter of semantics, but entailed a crucial distinction about who could act under the circumstances contemplated in the Third as opposed to the Seventh resolution.[71]

Even before South Carolina passed its Ordinance of Nullification in November, 1832, Madison was elaborating crucial distinctions that seemed obvious to him but continued to elude others. Virginia's Third resolution, Madison explained, expressed the "collective" right of the parties to the constitutional compact. The parties entitled to act were not individual states or state governments, but a plurality of the states understood as the people of those states in their highest sovereign capacity exercising a collective right. Once again Madison stressed that he had scrupulously used the plural in speaking of "the *ultimate* right of the States to interpose." Madison rationalized not being more explicit in 1798, because "Who could, at that day, have foreseen some of the comments on the Constitution advanced at the present?"[72]

State Response to South Carolina's Nullification

After South Carolina nullified the tariff in 1832, eight Southern state legislatures passed resolutions condemning nullification and no states supported South Carolina's act of nullification. Even so, some Southern legislatures, including Virginia, North Carolina, Alabama, Georgia, and Kentucky, asserted the right of their legislatures to express their opinion about the unconstitutionality of the tariff. Other Southern states recognized the right of state legislatures to declare their constitutional opinions through such resolutions, but rejected nullification because it violated their understanding of the nature of American constitutionalism. As Bradley Hays has suggested, states were entitled to express their view of the proper construction of the Constitution, as part of the process of "offering alternative interpretations and fostering dialogue among political officials and the various departments of government." On the other hand, nullification "turned the politics of interpretation into the politics of the threat."[73]

Some Northern states, like New York, while rejecting nullification, also rejected the assumption that only the Supreme Court could identify the proper constitutional division of authority between the federal government and the states. Indeed, when Martin Van Buren drafted the New York legislature's report on South Carolina's nullification, he rejected both nullification and the Supreme Court's interpretative monopoly. That position left room for states, and state legislatures in particular, to offer their opinions.[74]

Nonetheless, other New York legislators, including William H. Seward, objected to Van Buren's report because, despite its repudiation of nullification, it still endorsed the 'Principles of '98.' Seward considered the Virginia and Kentucky Resolutions "the text-book of the heresy" of nullification. Seward, along with many other Americans before the Civil War, lived with the fear of the potential use of the Virginia and Kentucky Resolutions to create cataclysmic national divisions. Those Americans – as well as subsequent scholars looking back at the horrors of secession – saw dangers lurking in those early resolutions, but in the process lost sight of the positive values found in their history and the original meaning of traditional interposition.[75]

After Virginia offered to mediate the dispute between South Carolina and the federal government, Madison worried the state would be drawn into the conflict with consequences that included disunion. In the end, Andrew Jackson facilitated a congressional resolution to the crisis in 1833 by coupling a lower tariff with greater enforcement power. Congress passed a Force Bill that enhanced presidential authority to collect federal revenues as well as a Compromise Tariff that reduced tariff rates. After Jackson signed both bills, South Carolina rejected the authority of the Force Bill but accepted the Compromise Tariff. These joint maneuvers and symbolic gestures effectively ended the confrontation between South Carolina and the national government. Calhoun proclaimed nullification a "success" and "triumph" because a political majority had responded to the grievances of a minority.[76]

After South Carolina's Ordinance of Nullification, both its defenders and critics began to use the terms interposition and nullification interchangeably. For opponents of nullification, like William Seward, Madison's terminology in Virginia's Third resolution embraced nullification. Another critic thought Virginia's Resolutions, if only in the "abstract," hinted "strongly of nullification doctrines."[77]

Madison's Final Campaign against Nullification

Despite the compromise resolving the crisis, Madison could not give up his fight against nullification. Along with allies, Madison instigated a letter-writing campaign to overcome the taint of nullification, motivated by nullifiers like Calhoun who gloated about nullification's effectiveness and by critics who challenged Madison's consistency. The essays of one critic writing as "A Friend of Union and State Rights" illustrated how the context of his resolutions and Report had been forgotten. Madison reminded "A Friend of Union" that state legislatures responding to Virginia's Resolutions insisted that states "had no right to interpose a *legislative* declaration of opinion on a constitutional point; nor a right to interpose at all against a decision of the Supreme Court of the United States, which was to be regarded as a tribunal from which there could be no appeal." That position missed the dual objectives of the resolutions. One purpose was "to vindicate legislative declarations of opinion" and "to designate the several constitutional modes of interposition by the States against abuses of power." But the resolutions also sought "to establish the ultimate authority of the States as parties to and creators of the Constitution, to interpose against the decisions of the judicial as well as other branches of the Government."[78]

Despite his declining health, Madison never wavered in his crusade against nullification since that doctrine put "powder under the Constitution and Union, and a match in the hand of every party to blow them up at pleasure." Madison gradually accepted the futility of correcting misconceptions about Virginia's Resolutions and his Report. In 1834 he lamented that his views were no longer subject to respect. During his final years, Madison devoted what energy he could muster to composing a memorandum entitled "On Nullification." The last political production of his life, the draft summarized his understanding of the formation of the Constitution, how the federalism it established could be monitored, and why nullification remained fundamentally inconsistent with Virginia's Resolutions and his Report. A close reading of the memorandum suggests Madison's anxiety that his words had inadvertently furnished support for nullification and disunion.[79]

In his memorandum, Madison again explained that the Third resolution restated a constitutional principle based on the sovereignty of the people who constituted the critical parties to the constitutional compact. As one of America's fundamental maxims of government it was deserving of solemn repetition whether in a Bill of Rights or other public declaration of principle. Thus, the Third resolution simply served to remind Americans that popular sovereignty lay at the heart of American constitutionalism. Madison further explained why he had not been more specific about how "the States could interpose in their collective character as parties to the Constitution against usurped power." According to Madison, "the object and reasoning of the resolutions and report" did not require detailing "the mode" the people might use. "It was sufficient to show that the authority to interpose existed and was a resort beyond that of the Supreme Court." Since the parties to the Constitution retained "plenary" authority, how they interposed remained their "own choice." Whatever Madison's reasons were for not being more specific about how "the people" might interpose under the Third resolution, the failure to explain undermined the utility and comprehensibility of his constitutional thought and led to various, dangerous interpretations.[80]

Nullification and Madison's Disturbing Legacy

Madison's death on June 28, 1836 ended his efforts to disown any connection with nullification. John Quincy Adams gave a eulogy that discussed the friendship of Jefferson and Madison and stressed Madison's "calmer sensibility and cooler judgment." In a private letter, Adams identified the "wide difference of opinion" between them on "the *interposition* of the State Legislatures, to withstand or controul the unconstitutional Legislation of Congress." Adams thought both of them misguided, but "the error of Madison was comparatively harmless" because he limited a "right of interposition by the State Legislatures to mere declarations, remonstrances, and arguments" and thus lacked "the deadly venom of Jefferson's nullification." Nevertheless, Madison's and Jefferson's writings served as a touchstone for the often-lauded 'Principles of '98', which in the hands of sovereign states' rights theorists ultimately helped justify secession.[81]

Before he died, Madison called secession a "twin" to the "heresy" of nullification with both doctrines springing "from the same poisonous root." He rightly predicted that growth from this evil source would bring "disastrous consequences." Unfortunately, in the aftermath of the debate over South Carolina's Exposition, the positions and actions taken by many state legislatures often reflected a dim understanding of traditional interposition and displayed their willingness to consider extra-constitutional actions.[82]

* * * * * *

Richard Ellis has identified ambiguities in thinking about the origins and nature of the Union and observed that many Americans were undoubtedly "confused by the abstract and inconclusive nature of the [Webster–Hayne] debate." Indeed, the complexities and conceptual distinctions of Madison's understanding of the Constitution have proven too much for many. Amidst fierce partisanship, people gravitated towards the more simplified and understandable extremes of Webster's and Calhoun's positions instead of Madison's views. As David Ericson has noted, Madison's description of the Constitution as partly federal and partly national proved "unstable" as an explanation to capture the imagination of Americans. Moreover, Madison's suggestion that Americans could somehow take action in the last resort when they believed they had exhausted their constitutional remedies became an attractive danger for nullifiers and later secessionists. The struggle over the nature of the Union during the South Carolina nullification crisis was "resolved through a political compromise that failed to provide answers to the complex constitutional questions that had been raised in the debate over the legitimacy of nullification." Thus, the disturbing legacy of Madison's views and the Virginia Resolutions persisted long after Madison passed from the scene and as America moved towards civil war.[83]

8

State Interposition and Nullification on the Path to Secession

While James Madison was engaged in his last efforts to discredit nullification and secession, President Andrew Jackson's Proclamation of 1832 rejected South Carolina's Ordinance of Nullification, stating that "Secession, like any other revolutionary act, may be morally justified by the extremity of oppression; but to call it a constitutional right" confounded "the meaning of terms." Jackson's description of the nation's divided sovereignty resonated with Americans who believed that the Constitution did not intend to maintain a confederation of sovereign states. For Jackson, Americans' allegiance should be first and foremost to the nation, fearing that resistance to some national laws would inevitably mean resistance to all of them. Others, such as Robert Hayne, Webster's debating opponent and now Governor of South Carolina, issued what one newspaper called a "Counter-Proclamation" that contended the citizens of states did not owe their chief allegiance to the national government, but to their state and were duty-bound to maintain the state's sovereign rights.[1]

Increasingly, Americans could not find common ground in their shared constitutional history – and some Americans were determined to lay the groundwork for disunion. Ultimately, it was the bitter struggle over slavery that intensified the opposing views of the Constitution. In particular, the enforcement of the Constitution's Fugitive Slave Clause that granted enslavers a right to reclaim an enslaved person who escaped into a free state brought the conflict between national and state authority into stark relief. That conflict generated important Supreme Court cases including *Prigg v. Pennsylvania* (1842) and *Ableman v. Booth* (1859) fueling public uproar and extreme rhetoric on both sides of the issue. Ironically, the traditional, conflicting parties ended up switching sides in their views of the appropriate equilibrium of federalism as Southern states sought to enforce the slave clause through federal legislation.

The Southern effort to utilize federal law to defend slavery spurred many Northern legislatures to pass laws governing the surrender and return of fugitive slaves. To justify personal liberty laws, those legislatures appealed to the authority reserved to states under the Constitution, citing the Virginia and Kentucky Resolutions. While personal liberty laws were not traditional, sounding the alarm interposition, those laws were passed by state legislatures intent on resisting the enforcement of an intrusive federal law that would extend the authority of enslavers beyond the South. The Northern legislatures also sought to protect all persons within the state, whether free or fugitive, who were in danger of being seized and enslaved without due process. For their part, Southern states became enraged by personal liberty laws that they considered a nullification of legitimate federal law. Those Southern legislatures also condemned the federal government for failing to use greater national power to enforce the Fugitive Slave Clause.

Slavery, secession and the coming of the Civil War exposed the newly divergent views of the Constitution. Southern states considered themselves entitled to secede and opt out of the compact as the right of sovereign states since the North was intent on eradicating slavery, violating longstanding constitutional accommodations. Northern states rejected any right of secession on grounds that a national people, not sovereign states, had created the Constitution which was intended to be perpetual. That debate revealed just how entrenched the revised constitutional positions of the North and South had become.

But more than insight into the divided sovereignty that accompanied the Constitution's framing was lost in the process. Another casualty during the pre–Civil War period was sounding the alarm interposition. Repudiating the idea that state courts might have an independent right to assess the constitutionality of acts of the federal government left little room for the concept that monitoring federalism could be a collaborative process involving state legislative interposition and state courts, as well as the federal government. Instead, much more was heard of the Supreme Court serving as not just the final judge of constitutionality, but rightly the only judge.

* * * * * *

Jackson's 1832 Proclamation

In response to the South Carolina Ordinance of Nullification, President Andrew Jackson's Proclamation of 1832 declared secession a "revolutionary act" and not "a constitutional right." Likewise, the "the absurd and dangerous doctrine" of nullification was not "a peaceable remedy." Both nullification and secession were treason that threatened the Union. The President challenged South Carolina's claim that it was acting consistently with Madison's Third Virginia resolution when the state nullified the tariff as "a deliberate, palpable and dangerous" violation of the Constitution. The President denied that Madison justified nullification. He described how states had frequently objected to federal laws – including during the War of 1812. However, according to Jackson, New England states did not assert the right to nullify when they denounced measures they perceived to be unconstitutional. The "discovery" and "invention" of the theory of nullification, he concluded, could not be traced to Madison, but was the brainchild of present-day South Carolinians.[2]

Jackson's understanding of nullification and secession reflected his view of the Constitution, with the Constitution's Preamble providing evidence of its formation by "the people of United States" and not by the states. Although Jackson described the Constitution as a compact, it was not as South Carolina nullifiers alleged, a compact between sovereign states that retained their sovereignty. Instead, with ratification, states transferred some, but not all of their sovereignty to create the government of the United States. That partial transfer of authority meant that the states could not have "retained their entire sovereignty" or "reserved an undivided sovereignty." Because states were not independent sovereigns, no state possessed a unilateral and constitutional right either to nullify an act of the national government or to secede from the Union.[3]

As Christopher Childers has expressed it, Jackson's formulation "sought a middle ground between the two extreme positions of ultra-states' rights and nationalism." Nonetheless, Jackson's depiction of the formation and nature of the Constitution stressed its national qualities and the subordination of the states. For example, Jackson thought that House members represented the United States and not their own states. Moreover, Jackson asserted that with the Constitution's ratification, the "allegiance" of all citizens "transferred ... to the Government of the United States." This new allegiance meant that no state could claim to be sovereign and independent since its citizens owed "obedience to laws not made by it" and local magistrates were "sworn to disregard" state laws in conflict with those passed by the federal government. Jackson also minimized the existence of state sovereignty before the formation of the Constitution, emphasizing the united and national nature of the colonial resistance during the Revolution. His belittlement of the role of states in the American constitutional order was challenged not only by South Carolina's nullifiers, but also many defenders of states' rights who rejected nullification.[4]

Hayne's Counter-Proclamation

South Carolina Governor Robert Hayne responded to the "dangerous and pernicious doctrines" in Jackson's Proclamation with his own "Counter-Proclamation." Hayne thought Jackson's Proclamation might lead South Carolinians astray and to forget their obligations to the state. Hayne disputed Jackson's position that the Constitution did not create "a confederated republic" of sovereign states that "retained their entire sovereignty." Jackson's denial of state sovereignty – according to Hayne – led to a consolidated government that would "annihilate the rights of the States."[5]

For Hayne, Jackson was suggesting that "the General Government is unlimited and supreme" and served as "the exclusive judge of the extent of its own powers." As such, congressional acts – even if they were unconstitutional – might persist as the supreme law of the land. In a compact of sovereign states, each state retained the right to judge when and how the compact was being violated and which remedies were appropriate. Hayne quoted the Virginia and Kentucky Resolutions and along with other nullifiers, assumed that Virginia's

'Principles of '98' were identical to those in Kentucky's Resolutions and that both resolutions justified South Carolina's nullification. Nearly a year later, Hayne insisted that "State interposition" or "the rightful remedy of nullification" was inherent in state sovereignty, and that every state possessed this remedy when it identified "gross, deliberate ... and palpable usurpation" by the federal government. For nullifiers like Hayne, it was irrelevant if "State interposition" or nullification was deemed "a constitutional, a sovereign, or a reserved right" and he used the phrase "state interposition" interchangeably with nullification.[6]

Advocacy for States' Rights without Nullification

When states' rights advocates who opposed nullification responded to Hayne's "Counter-Proclamation," they faced an intriguing challenge. They navigated a course that preserved the Union by rejecting the legitimacy of an individual state veto while at the same time asserting a role for states in assessing the proper exercise of powers delegated to the national government and those reserved to the states. One example was Thomas Ritchie, the editor of the *Richmond Enquirer*, who agreed with Jackson that nullification was not "a peaceful, *constitutional* remedy." After the "Counter-Proclamation," however, Ritchie considered Hayne's description of the federal compact to be more accurate than what President Jackson described. Still, he disagreed with how Hayne and nullifiers invoked Virginia's Third resolution of 1798.[7]

The Third resolution, as understood by Ritchie, referred to a revolutionary right should the federal government overreach its powers in a deliberate, palpable and dangerous fashion. Ritchie asserted that Hayne and nullifiers had misapplied Virginia's resolutions – which "merely *declare* the laws [the Alien and Sedition Acts] unconstitutional" but which "took *no measures* to arrest their execution in Virginia." Virginia's legislature had only appealed to public opinion and sought interstate cooperation that might involve elections, constitutional amendments, or even a constitutional convention with no intent of using force or resistance. Virginia's action in 1798 provided no precedent for nullification. For Ritchie, the Virginia and Kentucky Resolutions – and not South Carolina's nullification – embodied the "conservative principle of peaceable and constitutional State Interposition." Thus, for Ritchie a crucial difference existed between nullifiers and those who support "State Rights principles generally," but not "the particular *remedy* of Nullification."[8]

Others who supported states' rights but denied nullification also stressed the importance of traditional interposition. The editor of the *Southern Patriot* noted that the resolutions of New England legislatures condemning the Virginia and Kentucky Resolutions illustrated how people failed to understand the difference between a legislative declaration of unconstitutionality and "a Judicial Decision that Acts of Congress are unconstitutional." In thinking a declaration of unconstitutionality was "a right reserved . . . to the Supreme Court *exclusively*," New England legislators missed the fact that Virginia's interposition was a legislative declaration that did not interfere with "the functions and duties of the Supreme Court."[9]

Virginia Senator William C. Rives echoed Ritchie's characterization of Madison's Third resolution as an expression of the natural law right of revolution. Rives joined Ritchie in rejecting Webster's view of the Constitution and asserted that ratification occurred through the collective action of "the States" as the people of those states in their highest sovereign capacity. As such, the constitutional compact could not be altered or annulled by individual states. Rives thought nullifiers missed the connection between Virginia's Third and Seventh resolutions. Reading them together established that Virginia's legislature had only "*protested*" against laws deemed to be "palpable and alarming infractions" of the Constitution and asked other states for similar declarations to facilitate the "revision and repeal" of those laws.[10]

The Struggle over Terminology

Nullifiers continued to argue that nullification and interposition were identical and indispensable for preserving a federal government wherein states retained their sovereignty. Nullifiers touted interposition as "the great paramount conservative right" without which all other state rights were rendered precarious. For them, the nationalism of Jackson's Proclamation presented a stark choice. Either nullification or "Jackson's doctrine of Consolidation is true." Nullifiers denied any "middle ground" between their position and the view that the Constitution created a consolidated government.[11]

States' rights opponents of nullification were not unmindful of the danger of governmental consolidation. Thomas Ritchie thought the nullification crisis had stoked the desire of the national government to acquire additional powers. The tone of Jackson's Proclamation contributed to that trend by undercutting "the true doctrine of *State Rights*." Ritchie considered nullification unjustified even if the national government took the extreme step of emancipating the enslaved. Ritchie thought that such action – if left uncorrected – might lead a state to secede, but it still would not justify nullification.[12]

Reframing Jackson's Proclamation

In late September 1833, states' rights advocates such as Ritchie and Rives felt vindicated when the *Washington Globe* published a supposedly "authorized exposition" of Jackson's Proclamation. That exposition tried to dispel concerns that the Proclamation implied that the federal compact emerged from the people in the aggregate, and not from the states. The *Globe* reminded its readers that President Jackson had described the Constitution as a compact created as "the off-spring of the people of the several states, acting through their respective legislatures." That formulation refuted the idea that the Constitution was the work of one undifferentiated American people. Nothing in the proclamation, the *Globe* insisted, was intended to endorse "consolidating principles." The *Globe* pointed out that rejecting nullification still left the possibility of constitutional amendments. Moreover, in the Proclamation, President Jackson supposedly accepted the proposition that if the federal government exercised powers not granted it by the Constitution, state governments had "the right to interpose to arrest the evil" as explained in the Virginia Resolutions. Finally, "the people of the several states" were always entitled to invoke the natural law right of revolution.[13]

The Threat of Abolitionism

A vast gulf remained between nullifiers and their opponents. When Georgia's Governor William Schley addressed the legislature in November 1835, he thought there were "no remedies *known to the Constitution*" except to change "opinion" or "representatives" through "remonstrance and the ballot-box." The present danger that demanded the cooperation of "every Southern Patriot" did not come from the national government, but from abolitionists who formed "a sect of crazed enthusiasts" seeking "insurrection" and "massacre, under the banners of philanthropy."[14]

Abolitionists presented the biggest threat to slavery because their objections rested on moral grounds. Unlike Americans who questioned the scope of the Constitution's protection of slavery, many abolitionists opposed slavery as a violation of God's law. In their view, the legal and constitutional rights that enslavers claimed protected their 'property' were irrelevant since slavery was an abomination and incompatible with the doctrine of 'higher law.' As stated in a plank of the abolitionist Liberty Party's platform, because slavery conflicted with the laws of God and natural right, the Fugitive Slave Clause was "utterly null and void" and formed "no part of the Constitution." Abolitionists embracing a higher law doctrine occupied an extreme end of the spectrum of opposition faced by defenders of slavery. One example was the abolitionist William Lloyd Garrison who described the Constitution as a "covenant with death" and an "agreement with hell" because it protected slavery. He willingly accepted disunion as the price for slavery's abolition.[15]

The Struggle to Implement the Fugitive Slave Clause

The Fugitive Slave Clause in Article IV, section 2 of the Constitution granted enslavers the right to recover enslaved persons that fled to another state. But in passively phrasing the right of enslavers to have their 'property' "delivered up," the Constitution was unclear about whether the return of fugitive slaves was the responsibility of state or federal authorities. Congress' attempt to implement that ambiguous clause through two acts, one enacted in 1793 and the other in 1850, precipitated an intense and protracted legal struggle over slavery before the Civil War.[16]

When Congress passed the Fugitive Slave Act of 1793 it perpetuated the ambiguity of the clause by not establishing a national procedure for the recovery of runaway enslaved persons. Instead, the act empowered enslavers or their agents to seize or arrest fugitive enslaved persons within the states to which they had fled. The captors were authorized to bring such enslaved persons before a federal judge of that state or any local magistrate where the seizure was made. Those officials could then issue a certificate authorizing the removal of those captured persons from the state. From the perspective of free states trying to protect their freed citizens and others within their jurisdiction from potential abuse and kidnapping by slave captors, the act of 1793 was problematic.[17]

The result was that free states began passing personal liberty laws. By 1820 seven Northern states (Vermont, New York, New Jersey, Maine, Massachusetts, Pennsylvania, and Ohio) had enacted laws to protect free Blacks from being returned to slavery under the 1793 act by establishing procedures governing their recovery. By the end of that decade, both Pennsylvania and New York statutorily withdrew state assistance in enforcing the 1793 act. The liberty laws could be depicted as minimal compliance with the federal act requiring the return of fugitive slaves, while also protecting the personal liberty of people within the state. From the perspective of the Northern states, their legislative efforts were less a challenge to the constitutionality of the 1793 act than a statement that the national government could not "override traditional state police powers that protected the liberty of their citizens." While not fitting the pattern of traditional interposition, personal liberty laws resisted a federal law that compromised the ability of the states to provide due process for their citizens.[18]

The practical effect of personal liberty laws made reclaiming fugitive slaves more difficult and expensive while at the same time subjecting slave catchers to legal penalties for violating state laws. From the perspective of slave states, those early personal liberty laws were designed by Northern state legislatures to evade the constitutional obligations of the Fugitive Slave Clause and amounted to a nullification of congressional legislation seeking to enforce that clause. Many scholars have reached the same conclusion. From the perspective of Southerners, such legislation was as despicable as when abolitionists took matters in their own hands and interfered with efforts to recover fugitives. While Southerners considered personal liberty laws acts of nullification, they might more accurately be described as a form of "uncooperative federalism," acts of civil disobedience in which states refused to comply with the federal fugitive slave laws and otherwise obstructed them.[19]

Prigg v. Pennsylvania *(1842)*

Before the passage of the Fugitive Slave Act of 1850, the Supreme Court in *Prigg v. Pennsylvania* (1842) considered the issue of slave recovery under the Fugitive Slave Clause and the 1793 act. The case pitted enslavers against those supporting personal liberty laws. As Robert Baker has put it, "Slaveholders claimed a constitutional right to the return of their property without delay, and abolitionists demanded that black people ensnared by the law had a right to have their liberty determined in a court of law." Specifically, the *Prigg* case involved Pennsylvania's 1826 personal liberty law designed to prevent the kidnapping of free Blacks. Justice Joseph Story, in his majority opinion for the Court, struck down the state law on the grounds that it violated both the Fugitive Slave Clause and the 1793 act by intruding on what he asserted was the federal government's exclusive jurisdiction over fugitive slaves.[20]

For Story, the Fugitive Slave Clause was a "fundamental article" of the Constitution without which the Union "could not have been formed." It guaranteed the "unqualified right" of enslavers to recapture enslaved persons in any state – without interference or restraint – absent a breach of the peace. As such, Pennsylvania's law was unconstitutional and void because it punished the "act of seizing and removing a slave by his master, which the Constitution of the United States was designed to justify and uphold." Since the clause conferred congressional authority, the 1793 act was "clearly constitutional in all its leading provisions."[21]

Story's construction of national power over fugitive slaves received a warm reception from Southern slave states that had traditionally favored a strict construction of the Constitution. The irony that Southern states were now lobbying for national authority while Northern states were asserting state sovereignty was not lost on contemporaries or later scholars. But if Story's opinion in *Prigg* strengthened federal power at the expense of the states on the issue of fugitive enslaved persons, it was not a complete victory for pro-slavery forces. Despite Story's nationalism, he acknowledged authority reserved to the states on the subject of fugitive slaves consistent with his view of federalism. Story hinted that one section of the 1793 act – although not one of its "leading provisions" – was constitutionally doubtful in authorizing state magistrates to administer the act. Whether or not state magistrates were bound to act under the 1793 law, Story noted that "state magistrates may, if they choose, exercise the authority, unless prohibited by state legislation." Story thus suggested that states retained the right to opt out and bar state and local officials from participating in the process of recovering fugitive enslaved persons.[22]

Some Northerners focused on the pro-slave aspects of Story's opinion, including William Lloyd Garrison who called for the decision "to be spit upon" and "trampled in the dust." But if *Prigg* infuriated abolitionists, some Southerners were troubled by the decision's implications. Among them was Chief Justice Roger B. Taney who had assigned the opinion to Story. Taney was worried about Story's five-word caveat: "unless prohibited by state legislation." Taney thought the 1793 act "scarcely deserves the name of a remedy" if enslavers had to rely on the relatively few federal judges for its enforcement and if state authorities were "absolved from all obligation to protect this right, and may stand by and see it violated without an effort to defend it." Story reached the same conclusion about the deficiencies in federal enforcement. After his opinion, Story drafted a bill that he shared with Senator John M. Berrien of Georgia. The bill created a cadre of U.S. Commissioners to be appointed by federal judges authorized to exercise all the powers that "any State judge, Magistrate, or Justice of the Peace may exercise under any other Law or Laws of the United States." Story's idea for commissioners would later be incorporated in the 1850 Fugitive Slave Act.[23]

Resistance to Prigg

Northern state legislatures with personal liberty laws similar to those struck down in *Prigg* also noticed the "clue" provided in Story's opinion that might partially "heal" the "wound" inflicted by the case. One year after *Prigg*, legislators in Massachusetts acknowledged the

Court's insistence on the right of the federal government to execute the 1793 act, but noted the opinion "leaves the States perfectly free to refuse the cooperation of their magistracy, whenever they shall think it right to do so." As Andrew Delbanco has put it, Massachusetts' legislature promptly "walked through the door that Justice Story had opened." It did so by passing a law – subsequently copied by other Northern legislatures – prohibiting state officials from detaining anyone charged under the 1793 act and using any state facility for that purpose. State legislatures in the North thus anticipated the non-commandeering principle – prohibiting the federal government from requiring state officials to enforce federal law – that the Supreme Court would embrace more than a century and a half later.[24]

Ultimately *Prigg* stimulated a new wave of personal liberty laws. Opponents of slavery described that legislation as Northern states observing the "narrowest limits which will satisfy the Constitution." Southerners, however, considered those laws nullification pure and simple. After Pennsylvania passed a law copying the one in Massachusetts, a Southerner called it "the most deliberate & perfidious violation of all the guarantees of the Constitution ... & the most serious & dangerous attack yet made on the institution of slavery."[25]

By 1849, complaints about "Northern Nullification" culminated in an "Address of Southern Delegates in Congress, to their Constituents." The address, drafted by John Calhoun, identified hostile acts intended to nullify the Fugitive Slave Clause. Those acts rendered the clause "practically expunged" from the Constitution. Calhoun summarized the frustration of the Southern slave states at the lack of enforcement of the Fugitive Slave Act of 1793 which faced northern "resistance in every form." Southern politicians had long threatened disunion in response to attacks against slavery. Heightened grievances over the enforcement of the Fugitive Slave Clause coupled with resolutions from some states, like Vermont, that Congress had the authority to abolish slavery intensified the situation. The result was the sectional Compromise of 1850.[26]

Fugitive Slave Act of 1850

The political compromise over slavery in 1850 admitted California as a free state and created the territories of New Mexico and Utah in which the status of slavery remained uncertain. The political maneuvering included passage of the Fugitive Slave Act of 1850 that fully capitulated to enslavers' grievances about ineffective enforcement under the 1793 act. During debate, a chief architect of the compromise, Henry Clay of Kentucky, described the unconstitutional "obstructions and impediments" that had been "thrown in the way of the recovery of fugitive slaves." Soon thereafter Justice Robert C. Grier of the Supreme Court privately confided to James Buchanan that the Court was inclined to consider personal liberty laws withdrawing state participation from enforcement of the fugitive slave legislation as "entirely unconstitutional, null and void."[27]

The act of 1850 greatly expanded federal power over the return of fugitive enslaved persons in the free states. It created a system of federal commissioners with authority to appoint assistants to administer the law. The act not only precluded free states from burdening the efforts at recovering fugitive enslaved persons by providing procedural protections such as trial by jury and the writ of habeas corpus, but brought ordinary citizens into the process. Commissioners and their appointees were authorized to summon bystanders as a *posse comitatus* to enforce the return of fugitive enslaved persons. Every citizen had "to aid and assist in the prompt and efficient execution" of the law "whenever their services may be required." This measure, making everyone complicit in the sordid business of slave catching, proved particularly offensive. Northerners, who might have been tacitly willing to tolerate slavery for the sake of the Union, were now subject to direct and personal involvement in maintaining human bondage. The act also made federal officials liable for their failure to facilitate the recovery of fugitive enslaved persons and sought to deter slave rescues by imposing greater penalties on would-be rescuers.[28]

Some free state politicians, like Daniel Webster, chose appeasement of slavery in order to preserve the Union. For Webster that objective was more important than the liberty of free Blacks victimized by slave catchers. Webster declared the South "right" and the North "wrong" on the question of fugitive enslaved persons. He thought state legislators violated their oath to uphold the Constitution by finding "excuses" to avoid their obligation to "deliver up fugitives from service." Those hoping the 1850 act would "quiet the explosive slavery issue" and "remove it from the realm of political discussion" were soon disappointed. Within a year, the act "stirred passionate opposition and defiance."[29]

Vermont's legislature declared that the act of 1850 violated "the great principles of civil liberty" and urged every "constitutional means" to procure its repeal or modifications so as "to protect the rights of our own citizens." A Vermont law that provided suspected fugitive enslaved persons with jury trials and made the writ of habeas corpus available was widely perceived as nullification of the 1850 law, and Southerners found the willingness of the North to "burden its execution with all possible legal difficulties" most egregious.[30]

Daniel Webster tried to quell resistance to the 1850 act by touring several New York towns where hostility toward the act was particularly strong. Speaking in Syracuse in May 1851, Webster characterized attempts to frustrate the act in dire terms. As he told crowds, "If men get together and declare a law of Congress shall not be executed in any case, and assemble in numbers to prevent the execution of such a law, they are *traitors*, and are guilty of treason, and bring upon themselves the penalties of the law." After Massachusetts returned a fugitive slave to Georgia, President Millard Fillmore congratulated the state for redeeming itself from "the stain" of earlier slave rescues and "the reproach of *nullification*."[31]

Challenges to Its Constitutionality

Even as Webster and others sought to enforce the 1850 act, opponents challenged the act's constitutionality. Many abolitionists and those engaging in slave rescues considered any congressional law protecting slavery null and void. Other opponents of the 1850 act argued that Congress lacked constitutional authority over the 'local institution' of slavery and thus could not enact policies regulating the surrender of fugitive enslaved persons in the Northern states. The editor of the *Syracuse Standard* suggested that if Congress could dictate policy for the enslaved in the North, it had the ability to abolish slavery in the South. This possibility highlighted the paradox of Southern champions of states' rights advocating the vigorous use of national authority to protect slavery: if federal power could be invoked to defend slavery, it could be invoked to destroy it.[32]

In 1851, Chief Justice Lemuel Shaw of the Supreme Judicial Court of Massachusetts provided the "first full-scale judicial examination" of the 1850 act. Even as Shaw upheld the law's constitutionality, Ohio's legislators adopted resolutions calling the act "utterly unconstitutional." In August 1852 the Free-Soil Party adopted a plank in its national platform claiming the 1850 act lacked "binding force upon the American People" since it was "repugnant to the Constitution."[33]

Notwithstanding some resistance, most Northern state legislatures were willing to give the Compromise of 1850 a chance. While efforts to undercut the Fugitive Slave Act of 1850 were made in some states, including Massachusetts and Pennsylvania, they ultimately failed to pass procedural protections such as those of Vermont's 1850 act. State actions thus demonstrated an initial willingness to achieve political compromise even as they offered "important indications that many people within the state legislatures were seriously agitated by the federal law of 1850." Norman Rosenberg summarizes the legislative response soon after the 1850 act: "Most advocates of state action did not contemplate real interposition or nullification but supported personal liberty laws primarily as a symbol of northern resistance to 'aggression' by the 'slave power.'"[34]

Impact of the Kansas–Nebraska Act of 1854

The initial "forbearance" that met the 1850 law was "shattered" with the passage of the Kansas–Nebraska Act of 1854. That act allowed settlers in the territories of Kansas and Nebraska to decide whether or not to permit slavery. It thus repealed the Missouri Compromise of 1820 that had prohibited slavery above the latitude that included those territories. The Kansas–Nebraska Act, along with outrage directed at the highly publicized surrender of the enslaved fugitive Anthony Burns and his shipment from Boston to Virginia, prompted Northern legislatures to pass additional personal liberty laws. Connecticut, Vermont, and Rhode Island passed laws in 1854 while Michigan, Maine, and Massachusetts did so in 1855. After the Burns case, the abolitionist Theodore Parker called for action, "not rash, crazy action, but calm, deliberate, systematic action – organization for the defense of personal liberty and the State Rights of the North." Parker wanted laws to punish anyone invading "our soil."[35]

The reformer Carl Schurz, who later served as a Union General and a Senator from Missouri after the war, recalled the impact of the Kansas–Nebraska Act. Its passage drove opponents of slavery to "seek refuge in the extreme States' rights doctrine" that was "first elaborately formulated" in the Virginia and Kentucky Resolutions. The North became, in Schurz's words, "the 'nullifying' section of the country." Not only was the Fugitive Slave Act of 1850 declared unconstitutional and void in mass meetings in the North, but the personal liberty laws passed by Northern legislatures prevented the act's implementation.[36]

Opposition to the Fugitive Slave Act of 1850 and increasing alarm over attacks on slavery prompted Southerners to call for another type of interposition without specifying what form that intervention might take. The *Richmond Enquirer* noted that Virginia's constitutional convention of 1850 debated interposition designed to combat "the mad schemes of the abolitionists of the North." As late as December 1860, a would-be delegate to Georgia's Democratic Convention identified "State interposition" as the South's "remedy" for the "abuses and usurpations" of Northern states "rabid with 'liberty laws.'"[37]

Even as Southerners considered ways to combat abolitionism, some Northerners worried that the fragile political compromise over slavery might fall apart if the North caught "the infection of Nullification." The *National Intelligencer*'s editor wanted strict enforcement of the 1850 act and warned against interposition "to the Federal laws ... in *any* part of the Union." Advocates of personal liberty laws described them as a form of interposition justified by a legitimate opposition to Southern slave power. Increasingly, Northerners came to believe that their own liberty and economic well-being required resistance to slavery's influence and opposition to federal laws that supported slavery.[38]

Wisconsin's Challenge to the Fugitive Slave Act of 1850

Resistance to the Fugitive Slave Act of 1850 rekindled controversy over interposition, nullification and the right of states to question the constitutionality of acts of the national government. A dramatic occasion for that debate arose in *In Re Booth* (1854), leading to a decision by the Wisconsin Supreme Court declaring the 1850 act unconstitutional.[39]

The *Booth* case involved the rescue of Joshua Glover, an enslaved fugitive from Missouri who sought asylum in Wisconsin in 1852. Glover's enslaver learned of Glover's whereabouts in 1854 and attempted a recovery under the 1850 act. After Glover was arrested and placed in federal custody in a Milwaukee jail, a large crowd encouraged by the abolitionist and newspaper editor Sherman Booth broke in and rescued Glover. Although not personally participating in the rescue, Booth supported it through handbills and speeches. Booth was arrested, tried, and convicted of aiding and abetting the release of a fugitive slave under the 1850 act. Booth's lawyer, Byron Paine, sought a writ of habeas corpus from Abram Smith, justice of the Wisconsin Supreme Court and a known abolitionist.[40]

Paine argued that Congress lacked authority to legislate on the subject of fugitive enslaved persons. Even assuming Congress had such power, the 1850 act was unconstitutional because any person claimed as a fugitive was presumed to be enslaved without the benefit of a trial by jury. The key issue, according to Paine, was whether a state Supreme Court was as entitled as the U.S. Supreme Court to decide whether the national government had acted unconstitutionally. In taking that position, Paine cited Virginia's Court of Appeals 1814 holding in *Hunter v. Martin, Devisee of Fairfax*. Moreover, he quoted Madison's reference to interposition in the Third Virginia resolution as well as Jefferson's assertion in the First Kentucky resolution of 1798 that states as parties to the compact had a right to judge the existence of infractions of the Constitution. Paine believed that the Virginia and Kentucky Resolutions established the Constitution as a compact between states as "independent sovereignties." Knowing that John Marshall and the Supreme Court had repudiated the views of the Virginia judges, Paine conceded that his argument was unlikely to find favor with the federal courts.[41]

After oral argument, Wisconsin's Justice Smith discharged Booth because the warrant issued by the commissioner of the U.S. District Court pursuant to the Fugitive Slave Act of 1850 lacked due process. Consequently, the warrant was "clearly, substantially and radically insufficient." Smith proceeded to examine the 1850 act's constitutionality because the Constitution made it "the sworn duty of every State officer" to support "every power constitutionally exercised by the Federal Government." Implicitly, that oath also made it the duty of state officers "to interpose a resistance ... to every assumption of power on the part of the General Government, which is not expressly granted or necessarily implied in the Federal Constitution." Smith rejected the idea that the Supreme Court was the final arbiter of the equilibrium of federalism.[42]

Justice Smith believed that by failing to provide due process including a jury trial in the 1850 act, Congress had exceeded its powers. As such, he declared the act unconstitutional and void. Smith found that the Supreme Court's decision in *Prigg* offered no "authoritative judicial guide" with respect to the 1850 act. Indeed, fundamental questions related to the 1850 act had been disputed for years and the issues sought to be settled in *Prigg* remained "fruitful subjects of bitter discussion, and discordant action." Therefore, Smith felt justified in asking the Supreme Court to review its decision in *Prigg*.[43]

The Review by Wisconsin's Supreme Court

Five weeks after Justice Smith discharged Booth, the three-member Wisconsin Supreme Court (including Justice Smith) upheld Smith's decision and opinion in a 2-to-1 ruling. Chief Justice Edward Whiton began the majority opinion by finding Smith's issuance of the writ of habeas corpus proper. Whiton then turned to the constitutionality of the act of 1850. Unlike Smith, Whiton did not claim that the state Supreme Court had a right to render a competing judgment on the constitutionality of the act of 1850. Whiton acknowledged that the U.S. Supreme Court had the ultimate power to decide any alleged violation of the Constitution by an act of Congress. However, Whiton asserted that the constitutionality of the 1850 act was an open question because the issue of whether due process was violated if federal commissioners could surrender alleged fugitive enslaved persons without a Court appearance or jury trial was not addressed in *Prigg*. Wisconsin's high court thus had a duty to consider if Congress exceeded its constitutional powers by authorizing commissioners to act in such a manner. Whiton concluded that granting federal commissioners judicial powers allowing them to deny alleged fugitives a jury trial under the act of 1850 was "repugnant to the constitution" and "void."[44]

Justice Samuel Crawford dissented, believing that Justice Smith lacked jurisdiction to issue the writ of habeas corpus because the case was before a federal commissioner. He then turned to the constitutionality of the act of 1850. Unlike Whiton, Crawford thought *Prigg* established the act's constitutionality. Moreover, since the U.S. Supreme Court was the final arbiter on constitutional questions, Justice Smith's request that the Court revisit its decision in *Prigg* was "neither becoming nor proper." While upholding the constitutionality of the 1850 act, Crawford agreed that Booth's release was proper, and his detention unlawful, because he had not been charged with interfering with the return of a fugitive slave.[45]

Justice Smith's concurring opinion sought to vindicate his behavior as a judge subordinate to the U.S. Supreme Court. Smith thought Story's assertion of congressional authority demonstrated a "zeal for federal supremacy" that altered the intended equilibrium of federalism. While the U.S. Attorney for Wisconsin characterized *Booth* as "practical nullification" of the act of 1850, Smith thought that questioning the precedential value of *Prigg* was a legitimate state judicial interposition to maintain the proper balance of federalism. He described his stance as a "medium ground" between submitting to unconstitutional rulings by the Supreme Court and resorting to the right of revolution.[46]

Smith agreed that decisions of the U.S. Supreme Court within the scope of their jurisdiction were binding. However, he rejected the need to accept the Court's constitutional reasoning "without thought or inquiry." Smith described a collaborative tension in monitoring the equilibrium of federalism that implicitly included sounding the alarm interposition by state court opinions. Ideally, each level of government would operate to check the other and occasional conflicts would "sharpen investigation, whet official conscience, and thus lead to a correct understanding of the true boundary of jurisdiction." While Smith's ideas might seem unrealistic, his views were similar to a process that James Madison had described after *Cohens v. Virginia* (1821). Based on his view of divided sovereignty and federalism, Smith concluded that the act of 1850 was unconstitutional.[47]

The Burns *case and Further Congressional Debates*

Even as the Wisconsin courts considered the *Booth* case, other events prompted further agitation over the Fugitive Slave Act of 1850. On May 26 – the same day that a writ of habeas corpus was sought for Sherman Booth – a crowd of abolitionists stormed a Boston jail and unsuccessfully tried to rescue a Virginia fugitive slave. The case of Anthony Burns became a *cause célèbre* for resistance against the 1850 act. Thousands of Bostonians lined the streets to watch Burns being marched under military guard to a ship in the city's harbor. He was being returned to Virginia after a trial under the act ended with a remand to his so-called owner. The case mobilized renewed opposition to the act far beyond Boston and Massachusetts. At about the same time, on May 30, 1854, Congress passed the Kansas–Nebraska Act. By permitting inhabitants within those territories to decide whether or not to permit slavery, the 1854 act undid the Missouri Compromise of 1820, the effort to accommodate both defenders and opponents of slavery.[48]

The aftermath of these events stimulated a further wave of personal liberty laws. The laws passed between 1854 and 1858 formed an "interposition," according to Thomas Morris, in the sense of state legislators intervening by offering procedural justice to citizens of their state who might be subject to the Fugitive Slave Act of 1850. Six New England states along with Michigan and Wisconsin all passed such statutes, some of which provided for the writ of habeas corpus and a jury trial. The legislation infuriated Southerners, who accused Northern states of repudiating their constitutional obligations, and prompted the introduction of a bill in the Senate seeking to facilitate the enforcement of the 1850 act.[49]

In February 1855 the Senate debated a bill permitting the removal to federal court of any lawsuit brought in state courts against anyone engaged in enforcing federal law. While neutral on its face, the bill was designed to prevent state courts from failing to enforce the Fugitive Slave Act. Senator Benjamin Wade of Ohio, a Radical Republican, denounced the bill as "an attempt to trample upon the rights of the States and deprive them of the power to protect her own citizens from aggression and abuse." He chided Southern senators with "State rights constantly on their tongues" who were "now ready, prompt and eager, to beat down the rights of the States, and make them bow their sovereign heads to this miserable enactment."[50]

In response, Southern senators, including Judah P. Benjamin of Louisiana, castigated Northern courts for declaring the Fugitive Slave Act of 1850 unconstitutional and "maintaining the right in the States to nullify that legislation by State jurisprudence." Benjamin found it ironic that now Northern Senators were saying "that State tribunals were vested with jurisdiction, in the last resort, to determine upon the constitutionality of laws enacted by the Congress of the United States."[51]

During the debate, Senator Wade had asked whether "The General Government, or the States in their sovereignty" was the final arbiter of constitutionality. For Wade, the Virginia and Kentucky Resolutions stood for the proposition that if a state believed the federal government had constitutionally overreached its powers "a State must not only be the judge of that, but of the remedy in such a case" – a position that drew on language in Jefferson's First Kentucky resolution. Wade offered what he called "the true interpretation" of the 1798 Virginia Resolutions and, especially, Madison's Third resolution, under which "a State in the last resort, crowded to the wall by the General Government seeking by the strong arm of its power to take away the rights of the State, is to judge of whether she shall stand on her reserved rights."[52]

Democratic Senator John Pettit of Indiana accused Wade of claiming that the states of the Union are "absolute, unconditional, unrestricted, unlimited sovereignties." Instead, Pettit asserted that states are "sovereign only in things reserved to them" while the national government was "sovereign in things that are delegated to it." Even opponents of the enforcement bill, like Republican Senator William Seward of New York, described the Constitution as creating a system of divided sovereignty. Under the "Federal Union" the states "remain equal and qualified sovereignties" and at the same time they "constitute, in the aggregate, another qualified sovereignty." Such labored iterations of federalism and Wade's strained efforts to square his position with the Virginia and Kentucky Resolutions underscored what Democratic Senator Stephen Douglas of Illinois called "our complex system of government."[53]

After more than twelve hours of debate, the Senate passed the bill by a vote of 29 to 9 after a motion to repeal the Fugitive Slave Act of 1850 was defeated by the same margin. The Senate was willing to enhance enforcement of the 1850 act despite Northern state opposition[54]

Taney's Opinion in Ableman v. Booth (1859)

After the Wisconsin Supreme Court decisions dealing with Booth and the constitutionality of the Fugitive Slave Act, the U.S. Attorney General petitioned the Supreme Court for review in 1856, and the Court issued a writ of error to the state Supreme Court. Wisconsin's Supreme Court, however, never responded to the writ, and refused to send the case record to the U.S. Supreme Court. The case was nonetheless docketed and argued without the presence of counsel for Wisconsin. In 1859 the Supreme Court issued its opinion in *Ableman v. Booth*, overturning the *Booth* case and emphatically endorsing the Fugitive Slave Act.[55]

Writing for the majority, Chief Justice Taney accused the Wisconsin state court of having wrongfully assumed habeas jurisdiction over a federal prisoner and "determined that their decision is final and conclusive upon all the courts of the United States." Taney's characterization of the *Booth* decisions merged two separate issues: jurisdiction of a state court to grant a writ of habeas corpus to a federal prisoner and whether the U.S. Supreme Court alone could rule on the constitutionality of acts of Congress or if they shared that function with state supreme courts.[56]

Ableman was the first U.S. Supreme Court decision to hold that federal prisoners were *not* eligible for release on habeas corpus writs issued by state tribunals, representing "a major step in the consolidation of national government power." Taney saw the jurisdiction exercised by Smith as patently over "the line of division" traceable "by landmarks and monuments visible to the eye." For Taney, the Supremacy Clause was dispositive. By issuing writs of habeas corpus to federal prisoners, state courts clearly intruded into the sovereign "sphere of action" of the national government.[57]

Taney thought it well established that the Supreme Court alone was the final arbiter over the demarcation of power between the state and national governments. Lack of uniformity in all states would undermine the supremacy of the Constitution and the laws enacted thereunder. Taney asserted that the framers established the Supreme Court to render final and conclusive decisions in order to avoid serious controversies between state and federal authorities from being settled "by force of arms." Accepting the Supreme Court as the common arbiter of controversies over the federal–state boundary did not necessarily mean that monitoring federalism was exclusively the job of that Court even if Taney's opinion implied as much and suggested that resolving constitutional controversies was solely a matter of judicial decision-making. That conclusion ignored the long history of scrutiny and involvement by many other parties, including state legislators and judges as well as the people themselves. Moreover, Taney's view also buried from sight sounding the alarm interposition.[58]

Taney's understanding of the constitutional requirement that state officials take an oath to support the federal Constitution illustrated his belief that issues of contested federalism were the Supreme Court's business. For Taney the question of whether the national government was overreaching its authority remained the job of the federal judiciary and did not involve state judges or others. Therefore, Taney argued that the oath to support the Constitution was intended "to guard against resistance to or invasion of" the national government's authority "on the part of a State." For others, however, the oath to support the Constitution *also* meant the duty of state officials to monitor the equilibrium of federalism and weigh in on perceived overreaching by the federal government.[59]

According to Taney, the Wisconsin Supreme Court's judgment would "subvert" American government, which was why the Court provided an extensive examination of the Wisconsin cases. But it bears noting what Wisconsin's Supreme Court did and did not do. It did assert the state court habeas jurisdiction over federal prisoners – jurisdiction that *Ableman* denied. But Chief Justice Whiton and Justice Crawford also rejected Justice Smith's position that the Wisconsin Supreme Court could render competing judgments on the constitutionality of the Fugitive Slave Act. After *Ableman* and Taney's opinion upholding the 1850 act, Wisconsin's Supreme Court would, by Whiton's and Crawford's admission, be bound by that decision. As such, Whiton's opinion seemed unlikely to shake the "foundations" of the federal government.[60]

Wisconsin's Response to Ableman

In the end, a greater challenge to the national government came from Wisconsin's legislature than from its judiciary. Within two weeks of the *Ableman* decision, Wisconsin's state legislature passed a joint resolution rejecting the Supreme Court's authority to reverse the state court's grant of the writ of habeas corpus to Sherman Booth. According to the legislators, *Ableman* undermined the Constitution's guarantee of "the great writ of liberty" and thus was "without authority, void, and of no force." The legislature relied on the compact theory articulated in Kentucky's First resolution of 1798 and quoted from that state's resolution of 1799 asserting that states had "the unquestionable right to judge" infractions of the Constitution. Sensitive to the repudiated language of the 1799 resolution, the legislators altered their wording to read that a *"positive defiance"* instead of 'a nullification' by those sovereignties was the remedy for all unauthorized acts attempted under the Constitution. In that form the resolutions became known as Wisconsin's "Resolves of '59."[61]

After *Ableman*, Wisconsin citizens also weighed in on the constitutionality of the Fugitive Slave Act when they elected a new member of the state's Supreme Court in 1859. That election became a referendum on the state Supreme Court's decision in *Booth*. The vacancy arose when Justice Smith, who had granted Booth's writ of habeas corpus five years earlier, withdrew as a candidate. Republicans nominated Byron Paine, Booth's lawyer, to fill Smith's seat.[62]

One of Paine's staunchest advocates was the future Union General Carl Schurz, who delivered a speech in Milwaukee on March 23, 1859 entitled "State Rights and Byron Paine" that received wide distribution among Republicans throughout the country. In linking Paine with states' rights, Schurz was not endorsing nullification, but reaffirming what he considered the principal point of the Virginia and Kentucky Resolutions: the need for states to express their views about the extent of the national government's delegated powers. Schurz denied that the Supreme Court's appellate jurisdiction gave the Court exclusive and final authority "to decide what powers the States have delegated and what powers they have reserved" and claimed the doctrine of states' rights meant states possessed "concurrent jurisdiction" to decide whether "that narrow line which divides the delegated powers of the general government from the powers reserved to the States" had been "overstepped by one party or the other."[63]

Schurz recognized that "co-ordinate powers and concurrent jurisdictions" entailed "collisions and conflicts." Nonetheless, by not submissively forfeiting states' rights, those conflicts would be settled by a tribunal higher than the Supreme Court, namely, "the tribunal of public opinion." Schurz claimed that this was how earlier conflicts – including the one over the Alien and Sedition Acts – had been resolved. In touting Paine's adherence to states' rights, Schurz helped him win the election, but the Civil War changed Schurz's mind. When he published his speeches in 1865, Schurz omitted the Milwaukee address because a "more matured judgment" convinced him that his earlier views were mistaken.[64]

Republicans Flirt with Nullification

Well before the Civil War, Americans devoted much thought to nullification and the elusive legacy of the Virginia and Kentucky Resolutions. Despite Taney's assertion of federal supremacy and the constitutionality of the Fugitive Slave Act of 1850, abolitionists and some radical Republicans persisted in trying to nullify the 1850 act through even more wide-ranging personal liberty laws. As one Ohio judge wrote to Ohio's Governor Salmon P. Chase in 1859, "we have got to come to Calhoun's ground." Several explicit efforts to nullify the Fugitive Slave Act failed in New Hampshire and New York in 1859 and in Massachusetts in 1860. Those efforts were accompanied by invocations of the authority of the Virginia and Kentucky Resolutions and the contention that the Constitution was a compact among sovereign states.[65]

Moderate Republicans recoiled at that approach since, as one put it, "Almost the whole country has declared *nullification* to be an unconstitutional remedy." According to the *Daily National Intelligencer*, the resolutions of 1798 were "the traditional heirloom of the Virginia Democracy" only now "somewhat the worse for wear" and furnishing "an indifferent disguise by which to hide the deformity of *nullification*." If "Virginia precedents are now so highly in vogue north of the Potomac," the newspaper reminded its readers that Virginia's legislature in 1810 had declared the Supreme Court the only legitimate umpire to settle constitutional controversies. The *Intelligencer* also reported that attendees at a large "State rights meeting" in Cleveland had passed resolutions calling for the invalidation of the Fugitive Slave Act and declared their attachment to the Virginia and Kentucky Resolutions. The connection the newspaper made between the resolutions of 1798 and nullification continued a familiar pattern. Very few voices questioned that assumption and called for a more careful reading of those resolutions.[66]

On the Eve of Secession

Slavery dominated the 1860 presidential election and that issue produced a four-way contest. The Republican Party with Lincoln as its candidate promised not to interfere with slavery in the states, but opposed its further extension into the territories. The Republican platform rejected the so-called "new dogma" that the Constitution "of its own force, carries slavery into any or all of the territories." Southerners therefore perceived Lincoln's candidacy and the Republican Party to be hostile to slavery and associated with abolitionism.[67]

The Democratic Party selected Stephen A. Douglas of Illinois as their candidate. Their national platform described personal liberty laws as "subversive of the Constitution, and revolutionary" and the party endorsed the Supreme Court's 1857 decision in *Dred Scott* that had declared the Missouri Compromise's prohibition of slavery in the territories unconstitutional. Nonetheless, Douglas' advocacy of so-called 'popular sovereignty' – under which each individual territory could itself determine the status of slavery – alienated many Southern Democrats. Indeed, Southern Democrats split off and held their own convention where they nominated the current Vice President, John C. Breckinridge of Kentucky, as their candidate. The platform of the Breckinridge Democrats also denounced personal liberty laws and declared the right of citizens to settle "with their property" in any territory without molestation.[68]

Finally, in May of 1860, a fourth party emerged that claimed to solve the sectional crisis. The Constitutional Union party nominated John Bell of Tennessee and vowed "to *recognize* no political principle other than THE CONSTITUTION OF THE COUNTRY, THE UNION OF THE STATES, AND THE ENFORCEMENT OF THE LAWS." Responding to the polarizing nature of slavery, the unrealistic approach of the Constitutional Unionists was simply to ignore the issue.[69]

The 1860 election developed two different campaigns, with Lincoln and Douglas vying for support in the North and Breckinridge and Bell competing in the South. The election on November 6, 1860 gave Lincoln a plurality of the popular vote and a majority of the electoral vote but with minimal support from the South. Between them Breckinridge and Bell garnered some 30 percent of the popular vote.[70]

On December 3, 1860, three weeks before South Carolina seceded, President James Buchanan delivered his Fourth Annual Message seeking to quiet the political waters in a speech that satisfied neither Northerners nor Southerners. He identified Southern "sovereign States" as bearing the sole responsibility for slavery "existing among them" free from interference by "the people of the North." However, he rejected secession as "a constitutional remedy" and insisted on the "perpetual" nature of the Union. At the same time, he condemned Northern state efforts to defeat the Fugitive Slave Act and the region's "incessant and violent agitation of the slavery question." He considered personal liberty laws "palpable violations" of the Constitution and thus "null and void." Hopefully their repeal would avoid "revolutionary resistance" by Southern states, but should secession occur, Buchanan thought the federal government lacked authority to coerce seceding states into submission. He wanted a constitutional amendment to explicitly protect slavery in the states where it currently existed as well as in the territories. He noted that Madison had described amendments as one of the constitutional means to resolve conflicts between the two levels of government and hoped that such an amendment would avert disunion.[71]

When Buchanan delivered his Annual Message, Lincoln was president-elect. Any potential reconciliation with the South rested with the new administration's approach to the fugitive slave issue as well as with Southern perceptions of Lincoln's election. In responding to an inquiry about his political views, Lincoln claimed he knew "very little" about personal liberty laws, having "never ... read one." If they conflicted with the Constitution, he was happy to see them repealed, but thought as President he "could hardly be justified ... to recommend the repeal of a statute of Vermont, or South Carolina." Lincoln's flexibility on the fugitive slave issue was also on display five days later when he drafted resolutions for Republican members of a Senate committee. The first resolution combined two purposes that political experience had shown to be "incompatible" – calling for the effective enforcement of the Fugitive Slave Clause, without forcing private persons to participate in its enforcement, and "punishing all who resist it" while also providing procedural "safeguards to liberty" to ensure freed people would not be enslaved.[72]

During his presidential campaign Lincoln shared his moral objections about slavery while indicating a willingness to adhere to the Fugitive Slave Clause and not interfere with slavery in states where it already existed. As he said in his inaugural address, he had "no purpose, directly or indirectly, to interfere with the institution of slavery in the States where it exists" believing he had "no lawful right to do so" as well as "no inclination to do so." That statement satisfied neither abolitionists nor defenders of slavery. The problem with Lincoln's pledge was that it did not account for the desire of many Republicans to constrain slavery, and ultimately drive it out of existence. Pro-slavery Southerners were not appeased when Republicans asserted that their party had not been organized for "putting down slavery in the States, nor in any manner to interfere with it within the States" but instead to "prevent" the aggressive use of federal power "to propagate and extend the institution of human slavery." As Arthur Bestor explained, for Southerners the issue was not that Lincoln and fellow Republicans intended to abolish slavery by direct federal action. From the Southern perspective, "there was no difference between direct and indirect action" since any measure that was "deliberately designed to undermine slavery made it automatically unconstitutional, no matter how indirect the means employed."[73]

Secession

Southerners such as Senator Robert Toombs of Georgia could praise the federal government in early 1860 for having never "been truer to its obligations" or "more faithful to the Constitution, than within the last seven years" in its efforts to protect slave interests. Southerners were mainly aggrieved with the Republican Party and especially with Northern state legislatures willing to frustrate, undermine, and effectively nullify the efforts of all three branches of the federal government to uphold the Fugitive Slave Clause. A report by Virginia's legislature in 1860 captured Southern frustration by complaining that from the time of the passage of the Fugitive Slave Act in 1850 "the Legislatures of almost all the Northern States have passed acts to nullify or evade its practical execution." The report detailed the range of "enactments conceived in a spirit of hostility to the institutions of the south." The South's "enemies in the North," Senator Toombs warned, "hate the Constitution, and daily trample it under their feet." By December 1860 Toombs saw overwhelming evidence of the "open and avowed object" of Lincoln's party to abolish slavery in the states by abrogating the Fugitive Slave Clause by state laws.[74]

The impasse presented by slavery was underscored when U.S. Senator John J. Crittenden of Kentucky proposed to resolve the crisis on December 18, 1860 by entrenching slavery in the Constitution, a proposal that was met with little interest by Northern politicians. South Carolina then led the Southern response by seceding on December 20, 1860. Southern secession declarations, including South Carolina's, highlighted personal liberty laws as a principal grievance and threat to slavery.[75]

On March 21, 1861, six weeks after being elected Vice President of the Confederacy, Alexander H. Stephens praised the new Confederate government and explained that slavery was "the immediate cause" for secession. Seven years later, in the midst of Reconstruction, Stephens chose to ignore that rationale in his two-volume study entitled *A Constitutional View of the Late War Between the States* and claimed that states' rights and not slavery had been the issue underlying the Civil War. According to him the "whole subject of Slavery" was, "to the Seceding States, but a drop in the ocean" compared to other considerations. By his later account, the Civil War occurred because Southerners resisted "Federal authorities" seeking to assume "absolute Sovereign power over the whole country" and to destroy federalism by establishing a consolidated government.[76]

In writing slavery out of the Civil War, Stephens joined apologists for the institution of slavery who contributed to the myth of the 'Lost Cause'. Besides distorting the war's history, the invocation of states' rights by Stephens and others additionally obscured the importance of sounding the alarm interposition. The history and practice of interposition – contested, manipulated, and frequently misunderstood – retreated even further from view with the war.[77]

* * * * * *

The outcome of the Civil War fully delegitimized the idea that the Constitution was a compact of sovereign states. Nonetheless, there was content and meaning to states' rights and state sovereignty independent of the issue of slavery. The supposed plot to create a consolidated national government feared by some was never fully realized and the divided sovereignty that underlay the creation of the Constitution continued to present the challenge of monitoring the federalism it established in 1787 – involving questions that had long arisen outside the context of slavery and that would persist long after slavery's demise.

Undeniably, nullification, secession, and above all the Civil War tainted discussions over states' rights. Nonetheless, few were willing to deny – even after the travail of the war – that the states still retained an important measure of reserved rights and sovereignty under the Constitution, which implicitly included the use of the constitutional tool of interposition.

9

State Interposition during and after the Civil War

The Civil War marked the high point of state protests against perceived excesses of national governments – including power exercised by both the United States and the Confederacy. Relying on what Americans took to be the 'Principles of '98,' opposition to apparent overreaching by national authorities during this period reveals how ingrained state interposition had become, even as its historical origins were lost.

Sounding the alarm interposition occurred whenever Governors and state legislators believed their national government was exceeding its powers, including the highly controversial use of martial law and the suspension of the writ of habeas corpus. Moreover, Lincoln's decision to employ emancipation as a war measure was criticized in Northern as well as 'border states' (states that recognized slavery but which remained in the Union). State opposition to policies of Lincoln's administration during the war is often traced to Copperheads (Southern sympathizers in the North) or to the Peace Movement that sought to avoid armed conflict altogether. Frequently that opposition is seen as a struggle between the pro- and antiwar wings of the Democratic Party. Opposition to the measures of Jefferson Davis' administration has also been traced to the Peace Movement, lack of commitment to the Confederate cause, or political rivalries. Missing in the scholarship is an appreciation of how much of this opposition from states relied on interposition.[1]

The Civil War saw Northern Democrats invoking the 'Principles of '98' and the slogan of 'States' Rights' to justify secession and to resist the consolidation of national power they saw in Lincoln's war measures. Allegedly those measures violated a strict construction of the national government's constitutional powers and distorted the balance of federalism under which states retained powers not granted to the national government. The Virginia and Kentucky Resolutions were pressed into service to support strict construction *and* states' rights. At the same time, states' rights advocates helped fuel the argument that Lincoln had converted a war to preserve the Union into a moral crusade that threatened both the existence of states and white supremacy.[2]

The Civil War greatly enhanced the power of the national government and accelerated the 'lawyerization' of the Constitution. After the war, Democrats – both in the North and the South – continued to invoke states' rights and the 'Principles of '98.' They opposed the Thirteenth, Fourteenth, and Fifteenth Amendments, the policies of Reconstruction, racial equality, and more generally the increase in national power. The slogan 'States' Rights' came to be adopted by those who opposed conducting the Civil War and by advocates of white supremacy. But even as racism was inextricably and explicitly part of the disputes between the federal and state governments, addressing the appropriate balance of federalism remained integral to ongoing debates over American constitutionalism. Because the Reconstruction amendments shifted power to the national government, the prospect of constitutional overreaching and the need to monitor federalism became even more of a concern for states.[3]

As Democrats enshrined the Virginia and Kentucky Resolutions in their party platforms, the connection of those resolutions to the longstanding practice of sounding the alarm interposition was largely forgotten. The loss of that history, however, did not stop its practice. The postwar period saw a continued use of interposition – primarily directed at questioning the constitutionality of Reconstruction measures. In addition, both Northern and Southern legislatures occasionally sounded the alarm about perceived overreaching by the national government on issues unrelated to the war, but largely seemed unaware of their role as monitors of federalism. By the end of Reconstruction, the practice of interposition died out and lay dormant before its resurrection in the twentieth century.

* * * * * *

The Political Legacy of the Virginia and Kentucky Resolutions

Even before South Carolina seceded, the Virginia and Kentucky Resolutions had become one of the "main foundations" of the Democratic Party's "political creed." In their party platforms of 1852, 1856, and 1860, Democrats declared their allegiance to the principles in those resolutions and Madison's Report without fully understanding the events of 1798.[4]

As the country moved closer to civil war, the resolutions and in particular Madison's authority were invoked in two principal ways: to question the Supreme Court as the arbiter of constitutional controversies and to determine whether states were constitutionally entitled to secede. As with earlier efforts to justify nullification, attitudes about the role of the Court and right of secession were shaped by how one understood the Constitution's founding. Debates over the Supreme Court and secession frequently described the Constitution as either the creation of one national people or the product of sovereign and independent states – with no middle ground. Virginia's Governor John Letcher thought a constitutional amendment was required to resolve the issue of slavery because he denied the Supreme Court was the final arbiter of disputes over constitutional interpretation. Others believed that Madison had endorsed a right of individual states to judge infractions of the Constitution and construed Virginia's Third resolution to mean that individual states could "pronounce against" a decision of the Supreme Court.[5]

The Constitutionality of Secession

Lincoln's election on November 6, 1860 triggered the first wave of secession by seven Southern slave states in December 1860 and January 1861. Delegates from those states gathered at Montgomery, Alabama to frame a provisional constitution for the Confederate States of America. What they adopted largely duplicated the U.S. Constitution with a major exception being the statement in its Preamble that "*each State acting in its sovereign and independent character*" formed the new Confederate Constitution.[6]

With secession, delegates to a so-called Peace Conference assembled at Willard's Hotel in Washington on February 4, 1861 in order to avert war. Seven slave states and fourteen free states out of a total of thirty-four attended. The convention proposed a constitutional amendment similar to the failed compromise that John Crittenden had advanced the month before that neither limited the expansion of slavery into all of the territories, nor protected slavery in any territory. The proposed amendment was soundly rejected in the Senate on March 4, 1861 and never came to a vote in the House.[7]

Arguments Supporting Secession

The Confederate Constitution based its existence on a compact among sovereign states. The case for secession relied on a sovereign states' rights theory of the Constitution asserting that independent and sovereign states could secede as a matter of constitutional right, which was allegedly described in the Virginia and Kentucky Resolutions and Madison's Report.

Jefferson Davis, the provisional president of the Confederacy, expressed this idea soon after the attack on Fort Sumter. In a message to the Confederate Congress, Davis described the Constitution as "a *compact between* independent States," implicitly leaving a right of secession intact. He claimed that the Virginia and Kentucky Resolutions and Madison's Report clearly embraced "the right of each State to judge ... and redress the wrongs of which it complains." Overlooked was the fact that one could describe the Constitution as a compact without embracing a sovereign states' rights theory of its formation.[8]

Arguments Rejecting Secession

Northern newspapers anticipated that the Virginia and Kentucky Resolutions would figure prominently in secession's justification. Even before South Carolina seceded, an editorial appeared in the *Daily National Intelligencer* on "The Assumed Right of Secession." After analyzing the resolutions and Madison's Report, the editor concluded that they neither justified nullification nor secession and did not establish the Constitution as a mere league of sovereign states. The creation of "a Government of *the People*" precluded secession. However, the *Intelligencer* did recognize that the 1798 resolutions supported sounding the alarm interposition rather than nullification and were attempts by Virginia and Kentucky only to secure "a *constitutional redress of grievances*" by appealing to "the public opinion of their sister States."[9]

President James Buchanan summarized the case against the constitutionality of secession a few weeks before South Carolina seceded, noting the absence of an express clause in the Constitution supporting a right of secession. He also quoted Madison that the nation was formed by "the people in each of the States acting in their highest sovereign capacity." For Buchanan, the divided sovereignty under the Constitution created a national government in which states yielded some of the sovereign rights they possessed prior to ratification, including the right of secession. The government created by the Constitution, Buchanan concluded, was "intended to be perpetual, and not to be annulled at the pleasure of any one of the contracting parties."[10]

Others who accepted the perpetual nature of the Constitution occasionally relied on its amendment provisions. With ratification, each state "bound itself not only legally, but morally, to abide by any amendment to the constitution" supported by three-fourths of the states. If a state was aggrieved by the national government, the remedy was getting other states to support a constitutional amendment and not to overturn the Constitution through secession. Secession was unlawful without the consent of "the *whole* family of States."[11]

Harvard law professor Joel Parker addressed Jefferson Davis' claim that Madison offered support for secession. Parker insisted that the Virginia Resolutions did not identify a constitutional right of secession "as a State remedy." Parker acknowledged that if Davis was talking about the right of revolution he might be "in accordance with received principles," but claiming a constitutional right to secede was completely different. Parker noted that Virginia's Third resolution said nothing about secession and that Madison had denied that the resolutions sanctioned nullification. Virginia's legislators merely wanted other states to make similar declarations in support of a congressional repeal of the Alien and Sedition Acts.[12]

When the Civil War began, an old acquaintance of Madison's discussed secession and captured a prevailing sense of how

Northerners viewed the Union, but in terms that pushed Madison's efforts in the Virginia Resolutions even further from view. In 1861 Edward Everett delivered a Fourth of July oration in New York on the question, "Is Secession a Constitutional Right, or is it Revolution?" Everett dismissed the "imaginary right" of secession because it rested on the false "doctrine that the Union is a compact between Independent States, from which any one of them may withdraw at pleasure by virtue of its sovereignty."[13]

Everett quoted Madison's Third resolution about the right of the states to interpose and observed that the "sort of interposition intended was left in studied obscurity." Everett focused on the absence of any discussion of secession and Madison's denial of any "extra constitutional measures." For Everett, the "metaphysics" of the Virginia and Kentucky Resolutions had planted seeds in the minds of a later generation that had grown into the "deadly paradoxes of 1830 and 1860." The "monstrous absurdity" of nullification and "the still more preposterous doctrine" of secession were "kindred products of the same soil." Thus, it was time to shed "a little plain truth" on Virginia's resolutions, "the subject of so much political romance," and he argued that the resolutions of 1798 were only political slogans to support Jefferson's election.[14]

Everett's determination to deny secessionists any precedential value from the Virginia and Kentucky Resolutions left little room for sounding the alarm interposition. Implicitly, Everett advanced the idea of 'the lawyer's Constitution' that assumed monitoring the constitutional order and the equilibrium of federalism was the sole responsibility of the Supreme Court. That view of the Court's role, along with the disrepute of the resolutions because of their association with nullification and secession, made it harder to recognize the legitimacy of the traditional practice of interposition.

Denying the Right to Coerce Seceding States Back into the Union

Assuming secession was not a constitutional right, it remained to be seen how the national government could respond. Some Democrats, including outgoing President Buchanan, believed that neither the executive nor Congress possessed constitutional authority "to coerce a State" back into the Union, a position also taken by his Attorney General Jeremiah S. Black. For Buchanan, the Union rested on public opinion and could never be "cemented by the blood of its citizens shed in civil war." Congress was entitled to maintain the Union through conciliation – including a constitutional compromise over slavery. But Buchanan did not believe the Constitution placed "the sword" in the hands of Congress to preserve the Union by force. Likewise, a Southern critic of secession dismissed the idea of compelling states to remain in the Union "by violence and bloodshed," because a "conquered State, in a voluntary Union of States, would be an absurdity."[15]

Interposition in Border States during the War

Unlike Buchanan, Lincoln had no doubt about his right to wage war against seceded states. Lincoln's call for troops on April 15, 1861 forced the issue of whether the eight remaining slave states would stay in the Union or secede. Within two months, Virginia, Arkansas, North Carolina, and Tennessee chose secession while four border states, Maryland, Kentucky, Missouri, and Delaware did not. In those states that remained in the Union, sounding the alarm interposition was vigorously used during the war to protest perceived unconstitutional actions by the national government.[16]

Interposition in Maryland

Maryland was crucial for the Union war effort because once Virginia seceded, federal troops and supplies could only reach Washington, D. C. through Maryland. The fact that Maryland remained in the Union was hardly inevitable, with Lincoln receiving less than 3 percent of the state's popular vote and the remainder divided between Breckinridge, Bell, and Douglas.[17]

By the time of the secession winter of 1860 and the initial military preparations of Lincoln's administration, Maryland's legislature had already adjourned and would not reconvene until 1862 unless the Governor called a special session. Despite pressure from Democrats, Governor Thomas Hicks – who had been elected in 1857 as a Know-Nothing Party candidate – resisted reconvening. Worried that Democrats would seek secession, Hicks favored compromising with the South. Hicks supported the Washington Peace Conference and chose a policy of neutrality even as clashes erupted in Maryland between Southern sympathizers and supporters of the federal government. Eventually, Hicks relented and a special legislature convened on April 26, 1861 in western Maryland, instead of Baltimore where a mob had recently attacked a Massachusetts regiment headed to Washington.[18]

On the eve of that session, President Lincoln ordered General Winfield Scott "to watch, and await" the action of the Maryland legislators, who he acknowledged had a legal right to assemble. But at the first appearance of hostility, Lincoln expected Scott to take decisive action, including, if necessary, "the bombardment of their cities" and "the suspension of the writ of habeas corpus." On April 27, 1861 Lincoln explicitly authorized General Scott to suspend habeas corpus anywhere along troop transportation lines between Philadelphia and Washington.[19]

After convening the legislature, Hicks favored taking "a neutral position between our brethren of the North and South" with Maryland remaining "loyal to the Union." Hicks asked the legislature not "to take sides against the General Government" unless it committed "outrages upon us which would justify us to resist its authority" and instead to "array ourselves for Union and peace" and thus preserve "our lives and property."[20]

Although Democrats dominated the legislature, they quickly resolved one of Governor Hicks' concerns. On the first day of the session, the Senate unanimously passed a resolution rejecting secession and three days later the House adopted a report from the Committee on Federal Relations concluding that the legislature had no authority to secede. That Maryland Democrats who recently supported Breckinridge now opposed secession was not too surprising since the preservation of the Union had been a major theme in the recent presidential campaign. Despite rejecting secession, Maryland's legislators still criticized the war and Lincoln's policies. They eventually passed resolutions sounding the alarm about actions of the executive branch. On May 9, 1861 the House condemned the war as "unconstitutional in its origin, purposes, and conduct," and resolved to take no part "directly or indirectly" in the war's prosecution. The legislature wished to recognize the Confederacy because the military coercion of seceded states was unlawful and only led to "slaughter and hate."[21]

In addition, Maryland's legislature had a specific grievance after Lincoln suspended the writ of habeas corpus. On May 25, 1861 a Maryland citizen, John Merryman, was arrested for treason and expressing secessionist views, taken into custody, and confined at Fort McHenry, near Baltimore. Merryman immediately sought a writ of habeas corpus from the Maryland native Chief Justice Roger B. Taney since the Supreme Court had adjourned for the year. Taney issued a writ for Merryman on May 26, which the commanding officer of the fort refused to acknowledge given Lincoln's suspension. On May 28, Taney issued a bench ruling that the President lacked constitutional authority to suspend the writ of habeas corpus and issued an opinion a few days later asserting that only Congress could authorize that suspension. Taney left the President to "determine what measures he will take to cause the civil process of the United States to be respected and enforced." Lincoln ignored Taney's opinion even though the Chief Justice ordered the clerk of court to send a copy of the proceedings to the President.[22]

The confinement of Merryman and others in Fort McHenry triggered Maryland's interposition. On June 10, 1861, James U. Dennis introduced resolutions in the legislature that prompted extensive debate. After alleging that the Union army had violated the constitutional rights of Maryland citizens, the resolutions expressed the legislature's "solemn protest" against the actions of the President and declared them to be "gross usurpation, unjust, oppressive, tyrannical and in utter violation of common right and of the plain provisions of the Constitution." The resolutions asserted that the federal government had no constitutional power "to wage war against a State for the purpose of subjugation or conquest." Moreover, the President's suspension of habeas corpus, "the great safeguard of personal liberty," lacked congressional authorization. Indeed, it was nearly two years before Congress enacted a law in 1863 authorizing Lincoln to suspend the writ of habeas corpus.[23]

Maryland's House of Delegates then passed interposition resolutions protesting "the unconstitutional and arbitrary proceedings of the Federal Executive" and wanted the state's congressional delegation to endorse them. The resolutions passed the Senate with a bare quorum after pro-Union senators deserted the chamber before the vote. When the resolutions reached the U.S.

Senate, some Republicans objected to printing them because they were "an insult" to the government and neither "respectful" nor "truthful" to the President. Other Republicans reminded their colleagues about the long tradition of printing state resolutions criticizing actions of the national government, even with language that some deemed offensive or improper. When the Senate printed the Maryland resolutions it implicitly endorsed sounding the alarm interposition whether directed at Congress, the President, or the Supreme Court.[24]

Interposition in Kentucky

Another classic instance of interposition arose in the border state of Kentucky. Like Maryland, Kentucky was a slave state and its 1850 Constitution proclaimed that enslavers possessed an "inviolable" right of property. As such, Kentucky's commitment to the Union was hardly certain and following the attack on Fort Sumter in April 1861, a states' rights faction surfaced. Kentucky's Governor, Beriah Magoffin, while appearing neutral in demanding that neither Northern nor Southern troops enter the state, revealed his sympathies in a terse telegraphic response to Lincoln's request for military support: "Kentucky will furnish no troops for the wicked purpose of subduing her sister Southern States." Kentucky remained ambivalent about the war even as it opposed secession.[25]

As the war increasingly became seen as the means of freeing enslaved persons, many Kentuckians questioned the actions of Lincoln's administration. Uncertainty about the loyalty of its citizens led Union military commanders in Kentucky to transform it by 1862 into what one scholar has called a "police state." On September 22, 1862 Lincoln issued his preliminary emancipation proclamation warning the states in rebellion that unless they returned to the Union by January 1, 1863, enslaved people in those states "shall be then, thenceforward, and forever free." Some Kentuckians who had joined the Union cause felt betrayed. As one soldier put it, "I enlisted to fight for the Union and the Constitution, but Lincoln puts a different construction on things and now has us Union Men fighting for his Abolition Platform."[26]

One week after the Emancipation Proclamation freed enslaved people in Confederate-held territory, Kentucky's legislature responded. Governor James F. Robinson addressed the legislature in

January 1863 concerned about the sudden appearance of "a theory outside of and above the Constitution." This "new doctrine" asserted "that *military necessity* is not to be measured by *Constitutional* limits." He recommended the passage of resolutions protesting unconstitutional actions of the federal government.[27]

The legislature's Committee on Federal Relations issued a report condemning what it considered unconstitutional acts of Lincoln and the Republican Party. The report denounced the President's "anti-slavery fanaticism" and his willingness to embrace unlimited "war measures to put down the rebellion." Among the acts condemned were the passage of confiscation bills, the suspension of the writ of habeas corpus, and the Emancipation Proclamation. Remedying these "evils" lay with "the ballot-box" and turning out the "men at Washington" who were but "temporary trustees of power" for the people. The report saw hopeful electoral signs and thought Kentucky should "wait with the Democrats of the North" in order to reestablish the Constitution "as it is." In the meantime, the legislators rejected "all lawless and unconstitutional remedies which would only prove worse than the disease."[28]

In resolutions overwhelmingly adopted in early March, Kentucky's legislature highlighted the national government's infractions and sought to rally political support to reverse them. The resolutions identified the "unconstitutional acts of Congress, and startling usurpations of power by the Executive" that they hoped might be corrected through "the ballot-box." In addition, they called for constitutional amendments to clarify the Constitution's meaning and asked the Governor to send the report and resolutions to all the other Governors for the consideration of their legislatures. Finally, the state's congressional delegation was instructed and requested to advance the objects of the resolutions.[29]

West Virginia, the Draft and other War Powers

One early sign that the national government was disregarding constitutional requirements was the recognition and eventual statehood of West Virginia. Sentiment against secession ran high in northwestern Virginia and soon after the state seceded, a convention was convened at Wheeling to seek separate statehood. Article IV, section 3 of the Constitution required that no new state "shall be formed or erected within the jurisdiction of any other State" without the consent of the legislature of the state concerned – consent that Virginia would never give. Undeterred, the Wheeling convention formed its own "restored government" and declared all state offices vacant while appointing new state officials including Francis Pierpont as Governor. After Lincoln recognized Pierpont's administration as the "de jure government of Virginia," the new Virginia legislature elected two U.S. Senators. While the Wheeling convention met, Union forces invaded western Virginia and defeated a smaller Confederate army, thus permitting a referendum on statehood. After statehood bills passed the U.S. Senate and House in 1862, West Virginia entered the Union on June 20, 1863.[30]

During the war Lincoln exercised wide-ranging powers that proved controversial in Northern states as well as the border states. Lincoln believed Presidential authority allowed him to take whatever steps he deemed necessary to suppress the Southern rebellion. After suspending the writ of habeas corpus in Maryland, Lincoln defended his action to Congress and asserted that even if his suspension of habeas corpus was illegal, it was indispensable to preserve the Union. After draft resistance surfaced in Pennsylvania and Wisconsin, Lincoln issued a proclamation on September 24, 1862 that suspended the writ of habeas corpus throughout the nation. Aggressively enforced by Secretary of War Edwin M. Stanton, the decree subjected to martial law "all Rebels and Insurgents, their aiders and abettors within the United States, and all persons discouraging volunteer enlistments, resisting militia drafts, or guilty of any disloyal practice, affording aid and comfort to Rebels against the authority of the United States."[31]

Northern Democrats questioned the constitutionality of Lincoln's suspension of habeas corpus and his sweeping use of martial law that impinged on freedom of speech. Allegations of civil liberties violations swelled after the military arrest and conviction of the prominent Ohio Copperhead leader Clement Vallandigham in 1863 for disloyalty. Vallandigham was convicted of expressing "sympathy" for the enemy and uttering "disloyal sentiments and opinions" that undermined the government's efforts to suppress "an unlawful rebellion." Lincoln defended his administration from Democratic critics with two public replies that dismissed the claim that Vallandigham had been arrested only for "words addressed to a public meeting." Instead, his crime entailed "damaging the army" on whom "the life of the nation depends" and "warring upon the military." Lincoln came to the gist of his argument for military necessity by rhetorically asking, "Must I shoot a simple-minded soldier boy who deserts, while I must not touch a hair of a wiley agitator who induces him to desert?" By the summer of 1863, Lincoln came to believe, according to James McPherson, that "the whole country was a war zone and military arrests in areas far from the fighting front were justified."[32]

Interposition in the North

Interposition in Indiana

When Indiana's legislature convened in early January 1863, it considered both the Emancipation Proclamation and Lincoln's general prosecution of the war. Although Democrats enjoyed a substantial majority in both houses because of the negative reaction to Lincoln's preliminary emancipation proclamation in the 1862 election, the state's Governor, Oliver P. Morton, was a Republican. The session was marked by political acrimony and a feud between the Governor and Democrats that produced a deadlock. Despite their majority, Democrats in the Indiana legislature could not pass resolutions objecting to the policies of Lincoln's administration because Republicans intentionally deprived the House of a quorum. Nonetheless, from the start of the session, resolutions were introduced condemning Lincoln's "infamous Abolition Proclamation" and for conducting of the war "under the tyrants' plea of 'military necessity'" which "has usurped powers unwarranted by the constitution" – including the suspension of the writ of habeas corpus. Indiana's legislators were sounding the alarm.[33]

Along with other Northern Democrats who opposed the proclamation, Indiana's legislators accused Lincoln of converting a war to save the Union into a crusade for racial equality. Instead of their promise to crush the rebellion and restore the Union "as it originally existed under the Constitution," Republicans were tampering with the rights of the states and eliminating the protection of slavery. Democrats rejected secession, but favored a suspension of hostilities and a national convention to return Southern states to their prewar status.[34]

Racism and the desire to maintain white supremacy were never far from the surface of objections to the Emancipation Proclamation. As the text of one resolution complained, Indiana's Republican Governor and President Lincoln had "lost all regard for the white race of the North, and have turned their attention to the black race." Another proposed resolution thought Indiana's motto should be "millions to restore the Union as it was, not a dollar to emancipate the negro." Indiana Democrats feared that freed Blacks would move into "the free communities of the North and West." Both Whites and Blacks could see change looming.[35]

All of these resolutions were referred to the House Committee on Federal Relations which presented a joint resolution declaring the Emancipation Proclamation "unconstitutional, unwise, and calculated to do the cause of the Union incalculable injury." The resolutions called for the Secretary of State (and not Republican Governor Morton) to share the preamble and resolutions with the state's congressional delegation. The documents were to be sent to the Governors of the states "not in rebellion" requesting their legislatures' consideration. Had Republicans not deprived Democrats of a quorum by leaving the capitol, the interposition resolutions would undoubtedly have passed. Instead, no legislative business was conducted before the legislature adjourned.[36]

Interposition in Illinois

Like Indiana, Illinois responded to Lincoln's Emancipation Proclamation with a similar split between its executive and legislative branches. The state's Republican Governor, Richard Yates, supported a more aggressive campaign against the South, including policies aimed at slavery. While the state had backed Lincoln and the Republicans in 1860, two years later saw a reversal with Democrats taking control of both the House and Senate, reflecting misgivings about emancipation and the belief that Lincoln was focused more on slavery than on reestablishing the Union. Republicans thought the Democratic-dominated legislature might try to pass some "rash or vicious legislation." The contrasting messages of the Speaker of the House and Governor Yates illustrated the gulf between the executive and the legislature. The Speaker, Democrat Samuel Buckmaster, criticized "a disastrous civil war" that failed to subdue the

South's rebellion. Governor Yates, however, applauded Lincoln's "vigorous prosecution of the war" including the Emancipation Proclamation – a crucial policy needed for victory.[37]

Democrats disagreed with their Republican Governor in a proposed joint resolution that simultaneously sounded the alarm, rejected the Emancipation Proclamation, and advanced the Peace Movement by calling for a national constitutional convention. The partisanship was real, but scholars who assert that Democrats only sought to undermine Republicans and hamstring Governor Yates fail to appreciate how the legislators' protest was a form of state interposition even if motivated by white supremacy.[38]

The preamble of the legislative resolution asserted that Lincoln's administration was exercising "arbitrary and unconstitutional" powers by suspending the writ of habeas corpus, denying criminal due process, abridging free speech, and imposing martial law in states not in rebellion. The protest served "to warn our public servants against further usurpations." The Democratic legislators denounced the "monstrous usurpations of the administration, and the encroachments of abolitionism," but also branded the "heresy of secession" as unconstitutional. The joint resolution was to be sent to the President, members of the state's congressional delegation, and to the other states' Governors and members of their legislatures.[39]

As in Indiana, the attempt by Democratic legislators in Illinois to pass an interposition resolution was foiled when Senate Republicans boycotted the chamber. While that maneuver succeeded, two days earlier the House had concurred with the Senate in adopting a resolution that described a proposed bill for congressional appropriation to compensate enslavers in border states who agreed to emancipate enslaved persons as "unconstitutional and void." The resolution instructed and requested the state's congressional delegation to vote against that bill and copies of the resolution were sent to the Governors of Kentucky, Missouri, Maryland, and Delaware.[40]

Interposition in Wisconsin

Yet another attempt at interposition occurred during Wisconsin's legislative session of 1863 that assembled on January 14, one day after the Wisconsin Supreme Court declared Lincoln's suspension of

the writ of habeas corpus unconstitutional. Democrat Alden
S. Sanborn introduced resolutions in March 1863 calling the
Proclamation "unwise, unconstitutional, and void" and declaring
Lincoln's extension of martial law and the suspension of the writ of
habeas corpus "unwarranted by the constitution." Sanborn's
resolutions asserted the right of the legislature to disagree with the
President. The state's congressional delegation was directed to support
the resolutions and copies were sent to state Governors for
presentation to their legislatures. Ultimately, a motion to table
Sanborn's resolutions narrowly passed, reflecting the slight majority
by which Republicans held both houses of the legislature.[41]

Interposition in Pennsylvania

A more determined effort to question the constitutionality of Lincoln's
war policies surfaced in the complicated political context of
Pennsylvania. During the Civil War, that state not only featured
rivalry between Democrats and Republicans, but opposing factions
within both parties. A centrist Republican, Andrew Gregg Curtin, was
elected Governor in 1860. Before addressing the legislature, Curtin
reached out to President-elect Lincoln who advised Curtin "to
maintain the Union at all hazzards." In his address, Curtin stressed
Pennsylvania's ties with its Southern neighbors, but asserted that no
state "can voluntarily secede from the Union."[42]

Subsequent electoral results eroded Republican strength in the
legislature. The start of the session in 1863 saw the two parties
roughly balanced, with Democrats enjoying a slight edge in the
House while Republicans retained control of the Senate. With the
legislature meeting shortly after the Emancipation Proclamation,
Democrats were determined to respond both to the proclamation and
other policies of Lincoln's administration. Aware that their resolutions
stood little chance of approval in the Senate, Democrats chose to act
independently. In April 1863 the House approved resolutions that
were never sent to the Senate, but signaled objections to perceived
constitutional overreaching by the national government.[43]

The resolutions described Pennsylvanians as facing an armed
rebellion on one side and confronting unconstitutional acts of
Congress and "startling usurpations of power" by the President on

the other. In exercising its "right to differ" with the President, the House agreed with Wisconsin's Democratic legislators that the Emancipation Proclamation and the suspension of the writ of habeas corpus was "unwise, unconstitutional, and void." Although the resolutions lacked the Senate's approval, Pennsylvania's 1863 Democratic State Convention incorporated them in their party's platform.[44]

Interposition in New Jersey

New Jersey's legislature also responded to Lincoln's Proclamation, and its Democratic members passed interposition resolutions. New Jersey's legislative session in 1863 has been depicted as a victory for pro-war Democrats who rejected the demands for an immediate armistice by the radical Copperhead, antiwar faction of their party. The radical and moderate wings of the party were certainly at odds, but focusing on that conflict ignores a shared commitment to monitor federalism through interposition. Despite different approaches to the prosecution of the war, New Jersey's resolutions were not "an empty and ultimately meaningless gesture." While not demanding an end to the war, the resolutions brought attention to perceived constitutional overreaching and called for interstate cooperation.[45]

The resolutions that New Jersey's legislature eventually passed originated as an effort by the antiwar faction within the state's Democratic Party. On the first day of the session, a leading Copperhead in the state Senate, Daniel Holsman, introduced resolutions calling for a six-month armistice and a National Convention to discuss ending the war. The resolutions cited a series of "gross violations of the Constitution" demanding condemnation by the legislature, including the Emancipation Proclamation, the recognition of West Virginia, the suspension of habeas corpus, and an abridgement of due process and free speech.[46]

Holsman's resolutions – particularly the call for a unilateral armistice and peace negotiations – provoked immediate opposition from Democratic legislators supporting the war. Republicans thought those resolutions gave "aid and comfort to traitors in arms" and believed the best route to peace was "more vigorous prosecution of the war." Republican Senators also introduced resolutions that were never adopted, including one that supported Lincoln "in all measures he may think necessary" to suppress the rebellion. Pro-war Democrats eventually submitted resolutions to compete with those of Holsman, but before then, New Jersey's Democratic Governor, Joel Parker, delivered his inaugural address.[47]

Scholars have noted that Parker's address was favorably received by both wings of his party because he supported the war but was open to peace whether it came "by the exercise of power or by the exercise of conciliation." Less appreciated is Parker's description of federalism in New Jersey's interposition resolutions: "We should take care that both the National and State governments confine their action within the sphere of their respective power." The reserved rights of the states required protection particularly during times of war when "power is prone to encroach on law."[48]

Parker concluded that Lincoln's suspension of the writ of habeas corpus was unconstitutional and that the President's exercise of war powers "virtually suspends the Constitution in time of war." He questioned the Emancipation Proclamation in racial terms, envisioning millions of Black freedmen migrating to the North. Despite believing that Lincoln's administration had acted unconstitutionally, Parker insisted that citizens were still obliged to support the government while hoping that such constitutional overreaching would stimulate the election of representatives who might return the government to "true principles."[49]

When pro-war Democrats in New Jersey's legislature replaced Holsman's resolutions with a majority report of the Committee on Federal Relations, they rejected an immediate armistice. New Jersey's resolutions "Relative to National Affairs" claimed that Lincoln had promised not to fight "for conquest or subjugation" or to interfere with "the rights or established institutions of the states [that is, slavery], but to maintain and defend the supremacy of the constitution." They urged him to keep that pledge. The legislature also protested the President's use of unconstitutional war powers that included the Emancipation Proclamation, the suspension of the writ of habeas corpus, the exercise of powers under the claim of military necessity, the domination of the military over civil law, and the creation of West Virginia. In addition, the legislature objected to the federal government exercising power that was not "clearly given and expressed in the federal constitution."

The resolutions were to be sent to the other Governors and legislatures for their attention. In every particular, New Jersey's resolutions epitomized sounding the alarm interposition.[50]

Confederate Interposition

Just as gubernatorial and legislative actions in the border and Northern states have not been identified as interposition, the same is true of Confederate interpositions. Scholars have ignored how Confederate Governors and legislatures monitored the federalism created by their Confederate Constitution. Their responses were not simply actions of "[d]isgruntled politicians hiding behind State's rights" and engaged in nullification. Instead, when Confederate Governors and legislatures resisted measures of the Confederate government, they continued the American tradition of defending states' rights and the liberties of their citizens against what they believed were oppressive acts of a national government.[51]

Southern history during the Civil War has largely focused on why the South lost, whether the Confederacy "Died of State Rights," or unintentionally created an overly centralized government. Indeed, Confederate Governors and legislatures resisted and questioned the national policies of Jefferson Davis' administration in part because of heightened legislative activity at the state level. The war prompted six Confederate states to institute annual legislative sessions, and those that retained biennial systems frequently called extra sessions. As a result, the war years found Confederate Governors deeply engaged in negotiating the terms of the federalism established by the Confederate Constitution.[52]

One dilemma of the Confederacy has been described as "the issue of states' rights versus national interests within a system based on the sovereignty of the states." Although largely modeled on the Federal Constitution, the Confederate Constitution explicitly identified the authority of sovereign states over the Confederate government. That principle was reflected in the Preamble and the Confederate versions of the Ninth and Tenth Amendments to the U.S. Constitution that shifted an emphasis from "the people" to "the people of the several States." That change, G. Edward White has argued, sought to preclude "a possible reading of individual citizenship in the Confederacy as existing independent of state citizenship, or of the Confederate government as representing a national entity." Thus, Confederate interpositions were based on the premise that "the collective interests of the Confederacy could not be [a] justification to override the particular interest of a state in the minority."[53]

One measure of the Confederate Congress that provoked early adverse reaction from state officials was a Conscription Act of April 16, 1862, passed nearly a year before the North adopted a similar measure. The law bypassed states as the traditional conduit for raising troops and subjected all able-bodied white males between eighteen and thirty-five to service in the Confederate army for three years. Georgia's Governor Joseph E. Brown accused the Confederate Congress of transferring to the executive branch what the states had "expressly and carefully denied to Congress and reserved to themselves." Although aware of the argument that "State rights and State sovereignty must yield . . . to the higher law of necessity," Brown did not think wartime justified the Conscription Act. Governor John Letcher of Virginia also considered national conscription a "palpable violation of the rights of the states" and thought it was "*unconstitutional*." But unlike Brown, Letcher did not challenge the Confederate government. "When the war is ended, we can discuss these questions, and so settle them as to preserve the rights of the States." Independence took priority; thereafter, "we can mark clearly and distinctly the line between state and Confederate authority." Governor Brown, however, continued to criticize the Conscription Act and its adverse impact on the equilibrium of federalism under the Confederate Constitution. In a special message to the Georgia legislature in November 1862, Brown declared the act "not only a palpable violation of the Constitution of the Confederacy, but a dangerous assault upon both the rights and the sovereignty of States."[54]

Concerns about tyranny surfaced early in the war with the implementation of martial law and congressional authorization allowing President Davis to suspend the writ of habeas corpus. After the first Suspension Act and the declaration of martial law in Atlanta, Governor Brown wrote to his fellow Georgian and Vice President of the Confederacy, Alexander H. Stephens, saying he was more afraid of "military despotism" at home than subjugation by the enemy. Two months later, Governor Zebulon Vance of North Carolina saw similar dangers. In November 1862 he wrote to Jefferson Davis about the arrest of North Carolina citizens suspected of disloyalty. As Governor, it was his "duty" to protect their rights, foremost being "the right of a trial for their alleged offences." A week later, Governor Vance told his state legislators about the passage of the second act authorizing the suspension of the writ of habeas corpus and urged them to sound the alarm. If Davis could suspend the writ in all arrests made by the Confederate authorities, he could then "at pleasure seize any citizen of the State, with or without excuse, throw him into prison, and permit him to languish there without relief." Vance thought North Carolina's legislators would protect "the rights of our people." While not passing interposition resolutions on this occasion, North Carolina and other Confederate state legislatures eventually did so, prompted by war weariness and the prospect of a third Suspension Act in early 1864.[55]

Indeed, as the third Suspension Act was being considered by Congress, Governor Vance again complained to Davis about its enactment and predicted it would be "resisted" in the state. After Davis replied, Vance criticized the President for his "studied exclusion" of North Carolinians from offices and objected to military "outrages." Davis grew fed up with Vance's complaints and restricted any future communication to matters requiring "official action." But even as President Davis dismissed Vance's concerns, interposition surfaced in other Confederate state legislatures.[56]

Georgia acted first. Soon after the Confederate Congress authorized the third suspension of the writ of habeas corpus, an open letter by "A Georgian" declared: "When this war broke out our people thought they had something to fight for, but now they have nothing, but to keep the Yankees checked, so that our own Government may oppress them more." Governor Brown wanted all states to "denounce and condemn" suspension and he prepared an address raising concerns about unconstitutional acts after consulting with Alexander Stephens and his brother Linton Stephens who served in the Georgia legislature. Brown reminded legislators of their duty to monitor federalism as "the guardians" of the people's rights. He accused the Confederate Congress of passing a law that permitted the President "to make *illegal and unconstitutional arrests*," effectively creating a "Confederate Star

Chamber." Such unauthorized actions obliged state legislatures to "sound the alarm."[57]

Georgia's legislature responded to Governor Brown after Linton Stephens introduced resolutions questioning the constitutionality of the latest suspension of the writ. During the legislative debate, Vice President Stephens described the Confederacy as being beset by the external danger of "a strong, unscrupulous and vindictive foe" seeking the "subjugation, degradation and extermination" of the South – and the internal challenge to "maintain and keep secure our rights and liberties." Stephens called the suspension of the writ of habeas corpus "unwise, impolitic and unconstitutional" and "exceedingly dangerous to public liberty." Like Brown, Stephens distinguished congressional authority to suspend the writ from granting the President dictatorial powers "to order the arrest and imprisonment of any man, woman, or child in the Confederacy."[58]

Stephens hoped the legislators would exercise their "deliberate judgment" about the act's constitutionality much as the Virginia and Kentucky Resolutions had condemned the Alien and Sedition Acts. That action in 1798 had "saved the old government" in those states and he thought Georgia's legislators could play a similar role for the Confederacy. They could demand the repeal of the Suspension Act and have "the question of constitutionality" submitted to the courts. Stephens concluded by reminding legislators of their role as "faithful sentinels" who were duty bound to sound the alarm about the present constitutional infractions.[59]

Notwithstanding Stephens' plea, Georgia's legislators resisted passing Linton's resolutions. With adjournment looming, Governor Brown threatened to convene another extra session if the legislators failed to act, and the legislature complied by passing the resolutions on the last day of the session. Those resolutions declared warrantless seizures and the writ's suspension "a dangerous assault upon the constitutional power of the courts" and "the liberty of the people," and the state's congressional delegation was urged to repeal the act.[60]

While Governor Brown and Georgia's legislature were criticized for their resolutions, defenders argued they were not hostile acts directed at the Confederate government. Some thought the resolutions raised the broader question: "[W]ho are to keep watch upon the General Government, and see that the Constitution is not so set aside?" The answer, those defenders suggested, was to be found in words James Madison had spoken during the first Congress: that "the State Legislatures will jealously and closely watch the operations of this Government, and be able to resist, with more effect, every assumption of power, *than any other power on earth can do.*" Georgia's legislature was simply acting as one of the monitors of federalism, consistent with what had been anticipated by the framers.[61]

Three weeks later, Mississippi joined Georgia in passing interposition resolutions. On the last day of a special session called in March 1864, the state's legislature unanimously declared the Suspension Act "dangerous to the liberty of the citizen" and "unconstitutional in some of its features," noting that the act tended "to make the civil power subordinate to the military." The legislature instructed and requested members of their congressional delegation to seek the repeal of the overreaching act and to oppose any suspensions of the writ.[62]

Mississippi's legislators did not want their adoption of the resolutions to "impute to the President of the Confederate States any desire to arrogate to himself more power than the Constitution has conferred." All citizens were obliged to support President Davis "in the legitimate exercise" of his constitutional powers. In May 1864, Mississippi's joint resolutions reached the Confederate Congress, where they were ordered to be printed before being tabled.[63]

In May, North Carolina's Governor Zebulon Vance raised concerns about the most recent suspension of habeas corpus and recommended that legislators either urge Congress to repeal the act or remove its unconstitutional features. North Carolina's legislature responded by passing resolutions calling the Suspension Act a violation of "solemn guarantees of the constitution" and the latest Conscription Act passed by the Confederate Congress "destructive of State sovereignty." The Confederate government seemed headed toward "a consolidated military despotism" and the legislature wanted the state's congressional delegation to repeal the Suspension Act and modify the Conscription Act.[64]

After the third suspension law expired on August 1, 1864, President Davis sought yet another Suspension Act. That request was ultimately "laid aside as unimportant and inexpedient." A report of a select committee of the Senate noted the "great repugnance" to the suspension of the writ expressed by the legislatures of Georgia, Mississippi, and North Carolina and by many Southerners. The report rejected the argument that suspension was an indispensable war measure. In the Confederate House of Representatives in May 1864, Henry S. Foote of Tennessee urged the repeal of the "unconstitutional and dangerous" Suspension Act to remove a "dark and portentous precedent." Despite Davis' urging, the Confederate Congress did not pass another Suspension Act.[65]

Interposition and States' Rights after the War

The attempt to reconstruct the Union after the Civil War and achieve legal equality for previously enslaved Blacks through the Thirteenth, Fourteenth, and Fifteenth Amendments is a well-studied chapter of American history. Resistance to these efforts by Democrats, both in the North and the South, is also well documented. Less well known are the assertions of political rights by Black Americans and the complex suppression of those rights. Laura Edwards describes how for the white hierarchy in North Carolina, the political participation "of poor white and African-American men appeared as pointless as that of women" and in the end, white supremacy campaigns pushed Blacks, women and poor whites out of "public space" and into economic and personal vulnerability.[66]

Scholars have also not appreciated how resistance to Reconstruction included interposition resolutions passed by Southern and Northern legislatures in the 1860s and 1870s, objecting to Reconstruction on constitutional as well as policy grounds. Such resistance surfaced in Northern states where Democrats opposed the efforts of Radical Republicans to grant freed Blacks political equality. In New York, for example, Republicans tried to amend the state constitution's racially discriminatory property qualification that effectively disenfranchised Black men. Democrats had political success in arguing that Black political equality meant Black political dominance – and that the freedom of white New Yorkers depended on continued Black disenfranchisement. The state's Democratic Chairman, Samuel J. Tilden, endorsed that strategy by insisting in early 1868 that the party's position "must be *condemnation and reversal of negro supremacy.*" Opposing political equality for Blacks also became a national issue for the Democratic Party during the Reconstruction era and central to former New York Governor Horatio Seymour's presidential bid against Republican Ulysses S. Grant in 1868.[67]

In January 1868, Democrat William S. Clark, citing his oath to uphold the Constitution, introduced resolutions in New York's Assembly condemning congressional Reconstruction measures as a "scheme of usurpation" designed "to extinguish ten States of the Union." Republican newspapers called them "lunatic resolutions," but the Democratic press saw them as an important check on "the Radical cabal in Congress" and a protest of unconstitutional acts. Despite support from Democrats, Clark's resolutions were ultimately tabled. If New York's legislature chose not to pass interposition resolutions on that occasion, other legislatures were less reticent.[68]

In Ohio, the legislative control that allowed Republicans to ratify the Fourteenth Amendment in early 1867 evaporated with the fall elections – a rout by Democrats that was replicated in many other states. A proposed constitutional amendment to enfranchise Black men also served the purposes of the state's Democratic Party. A prominent feature of Democratic processions and parades was "wagons filled with young girls, dressed in white, carrying banners inscribed with the appeal: 'Fathers, save us from negro equality.'" Not only was the suffrage amendment defeated, but Democrats carried both houses of the legislature and nearly won the governorship, with the Republican Rutherford B. Hayes clinging to a slight lead. The legislative session of 1868–1869 saw Ohio's Democrats poised to roll back efforts seeking racial equality.[69]

Early in the January 1868 session of Ohio's legislature, joint resolutions were introduced and passed rescinding the state's ratification of the Fourteenth Amendment. The resolutions demanded that the executive branch return to Ohio all the documents related to the state's 1867 certification of the amendment. The rescinding resolution was to be sent to all Governors. Secretary of State William Seward replied that his department was charged with "the safe-keeping of the public archives" and that legally he could not release any document in his custody. Seward later certified the Fourteenth Amendment, finding that Ohio's ratifying resolution remained in force. Ohio's legislature also rejected the Fifteenth Amendment in May 1869, after a report concluded that the amendment "centralizes too much power in the General Government," and opposed the Fifteenth Amendment's protections for Black political participation.[70]

While scholars have noted Ohio's attempt to rescind the Fourteenth Amendment and its rejection of the Fifteenth Amendment, largely overlooked are the interposition resolutions passed that same session. After voting to rescind the Fourteenth Amendment, the legislature considered resolutions offered by Hugh J. Jewett, a Democratic member of the House, protesting congressional Reconstruction acts as being "in direct conflict with the plainest provisions of the Constitution" and "subversive of the rights of the States." The state's congressional delegation was instructed and requested to vote for their repeal. The Senate adopted Jewett's resolutions on February 13, 1868 and described congressional Reconstruction as seeking "to overthrow by force or fraud the Constitution of the United States."[71]

Republicans in Iowa's legislature weighed in on the struggle between President Andrew Johnson and congressional Republicans over the shape of Reconstruction. Johnson's dismissal of Secretary of War Edwin Stanton and his perceived mistreatment of General Grant contributed to Johnson's impeachment in February 1868. Resolutions were passed in Iowa's House and Senate supporting Stanton and Grant and condemning Johnson. After Stanton's dismissal, resolutions were passed accusing the President of being willing to "disregard existing laws" and "override the law-making power of the land." Because he failed to protect the Constitution in violation of his oath of office, Iowa's legislature called for Johnson's impeachment.[72]

Opposition to Reconstruction continued under President Grant's administration and reached a peak in 1875. Politics in Reconstruction-era Louisiana was particularly contentious, but also a classic example of Southern resistance to Reconstruction. According to Eric Foner, every state election between 1868 and 1876 was marked by "rampant violence and pervasive fraud." The election of 1874 was particularly vicious, with Democrats determined to displace the Republican administration of Governor William J. Kellogg through the formation of the White League, an organization "openly dedicated to the violent restoration of white supremacy." The level of vote tampering and intimidation of Black voters led Erik Mathisen to call it "one of the most fraudulent elections in the nation's history." Republicans and Democrats confronted one another when the Louisiana legislature met on January 4, 1875. After Democrats tried to seize control of the House by forcefully installing five of their members whose elections were contested, federal troops entered the chamber and ejected them, allowing the Republicans to resume control and prompting the Democrats to walk out.[73]

The military enforcement of Reconstruction in Louisiana not only outraged Southerners but "aroused more Northern opposition than any previous federal action in the South." The response of Southern legislatures to the events in Louisiana has been characterized as "states' rights resolutions." Virginia's legislature passed a joint resolution on January 15, 1875 in response to the federal government's "gross and wanton usurpation of power." It protested the violation of Louisiana's "sacred right of self-government," hoping that other state legislatures would defend "the principle of popular representation." Virginia's Governor was directed to telegraph all the other Governors urging them to defend their sovereign rights.[74]

When West Virginia's Governor John Jacob addressed his state's legislators in 1875, he urged them to protest the federal government's assertion of powers which "if admitted, would be subversive of the rights of all the States." One proposed resolution denounced federal actions as contributing to "the overthrow of republican government and the establishment of a military despotism." In January 1875 the legislature adopted resolutions calling the use of federal troops in Louisiana "a gross violation of the Constitution."[75]

When Georgia's legislature assembled on January 12, resolutions were referred to the "Committee on the State of the Republic" condemning the "Federal interference" in Louisiana as threatening "the destruction of the Union and the subversion of the Constitution." The President of the Senate, T.J. Simmons, warned about "Centralism" displayed in the "crowning outrages" committed in Louisiana. "For the first time in the history of our country, a Legislature elected by the people has been dispersed by Federal bayonets." Simmons' description ignored the rampant fraud, racial violence, and intimidation of that election, but it captured how preoccupied Democrats were with the consolidation of national power and the pro-Black policies they attributed to the Republican Party. The joint committee reported that President Grant's expulsion of the Louisiana legislators constituted "a palpable and dangerous usurpation of power." Georgia's legislators called on the citizens of all the states "to resort to legal means for the redress of grievances" and urged the national government to return to "the principles of constitutional law." The resolutions were to be sent to the state's congressional delegation and the other state Governors.[76]

Various interposition efforts continued after the war on subjects unrelated to Reconstruction policies, though with less fervor. For example, resolutions were introduced in Ohio's legislature by Senator M.R. Willett in early 1866 to instruct and request the state's congressional delegation to oppose the tax-free status of federal bonds on constitutional grounds. Willett's resolution asserted an inherent right of states to tax their citizens, and hence all federal laws infringing that right were "infractions of the organic law – palpable violations of the reserved rights of the States and the people, and destructive of that just and proper equilibrium between State and Federal authority." Willett's resolutions were tabled, as were those offered four years later in Ohio's House by Llewellyn Baber directed at a tariff on agricultural products. Baber's resolutions revived the longstanding argument that a tariff levied for any other purpose than revenue "is unauthorized by the Constitution."[77]

While these resolutions failed, others opposing the possible nationalization of the telegraph system and federal judicial jurisdiction over municipalities succeeded in Pennsylvania and Alabama. In 1873 Pennsylvania's legislature passed a joint resolution instructing and requesting its congressional delegation to oppose any bill permitting the federal government to build and operate national telegraph lines. That position was contrary to resolutions passed earlier by numerous other state legislatures favoring a national system. While not sounding the alarm about alleged unconstitutional actions of the federal government, Pennsylvania's resolutions of 1873 were noteworthy for how their author defended them.[78]

After Republican James S. Rutan, Speaker of Pennsylvania's Senate, resolved to oppose telegraph nationalization, he was challenged both about the propriety and need for such a resolution. Rutan denied that he was "meddling with a question that did not concern the Legislature" and reminded his colleagues that "It has been the custom in every State in the Union, since the adoption of the Federal Constitution, for the Legislatures to instruct their Senators in Congress on questions of national importance." He pointed out that only a few days earlier the legislature had instructed and requested the state's congressional delegation about a homestead bill. Moreover, a resolution was appropriate not only because nationalization was bad policy, but because it amounted to "an assumption of power on the part of the General Government not warranted in the Constitution" and ignored "the rights of States altogether." Nationalization greatly enhanced the powers of President Grant's administration and was part of a dangerous trend toward "a strong consolidated government."[79]

In defending states' rights, Rutan distinguished the early, laudable efforts of Madison and Jefferson in their Virginia and Kentucky Resolutions "to preserve the liberties of the country by protecting the States against Federal encroachment" from the later misinterpretation of those resolutions that tried "to authorize the nullification of national laws and secession." The Civil War rejected the distorted meaning of those resolutions, but Rutan wondered if that reaction had gone too far. In repudiating the heretical claims made for states' rights, the federal government "was compelled to assume large and dangerous powers during the war," contributing to a pattern of ever-increasing national power.[80]

If Pennsylvania's 1873 resolution was not a traditional interposition because it did not identify an unconstitutional act by the national government, resolutions of Alabama's legislature in 1879 clearly fit the bill. In perhaps one of the last examples of state interposition in the nineteenth century, Alabama protested against perceived constitutional overreaching by the federal government. Alabama's legislators asserted that federal judicial jurisdiction over municipal corporations including counties, cities, and towns, invaded "the exclusive jurisdiction of the State over its own officers" as a matter of "the highest attribute of sovereignty." It violated "the spirit and purpose of the Constitution," including the Eleventh Amendment. The legislators urged Congress to revoke federal jurisdiction and wanted copies of the resolutions sent to every Governor, requesting they be placed before their state legislatures "for such action as may be deemed expedient."[81]

* * * * * *

Despite the continuing practice of interposition during the post–Civil War period, the use of interposition occurred without a sense of its history. After the war, the phrase 'state interposition' came to be associated with the widely discredited notion of state nullification of federal law. Indeed, by the end of the 1870s, the practice of interposition largely died out, along with any appreciation of its use as a tool to monitor federalism by state legislatures. When the Virginia and Kentucky Resolutions were remembered, they served as part of the Democratic slogan of states' rights.

After the Civil War, the 'Principles of '98' were stigmatized by their association with nullification and the discredited doctrine of secession, a connection that continued into the early twentieth century. For Robert Baker "secession tainted the states' rights doctrine, and the Civil War stained it in blood." The Virginia and Kentucky Resolutions remained a political mantra for Democrats who opposed the consolidation of federal power, Black rights, and national centralization – and who claimed the resolutions of 1798 as the genesis of states' rights. Lost was how those resolutions were but one example of the role that state legislators – whatever their political persuasion – historically played as important monitors of federalism. However, interposition was so deeply woven into the American constitutional fabric that it was bound to surface at various junctures in the twentieth century and beyond as states sought to voice their concerns about actions of the federal government.[82]

To the extent that state legislatures continued to monitor federalism, the nature of that balance fundamentally changed with the Civil War and a redistribution of powers and authority between the federal and state governments. The Reconstruction amendments after the Civil War significantly expanded the powers exercised by the federal government. The powers retained by the states under the Tenth Amendment of 1791 were shrunk by the grant of national power in the Thirteenth, Fourteenth, and Fifteenth Amendments along with their "power to enforce clauses." While federalism persisted after the Civil War, the equilibrium between the national and state levels was no longer that struck by the 1787 Constitution and its amendments in 1791.[83]

10

Modern Interposition by States and "Nullification"

While Americans had largely forgotten the history of the constitutional tool of interposition by the late nineteenth century, the dynamic tensions of federalism that underlay the practice of interposition persisted. In 1908 Woodrow Wilson considered "the relation of the States to the federal government" to be "the cardinal question" of America's constitutional system and that a loss of "confidence in our state legislatures" meant losing "faith in our very system of government." Struggles over the social and economic reforms called for by Populists and Progressives underscored Wilson's statement. Sidney Milkis suggests that many Progressives were profoundly uneasy about the "prospect of expanding national administrative power" due to "a celebration of local self-government that was deeply rooted in American political culture."[1]

Debates over the Progressive movement, the New Deal, and America's involvement in two world wars revealed ongoing tensions of federalism that encouraged traditional sounding the alarm interposition. If during these later periods interposition functionally existed without being identified by name, the Civil Rights movement of the twentieth century saw a different pattern emerge. While systemic racism existed from the birth of the nation, resistance to national efforts to combat racial inequalities after World War II spawned a revival and reinvention of state interposition that resurfaced as an attempt to foil the federal government's efforts to advance equal justice. The invocation of "interposition" in the 1950s by state-based opponents of integration was firmly rejected by the federal courts. However, a new version of interposition termed "Judicial Federalism" emerged in the 1990s as a constraint on federal legislative power. The doctrine of "Judicial Federalism" joined traditional modes of interposition and both continue to be utilized by state officials who have concerns about the undue expansion of federal power or think the national government is acting unconstitutionally.[2]

* * * * * *

State Opposition to Early Twentieth-Century Exercises of Federal Power

Soon after 1900, state interposition resurfaced as a key component of American political life. Examples of modern interposition included: state legislative resistance to the Supreme Court's liberty-of-contract cases undermining Progressive Era economic regulations; objections to the expansion of federal powers including a mandatory national draft and prohibition during the First World War; opposition to the federal government's New Deal programs in the 1930s; and renewed struggles against wartime measures imposed during the Second World War. The urge to respond to all of those issues stimulated interposition actions by states to check what they viewed as the unconstitutional exercise of authority by the federal government.

After the Supreme Court overturned a New York law restricting the working hours of bakers in *Lochner v. New York* (1905), state officials rejected the Court's monopoly on interpreting the Constitution. As the pre–New Deal Court continued to invoke the doctrine of liberty of contract to strike down state minimum wage laws, states defending those laws called for constitutional amendments to restore local control. Three western states, California, Oregon, and Washington, created wage commissions to provide state oversight of labor issues, ignoring without defying the Court's liberty-of-contract rulings.[3]

The First World War "profoundly" affected America's constitutional order "by increasing the powers of the federal government at the expense of the states." A conscription act was one of many congressional measures that challenged traditional states' rights, by authorizing a compulsory military draft administered by both state and federal officials. During debate over the act, Wisconsin's Progressive Senator Robert M. LaFollette argued that granting presidential authority to force men into military service "marks the beginning of the end of our constitutional government." LaFollette recalled Daniel Webster's objections to conscription in 1814 when Webster asserted that any such attempt by the national government should trigger "the solemn duty of the State Governments to protect their own authority over their own militia, and to interpose between their citizens and arbitrary power." After the conscription law was enacted in 1917, the constitutional scholar Edward Corwin considered that law a radical transgression of "the principle of dual sovereignty which has hitherto underlain our federal system." Specifically, the law reversed the traditional understanding "that the national government can impose legal duties upon state officers only with the consent of and upon the terms imposed by the states themselves."[4]

Numerous organizations denounced conscription, and resistance movements surfaced in many states. Leaders of the anti-draft movement considered conscription an unconstitutional extension of federal power. The former Populist Tom Watson led an antiwar and anti-draft crusade in the South. As editor of *The Jeffersonian*, "known nationally as a vicious race-baiting, anti-Catholic, anti-Semitic sheet," Watson proposed a "state convention" to be held in Macon, Georgia, to protest "the recent usurpations of power by Congress, the President, and the Post Office Department." The convention was cancelled after death threats against Watson, but anti-draft meetings and letter campaigns to Congress continued in Georgia, Alabama, Tennessee, Arkansas, Mississippi, Kentucky, and Texas.[5]

The war also saw increased restrictions on alcohol that culminated in the enactment of the Eighteenth Amendment in 1919. According to William Ross, "The need to conserve food and to encourage sobriety during a time of national crisis provided both political and constitutional justifications for wartime restrictions on alcohol that eased the path of the amendment." Nonetheless, the political struggle over prohibition between 1913 and 1933 was arguably "one of the major battles over the contours of American federalism."[6]

Opponents of national prohibition in the House of Representatives asserted the policy contravened basic principles of federalism and impaired the police power of the states. Congressman George

Graham of Pennsylvania argued that the Tenth Amendment demonstrated that the Framers never intended "that the States should surrender their police power over the regulation of their internal affairs." In essence, opponents of prohibition contended that the Eighteenth Amendment "threatened to sweep away state sovereignty by establishing a federal police power and commandeering the states to do the federal bidding."[7]

After the Amendment's ratification, enforcement of prohibition faced considerable resistance from states with 'wet' legislative majorities arguing that the concurrent scheme of enforcement under the Amendment allowed an independent regulation of intoxicating liquors under a state's police powers. Several state Governors sounded the alarm about the importance of distinguishing "between federal and state obligations and the need to zealously observe them lest federalism be replaced by an undifferentiated nationalism." In the end, because the Twenty-First Amendment repealed the Eighteenth Amendment in 1933, the most enduring legacy of prohibition might be, as David Kyvig has suggested, that it "gave the national government direct responsibility over the routine activities of ordinary citizens, a notable extension of its authority."[8]

With President Franklin D. Roosevelt's election in 1932, his administration greatly expanded the national government's activities to cope with the effects of the Depression. "New Deal reforms that threatened powerful, entrenched economic interests or that attempted to redistribute social benefits often provoked fervent pleas on behalf of 'states' rights' and angry denunciations of 'federal tyranny.'" Moreover, concerns that Roosevelt's agenda was leading the country toward socialism prompted conservative Senators to draft "An Address to the People of the United States." Soon dubbed a "Conservative Manifesto," one of its ten "paramount principles" was a commitment to "the vigorous maintenance of States rights, home rule and local self-government" except in those cases "where State and local control are proven definitely inadequate." The "Address" or "Manifesto" was endorsed by hundreds of Chambers of Commerce and citizens' organizations throughout the country, and members of Congress were flooded with petitions from every state in the Union. Yet the federal government identified a critical need to serve the millions of Americans who were in Roosevelt's words "ill-housed, ill-clad" and "ill-nourished" – and embarked on an unprecedented effort to provide work for the unemployed.[9]

World War II prompted further efforts to nationalize a wide range of strategic military and economic measures, including oil production. One national agency, the Petroleum Administration for War (PAW), began to exert considerable control over refining and transporting petroleum even as the oil-producing states "believed they did not require the aid of Washington in developing petroleum resources." Indeed, while PAW set production limits during the war, some states ignored them and "states' officials and regulatory commissioners complained regularly about federal controls." In seeking "to forestall national control of oil, state officials simultaneously promoted and regulated their oil and gas industries" with the effect that "the states, not PAW, controlled production." As William Childs has concluded, "State officials took seriously the divided powers embodied in the Constitution" and "throughout the war period, they engaged in an on-going discourse" over oil and gas production.[10]

Historians have described the changes following the Depression and the New Deal as a "constitutional revolution," with the Supreme Court adopting a much broader notion of the scope of federal power. Eventually, the Court endorsed wide-ranging congressional powers to regulate interstate commerce, leading Edward Corwin to assert that "whatever validity" dual federalism once possessed "as a canon of constitutional construction," that idea was "outmoded" due to "modern decisions" and "business conditions." In 1950, Corwin announced that the principle of dual federalism had been "superseded by a concept favorable to centralization" and he considered it was an open question "whether the constituent States of the System can be saved for any useful purpose." Corwin's epitaph for dual federalism proved premature.[11]

Resurrection of "Interposition" in the Aftermath of *Brown*

Given the centrality of race and racism in America's history, it was not surprising that interposition, albeit in a modern form, resurfaced in the context of race relations following World War II. After President Harry S. Truman ordered the racial integration of American military units, the Democratic Party adopted a strong civil rights plank at its

1948 national convention with a commitment to "eradicate" racial discrimination and insure "the full and equal protection of the laws." Southern delegates supporting segregation walked out of the convention, formed the States' Rights Democratic Party, often called Dixiecrats, and chose Senator Strom Thurmond of South Carolina as their presidential candidate. Thurmond won four Southern states – South Carolina, Mississippi, Louisiana, and Alabama – and thirty-nine electoral votes. As their party's "cornerstone," Dixiecrats embraced the Democratic Party's 1840 resolution that "Congress has no power under the Constitution to interfere with or control the domestic institutions of the several states, and that such states are the sole and proper judges of everything appertaining to their own affairs not prohibited by the Constitution."[12]

In going back to a time when slavery was protected under the Constitution, Dixiecrats sought to undermine the outcome and constitutional consequences of the Civil War and wishfully imagined themselves back to an era of unrestricted white supremacy. They chose to ignore the adoption of the Thirteenth, Fourteenth, and Fifteenth Amendments that abolished slavery, gave the national government the power to protect voting rights irrespective "of race, color, or previous condition of servitude," and ensured that "any person" received due process and the equal protection of the laws. Dixiecrats were following the example of Mississippi legislators in 1890 who sought to annul the Fifteenth Amendment because Black suffrage had allegedly failed in "theory and practice."[13]

What galvanized Southern segregationists and resurrected interposition was opposition to two landmark decisions of the Supreme Court. In 1954 in *Brown v. Board of Education of Topeka* (*Brown* I) the Court rejected the 'separate but equal' doctrine and held that racial segregation in public education violated the Equal Protection Clause of the Fourteenth Amendment. One year later, in *Brown v. Board of Education of Topeka* (*Brown* II) the Court ordered school boards to make a "prompt and reasonable start" to desegregate and held that *Brown* I was to be implemented "with all deliberate speed."[14]

The prospect of integration led segregationists to advance their version of interposition to challenge the federal government and resist the Court's rulings. Although the term "interposition" began to appear in segregationist pamphlet literature by August 1955, interposition received its greatest elaboration and prominence through the *Richmond News Leader*. The newspaper became a central forum for critics of the Civil Rights Movement in general and *Brown* in particular. In a series of editorials beginning in November 1955, the newspaper's editor, James J. Kilpatrick, identified interposition as a constitutional means of opposing the rulings of the Supreme Court and federal intervention.[15]

According to Kilpatrick the "right of interposition" was "enunciated" by Thomas Jefferson, James Madison, and John C. Calhoun, among others, and consisted of "the States' right to interpose their sovereignty between the Federal Government and ... powers reserved to the States." Kilpatrick thought that interposition rested on the "incontrovertible" theory that the Constitution was "a Union of sovereign States" and "a solemn compact among the States." Since every state was "a coequal party" to the compact, if the federal government violates the compact, "every State has a right to judge of the infraction," and on contested issues of power "*only the States themselves*, by constitutional process, may finally decide the issue."[16]

Seeing *Brown* as a "flagrant" violation of the Constitution, Kilpatrick wanted states to interpose their sovereignty and halt the enforcement of *Brown* until the states passed an amendment that either sustained or denied the Court's interpretation. In support of these claims, the *Richmond News Leader* reprinted the Virginia and Kentucky Resolutions of 1798, excerpts from Madison's Report of 1800, and other documents from the Nullification crisis. The newspaper described interposition as "the basic right of a State to assert its sovereignty against Federal encroachments." Interposition "may take many forms – mild, moderate, and strong" – and could be invoked by all the branches of state government. Assertions of the right to interpose "may range from temperate protest at the one extreme to flat nullification at the other." Kilpatrick accepted Madison's explanation that the Virginia Resolutions were only a protest intended "to excite reflection." Neither the Virginia nor the Kentucky resolutions involved nullification, but he thought they underlay a concept of interposition that included the eventual option of nullification. Kilpatrick's editorials argued that Madison had implicitly endorsed the constitutionality of nullification in the Virginia Resolutions, paving the way for Calhoun to invoke the doctrine explicitly.[17]

Kilpatrick's mythologized version of state interposition also appeared in resolutions that Southern legislatures subsequently passed. Those resolutions identified what they called the Supreme Court's deliberate and palpable overreaching in *Brown* that justified Southern states in interposing their sovereignty. Kilpatrick appreciated that interposition elevated the debate over racial equality from "the regional field of segregation to the transcendent, national field of State sovereignty." By asserting that interposition was central to America's constitutional system, segregationists attempted to distance themselves from the local and racial issue of school desegregation while "claiming to defend the very foundations of the nation." Kilpatrick understood the South's desperate need for "a rallying cry of some sort" that would "get this dispute on a high ground of constitutional principle, and away from the muck of the race issue."[18]

Once Kilpatrick and others exhumed interposition, it served segregationists as "the theory and the battle cry of massive resistance." Interposition had the capacity, as George Lewis put it, "to unite the disparate strands of the southern battle to maintain segregation." After four months of editorials, the result was even more dramatic: "Whites across the South, from Virginia to Texas, from political elites to grassroots activists, and from moderates to radical white supremacists, breathed life into the [interposition] concept."[19]

Despite unifying segregationists, interposition's meaning remained unclear. Much confusion centered on whether interposition necessarily involved nullification. A writer in the *Atlanta Journal* in January 1956 called interposition a legal and constitutional means "to nullify the Supreme Court's order." At a closed door meeting that same month, political leaders from four Southern states struggled to understand interposition, with the Governors and representatives from North and South Carolina uncertain about "the legal position of nullification." Indeed, when the *Race Relations Law Reporter* printed the resolutions passed by state legislatures in the wake of the call for interposition, it grouped them under the heading "Interposition and Nullification."[20]

The linkage between interposition and nullification made some Southern leaders nervous if not contemptuous. James Folsom, the Governor of Alabama, described his state legislature's vote for interposition as "a bunch of hogwash" and James Coleman, Mississippi's Governor-elect in 1956, thought calls for nullification were "foolish, ruinous, and legal poppycock." The Mississippi *Delta Democrat-Times* similarly described interposition, which it equated with nullification, as "hysterical bravado which is making our state a laughing-stock."[21]

Despite uncertainty over the legal and constitutional basis for interposition, when Southern states challenged federal efforts to overcome racial inequality, they clearly went beyond the traditional practice of sounding the alarm resolutions. Numan Bartley observed that interposition in the hands of segregationists rested on a commitment to use state power to oppose the *Brown* decision. When segregationists consolidated public school authority in the state as an act "interposing the 'sovereignty' of the state between local school officials and federal courts," they "sought not so much to avoid or evade the Court order as they did to defeat it – to achieve total victory." Nullifying the *Brown* decision was the primary objective of state laws during the campaign of massive resistance.[22]

Southern state legislatures began passing interposition resolutions in early 1956. Invariably, those resolutions described *Brown* as a "deliberate, palpable, and dangerous" exercise of power by the Supreme Court, words that echoed Madison's language in the Third Virginia Resolution, but which ignored his purpose in that resolution. Instead, these twentieth-century resolutions claimed a right of individual states to nullify acts of the federal government. The first state to pass such a resolution was Virginia in February 1956. In what became a pattern for other Southern resolutions, Virginia's legislature invoked the compact nature of the Constitution and emphasized that the delegated powers of the federal government and those reserved to the states could only be altered by constitutional amendment. *Brown*, they concluded, had amended the Constitution through a judicial interpretation that Virginia rejected. Virginia invited other states to support a constitutional amendment to "settle the issue of contested power" presented by the Supreme Court's ruling. Until then, the legislature vowed "to take all appropriate measures ... to resist this illegal encroachment upon our sovereign powers" and urged other states to do likewise. The day after Virginia's legislature acted, Kilpatrick celebrated the effort of Southern states to "bring us back to the principles of sound constitutional government and dual sovereignty, established by our fathers and abandoned in our own time."[23]

Two weeks later, Virginia's Attorney General rendered an opinion denying that the resolution amounted to nullification: the legislature lacked the power to "legally nullify" *Brown*. Rather, the Supreme Court had embraced that doctrine "when it nullified basic provisions of the Constitution." Even so, Virginia's resolution was more than a "stern protest and a memorial" seeking "corrective action" from the federal government. The Attorney General defended Virginia's "declaration of right invoking and interposing the sovereignty of the State against the exercise of powers seized in defiance of the creating compact." The resolution constituted "an appeal of last resort against a deliberate and palpable encroachment transgressing the Constitution."[24]

The day after Virginia's legislature acted, Alabama's legislature followed suit, although with a different twist. Like Virginia, Alabama's legislature thought segregation posed "a question of contested power" and considered *Brown* "a deliberate, palpable, and dangerous attempt by the court to prohibit to the states certain rights and powers never surrendered by them." Alabama's resolution quoted Madison's Report for the proposition that the states "must decide themselves, in the last resort, such questions as may be of sufficient magnitude to require their interposition." But unlike Virginia's legislators hoping to enshrine segregation through a constitutional amendment, Alabama's legislature declared the *Brown* decision "null, void, and of no effect" and hence not binding on the state. The legislature advocated all "constitutionally available" measures "to avoid this illegal encroachment" and urged other states to join their nullification.[25]

The approaches taken by Alabama and Virginia prefigured a division among other Southern states that subsequently passed interposition resolutions. The legislatures of Georgia, Mississippi, and Florida followed Alabama by nullifying *Brown* within their states. Legislators in South Carolina and Louisiana followed Virginia's example of invoking interposition but stopped short of nullification. The significance of the divide was minimal: the states that followed Virginia's lead may not have proclaimed *Brown* null and void, but they crafted laws designed to eviscerate the decision. Louisiana's legislators endorsed measures "to void" the decision and when citizens of Arkansas approved a constitutional amendment, they directed their legislature to pass laws "interposing" the state's sovereignty to nullify federal decisions on desegregation.[26]

Tennessee's opposition to *Brown* came closest to traditional sounding the alarm interposition after its legislators accused the Supreme Court of amending the Constitution through its decision. However, they neither invoked the language of Madison's Third resolution nor did they call for legislative measures to thwart *Brown*. Instead, they registered their "condemnation and protest" of the Court's "usurpation of power." The legislature identified "its solemn duty to help alert the Nation" to such constitutional overreaching and invited "all States and the Congress" to oppose the Court's decision.[27]

Southern "state 'interposition' laws" included a wide range of efforts to maintain school segregation: privatizing public schools, punishing those who attended or taught in racially mixed schools, pupil assignment schemes, and gerrymandering school districts to maintain segregation. Within three years of *Brown*, former Confederate states collectively passed more than 130 legislative measures "designed to counteract some aspect of federally mandated desegregation." Another estimate identified the passage of some "450 laws and resolutions maintaining segregation" in the decade after *Brown*.[28]

On March 13, 1956, nearly one hundred members of the Southern congressional delegation signed a Declaration of Constitutional Principles. In what became known as the Southern Manifesto, they objected to federally mandated desegregation. The Manifesto declared *Brown* "a clear abuse of judicial power" that overturned the constitutionally protected 'separate but equal' principle. The signers denounced the Court's "encroachments on rights reserved to the States and to the people" and promised "to use all lawful means to bring about a reversal" of *Brown* and "to prevent the use of force in its implementation."[29]

An early version of the Manifesto expressly endorsed interposition. Senator Strom Thurmond wanted Southern interposition resolutions to create "a solid front ... against the illegal and unconstitutional action of the Court." Similarly, Senator Richard Russell of Georgia called interposition "a solemn protest by a sovereign state of the invasion of its rights and powers," putting the federal government on notice that the state would use "all of its constitutional powers ... to defeat and reverse all illegal encroachments" of "a power-mad Judiciary." However, both Russell and Thurmond knew they would get fewer signatures if the Manifesto explicitly endorsed interposition. As Representative Brooks Hays of Arkansas explained, he and others refused to sign the document unless it removed all mention of "the doctrines of nullification and interposition." The historical disrepute of those terms and the perception that they were intertwined led to the omission of the word 'interposition.'[30]

In the end, the Manifesto only congratulated States that had declared their "intention to resist forced integration *by any lawful means*." That endorsement of the recent Southern resolutions, however, took a position well outside traditional sounding the alarm interposition. Indeed, unyielding segregationists thought the Manifesto endorsed nullification, despite not using the term. For Roy Harris, the Georgia editor of the *Augusta Courier*, signers of the Manifesto agreed that the Supreme Court decisions "are illegal and they are not binding on any citizen of this country."[31]

Civil rights advocates in Congress repudiated the Manifesto. Oregon's Senator Wayne Morse declared that "the doctrine of interposition means nothing but nullification." The Manifesto demonstrated that White Southerners were determined "to put themselves above the Supreme Court and above the Constitution." He challenged segregationists to propose a constitutional amendment denying Blacks equal rights, and "see how far they will get with the American people." The whole affair prompted Morse to think that "Calhoun was walking and speaking on the floor of the Senate." Morse's view was echoed by other Senators including Senator Hubert Humphrey of Minnesota, all of whom thought the principle of federalism "leaves no room for nullification" and that interposition "fully developed becomes nullification."[32]

While the Manifesto ignited a national debate over civil rights, it also split the Democratic Party. John Day observed that the Manifesto forced congressional candidates to either endorse interposition or support civil rights. Members of the Southern congressional delegation who signed the Manifesto "quickly issued press releases to distribute the statement" and employed it in their reelection campaigns "to promote resistance to desegregation."[33]

Many Southern states quickly moved from words to action. Arkansas Governor Orval Faubus deployed the state's National Guard in early September 1957 to prevent nine Black students from entering Little Rock's Central High School in defiance of a federal court order. Invoking a theory of states' rights, Faubus sought to nullify *Brown* just as earlier efforts at integration in Alabama, Texas and Tennessee had been met with open defiance of federal law based on the theory of a constitutional right of an individual state veto.[34]

President Dwight D. Eisenhower belatedly responded to *Brown* by sending federal troops to enforce the desegregation of Central High School. The resolution of the Little Rock crisis marked a turning point that dealt "a fatal blow to interposition and to the South's confidence that it could legally and 'respectably' escape integration." The employment of interposition and massive resistance by Southern states failed as a matter of constitutional law when the Supreme Court decided *Cooper v. Aaron* in 1958. In an emphatic sign of unanimity and resolve, all nine justices signed as authors (or co-authors) of the opinion in *Cooper*, holding that Arkansas officials were bound by federal court orders that rested on *Brown*. Moreover, the Court held that the *Brown* decision could "neither be nullified openly and directly by state legislators or state executive or judicial officers, nor nullified indirectly by them through evasive schemes for segregation."[35]

In so ruling, the Court issued what appeared to be the death knell to the assertion of state authority over federal constitutional interpretation. The Court cited the Supremacy Clause and noted that in *Marbury v. Madison* the Court had "declared the basic principle that the federal judiciary is supreme in the exposition of the law of the Constitution, and that principle has ever since been respected by this Court and the Country as a permanent and indispensable feature of our constitutional system." Based on this foundation the *Cooper v. Aaron* Court unequivocally ruled: "It follows that the *interpretation of the Fourteenth Amendment enunciated by this Court in the* Brown *case is the supreme law of the land*, and Art. VI of the Constitution makes it of binding effect on the States 'any Thing in the Constitution or Laws of any State to the Contrary notwithstanding.'" While the Court's expansive expression of judicial supremacy overlooked the fact that other institutions also possessed authority to interpret the Constitution and sometimes with practical finality, the opinion in *Cooper* underscored the unconstitutionality of circumventing *Brown*.[36]

A U.S. District Court ruling in Louisiana in the case of *Bush v. Orleans Parish School Board* (1960) provided the judicial coda for using interposition to resist *Brown*. In language endorsed by the Supreme Court, the district court concluded that the "amorphous concept" of interposition was "not a *constitutional* doctrine," but instead "illegal defiance of constitutional authority." However, neither *Cooper* nor *Bush* could banish the rhetoric of interposition and nullification from American legal and constitutional discourse or future actions to interpose and nullify.[37]

Indeed, little more than a quarter of a century after Edward Corwin delivered his epitaph for American federalism, the Supreme Court's decision in *National League of Cities v. Usery* (1976) suggested that Congress did not have nearly unlimited powers under the Commerce Clause. With that decision, and other opinions of the Court taking a similar view, scholars have detected the emergence of a "new federalism." Robert Schapiro noted that while the idea of exclusive and non-overlapping spheres of state and federal action may have "passed irrevocably into history," opinions of the Court have "generally spoken in the accents of dual federalism." "The Court has insisted on the existence of a 'truly local' sphere and a 'truly national' sphere and defined an important role for the courts in demarcating the boundaries of each."[38]

In analyzing the current state of American federalism, some legal scholars have suggested the need to "conceptualize federalism as a relationship between the states and the federal government, rather than as a means of building walls to divide them." Heather Gerken suggests that a new "operating system" is needed to think about federalism because the current reality demonstrates that "neither the state nor the federal government presides over its own empire." Instead, she argues, "they govern shoulder-to-shoulder in a tight regulatory space, sometimes leaning on one another and sometimes deliberately jostling each other."[39]

Modern "Nullification" and "Uncooperative Federalism"

Three decades after the Supreme Court rejected interposition and nullification in *Cooper v. Aaron*, those terms resurfaced – and continue to circulate today – in debates over state opposition to federal laws and policies. But contemporary state resistance to federal laws and policies seems to proceed as if unaware of the history of interposition. Some scholars have identified "a nullificationist (and even secessionist) impulse coursing through contemporary America." Such instincts have produced what some have called 'modern' nullification movements, with some state statutes embracing Calhoun's doctrine of nullification. Indeed, the recent passage of Missouri's so-called "Second Amendment Preservation Act" explicitly invokes Jefferson's compact theory to justify a supposed right of individual state legislatures to nullify federal gun control laws they consider unconstitutional.[40]

A handful of contemporary writers have even asserted the legitimacy if not constitutionality of nullification, while linking the doctrine to Jefferson's Kentucky Resolutions of 1798. Such advocates have argued that an individual state nullifying veto is implicit in the Tenth Amendment, which "originally meant to include a positive power of self-defense or Nullification." Overwhelmingly, however, scholars reject nullification as lacking constitutional authority. There is broad agreement, as Mark Graber has put it, that nullification has been "consigned to the dustbins of history."[41]

Most current state legislative actions responding to national laws and policies do not reflect Calhoun's theory of nullification or amount to an individual state veto. John Dinan finds that nearly all recent state measures "fall short" of nullification. A study of over 1,500 proposals introduced in state legislatures between 2010 and 2016 found less than 10 percent fell into the category of "pure" nullification, subscribing to the theory that "the states have the ability to invalidate national actions that they deem unconstitutional." Yet another analysis of "State Opposition Laws" produced a taxonomy of six different categories, only one of which entails purported nullification.[42]

If not amounting to nullification, state opposition to federal laws and policies in recent decades has ranged widely and includes issues related to national security, immigration, healthcare, gun control, abortion rights, education, the environment, and land policies. Three examples of modern-day state resistance include opposition to the Patriot Act of 2001, the Real ID Act of 2005, and the Affordable Care Act of 2010.[43]

The Patriot Act, passed overwhelmingly in the wake of the September 11 terrorist attacks, seeks to tighten national security. It prompted numerous state legislatures to pass resolutions denouncing the act as an assault on civil liberties, urging Congress to amend or repeal portions of the act that the states believe to be unconstitutional. "A primary criticism leveled at the Patriot Act is that its enforcement is shrouded in secrecy."[44]

The Real ID Act requires states to demand and verify certain forms of documentation before issuing drivers' licenses, and mandates the inclusion of specific information in those licenses. Some twenty-five states have enacted resolutions and statutes opposing the act, with some fifteen states declaring their non-acquiescence. Opponents of a national identification system have "highlighted privacy concerns" as well as claims that the act "violates state sovereignty."[45]

The Affordable Care Act (ACA) required nearly all individuals to purchase health insurance or face a financial penalty. That requirement prompted more than a dozen states to enact statutes and constitutional amendments challenging the constitutionality of the individual mandate. A central complaint was that the mandate "intruded upon personal liberty" and created a precedent for the federal government to "increasingly regulate and compel Americans' commercial choices." The individual mandate was invalidated by the Fifth Circuit, but the Supreme Court in *California v. Texas* reversed the Fifth Circuit and upheld the ACA in its entirety, holding that the plaintiffs lacked standing to challenge the individual mandate. As a result, the Court did not need to reach the merits of the constitutional challenge to the individual mandate, or determine whether the individual mandate was "severable" from the rest of the ACA.[46]

Even more recent instances of state resistance to perceived constitutional overreaching by the federal government have occurred during President Donald Trump's administration including issues involving immigration and federal police power. So-called "sanctuary" cities and states have refused to cooperate with the efforts of Immigration and Custom Enforcement (ICE) to remove aliens illegally residing in the United States. Additionally, after an Executive Order in the wake of Black Lives Matter protests directed federal law enforcement to enter Seattle for the purpose of protecting federal property, the federal force then extended its mission to undertake generalized police power to restrain violence. Seattle's City Attorney Peter Holmes criticized the assumption of "a federal law enforcement role which goes far beyond protecting federal buildings and instead improperly intrudes on local government roles and authority." Holmes raised the concern that the "federal intervention" in Washington state might result in the "disarray" of the "constitutionally mandated balance between federal and local government."[47]

Also concerned about intrusions into state police power, the city of Portland, Oregon brought suit in U.S. District Court against actions of federal agents during protests in 2020. In terms that echoed the defense of personal liberty laws by state legislatures that resisted the Fugitive Slave Act of 1850, Portland's lawsuit alleged that the federal actions "violate the state's sovereign interests in enforcing its laws and in protecting people within its borders from kidnap and false arrest."[48]

Most of the modern state measures of resistance do not constitute 'classical' or 'pure' nullification. John Dinan sees many state laws as falling into two broad categories: some that "vow non-acquiescence to, or are inconsistent with, federal law" and statutes that challenge "the legitimacy or applicability" of federal laws. Dinan's categories are consistent with John Nugent's observation that state officials have "a great many options as they promote their states' interests in dealing with the federal government" between "the extremes of armed rebellion and acquiescence."[49]

Much of the state activity in resisting federal laws and policies appears consistent with what Jessica Bulman-Pozen and Heather Gerken have called "uncooperative federalism," in the course of which "states use regulatory power conferred by the federal government to tweak, challenge, and even dissent from federal law." According to Bulman-Pozen and Gerken, the "strongest form of uncooperative federalism involves civil disobedience: states may simply refuse to comply with the national program or otherwise obstruct it." The alarms to be sounded are *only* political ones, to be answered exclusively in the realm of political conflict and not through purportedly 'legal' analyses written by judges. Uncooperative federalism is one of the various ways, according to Dinan, that "states can 'talk back' to federal officials, without running afoul of the Supremacy Clause by engaging in the discredited practices" of nullification. Uncooperative federalism can spill over into outright nullification, but it has not often crossed this constitutional line.[50]

Still, placing the recent state legislative resistance in historical context has been challenging. Scholars who have re-examined the Virginia and Kentucky Resolutions remain hard pressed to make sense of Madison's language in the Third Virginia resolution and are unclear about what precedents the resolutions offer for state legislative resistance to federal laws and policies today. Occasionally, scholars have taken notice of language in *The Federalist* suggesting a role for states to monitor the national government, though without an appreciation of the origins and the longstanding practice of sounding the alarm interposition.[51]

In assessing Madison's thought in the context of what Sanford Levinson has called the "21st Century Rediscovery of Nullification and Secession," he comes very close to describing the original dynamics of American interposition. "Interposition," Levinson writes, "can mean only that states – like any citizens – are free to articulate their views about the possible unconstitutionality of national laws and to attempt to generate a national movement to repeal those laws." In that process, state legislatures can sound the alarm, by serving "a certain Paul Revere function, announcing to the people – beginning with those from their own state and proceeding to the wider American community – that the national government has violated the Constitution and that a response is necessary."[52]

New Aspects of Judicial Federalism

At the same time that "new nullification" or "uncooperative federalism" was emerging in the states, developments were also taking place in Supreme Court jurisprudence that aided state resistance to perceived excesses of federal congressional power. Those developments resurrected the Tenth Amendment to constrain forced federal enlistment of state officers and entities to carry out federal obligations.

From the beginning of the republic, the Supreme Court has primarily addressed the meaning of the Tenth Amendment's recognition that the powers not delegated to the federal government "are reserved to the States respectively, or to the People," by asking whether that amendment imposes any internal limits on the scope of specific grants of federal power. During the late nineteenth and early twentieth century, reliance on the Tenth Amendment was a significant force in the arguments leading to the invalidation of Congress' power under the Commerce Clause to regulate local manufacture or other local incidents of commercial production. After the New Deal shift in favor of expanded commerce clause authority, the Court viewed the Tenth Amendment as a mere "tautology" – that is, the statement of a conclusion resulting from an analysis of whether power was granted to Congress, instead of an independent constraint on that power.[53]

The Tenth Amendment's new vitality – not only as an internal limit on one of Congress' powers – was expanded as an external constraint on the exercise of specific congressional powers that impose direct burdens on state governments themselves. In this expanded Tenth Amendment limitation on federal authority, the Court articulated an "anti-commandeering" principle, expressed most fully in *Printz v. United States* (1997):

The Federal Government may neither issue directives requiring the States to address particular problems, nor command the States' officers, or those of their political subdivisions, to administer or enforce a federal regulatory program. It matters not whether policymaking is involved, and no case-by-case weighing of the burdens or benefits is necessary; such commands are fundamentally incompatible with our constitutional system of dual sovereignty.

This newly articulated principle also adds grist to the mill for those seeking to support other state challenges to what are also perceived as excessive federal actions interfering with a state's sovereign powers.[54]

* * * * * *

Mark Graber has coined the phrase "partial nullification" to describe instances when a state legislature declares federal laws null and void but does not mandate behavior that violates the law, a practice he calls "interposition." Sanford Levinson has used the phrase "neonullification" to describe the various tactics other than declaring laws null and void that states can use to resist federal laws and policies they oppose. Both phrases identify state actions that are consistent with the theory and history of interposition. The question that remains is whether and to what extent the history of interposition should influence how we think about and practice federalism today.

One important contribution of interposition might be a reminder that the Constitution neither intended to create a consolidated national government nor perpetuate a system of states with independent sovereignty. Under such a federal system, it may well be natural for states to fear that an invigorated national government would unduly expand its powers, just as the national government might fear that states would shirk their responsibilities to the national system.

Given that inevitable dynamic, interposition offers the important insight that the national government cannot do whatever it wants and ride roughshod over the states. And at the same time, interposition reinforces the obligation that states owe to the "supreme law of the land" with the understanding that individual states lack any legitimate power to nullify national laws with which they disagree.[55]

Abbreviations

AJLH	*American Journal of Legal History*
ASP	*American State Papers: Documents, Legislative and Executive, of the Congress of the United States* (38 vols., 1832–1861). The series is divided into ten categories: *Foreign Relations, Indian Affairs, Finance, Commerce and Navigation, Military Affairs, Naval Affairs, Post-Office Department, Public Lands, Claims, and Miscellaneous.*
CP	Robert L. Meriwether et al., eds., *The Papers of John C. Calhoun* (27 vols., 1959–2003).
CTSC	Ulrich Bonnell Phillips, ed., "The Correspondence of Robert Toombs, Alexander H. Stephens, and Howell Cobb," *Annual Report of the American Historical Association for the Year 1911* (2 vols., 1913).
DHFFC	Linda Grant De Pauw et al., eds., *Documentary History of the First Federal Congress of the United States of America, March 4, 1789–March 3, 1791* (22 vols., 1972–2017).
DHRC	John P. Kaminski et al., eds., *The Documentary History of the Ratification of the Constitution, Digital Edition* (2009–2022).
DHSC	Maeva Marcus et al., eds., *The Documentary History of the Supreme Court of the United States, 1789–1800* (7 vols., 1985–2003).
ED	Jonathan Elliot, ed., *The Debates in the Several State Conventions on the Adoption of the Federal*

	Constitution as recommended by the General Convention at Philadelphia, in 1787 (5 vols., 1836).
HP	Harold C. Syrett et al., eds., *The Papers of Alexander Hamilton* (27 vols., 1961–1987).
JER	*Journal of the Early Republic*
JP	Julian P. Boyd et al., eds., *The Papers of Thomas Jefferson* (45 vols. to date, 1950–2021).
JSH	*Journal of Southern History*
ML	[William C. Rives and Philip R. Fendall, eds.], *Letters and Other Writings of James Madison* (4 vols., 1865).
MP	William T. Hutchinson et al., eds., *The Papers of James Madison* (17 vols., 1962–1991).
MPP	James D. Richardson, ed., *A Compilation of the Messages and Papers of the Presidents: 1789–1897* (10 vols., 1896–1899).
PJF	*Publius: The Journal of Federalism*
RFC	Max Farrand, ed., *The Records of the Federal Convention of 1787* (4 vols., revised ed., 1937, reprinted 1966).
RRLR	*Race Relations Law Reporter*
VMHB	*Virginia Magazine of History and Biography*
Web(SFW)	Charles M. Wiltse, ed., *The Papers of Daniel Webster, Speeches and Formal Writings* (2 vols., 1986–1988).
WL	Roy P. Basler, ed., *The Collected Works of Abraham Lincoln* (9 vols., 1953–1955).
WMQ	*William and Mary Quarterly*

Notes

Introduction

1. *Federalist* 51, p. 351 ("compound republic") (Madison), February 6, 1788.
2. Cornell, *Other Founders*, 303 ("tension and conflict").
3. Edward A. Purcell, Jr., *Originalism, Federalism, and the American Constitutional Enterprise: A Historical Inquiry* (2007), 6 ("inherent elasticity and dynamism"); Joseph J. Ellis, *His Excellency: George Washington* (2004), 179 (noting that the Constitution "has been most admired" over the years "for its artful ambiguities, in effect for refusing to resolve the question of state versus federal sovereignty" and "for establishing a framework in which constitutional arrangements could evolve over the years, rather than providing clear answers at that time").
4. The phrase "sovereign states' rights" is used to refer to those who asserted that the Constitution rested on a compact of sovereign states since the phrase "states' rights" only became commonplace in the twentieth century, while prior to that time Americans usually spoke of "state rights." For the sake of consistency, "states' rights" will be used outside of direct quotations describing "state rights."
5. On Native American populations and state sovereignty, see Gregory Ablavsky, "The Savage Constitution," 63 *Duke Law Journal*, (2014), 999–1089; Gregory Ablavsky, "Beyond the Indian Commerce Clause," 124 *Yale Law Journal* (2015), 1012–1090.
6. *Washington Reporter* [Washington, Pa.], February 19, 1873; Peverill Squire, *The Right of Instruction and Representation in American Legislatures, 1788 to 1900* (2021).

7. While well studied, instruction's connection with the practice of interposition has been overlooked. See, for example, Kenneth Colegrove, "The Early History of State Instructions to Members of Congress, 1774–1812" (Ph.D. diss., Harvard University, 1915); George H. Haynes, *The Senate of the United States: Its History and Practice* (2 vols., 1938, reprinted, 1960); William H. Riker, "The Senate and American Federalism," 49 *American Political Science Review* (1955), 452–469; Anderson, "Right of State Legislatures to Instruct"; Kenneth Bresler, "Rediscovering the Right to Instruct Legislators," 26 *New England Law Review* (1991), 355–394; Elaine K. Swift, *The Making of an American Senate: Reconstitutive Change in Congress, 1787–1841* (1996); Jay S. Bybee, "Ulysses at the Mast: Democracy, Federalism, and the Sirens' Song of the Seventeenth Amendment," 91 *Northwestern University Law Review* (1997), 500–572; Kris W. Kobach, "May 'We the People' Speak?: The Forgotten Role of Constituent Instructions in Amending the Constitution," 33 *U.C. Davis Law Review* (1999), 1–94; Halperin, "Special Relationship"; Christopher Terranova, "The Constitutional Life of Legislative Instructions in America," 84 *New York University Law Review* (2009), 1331–1374; Squire, *Right of Instruction*.

   State legislatures instructed their Senators and requested their Representatives in Congress on a wide variety of issues – both national and state-related – from the start of the republic. The much broader set of instructions issued to state lawmakers as well as to U.S. Senators mainly dealt with "policy priorities on matters of economic development," and a recent study suggests "that elected representatives usually followed instructions from their constituents because they could do so at a relatively low cost." Squire, *Right of Instruction*, 111.

8. In New York in 1787 and 1788, Alexander Hamilton, James Madison, and John Jay took the pseudonym "Publius" in coauthoring the now-famous eighty-five newspaper essays known as *The Federalist*.

9. Virginia Resolutions, December 21, 1798, *MP*, XVII:189 ("to interpose").

10. Maier, "Road Not Taken," 1 at 10; Phillip Shaw Paludan, "Hercules Unbound: Lincoln, Slavery, and the Intentions of the Framers," in Donald G. Nieman, ed., *The Constitution, Law, and American Life: Critical Aspects of the Nineteenth-Century Experience* (1992), 2; John J. Dinan, *Keeping the People's Liberties: Legislators, Citizens, and Judges as Guardians of Rights* (1998); Keith E. Whittington, *Political Foundations of Judicial Supremacy: The Presidency, The Supreme Court, and Constitutional Leadership in U.S. History* (2007); Lahav and Newmyer, "Law Wars," 326 at 329; Tony A. Freyer, *Producers versus Capitalists: Constitutional Conflict in Antebellum America* (1994); Powell, "Principles of '98," 689 at 740; David E. Engdahl, "What's in a Name?

The Constitutionality of Multiple 'Supreme' Courts," 66 *Indiana Law Journal* (1991), 457–510; Baker, "Fugitive Slave Clause," 1133 at 1173.

11. Donald G. Morgan, *Congress and the Constitution: A Study of Responsibility* (1966); Kermit L. Hall, *The Magic Mirror: Law in American History* (1989), 72; Thomas Jefferson to Spencer Roane, September 6, 1819, Paul Leicester Ford, ed., *The Writings of Thomas Jefferson* (10 vols., 1892–1899), X:141; Andrew Jackson, *Veto Message*, July 10, 1832, MPP, II:582 ("It is as much the duty of the House of Representatives, of the Senate, and of the President to decide upon the constitutionality of any bill or resolution which may be presented to them for passage or approval as it is of the supreme judges when it may be brought before them for judicial decision"); Larry D. Kramer, *The People Themselves: Popular Constitutionalism and Judicial Review* (2004).

12. Powell, "Principles of '98," 689 at 731 ("the 'lawyerizing'"); Leonard and Cornell, *Partisan Republic*, 85 ("legalist" and "the Constitution had entrusted"); Zarefsky and Gallagher, "Public Discourse," 247.

13. "Speech before the Elmira Chamber of Commerce, May 3, 1907," in *Addresses and Papers of Charles Evans Hughes, Governor of New York, 1906–1908* (1908), 139 ("the Constitution is"); Bradburn, "Public Mind," 565 at 590; Michael F. Conlin, *The Constitutional Origins of the American Civil War* (2019); McDonald, *States' Rights*, 224; *Cooper v. Aaron* 358 U.S. 1 (1958), 18 (asserting that "the federal judiciary is supreme in the exposition of the law of the Constitution").

14. Gienapp, *Second Creation*, 1 ("imaginings"), 4 ("fix"), 110–112, 139; *Federalist* 37, p. 236 ("discussions and adjudications") (Madison), January 11, 1788.

1   The Riddle of Federalism and the Genesis of Interposition

1. Despite the attention devoted to *The Federalist*, the genesis of interposition has been overlooked in part because the description of interposition must be gleaned from multiple essays, none of which deal with interposition per se or even use that terminology.

2. Gunther, *Marshall's Defense*, 2 ("the pervasive problem").

3. McDonald, *States' Rights*, viii ("Dividing sovereignty was generally regarded as impossible, until Americans devised a way of doing it"); Bodenhamer, *U.S. Constitution*, 22.

4. Martin Diamond, "*The Federalist* on Federalism: 'Neither a National Nor a Federal Constitution, but a Composition of Both'," 86 *Yale Law Journal* (1977), 1273 at 1274 ("the primacy"); Martin Diamond, "What the Framers Meant by Federalism," in William A. Schambra, ed., *As Far as Republican Principles Will Admit: Essays by Martin Diamond* (1992), 93 at 95 ("with the localities").

5. Amar, "Of Sovereignty," 1425 at 1449 ("third model"); Gienapp, *Second Creation*, 62; Michael Foley, *Laws, Men, and Machines: Modern American Government and the Appeal of Newtonian Mechanics* (1990); I. Bernard Cohen, *Science and the Founding Fathers: Science in the Political Thought of Jefferson, Franklin, Adams, and Madison* (1995).

6. George Washington to the President of Congress, September 17, 1787, W.W. Abbot and Dorothy Twohig, eds., *The Papers of George Washington, Confederation Series* (6 vols., 1992–1997), V:330 ("difficult to draw").

7. Diamond, "What the Framers Meant," 93 at 95 ("We now give"); Gordon S. Wood, *The Idea of America: Reflections on the Birth of the United States* (2011), 184 ("the remarkable"); Alison L. LaCroix, *The Ideological Origins of American Federalism* (2010), 6 ("new federal ideology"); David J. Bodenhamer, *The Revolutionary Constitution* (2012), 66 ("Federalism was the most novel doctrine to emerge from the Constitutional Convention").

8. A search on May 31, 2022 of Readex's "American Historical Newspapers" from 1787 to 1860 revealed the following usage: "general government" appeared 167,166 times; "federal government" appeared 84,838 times; and "national government" 41,312 times. For clarity for modern readers, we will use "national" or "federal."

9. LaCroix, *Federalism*.

10. *Federalist* 37, p.233 ("stability and energy"), 234 ("marking the proper line") (Madison), January 11, 1788; LaCroix, *Federalism*, 6 ("the belief"); *Federalist* 37, p.237 ("a certain degree"), 238 ("regular symmetry").

11. *Federalist* 39, p.257 ("partly federal") (Madison), January 16, 1788; *Federalist* 37, p.233 ("no other light"); James Madison to N.P. Trist, December, 1831, *ML*, IV:209 ("compound"); James Madison to Robert S. Garnett, February 11, 1824, *ML*, III:367; James Madison to N.P. Trist, December, 1831, *ML*, IV:209 ("technical terms"); James Madison to Thomas Jefferson, June 30, 1789, *MP*, Vol. XII:268 (after being elected to the First Congress Madison declared: "We are in a wilderness without a single footstep to guide us"); Alexis de Tocqueville, *Democracy in America* (Harvey C. Mansfield and Delba Winthrop, eds., 2000), 149; Tulis and Mellow, *Legacies of Losing*, 47 (the Constitution's invention of federalism "made it impossible to describe the regime as either a states' rights or a nationalist polity").

12. *Federalist* 39, p.250 ("evident"), 257 ("a composition").

13. Luther Martin, *Maryland Journal*, March 21, 1788, in Paul Leicester Ford, ed., *Essays on the Constitution of the United States, Published during Its Discussion by the People, 1787–1788* (1892), 367 ("the unsuspecting"), 368 ("to strike out"); *Annals of Congress*, House of

Rep., 1st Cong., 1st Sess., (August 15, 1789), 759 (Elbridge Gerry noting that during the ratifying conventions Anti-Federalists accused their opponents of falsely naming them because "they were in favor of a Federal Government" while "the others were in favor of a national one"); Tulis and Mellow, *Legacies of Losing*, 39.

14. Herbert J. Storing (with the editorial assistance of Murray Dry), *What the Anti-Federalists Were For* (1981), 32 ("new federalism"), 33 ("the primacy").

15. Bernard Bailyn, *To Begin the World Anew: The Genius and Ambiguities of the American Founders* (2003), 121 ("a great web"); Samuel H. Beer, *To Make a Nation: The Rediscovery of American Federalism* (1993), 300 ("established").

16. [James Monroe], *Some Observations on the Constitution* (1788), 11 ("mark the precise point"); James Wilson, Pennsylvania Ratifying Convention, December 4, 1787, *DHRC*, II:496 ("inaccuracy"), 496 (noting that "the line" between the two levels of government was not "drawn with mathematical precision"); James Madison to Edmund Pendleton, September 20, 1787, *MP*, X:171 (explaining that "tracing a proper line of demarkation between the national and State authorities, was necessarily found to be as difficult as it was desirable" and produced "an infinite diversity" of opinions).

The desire to draw clear lines establishing federalism persisted with constitutional commentators producing Venn diagrams seeking to specify the distribution of powers under the Constitution. For example, see Frederic Jesup Stimson, *The Law of the Federal and State Constitutions of the United States* (1908), "Diagram of State and Federal Power" (opposite title page).

17. LaCroix, *Federalism*, 178 ("as the central"); Leonard and Cornell, *Partisan Republic*, 40–41 ("The distribution").

18. Jackson Turner Main, *The Antifederalists: Critics of the Constitution, 1781–1788* (1961), 120 ("previously independent"); Cornell, *Other Founders*, 28–30, 52. Scholars credit the critics of the Constitution for anticipating the proposed system's tendency toward a more centralized government. See Harry N. Scheiber, "Federalism and the Constitution: The Original Understanding," in Lawrence M. Friedman and Harry N. Scheiber, eds., *American Law and the Constitutional Order* (1978), 85–98; Akhil Reed Amar, "Anti-Federalists, *The Federalist Papers*, and the Big Argument for Union," 16 *Harvard Journal of Law and Public Policy* (1993), 111–118; Charles J. Cooper, "'Independent of Heaven Itself': Differing Federalist and Anti-Federalist Perspectives on the Centralizing Tendency of the Federal Judiciary," 16 *Harvard Journal of Law and Public Policy* (1993), 119–128.

19. Rakove, *Original Meanings*, 182 ("a middle ground"), 193; George Washington to the President of Congress, September 17, 1787,

Washington Papers, Confederation Series, V:330 ("the Consolidation"); Samuel Adams to Richard Henry Lee, December 3, 1787, Harry Alonzo Cushing, ed., *The Writings of Samuel Adams* (4 vols., 1904–1908), IV:324 ("as I enter"); Massachusetts Ratifying Convention, January 24, 1788, *ED*, II:99 ("an actual consolidation") (Gilbert Dench).

20. Robert Yates and John Lansing, Jr., to the Governor of New York, Containing Their Reasons for Not Subscribing to the Federal Constitution, *ED*, I:480 ("consolidated government"). After 1801, an account of the convention based on Yates's notes portrayed the delegates as committed to national consolidation and seeking the abolition of state governments. See Cornell, *Other Founders*, 288–289; Bilder, *Madison's Hand*, 226–229; Gienapp, *Second Creation*, 330–331.

21. "Brutus I," *New York Journal*, October 18, 1787, *DHRC*, XIX:103–115; *DHRC*, XIII:411–412; Rakove, *Original Meanings*, 183; James Madison to Edmund Randolph, October 21, 1787, *MP*, X:199 ("new Combatant"); "Brutus I," *New York Journal*, October 18, 1787, *DHRC*, XIX:106 ("a confederated government"), 107 ("except so far"), 109 ("power retained").

22. Garry Wills, *Explaining America: The Federalist* (1981), 171 ("sweet talk"); Rakove, *Original Meanings*, 197 ("was already"); James Madison to George Washington, April 16, 1787, *MP*, IX: 383 ("a new system" to "middle ground"); Stampp, "Perpetual Union," 5 at 17 (describing Hamilton's "readiness to say almost anything that would assure Federalist success").

23. *Federalist* 39, p.256 ("controversies" and "clearly essential"); Rakove, *Original Meanings*, 176 (asserting that Madison's statement "accurately captured the original intention of the framers"); Oliver Ellsworth, Connecticut Ratifying Convention, January 7, 1788, *DHRC*, XV:278–279 (identifying the courts as a "constitutional check" against any overreach of authority).

24. *Federalist* 33, p.206 ("must judge") (Hamilton), January 2, 1788; *Federalist* 78, p.528 ("faithful guardians"), 524 ("the constitutional judges"), 525 ("designed") (Hamilton), May 28, 1788.

25. *Federalist* 80, p.534 ("proper extent" and "out of the laws"), 535 ("an authority") (Hamilton), May 28, 1788; "Brutus I," *New York Journal*, October 18, 1787, *DHRC*, XIX:109 ("out of the way").

26. *Federalist* 45, p.310 ("the balance") (Madison), January 26, 1788; *Federalist* 46, p.317 ("resist and frustrate") (Madison), January 29, 1788.

27. *Federalist* 46, p.319 ("executed" and "refusal"), 319–320 ("very serious").

28. *Federalist* 17, p.106 ("usurp") (Hamilton), December 5, 1787; *Federalist* 25, p.159 ("contest") (Hamilton), December 21, 1787.

29. James Wilson, Pennsylvania Ratifying Convention, December 4, 1787, *DHRC*, II:478 ("will not be able"); Charles Pinckney, South Carolina

Ratifying Convention, January 16, 1788, *ED*, IV:259 ("infringement" and "sufficiently energetic").

30. *Federalist* 16, p.103–104 ("would always") (Hamilton), December 4, 1787; *Federalist* 31, p.198 ("must be left") (Hamilton), January 1, 1788; *Federalist* 33, p.206 ("proper exercise" and "If the Federal Government").

31. *Federalist* 46, p.315 ("lost sight"), 315–316 ("the ultimate"); *Federalist* 49, p.339 ("only legitimate") (Madison), February 2, 1788; *Federalist* 44, p.305 ("in the last resort") (Madison), January 25, 1788; *Federalist* 51, p.349 ("the primary") (Madison), February 6, 1788.

32. *Federalist* 39, p.256 ("extends"); *Federalist* 40, p.261 ("distinct") (Madison), January 18, 1788; *Federalist* 9, p.55 ("implying") (Hamilton), November 21, 1787; *Federalist* 32, p.200 ("would clearly") (Hamilton), January 2, 1788.

33. Elaine F. Crane, "Publius in the Provinces: Where Was *The Federalist* Reprinted outside New York City?" 21 *WMQ* (1964), 589–592; Bailyn, *Begin the World Anew*, 100–125; Maier, *Ratification*, 84–85; Yazawa, *Contested Conventions*, 175–208.

Hamilton and Madison published their "Publius" essays between October 27, 1787 and May 28, 1788. For references to state legislatures before Hamilton and Madison published their essays, see "An Independent Freeholder," *Winchester Virginia Gazette*, January 25, 1787, *DHRC*, VIII:328 (state legislatures "will keep a watchful eye and take special care that congress do not exceed their powers"); "Poplicola," *Massachusetts Centinel*, October 31, 1787, *DHRC*, IV:181–182 (state legislatures would "form a formidable barrier against any possible encroachment of the sovereign power"); "An American," *Independent Chronicle*, November 30, 1787, *DHRC*, IV:337 (state legislatures would be a "powerful check" that along "with the people in every State will keep a fixed eye upon all the acts of Congress").

34. *Federalist* 26, p.168 ("exceed the proper"), 169 ("always be") (Hamilton), December 22, 1787. Mclean's 1788 edition of *The Federalist* describes action by "the state Legislatures" which Cooke's edition renders in the singular. See *The Federalist: A Collection of Essays Written in Favour of the New Constitution As Agreed Upon by the Federal Convention, September 17, 1787. In Two Volumes* (1788), I:166.

35. *Federalist* 26, p.169 ("constantly"); *Federalist* 44, p.305.

36. *Federalist* 28, p.179–180 ("select bodies" to "discover the danger"), (Hamilton), December 26, 1787; Alexander Hamilton, Speeches in the New York Ratifying Convention, June 21, 1788, *HP*, V:57 (describing state legislatures as "standing bodies of observation, possessing the confidence of the people, jealous of federal encroachments, and armed with every power to check the first essays of treachery" who would

"institute regular modes of enquiry" and serve as "vigilant guardians of the people's rights").

37. *Federalist* 44, p.305 ("[W]hat is to be").
38. *Federalist* 44, p.305 ("usurpation" to "ultimate redress").
39. *Federalist* 44, p.305 ("will be ever ready" to "watching").
40. *Federalist* 46, p.320 ("ambitious encroachments" and "Every Government").
41. *Federalist* 52, p.359 ("restrained") (Madison), February 8, 1788; *Federalist* 55, p.376 ("would fail") (Madison), February 13, 1788.
42. *Federalist* 84, p.581 ("large powers"), 582 ("the vigilance"), 582–583 ("The executive"), 583 ("sound the alarm") (Hamilton), May 28, 1788.
43. *Federalist* 85, p.593 ("local interests" and "We may safely") (Hamilton), May 28, 1788.
44. *Federalist* 26. p.169 (the ARM"; *Federalist* 46, p.320 ("appeal to a trial").
45. *Federalist* 28, p.180 ("opposition"); *Federalist* 46, p.320 ("resistance"); *Federalist* 46, p.319 ("legislative devices"); Beer, *Make a Nation*, 295; Chernow, *Hamilton*, 255–256; Stephen C. Neff, "Secession and Breach of Compact: The Law of Nature Meets the United States Constitution," in Cogan, *Union & States' Rights*, 88 at 103–104; Saul Cornell, "Mobs, Militias, and Magistrates: Popular Constitutionalism and the Whiskey Rebellion," 81 *Chicago-Kent Law Review* (2006), 883 at 890; Rakove, "Hollow Hopes," 81 at 89; Dennis A. Henigan, "Alarms, Anarchy and the Second Amendment," 26 *Valparaiso University Law Review* (1991), 107 at 120.

    In identifying the 'sounding the alarm' language in Madison's *Federalist* 44 and 46, Bradley Hays correctly identifies the alert that states might issue on the occasion of national overreaching, but overlooks Hamilton's part in describing interposition. See Hays, *States in American Constitutionalism*, 4, 39, and 96.
46. "Federal Farmer," Letter X, January 7, 1788, *DHRC*, V:296 ("will stand" to "by which"); "Federal Farmer," Letter XVII, January 23, 1788, *DHRC*, V:359 ("ready advocates"). For evidence that Melancton Smith was the "Federal Farmer," see Robert H. Webking, "Melancton Smith and the *Letters from the Federal Farmer*," 44 *WMQ* (1987), 510–528.
47. Alexander Hamilton, New York Ratifying Convention, June 24, 1788, *DHRC*, XXII:1864 ("natural strength"), 1865 ("shocking"); John Lansing, Jr., New York Ratifying Convention, June 24, 1788, *DHRC*, XXII:1872 ("only proved" to "None but to wait").
48. On whether *The Federalist* reflected a "split personality," see, for example, Douglass Adair, "The Authorship of the Disputed Federalist Papers: Part II," 1 *WMQ* (1944), 235 at 242; George W. Carey, "Publius – A Split Personality?" 46 *Review of Politics* (1984), 5–22; Todd Estes, "The Voices of Publius and the Strategies of Persuasion in *The Federalist*," 28 *JER* (2008), 523–558.

As to interposition, however, Hamilton and Madison shared the goal of ratification and jointly embraced a rhetorical argument in responding to Anti-Federalists warning about national consolidation. Hamilton's part in describing interposition originated as "sweet talk" and ever remained so for him while Madison would later, particularly in the course of the Virginia and Kentucky Resolutions of 1798, embrace the constitutional tool of interposition that he and Hamilton had described during the ratification debates.

49. Wood, *Empire of Liberty*, 31 ("the real problem"); James Madison, "Vices of the Political System of the United States," [April–June], 1787, *MP*, IX:345–358; James Madison to Thomas Jefferson, October 24, 1787, *MP*, X:212 ("mutability"); Alexander Hamilton, June 19, 1787, *RFC*, I:323 ("no boundary"); *Federalist* 71, p.483–484 ("the people themselves") (Hamilton), March 18, 1788; Gordon S. Wood, *The Radicalism of the American Revolution* (1992), 250–251; Larry D. Kramer, "Madison's Audience," 112 *Harvard Law Review* (1999), 611 at 625; Quentin Taylor, "The Mask of Publius: Alexander Hamilton and the Politics of Expediency," 5 *American Political Thought: A Journal of Ideas, Institutions and Culture* (2016), 55 at 68.

50. Rakove, *Original Meanings*, 189 ("in dispelling"); Wills, *The Federalist*, xii ("Publius" both "had to argue for a stronger government and at the same time quiet the fears of strong government"); George W. Carey, *The Federalist: Design for a Constitutional Republic* (1989), 97.

51. Alexander Hamilton to George Washington, July 3, 1787, *HP*, IV:224 ("thinking men"); "Conjectures about the New Constitution," [September 17–30, 1787], *HP*, IV:276 ("good administration" and "the general government"), 277 ("contests"). The essay was not printed or shared with his correspondents, and the editors of the Hamilton *Papers* speculate it may have been intended as a newspaper article but set aside once work began on the *Federalist* essays.

52. James Madison, June 8, 1787, *RFC*, I:165 ("controul"); James Madison to Thomas Jefferson, September 6, 1787, *MP*, X:163–164 ("neither effectually"); James Madison to Thomas Jefferson, October 24, 1787, *MP*, X:212 ("A constitutional negative"), 211 ("a recurrence"); Bilder, *Madison's Hand*, 74–77, 77 ("For Madison, a broad national negative was the linchpin of the new system"); Charles F. Hobson, "The Negative on State Laws: James Madison, the Constitution, and the Crisis of Republican Government," 36 *WMQ* (1979), 215–235.

53. Bilder, *Madison's Hand*, 115 ("constitutional protections" and "southern delegates").

54. Douglass Adair, "The Authorship of the Disputed Federalist Papers," 1 *WMQ* (1944), 97 at 100 (noting that Hamilton's "strange reluctance" to identify himself as one of the authors of *The Federalist* in 1802 undoubtedly stemmed from the fact that "some of his essays written in

1787–88 did not square with certain constitutional theories that he had come to espouse publicly after 1790").

55. U.S. Const., Art. VI ("by oath or affirmation").

56. Jack P. Greene, *Peripheries and Center: Constitutional Development in the Extended Polities of the British Empire and the United States, 1607–1788* (1986), 204 (the Constitution ensured that "both the national government and the state governments would have full authority within their respective spheres, authority deriving directly from grants by the people – in whom sovereignty continued to reside"); Martha Derthick, *Keeping the Compound Republic: Essays on American Federalism* (2001), 2 ("What the Framers settled on was an implausible compromise between a pure federation and a pure unitary or national government").

57. Banning, "Hamiltonian Madison" (pointing out that Hamilton's perspective differed from Madison's in terms of the potential source of disequilibrium); David J. Siemers, *Ratifying the Republic: Antifederalists and Federalists in Constitutional Time* (2002), 75 (noting Madison's and Hamilton's shared effort to adopt the Constitution, "but in doing so they seem to be back-to-back, facing in opposite directions").

2 Early State Use of Interposition: Testing the Powers of the New National Government

1. George Mason, September 12, 1787, *RFC*, II:587–588 ("prefaced"); J. Gordon Hylton, "Virginia and the Ratification of the Bill of Rights, 1789–1791," 25 *University of Richmond Law Review* (1991), 433 at 437–438 ("The principal problem"); Gienapp, *Second Creation*, 165 ("they tended"); John Marshall, *Life of George Washington* (2d. ed., 2 vols., 1836), II:205–206; Cornell, *Other Founders*, 162–163.

2. James Madison to Richard Peters, August 19, 1789, *MP*, XII:347 ("tacit compact"); James Madison to George Washington, August 11, 1788, *MP*, XI:230; Hylton, "Bill of Rights," 433 at 438; Robert A. Rutland, ed., *The Papers of George Mason, 1725–1792* (3 vols., 1970), III:1068–1072, 1115–1120. On Virginia's ratification convention, see Maier, *Ratification*, 255–319; Yazawa, *Contested Conventions*, 144–174; Broadwater, *Jefferson, Madison*, 172–177.

3. James Madison to Alexander Hamilton, June 27, 1788, *MP*, XI:181 ("highly objectionable"); James Madison to Thomas Jefferson, December 8, 1788, *MP*, XI:382 ("friends of the Constitution"); *Mason Papers*, III:1116–1117; Leonard and Cornell, *Partisan Republic*, 35 ("The one thing Madison adamantly opposed was any effort to weaken the powers of the central government and restore power to the states").

4. James Madison to George Eve, January 2, 1789, *MP*, XI:405 ("rights of Conscience"); Henry Lee to James Madison, November 19, 1788, *MP*, XI:356; James Madison to a Resident of Spotsylvania County, January 27, 1789, *MP*, XI:428. Madison won by a vote of 1,308 to 972. *MP*, XI:438n1.

5. George Mason to John Mason, July 31, 1789, Mason *Papers*, III:1164 ("some Milk & Water"); James Madison to Thomas Jefferson, October 17, 1788, *MP*, XI:297 ("parchment barriers").

6. James Madison to Thomas Jefferson, October 17, 1788, *MP*, XI:298 ("political truths"), 298–299 ("acquire by degrees"), 299 ("usurped acts"); Thomas Jefferson to James Madison, March 15, 1789, *MP*, XII:14 ("the subordinate"); Paul Finkelman, "James Madison and the Bill of Rights: A Reluctant Paternity," *Supreme Court Review* (1990), 301–347.

7. "Amendments to the Constitution, June 8, 1789, *MP*, XII:204 ("paper barriers"), 207 ("security").

8. "Amendments to the Constitution," June 8, 1789, *MP*, XII:200 ("That all power"); James Madison, August 31, 1787, *RFC*, II:476 ("The people were" and "first principles"); "Public Opinion," for the *National Gazette*, [*c.* December 19, 1791], *MP*, XIV:170 (Madison observing that matured public opinion limited "every government, and is the real sovereign in every free one").

9. Edward Dumbauld, *The Bill of Rights and What It Means Today* (1957), 33–44; Michael J. Klarman, *The Framers' Coup: The Making of the United States Constitution* (2016), 546–595; Gienapp, *Second Creation*, 164–201.

10. "Amendments to the Constitution," June 8, 1789, *MP*, XII:198 ("injure the constitution"), 199 ("the whole structure"); Helen E. Veit, Kenneth R. Bowling, and Charlene Bangs Bickford, eds., *Creating the Bill of Rights: The Documentary Record from the First Federal Congress* (1991), 41, 197; Klarman, *Framers' Coup*, 577–583; Gienapp, *Second Creation*, 190–196, 400n48.

11. Aedanus Burke, August 15, 1789, *DHFFC*, XI:1278 ("a tub"); Kenneth R. Bowling, "'A Tub to the Whale': The Founding Fathers and Adoption of the Bill of Rights," 8 *JER* (1988), 223–251; "Amendments to the Constitution," August 15, 1789, *MP*, XII:341; Tulis and Mellow, *Legacies of Losing*, 37 (Madison "realized that the main objective of the Anti-Federalists was not to secure the sorts of individual rights now contained in the Bill of Rights but rather to advance structural amendments to change the most fundamental features of the Constitution and thereby restore power to the states").

12. James Madison to Alexander White, August 24, 1789, *MP*, XII:352 ("ambiguities"); James Madison to Thomas Jefferson, June 30, 1789, *MP*, XII:272; James Madison to Edmund Pendleton, September 14, 1789, *MP*, XII:402.

13. Richard Henry Lee and William Grayson to the Speaker of the Virginia House of Delegates, September 28, 1789, Veit et al., *Creating the Bill of Rights*, 299 ("the annihilation"), William Grayson to Patrick Henry, September 29, 1789, p. 300 ("are so mutilated"); James Madison to George Washington, December 5, 1789, *MP*, XII:458 ("to keep alive"); Kenneth R. Bowling, "Overshadowed by States' Rights: Ratification of the Federal Bill of Rights," in Ronald Hoffman and Peter J. Albert, eds., *The Bill of Rights: Government Proscribed* (1997), 77 at 92–93.

14. "Location of the Capital," September 4, 1789, *MP*, XII:374 ("eccentric"), September 3, 1789, 372 ("moderation"); James Madison to Tench Cox, September 18, 1789, *MP*, XII:410 ("an overbearing").

15. *Journal of the Senate of the Commonwealth of Virginia; Begun and Held in the City of Richmond, On Monday, the 19th day of October, in the year of our Lord 1789, and in the Fourteenth Year of the Commonwealth* (Richmond, 1828), 62 ("much more materially"); Hardin Burnley to James Madison, November 28, 1789, *MP*, XII:456; Hylton, "Bill of Rights," 433 at 452–456; Bowling, "Overshadowed by States' Rights," 94–95.

16. Hylton, "Bill of Rights," 433 at 460–462.

17. J.R. Pole, *The Gift of Government: Political Responsibility from the English Restoration to American Independence* (1983), 117–130, 131; J. R. Pole, *Political Representation in England and the Origins of the American Republic* (1966), 278, 402.

18. Daniel Wirls and Stephen Wirls, *The Invention of the United States Senate* (2004), 166.

19. Willi Paul Adams, *The First American Constitutions: Republican Ideology and the Making of the State Constitutions in the Revolutionary Era* (1980), 250; Marc W. Kruman, *Between Authority and Liberty: State Constitution Making in Revolutionary America* (1997), 81; 1776 Pennsylvania Constitution, Sec. 13, Francis Newton Thorpe, ed., *The Federal and State Constitutions, Colonial Charters, and Other Organic Laws of the States, Territories, and Colonies Now or Heretofore Forming the United States of America* (7 vols., 1909), V:3085.

20. David Stuart to George Washington, July 14, 1789, W.W. Abbot and Dorothy Twohig, eds., *The Papers of George Washington, Presidential Series* (21 vols. to date, 1987–2020), III:199 ("much censured"); Paine Wingate to Timothy Pickering, April 29, 1789, in Goebel, *Supreme Court*, 444n163; Wirls and Wirls, *United States Senate*, 170; Anne M. Butler and Wendy Wolff, *United States Senate Election, Expulsion and Censure Cases, 1793–1990* (1995), 3–5; Roy Swanstrom, *The United States Senate, 1787–1801: A Dissertation on the First Fourteen Years of the Upper Legislative Body*, 87th Cong., 1st Sess., Senate Doc. No. 64 (1962), 238.

21. Elizabeth G. McPherson, "The Southern States and the Reporting of Senate Debates, 1789–1802," 12 *JSH* (1946), 223 at 228 ("free admission"); DHFFC, I:296–298; John Dawson to James Madison, May 14, 1790, *MP*, XIII:215; David Stuart to George Washington, June 2, 1790, Washington *Papers, Presidential Series*, V:461; Kenneth R. Bowling and Helen E. Veit, eds., *The Diary of William Maclay and Other Notes on Senate Debates* (1988), 255.

22. *Journal of the House of Delegates, of the Commonwealth of Virginia, Begun and Held at the Capitol in the City of Richmond, on Monday, the Eighteenth of October, in the Year of our Lord, One Thousand Seven Hundred and Ninety, and of the Commonwealth the Fifteenth* [Richmond, 1790], 82 ("among the important"); Editorial Note, DHFFC, VIII:749n5; *JP*, XVII:459 (referring to the introduction of resolutions seeking the opening of the Senate debates in conjunction with the resolutions dealing with assumption); Walter Clark, ed., *The State Records of North Carolina* (1788–1790), XXI:1029–1030; McPherson, "Senate Debates," 223 at 230–231; Bowling and Veit, *Diary of William Maclay*, 389 (reporting a resolution of January 22, 1791 passed by the House of Representatives of Pennsylvania calling for the opening of the U.S. Senate, defeated by the state's Senate by one vote on February 25, 1791); *Providence Gazette* [Providence, R.I.], February 12, 1791; Halperin, "Special Relationship," 267 at 282; *Pennsylvania Mercury* [Philadelphia], February 12, 1791. Maryland's House of Delegates voted to join Virginia's call for instructions to their Senators to open the proceedings of the Senate by a vote of 48 to 4. *Votes and Proceedings of the House of Delegates of the State of Maryland. November Session, 1790*, Maryland State Archives, 95.

23. Swanstrom, *United States Senate*, 166 ("could not be"); McPherson, "Senate Debates," 223 at 228; Wirls and Wirls, *United States Senate*, 167–168; Anderson, "Right of the State Legislatures to Instruct," 39; Halperin, "Special Relationship," 267 at 278–285; North Carolina, *State Records*, XXI:1029; Earl R. Franklin, "The Instruction of United States Senators by North Carolina," 7 *Trinity College Historical Papers* (1907), 1–15.

24. *Senate Journal*, 2nd Cong., 2nd Sess., (January 3, 1793), 468 ("the principles").

25. "OBSERVATIONS: On the policy of keeping shut the doors of the Senate of the United States," *Norwich Packet* [Norwich, Conn.], August 23, 1792 ("kept in the dark" and "If rulers").

26. *National Gazette* [Philadelphia], February 2, 1792 ("the people"); "To the Freemen of America," *National Gazette*, February 13, 1793 ("How are you"). Freneau had been recruited and supported by Jefferson and Madison in an effort to counterbalance the pro-administration newspaper *Gazette of the United States* edited by John Fenno. See Pasley, *"Tyranny*

of Printers," 60–66; Gerald L. Grotta, "Philip Freneau's Crusade for Open Sessions of the U.S. Senate," 48 *Journalism Quarterly* (1971), 667–671.

27. Jacob E. Cooke, *Alexander Hamilton* (1982), 77 ("a monolithic nationalism"); *HP*, VI:51–168; Forrest McDonald, *Alexander Hamilton: A Biography* (1979), 171; Chernow, *Hamilton*, 301–302.
    On Hamilton's vision for establishing the economic and financial foundation of a modern national state, see John C. Miller, *Alexander Hamilton: Portrait in Paradox* (1959), 46–56; John C. Miller, *The Federalist Era, 1789–1801* (1960), 39–41; Gerald Stourzh, *Alexander Hamilton and the Idea of Republican Government* (1970); Lance Banning, *The Jeffersonian Persuasion: Evolution of a Party Ideology* (1978), 129–140; Drew R. McCoy, *The Elusive Republic: Political Economy in Jeffersonian America* (1980), 146–152; Edling, *Hercules*, 81–107; Leonard and Cornell, *Partisan Republic*, 43; Act of August 4, 1790, ch. 34, 1 Stat. 138.

28. E. James Ferguson, *The Power of the Purse: A History of American Public Finance, 1776–1790* (1961), 289–343; McDonald, *Hamilton*, 163–188; Elkins and McKitrick, *Federalism*, 114–123; Edwin J. Perkins, *American Public Finance and Financial Services, 1700–1815* (1994), 199–234; *HP*, VI:78–81 (Hamilton's argument supporting assumption).

29. Alexander Hamilton to James Madison, October 12, 1789, *HP*, V:439 (*"least* unpopular"); James Madison to Alexander Hamilton, November 19, 1789, *HP*, V:526 ("buy out"); James Madison to Henry Lee, April 13, 1790, *MP*, XIII:147 ("faulty"), 148 ("Public Debt"). For Jefferson's scathing critique of Hamilton's financial plan, see Thomas Jefferson to George Washington, May 23, 1792, *JP*, XXIII:536–537; Thomas Jefferson to George Washington, September 9, 1792, *JP*, XXIV:353.

30. Brant, *Madison*, III:290–305; Ketcham, *Madison*, 308; Banning, *Sacred Fire*, 309–325.

31. Ferguson, *Power of the Purse*, 307–318.

32. James Madison to Thomas Jefferson, March 8, 1790, *JP*, XVI:213 ("already sufficiently great"); "General Defense of the Constitution," Virginia Ratifying Convention, June 6, 1788, *MP*, XI:85; Banning, "Hamiltonian Madison," 9.

33. James Madison to Thomas Jefferson, May 27, 1789, *JP*, XV:154; Banning, *Sacred Fire*, 318–319; Elkins and McKitrick, *Federalism*, 146 (arguing that the debate over assumption pitted Madison's ideological views as a Virginian against his instincts towards nationhood and that Madison no longer trusted Hamilton).

34. Speech of James Madison, April 22, 1790, *MP*, XIII:168 ("to be remedied"); *Federalist* 44, p.304–305 (Madison), January 25, 1788 ("No axiom is more clearly established in law, or in reason, than that

wherever the end is required, the means are authorized; wherever a general power to do a thing is given, every particular power necessary for doing it, is included").

35. David Stuart to George Washington, June 2, 1790, Washington *Papers, Presidential Series*, V:462 ("subversive"), 461 ("unwarrantable"), 462 ("blow"); Patrick Henry, Virginia Ratifying Convention, June 4, 1788, *ED*, III:22 ("That this is a consolidated government is demonstrably clear; and the danger of such a government is, to my mind, very striking");.

36. Richard Henry Lee to Samuel Adams, April 25, 1789, James Custis Ballagh, ed., *The Letters of Richard Henry Lee* (2 vols., 1911–1914), II:484 ("One Government"), Richard Henry Lee to Patrick Henry, September 14, 1789, Lee *Letters*, II:502 ("the friends of liberty" and "prevent a consolidating").

37. James Madison to James Monroe, April 17, 1790, *MP*, XIII:151 (noting "the zeal" of advocates for assumption who "intimate danger to the Union from a refusal to assume"); Thomas Jefferson to Thomas Mann Randolph, Jr., June 20, 1790, *JP*, XVI:540 (if Congress adjourned without assumption "there is an end of the government"); "Jefferson's Account of the Bargain on the Assumption and Residence Bills," [1792?], *JP*, XVII:205–208; Jacob E. Cooke, "The Compromise of 1790," 27 *WMQ* (1970), 523–545; Elkins and McKitrick, *Federalism*, 155–161; Kenneth R. Bowling, *The Creation of Washington D.C.: The Idea and Location of the American Capital* (1991).

38. North Carolina, *State Records*, XXI:877 ("consent"); *Federalist* 84, p.582 ("executive") (Hamilton), May 28, 1788.

39. *New Hampshire Spy* [Portsmouth, N.H.], January 5, 1791 (citing a newspaper reporting from Petersburg, North Carolina, December 9, 1790) ("violently opposed"); North Carolina, *State Records*, XXI:1055 ("an infringement"); *Salem Gazette* [Salem, Mass.], February 2, 1791 (including "Extract of a letter from Fayetteville," dated December 6, 1790); *Independent Gazetteer* [Philadelphia], January 1, 1791 (including "Extract of a letter from a gentleman in North Carolina to his friend in this city").

40. North Carolina, *State Records*, XXI:1029 ("the alarming measures"), 962 ("every excise"), 855–856, 961.

41. Virginia House of Delegates, *Journal*, 36 ("repugnant"); Beverley Randolph to James Madison, May 26, 1790, *MP*, XIII:230; Harry Ammon, "The Formation of the Republican Party in Virginia, 1789–1796," 19 *JSH* (1953), 283 at 291.

42. Virginia House of Delegates, *Journal*, 36 ("highly injurious"); Beveridge, *Marshall*, II:65–68; Ammon, "Formation of the Republican Party," 283 at 291.

43. Meriwether Smith to Thomas Jefferson, December 4, 1790, *JP*, XVIII:131 ("One party charges"); Virginia House of Delegates, *Journal*, 39, 45.

44. Alexander Hamilton to John Jay, Philadelphia, November 13, 1790, _HP_, VII:149 ("This is the first symptom" and "the collective"); John Jay to Alexander Hamilton, Boston, November 28, 1790, _HP_, VII:167 ("Every indecent"); Joanne B. Freeman, "'The Art and Address of Ministerial Management': Secretary of the Treasury Alexander Hamilton and Congress," in Kenneth R. Bowling and Donald R. Kennon, eds., _Neither Separate nor Equal: Congress in the 1790s_ (2000), 269–293, esp., 289–290.

45. "Notes of Objects for Consideration of the President" [December 1, 1790], _HP_, VII:173 ("Utility"); Benjamin Lincoln to Alexander Hamilton, December 4, 1790, _HP_, VII:196 ("to control"), VII:197 ("the doings"); Christian G. Fritz, _American Sovereigns: The People and America's Constitutional Tradition before the Civil War_ (2008), 106, 109–112; Robert A. Feer, _Shays's Rebellion_ (1988), 345–360; Robert J. Taylor, _Western Massachusetts in the Revolution_ (1954), 158–159; David B. Mattern, _Benjamin Lincoln and the American Revolution_ (1995), 166–169.

46. Maryland House of Delegates, _Proceedings_, 83 ("particularly injurious"), 84 ("authorized by the Constitution"), 104–105; L. Marx Renzulli, Jr., _Maryland: The Federalist Years_ (1972), 130–132.

47. Meriwether Smith to Thomas Jefferson, December 4, 1790, _JP_, XVIII:130 ("declaration"); William Waller Hening, _The Statutes at Large; Being a Collection of all the Laws of Virginia from the First Session of the Legislature, in the Year 1619 ..._ (13 vols., 1809–1823), XIII:234 ("not granted"), 235, 237–239; _Journal of the Senate of the Commonwealth of Virginia; Begun and Held in the City of Richmond, On Monday, the 18ᵗʰ day of October, in the Year of our Lord 1790, and in the Fifteenth Year of the Commonwealth_ (Richmond, 1828), 44, 78; Alexander Hamilton to John Jay, November 13, 1790, _HP_, VII:149.

    On January 3, 1791 Virginia's governor sent Madison (along with the other members of the state's congressional delegation) a copy of the resolutions and the memorial. _MP_, XIII:345–346.

48. Virginia House of Delegates, _Journal_, 45; Ammon, "Formation of the Republican Party," 283 at 291; Malone, _Jefferson_, II:337; Sharp, _American Politics_, 38; Gutzman, "Virginia and Kentucky Resolutions," 473 at 477; Richard R. Beeman, _Patrick Henry: A Biography_ (1974), 175.

49. Virginia House of Delegates, _Journal_, 82 ("the consent"), 142; Virginia Senate, _Journal_, 83–84; Hening's _Statutes_, XIII: 237–239.

50. _DHFFC_, VIII:300 ("an enormous debt"); Beeman, _Old Dominion_, 79 ("prerevolution rhetoric"); Miller, _Juries and Judges_, 48 ("a classic statement"), 10 ("drawing up").

51. _DHFFC_, VIII:301 ("During the whole" and "no clause"); Beeman, _Old Dominion_, 81 ("taking a step"); Ammon, "Formation of the Republican

Party," 283 at 292; Charles Pinnegar, *Virginia and State Rights, 1750–1861: The Genesis and Promotion of a Doctrine* (2009), 107–108; Gutzman, "Virginia and Kentucky Resolutions," 473 at 478; Bowling, "Overshadowed by States' Rights," 77 at 98; Tipton, *Nullification and Interposition,* 15.

52. *DHFFC*, VIII:301 ("the Guardians"); *Federalist* 26, p.169 (Hamilton), December 22, 1787; *Federalist* 44, p.305; *Federalist* 46, p.320 (Madison), January 30, 1788; *Federalist* 84, p.582 (Hamilton), May 28, 1788.

    Most of the scholars who have discussed the Virginia legislature's 1790 resolutions and memorial invariably describe them as a "remonstrance" patterned on colonial practices drawn from English political traditions without noting their connection with *The Federalist.* See Ammon, "Formation of the Republican Party," 283 at 291; Miller, *Federalist Era,* 52; Banning, *Jeffersonian Persuasion,* 150; Miller, *Juries and Judges,* 48; Gutzman, "Virginia and Kentucky Resolutions," 473 at 477; Edling, *Hercules,* 85.

    A rare example of identifying the action of Virginia's legislature with interposition described in *The Federalist* is William Wirt Henry, *Patrick Henry: Life, Correspondence, and Speeches* (3 vols., 1891), II:457 (noting that notwithstanding Hamilton's denunciation of the memorial, Hamilton himself had identified the state legislative guardianship role and function to sound the alarm in *Federalist* 26 and 28).

53. Edward Carrington to James Madison, December 24, 1790, *MP*, XIII:332; *DHFFC*, VIII:269–271.

54. The resolutions of the Pennsylvania House of Representatives of January 22, 1791 were reprinted in *Gazette of the United States* [Philadelphia], February 5, 1791.

55. *Dunlap's American Daily Advertiser* [Philadelphia], January 22, 1791 ("constitutional opposition" and "within the bounds") (Bingham).

56. *Dunlap's American Daily Advertiser*, January 24, 1791 ("that the state legislatures" to "blowing the trumpet") (Gallatin), ("the proceedings") (Findley); Caldwell, *Findley,* 230; *Gazette of the United States,* February 5, 1791. On June 22, 1791, Pennsylvania's legislature by a vote of 36 to 11 "requested their senators and representatives in Congress to oppose" all aspects of the excise that "shall militate against the rights and liberties of the people." See John Austin Stevens, *Albert Gallatin* (1884), 50. Pennsylvania's Senate "non-concurred" with the resolutions of the House by the narrow vote of 9 to 8. See *Gazette of the United States,* February 5, 1791.

57. *Gazette of the United States,* February 5, 1791 ("subversive"); Perkins, *American Public Finance,* 234 (noting that President Jefferson had eliminated all excise taxes by 1805).

58. Thomas P. Slaughter, *The Whiskey Rebellion: Frontier Epilogue to the American Revolution* (1986), 93–108; North Carolina, *State Records,*

XXI:962; Fisher Ames to Thomas Dwight, January 6, 1791, W.B. Allen, ed., *Works of Fisher Ames* (2 vols., 1983), II:845–846 (noting the "ferment" in North Carolina that had produced resolves "against direct and indirect taxes").

59. *Gazette of the United States*, January 22, 1791 ("the work of legislation"); "Civis," *Gazette of the United States*, February 5, 1791; Fisher Ames to Thomas Dwight, January 24, 1791, Allen, ed., *Works*, II:848; Fritz, *American Sovereigns*, 183–187.

60. "The Minority on the Vote respecting the Resolutions," *Gazette of the United States*, February 5, 1791 ("the particular objects" to "ultimate appeal"); *Dunlap's American Daily Advertiser*, January 18, 1791, *New York Daily Gazette*, January 20, 1791, *Gazette of the United States*, January 26, 1791; *Osborne's New Hampshire Spy* [Portsmouth, N.H.], February 12, 1791; "An Enquirer," *Gazette of the United States*, April 16, 1791.

61. "House of Representatives. Pennsylvania," *Gazette of the United States*, February 9, 1791 ("a duty" to "We know our rights"). In his 1796 *History of the Insurrection*, William Findley noted that "other state legislatures have frequently interfered by giving their opinion on important federal measures without being censured for it." See Steven R. Boyd, "William Findley, *History of the Insurrection*," in Steven R. Boyd, ed., *The Whiskey Rebellion: Past and Present Perspectives* (1985), 77 at 79.

62. "The Bank Bill," February 8, 1791, *MP*, XIII:386 ("constructions of the constitution"); "The Bank Bill," February 2, 1791, *MP*, XIII:376 ("essential characteristic" and "as composed"), 378 ("which is not evidently"); James Madison to Edmund Pendleton, February 13, 1791, *MP*, XIII:390–391; "Draft Veto of the Bank Bill," February 21, 1791, *MP*, XIII:395 ("expressly delegated").

63. "Consolidation," For the *National Gazette*, December 3, [1791], *MP*, XIV:138–139 ("a consolidation" to "Let the latter"); Leonard and Cornell, *Partisan Republic*, 53 ("to shift power"); Gienapp, *Second Creation*, 321–322.

64. Bilder, *Madison's Hand*, 200–201 ("may have wanted").

65. James Madison to Edmund Pendleton, January 21, 1792, *MP*, XIV:195 ("broaches"); James Madison to Henry Lee, January 21, 1792, *MP*, XIV:193 ("usurpation of power"); James Madison to Henry Lee, January 1, 1792, *MP*, XIV:180 ("If not only"); "Alexander Hamilton's Final Version of The Report on the Subject of Manufactures," December 5, 1791, *HP*, X:230–340; Douglas A. Irwin, "The Aftermath of Hamilton's 'Report on Manufactures,'" Working Paper 9943, National Bureau of Economic Research (August, 2003), 7–11.

66. The motion was lost by a vote of 55 to 26 in North Carolina's House of Commons on December 9, 1790. See North Carolina, *State Records*, XXI:1021; Banning, "Republican Ideology," 167 at 180n26 ("Nothing

frightened Hamilton so much as early attempts by state legislatures to instruct their federal senators and representatives or to pass legislative resolutions on federal laws").

On the politics of the early republic, see Marshall Smelser, "The Federalist Period as an Age of Passion," 10 *American Quarterly* (1958), 391–419; John R. Howe, Jr., "Republican Thought and the Political Violence of the 1790s," 19 *American Quarterly* (1967), 147–165; Richard Hofstadter, *The Idea of a Party System: The Rise of Legitimate Opposition in the United States, 1780–1840* (1970); Joanne B. Freeman, *Affairs of Honor: National Politics in the New Republic* (2001).

67. Alexander Hamilton to Edward Carrington, May 26, 1792, *HP*, XI:443 ("liberal construction"), XI:438 ("lost no opportunity").

68. Miller, *Federalist Era*, 35 ("the equilibrium"); Wood, *Empire of Liberty*, 141 ("Hamilton's kind"); Rakove, *Original Meanings*, 38 (Madison's congressional service left him "a 'nationalist' in this sense at least: He was convinced that Congress lacked the authority and resources to carry out even its existing duties under the Articles of Confederation. Whether he privately held more expansive notions of the potential scope of national power is less certain").

69. Alexander Hamilton to Edward Carrington, May 26, 1792, *HP*, XI:427 ("similarity of thinking"), XI:432 ("the *same point*"); McCoy, *Elusive Republic*, 134 ("they brought very different"); Stourzh, *Alexander Hamilton*, 160 ("the unitary state"); Banning, "Hamiltonian Madison," 3–28; Banning, *Sacred Fire*, 293–298, 315–316; Drew R. McCoy, "James Madison and Visions of American Nationality in the Confederate Period: A Regional Perspective," in Richard Beeman, Stephen Botein, and Edward C. Carter II, eds., *Beyond Confederation: Origins of the Constitution and American National Identity* (1987), 226 at 254 ("Madison's nationalist commitment had always differed substantially from the largely northern strain of Federalist nationalism that assumed dominance in the early 1790s").

3 State Interposition and Debates over the Meaning of the Constitution

1. Gienapp, *Second Creation*, 10 ("fixed").

2. Gienapp, *Second Creation*, 125–163, 142 ("the meaning").

3. Introduction, *DHSC*, V:1–2; John J. Gibbons, "The Eleventh Amendment and State Sovereign Immunity: A Reinterpretation," 83 *Columbia Law Review* (1983), 1889 at 1895–1899; Clyde E. Jacobs, *The Eleventh Amendment and Sovereign Immunity* (1972), 5–6; Massey, "State Sovereignty," 61 at 87–90.

4. Letter from an Anonymous Correspondent, Philadelphia *Independent Chronicle*, between February 13 and 19, 1791, *DHSC*, V:21 ("have relinquished").

5. U.S. Const., Art. III, Sec. 2.

6. Introduction, *DHSC*, V:2; "Federal Farmer, III," October 10, 1787, Herbert J. Storing, ed. (with the assistance of Murray Dry), The *Complete Anti-Federalist* (7 vols., 1981), II:245 ("to humble"); "Brutus, XIII," *New York Journal*, February 21, 1788, *DHRC*, XX:796 ("between a state"); *Federalist* 81, p.548 ("inherent"), 549 ("surrender") (Hamilton), May 28, 1788.

7. *DHRC*, X:1406 ("disgraceful"), 1414 ("It is not"), 1433 ("will think" to "this construction"), 1423 ("clear").

8. Introduction, *DHSC*, V:3, 4 ("between a state").

9. Maeva Marcus and Natalie Wexler, "Suits against States: Diversity of Opinion in the 1790s," 1993 *Journal of Supreme Court History* (1993), 73 at 84 ("the plaintiffs").

10. James Sullivan, *Observations upon the Government of the United States of America* [1791], *DHSC*, V:22 ("there were great" and "men of learning").

11. *DHSC*, V:28 "two sovereign powers"), 29 ("inconsistent"), 31 ("sovereign states").

12. *DHSC*, V:140; Thomas P. Carnes and John Y. Noel to Edward Telfair, March 31, 1791, *DHSC*, V:142; Plea to the Jurisdiction, October 17, 1791, *DHSC*, V:143; James Iredell's Circuit Court Opinion, October [21], 1791, *DHSC*, V:148–155; Summons, February 8, 1792, *DHSC*, V:155; Edward Telfair to the President of the Senate and Speaker of the House of Representatives, November 5, 1792, in *Augusta Chronicle* [Augusta, Ga.], November 10, 1792, *DHSC*, V:132n33.

13. Proceedings of the Georgia House of Representatives, *Augusta Chronicle*, December 14, 1792, *DHSC*, V:161("destroy"), 162 ("unconstitutional"); Journal of Proceedings of the Executive Department of Georgia, January 2, 1793, *DHSC*, V:132n36; John Wereat to Edward Telfair, February 14, 1793, *DHSC*, V:163.

14. *Chisholm v. Georgia*, 2 U.S. 419 (1793), 423 ("immediately" and "their powers"), 420 ("the letter of the Constitution"), 423 ("usual construction"), 425 ("no degradation"), 429 ("prostration").

15. 2 U.S. 419, 448 ("A state is altogether").

16. 2 U.S. 419, 435 ("powers surrendered" and "completely sovereign"); John V. Orth, "The Truth about Justice Iredell's Dissent in *Chisholm v. Georgia* (1793)," 73 *North Carolina Law Review* (1994), 255 at 265 ("divided sovereignty" and "endear him"); Jeff B. Fordham, "Iredell's Dissent in *Chisholm v. Georgia*: Its Political Significance," 8 *North Carolina Historical Review* (1931), 155 at 157.

17. 2 U.S. 419, 453 ("to be *sovereign*"), 462 ("confusion" and "the 'people of the United States'"), 465 ("that the people" and "repugnant").

18. 2 U.S. 419, 470 ("in what sense" and "the people, in their collective"), 471
    ("residuary sovereignty" and "this great compact"); Powell, *History and
    Politics*, 35–36 ("reference").
19. Proceedings of the Georgia House of Representatives, *Augusta Chronicle*,
    November 19, 1793, *DHSC*, V:235, 236; George Mathews to the
    Senators and Representatives of the State of Georgia, January 1, 1794,
    DHSC, V:237 ("too rigid"); Edward Telfair's Address to the Georgia
    General Assembly, *Augusta Chronicle*, November 4, 1793, *DHSC*,
    V:234; *American Minerva* [New York], January 15, 1794, *DHSC*,
    V:237–238.
20. John V. Orth, *The Judicial Power of the United States: The Eleventh
    Amendment in American History* (1987), 12; Editorial Note, *DHSC*,
    V:137 ("significance" and "unacceptable"); David P. Currie, *The
    Constitution in Congress: The Federalist Period, 1789–1801* (1997),
    196 ("just about"); Marcus and Wexler, "Suits against States."
21. Plea to the Jurisdiction, August 5, 1793, *DHSC*, V:92 ("a free");
    Proceedings of the Virginia House of Delegates, December 18, 1792,
    DHSC, V:322 ("a dangerous").
22. Jacobs, *Eleventh Amendment*, 71("for repudiation"); *The Mirror*
    [Concord, N.H.], August 12, 1793 (asserting that *Chisholm* struck
    "at the root of individual State Sovereignty"); Orth, *Judicial Power
    of the United States*, 7 (asserting the Amendment was "[a]lways
    a dollars-and-cents proposition"); Jacobs, *Eleventh Amendment*, 70
    (concluding that "there is practically no evidence that Congress
    proposed and the legislatures ratified the Eleventh Amendment to
    permit the states to escape payment of existing obligations"); Goebel,
    Supreme Court, 728, 741–756; William A. Fletcher, "A Historical
    Interpretation of the Eleventh Amendment: A Narrow Construction
    of an Affirmative Grant of Jurisdiction Rather Than a Prohibition
    against Jurisdiction," 35 *Stanford Law Review* (1983), 1033 at
    1045–1054, 1058; Gibbons, "Eleventh Amendment," 1889 at 1899–
    1920; Amar, "Of Sovereignty"; Vicki C. Jackson, "The Supreme
    Court, the Eleventh Amendment, and State Sovereign Immunity," 98
    Yale Law Journal (1988), 1–126; Lawrence C. Marshall, "Fighting the
    Words of the Eleventh Amendment," 102 *Harvard Law Review*
    (1989), 1342 at 1356–1361; Marcus and Wexler, "Suits against
    States," 73 at 85.
23. See Resolution of the Connecticut General Assembly, October 29, 1793,
    DHSC, V:609; Resolution of North Carolina General Assembly,
    January 11, 1794, *DHSC*, V:615; Proceedings of a Joint Session of the
    New Hampshire General Court, January 23, 1794, *DHSC*, V:618. For
    attempts to pass interposition resolutions, see Proceedings of the South
    Carolina Senate, December 17, 1793, *DHSC*, V:610–611 (Senate but not
    the House); Proceedings of the Maryland House of Delegates,

December 27, 1793, *DHSC*, V:611–612 (House of Delegates but not the Senate); Proceedings of the Pennsylvania House of Representatives, December 30, 1793, *DHSC*, V:612–613 (House committee proposed resolution but not acted upon).

24. Editorial Note, *DHSC*, V:597, *DHSC*, V:231n1.
25. Report of a Joint Committee of the Massachusetts General Court, *Independent Chronicle*, June [20], 1793, *DHSC*, V:230 ("repugnant").
26. Editorial Note, *DHSC*, V:352–369; Proclamation by John Hancock, *Independent Chronicle*, July 9, 1793, *DHSC*, V:387–389.
27. *Boston Gazette*, August 5, 1793 ("aimed a blow"); "Marcus," *Massachusetts Mercury* [Salem, Mass.], July 13, 1793; "Brutus," *Independent Chronicle* [Boston, Mass], July 18, 1793, The Crisis, No. XIII by "A Republican," July 25, 1793, and "Hampden," July 25, 1793, *DHSC*, V:389–390, 392–393, 395–401.
28. *Worcester Gazette* [Worcester, Mass.], September 26, 1793; John Hancock's Address to the Massachusetts General Court, *Independent Chronicle*, September 18, 1793, *DHSC*, V:419 ("force and efficacy" and "consolidation"); Editorial Note, *DHSC*, V:366n66 and n67 (suggesting that Hancock's Attorney General, James Sullivan, may have written the Address).
29. Report of a Joint Committee of the Massachusetts General Court, *Independent Chronicle*, September 23, 1793, *DHSC*, V:424 ("not expedient").
30. William Widgery's Speech in the Massachusetts House of Representatives, *Independent Chronicle*, September 23, 1793, *DHSC*, V:430 ("high time"); Account of John Davis' Speech in the Massachusetts House of Representatives, *Independent Chronicle*, September 23, 1793, *DHSC*, V:433 ("expression"); Account of William Martin's Speech in the Massachusetts House of Representatives, *Independent Chronicle*, September 23, 1793, *DHSC*, V:435; Charles Jarvis' Speech in the Massachusetts House of Representatives, *Independent Chronicle*, September 23, 1793, *DHSC*, V:437.
31. Resolution of the Massachusetts General Court, September 27, 1793, *DHSC*, V:440 ("dangerous"); Lorenzo Sears, *John Hancock: The Picturesque Patriot* (1912), 322.
32. Samuel Adams to the Governors of the States, October 9, 1793, *DHSC*, V:442 ("upon a principle"), 443 ("the federal principle").
33. *Boston Gazette*, June 7, 1790.
34. *DHSC*, V:442, 609n1.
35. *DHSC*, V:234–236.
36. Henry Lee to the Speaker of the Virginia House of Delegates, November 13, 1793, *DHSC*, V:338.
37. Henry Lee to Virginia House of Delegates, *DHSC*, V:334 ("fundamental principle"), 335 ("They are then" and "respective Sovereignties").

38. Henry Lee to Virginia House of Delegates, *DHSC*, V:337 ("a disavowal" and "forever crush").
39. Proceedings of the Virginia House of Delegates, November 28, 1793, *DHSC*, V:338 ("incompatible"); *DHSC*, V:339n3.
40. Goebel, *Supreme Court*, 735 ("addicted"); Proceedings of the Virginia House of Delegates, November 28, 1793, *DHSC*, V:338 ("a state cannot, under the constitution of the United States, be made a defendant at the suit of any individual"); Resolution of the Massachusetts General Court, September 27, 1793, *DHSC*, V:440.
41. St. George Tucker, *Blackstone's Commentaries: With Notes of Reference, to the Constitution and Laws, of the Federal Government of the United States; and of the Commonwealth of Virginia* (5 vols., 1803), Note D, "View of the Constitution of the United States," Vol. 1, appendix p.153 ("warranted" to "whose rights"); Charles T. Cullen, *St. George Tucker and Law in Virginia, 1772–1804* (1987); Cornell, *Other Founders*, 263–264; Davison M. Douglas, "Foreword: The Legacy of St. George Tucker," 47 *William and Mary Law Review* (2006), 1111–1122.
42. *Federalist* 44, p.305 ("[W]hat is to be" to "will be an invasion") (Madison), January 25, 1788; Tucker, *Blackstone's Commentaries*, "View of the Constitution," Vol. 1, appendix p.153. Tucker cited *The Federalist: A Collection of Essays, Written in Favour of the New Constitution, As Agreed Upon by the Federal Convention, September 17, 1787* (2 vols., 1788), II:74.
43. Proceedings of the South Carolina Senate, December 17, 1793, *DHSC*, V:610–611; Proceedings of the Maryland House of Delegates, December 27, 1793, *DHSC*, V:611–612; Proceedings of the Pennsylvania House of Representatives, December 30, 1793, *DHSC*, V:612–613.
44. Legislature of Pennsylvania, House of Representatives, September 6, 1794, *Daily Advertiser* [New York], September 10, 1794 ("in vain" to "a seasonable interposition"); Caldwell, *Findley*, 230.
45. Resolution of North Carolina General Assembly, January 11, 1794, *DHSC*, V:615 ("derogatory" and "secure the Sovereignty"); Proceedings of a Joint Session of the New Hampshire General Court, January 23, 1794, *DHSC*, V:618.
46. The amendment was proposed in the Senate on January 2, 1794 and passed that body by a vote of 23 to 2. The amendment subsequently passed the House on March 4, 1794 with another overwhelming vote, 81 to 9. Less than a year later, on February 7, 1795, the requisite number of states (twelve of fifteen) had ratified the Eleventh Amendment. Nonetheless, the formal Presidential Proclamation of the ratification of the Amendment only occurred nearly two years later, on January 8, 1798. See *DHSC*, V:601, 604, 617–618, 620–623, 626–627; Currie, *Federalist Period*, 196.

47. Todd Estes, *The Jay Treaty Debate, Public Opinion, and the Evolution of Early American Political Culture* (2006), 212 ("Because *both* sides"); Jeffrey L. Pasley, *The First Presidential Contest: 1796 and the Founding of American Democracy* (2013), 101–181.

48. *Senate Executive Proceedings*, I:152; *Boston Independent Chronicle* of April 28, 1794, quoted in Elkins and McKitrick, *Federalism*, 395; *General Advertiser* [Philadelphia], June 22, 1795 (complaining that senatorial secrecy smacked of a practice "borrowed *from Kings and their Ministers*").

49. *Richmond Chronicle* [Richmond, Va.], July 14, 1795 ("unconstitutionally invaded"); Currie, *Federalist Period*, 210; Amanda C. Demmer, "Trick or Constitutional Treaty?: The Jay Treaty and the Quarrel over the Diplomatic Separation of Powers," 35 *JER* (2015), 579–598; David M. Golove, "Treaty-Making and the Nation: The Historical Foundations of the Nationalist Conception of the Treaty Power," 98 *Michigan Law Review* (2000), 1075 at 1159n249; George Washington to Alexander Hamilton, July 3, 1795, *HP*, XVIII:398–400; Alexander Hamilton, "Remarks on the Treaty of Amity Commerce, and Navigation lately made between the United States and Great Britain," [July 9–11, 1795], *HP*, XVIII:428.

50. Sharp, *American Politics*, 117; Jerald A. Combs, *The Jay Treaty: Political Battleground of the Founding Fathers* (1970); Elkins and McKitrick, *Federalism*, 415–431; Estes, *Jay Treaty Debate*; Pasley, *First Presidential Contest*, 108–181.

51. James Madison to Robert R. Livingston, August 10, 1795, *MP*, XVI:47 ("a British party"); Gienapp, *Second Creation*, 252 ("on the underlying"), 255; Thomas Jefferson to Edward Rutledge, November 30, 1795, *JP*, XXVIII:542; Edling, *Hercules*, 50–80; Holger Hoock, *Scars of Independence: America's Violent Birth* (2017), 151–177, 186–201, 211–240; Joseph M. Fewster, "The Jay Treaty and British Ship Seizures: The Martinique Cases," 45 *WMQ* (1988), 426–452; Elkins and McKitrick, *Federalism*, 375–396; Pasley, *First Presidential Contest*, 102–103.

52. Gienapp, *Second Creation*, 253–255, 254 ("foreign affairs"); Demmer, "Trick or Constitutional Treaty?"; Golove, "Treaty-Making and the Nation," 1075 at 1161–1168.

53. Thomas Jefferson to James Monroe, September 6, 1795, *JP*, XXVIII:449 ("as constitutionally void"); From John Minor, Jr., and others, [post–August 25, 1795], "An Address, and Instructions from the People of Spotsylvania County, To James Madison," *MP*, XVI:59 ("in every point"); George Washington to the Boston Selectmen, July 28, 1795, John C. Fitzpatrick, ed., *The Writings of George Washington* (39 vols., 1931–1944), XXXIV:253 (asserting that neither the President nor the Senate should "substitute for their own conviction the opinions of others"); Demmer, "Trick or Constitutional Treaty?" 579 at 593; Golove, "Treaty-Making and the Nation," 1075 at 1162–1163.

For Washington's struggle over the treaty, see Combs, *Jay Treaty*, 164–170; Elkins and McKitrick, *Federalism*, 419–431; Thomas J. Farnham, "The Virginia Amendments of 1795: An Episode in the Opposition to Jay's Treaty," 75 *VMHB* (1967), 75 at 82.

54. Editorial Note, *MP*, XVI:62–77; "Petition to the General Assembly of the Commonwealth of Virginia," [October 12, 1795], *MP*, XVI:95 ("representations" and "constitutional right"), 103 ("such measures").

55. Joseph Jones to James Madison, October 29, 1795, *MP*, XVI:113 ("what course" and "declaring their opinions").

56. *Journal of the House of Delegates of the Commonwealth of Virginia*, November 10–December 29, 1795 (Richmond, Va., 1795), 19 ("are and should" and "unnecessary"); Joseph Jones to James Madison, November 22, 1795, *MP*, XVI:132 ("belonged" and "had no controul").

57. Joseph Jones to James Madison, November 22, 1795, *MP*, XVI:132 ("indirectly"); Virginia House of Delegates, *Journal*, 27 ("mature opinion"); Thomas Mann Randolph, Jr., to Thomas Jefferson, November 22, 1795, *JP*, XXVIII:535; Beveridge, *Marshall*, II:132–140. The substitute failed by a vote of 98 against and 52 in favor in the House and the original vote passed by a vote of 100 to 50, with the Senate approving the resolution four days later. See Virginia House of Delegates, *Journal*, 38.

58. James Madison to James Monroe, December 20, 1795, *MP*, XVI:170 ("firm example"); *Annals of Congress*, House of Rep., 4th Cong., 1st Sess., (April 5, 1796), 776 (James Madison) ("the sense of that body" and "the meaning"); *Washington Spy* [Hagers-Town, Md.], December 31, 1795; Joseph Jones to James Madison, November 22, 1795, *MP*, XVI:132–133; Stephen G. Kurtz, *The Presidency of John Adams: The Collapse of Federalism, 1795–1800* (1957), 21–33; Risjord, *Chesapeake Politics*, 457–460; Virginia House of Delegates, *Journal*, 91; Farnham, "Virginia Amendments of 1795," 75 at 85–88.

59. Samuel Adams to the Legislature of Massachusetts, January 19, 1796, Harry Alonzo Cushing, ed., *The Writings of Samuel Adams* (4 vols., 1904–1908), IV:389 ("the Constitutional rights").

60. Quoted in Farnham, "Virginia Amendments of 1795," 75 at 86 ("a respectful"); Joseph Jones to James Madison, February 17, 1796, *MP*, XVI:224 ("astonished"), 225 ("unconstitutional"); *Federal Intelligencer* [Baltimore, Md.], December 17, 1795 ("the indispensable duty"); *The Oracle of the Day* [Portsmouth, N.H.], January 9, 1796.

61. Farnham, "Virginia Amendments of 1795," 75 at 88 ("They accomplished").

62. Gienapp, *Second Creation*, 250 ("over the Constitution's"), 285 ("unique capacity"); *Annals of Congress*, House of Rep., 4th Cong., 1st Sess., (April 15, 1796), 989 (Samuel Lyman) ("sent here" and "it is a nullity"); Estes, *Jay Treaty Debate*, 29; Combs, *Jay Treaty*, 152–153;

Elkins and McKitrick, *Federalism*, 410–413; Bradford Perkins, *The First Rapprochement: England and the United States, 1795–1805* (1967), 12.

63. Gienapp, *Second Creation*, 290 ("archival Constitution"), 305 ("In appealing").

4 The Virginia and Kentucky Resolutions and Madison's Report of 1800

1. James Morton Smith, *Freedom's Fetters: The Alien and Sedition Laws and American Civil Liberties* (1956), 438 ("dangerous"), 441 ("to oppose"), 442 ("writing, printing").
2. Jeff Broadwater, *James Madison: A Son of Virginia & a Founder of the Nation* (2012), 107 ("Because Federalists"); John C. Miller, *Crisis in Freedom: The Alien and Sedition Acts* (1952); Michael Kent Curtis, *Free Speech, "The People's Darling Privilege": Struggles for Freedom of Expression in American History* (2000), 58–79; David Jenkins, "The Sedition Act of 1798 and the Incorporation of Seditious Libel into First Amendment Jurisprudence," 45 *AJLH* (2001), 154–213; Marc Lendler, "'Equally Proper at All Times and at All Times Necessary': Civility, Bad Tendency, and the Sedition Act," 24 *JER* (2004), 419–444; Terri Diane Halperin, *The Alien and Sedition Acts of 1798: Testing the Constitution* (2016).
3. Thomas Jefferson to James Madison, June 7, 1798, *JP*, XXX:393 ("no respect"); Thomas Jefferson to Stevens Thomson Mason, October 11, 1798, *JP*, XXX:560 ("experiment"); "Virginia Resolutions, December 21, 1798," *MP*, XVII:189–190 ("right of freely"); Alexander Hamilton to Oliver Wolcott, Jr., [June 29, 1798], *HP*, XXI:522 ("highly exceptionable").
4. Thomas Jefferson to Peregrine Fitzhugh, February 23, 1798, *JP*, XXX:130 ("beautiful equilibrium"); Brian Steele, *Thomas Jefferson and American Nationhood* (2012), 264 ("Jefferson's protest"); Douglas Bradburn, *The Citizenship Revolution: Politics and the Creation of the American Union, 1774–1804* (2009), 168–205.
5. Thomas Jefferson to John Wayles Eppes, April 21, 1800, *JP*, XXXI:531 ("cripple & suppress"); John K. Alexander, *The Selling of the Constitutional Convention: A History of News Coverage* (1990); Pasley, *"Tyranny of Printers."*
6. Wendell Bird, "Reassessing Responses to the Virginia and Kentucky Resolutions: New Evidence from the Tennessee and Georgia Resolutions and from Other States," 35 *JER* (2015), 519 at 520 (noting the widespread tendency to consider the Resolutions "abject failures"), 521–523n4 and 5; Peterson, *Jefferson Image*, 63; Tipton, *Nullification*

and Interposition, 15–16; Beeman, *Old Dominion*, 194; Harry V. Jaffa, "Partly Federal, Partly National: On the Political Theory of the American Civil War," in Harry V. Jaffa, ed., *The Conditions of Freedom: Essays in Political Philosophy* (1975), 161 at 163; Ellis, *Union at Risk*, 4–5; Sharp, *American Politics*, 194; Kevin R. Gutzman, "A Troublesome Legacy: James Madison and 'The Principles of '98'," 15 *JER* (1995), 569 at 571, 579; Peter S. Onuf, *Jefferson's Empire: The Language of American Nationhood* (2000), 145; Wood, *Empire of Liberty*, 269; James H. Read, *Majority Rule versus Consensus: The Political Thought of John C. Calhoun* (2009), 39; Mark E. Neely, Jr., *Lincoln and the Triumph of the Nation: Constitutional Conflict in the American Civil War* (2011), 43; Anderson, *Federalism*, 36; Jack N. Rakove, *A Politician Thinking: The Creative Mind of James Madison* (2017), 187; Benjamin E. Park, *American Nationalisms: Imagining Union in the Age of Revolutions, 1783–1833* (2018), 205.

7. The Third Virginia resolution provided that "in case of a deliberate, palpable and dangerous exercise of other powers not granted by the said compact, the states who are parties thereto have the right, and are in duty bound, to interpose for arresting the pro[gress] of the evil, and for maintaining within their respective limits, the authorities, rights and liberties appertaining to them."

The Seventh Virginia resolution invited other states to "concur with this Commonwealth in declaring, as it does hereby declare, that the acts aforesaid [the Alien and Sedition Acts] are unconstitutional, and that the necessary and proper measures will be taken by each, for cooperating with this State in maintaining unimpaired the authorities, rights, and liberties, reserved to the States respectively, or to the people." Virginia Resolutions, December 21, 1798, *MP*, XVII:189–190.

8. Rabun, "Interposition"; Malone, *Jefferson*, III; Merrill D. Peterson, *Thomas Jefferson and the New Nation: A Biography* (1970); Richard Buel, Jr., *Securing the Revolution: Ideology in American Politics, 1789–1815* (1972); Ketcham, *Madison*; Sharp, *American Politics*; David N. Mayer, *The Constitutional Thought of Thomas Jefferson* (1994); Wayne D. Moore, "Reconceiving Interpretive Autonomy: Insights From the Virginia and Kentucky Resolutions," 11 *Constitutional Commentary* (1994), 315–354; Banning, *Sacred Fire*; Cornell, *Other Founders*; Gutzman, "Virginia and Kentucky Resolutions"; Robert H. Churchill, "Popular Nullification, Fries' Rebellion, and the Waning of Radical Republicanism, 1798–1801," 67 *Pennsylvania History: A Journal of Mid-Atlantic Studies* (2000), 105–140; William J. Watkins, Jr., *Reclaiming the American Revolution: The Kentucky and Virginia Resolutions and Their Legacy* (2004); Colleen A. Sheehan, *James Madison and the Spirit of Republican Self-Government* (2009).

9. Neely, *Constitutional Conflict*, 6 ("the ultimate basis").

10. Adrienne Koch and Harry Ammon, "The Virginia and Kentucky Resolutions: An Episode in Jefferson's and Madison's Defense of Civil Liberties," 5 *WMQ* (1948), 145 at 148; Thomas Jefferson to James Madison, August 3, 1797, *JP*, XXIX:489–491; Petition to the Virginia House of Delegates, [on or before August 3, 1797]; James Madison to Thomas Jefferson, August 5, 1797, *JP*, XXIX:505–506.

11. Virginia Resolutions, December 21, 1798, *MP*, XVII:190 ("unconstitutional"); Resolutions Adopted by the Kentucky General Assembly, November 10, 1798, *JP*, XXX:551 ("not law"), 553 ("unconstitutional"); Banning, *Sacred Fire*, 534n65 (identifying no logical difference between the two sets of resolutions).

12. Samuel Brown to Thomas Jefferson, September 4, 1798, *JP*, XXX:510–511; "Philo-Agis," *Kentucky Gazette* [Lexington, Ky.], August 22, 1798; Editorial Note, *JP*, XXX:531–532.

13. *Virginia Herald* [Fredericksburg, Va.], September 18, 1798, Editorial Note, *JP*, XXX:532; *Alexandria Advertiser* [Alexandria, Va.], September 18, 1798; Thomas Jefferson to Wilson Cary Nicholas, October 5, 1798, *JP*, XXX:557; Beeman, *Old Dominion*, 189; Mayer, *Constitutional Thought of Jefferson*, 357n66.

14. Thomas Jefferson to George Wythe, September 16, 1787, *JP*, XII:128; Jefferson's Draft, [before October 4, 1798], *JP*, XXX:536 ("certain definite powers" to "the exclusive or final judge").

15. Jefferson's Draft, [before October 4, 1798], *JP*, XXX:536 ("as in all other cases").

16. For assumptions that Jefferson and Madison shared a similar understanding of the compact, see Freehling, *Prelude*, 207; Ellis, *Union at Risk*, 4–5; Jack N. Rakove, *James Madison and the Creation of the American Republic* (1990), 128; Elkins and McKitrick, *Federalism*, 719; McDonald, *States' Rights*, 42; Watkins, *Reclaiming*, 59; Saul Cornell and Gerald Leonard, "The Consolidation of the Early Federal System, 1791–1812," in Michael Grossberg and Christopher Tomlins, *The Cambridge History of Law in America* (3 vols., 2008), I:518 at 530; Steele, *Jefferson*, 245, 249; Anderson, *Federalism*, 19; Hays, *States in American Constitutionalism*, 23.

17. Resolutions Adopted by the Kentucky General Assembly, November 10, 1798, *JP*, XXX:550 ("co-states").

18. Jefferson's Draft, [before October 4, 1798], *JP*, XXX: 536, 537 ("not law"), 537–538 ("void"), 539 ("unlimited powers" and "immediate redress").

19. Jefferson's Draft, [before October 4, 1798], *JP*, XXX:539 ("a committee of conference"), 541.

20. Jefferson's Draft, [before October 4, 1798], *JP*, XXX:539 ("in cases of an abuse"); Koch and Ammon, "Virginia and Kentucky Resolutions," 145 at

168; Miller, *Crisis in Freedom*, 173; Beeman, *Old Dominion*, 200; Banning, "Republican Ideology," 167 at 185; Stampp, "Perpetual Union," 5 at 22; Jefferson Powell, *Languages of Power: A Sourcebook of Early American Constitutional History* (1991), 147; Mayer, *Constitutional Thought of Jefferson*, 201; Gutzman, "Troublesome Legacy," 569 at 579; Cornell, *Other Founders*, 240; Churchill, "Popular Nullification," 105 at 114; Joseph J. Ellis, *Founding Brothers: The Revolutionary Generation* (2001), 200; Watkins, *Reclaiming*, 72; Wilentz, *American Democracy*, 79; Robert G. Natelson, "James Madison and the Constitution's 'Convention for Proposing Amendments'," in Cogan, *Union & States' Rights*, 30 at 37; Halperin, *Alien and Sedition Acts*, 104; Read and Allen, "Nullification," 91 at 102; Childers, *Webster-Hayne Debate*, 6.

21. Jefferson's Draft, [before October 4, 1798], *JP*, XXX:539 ("constitutional remedy" to "a natural right").

22. Jefferson's Draft, [before October 4, 1798], *JP*, XXX:539 ("that nevertheless"), 540 ("necessarily drive"), 541 ("co-states").

23. Jefferson's Draft, [before October 4, 1798], *JP*, XXX:541 ("surrender" and "seizing the rights" to "the costates").

24. Jefferson's Draft, [before October 4, 1798], *JP*, XXX:539 ("nullification" and "a natural right"), 541 ("the costates").

25. Jefferson's Draft, [before October 4, 1798], *JP*, XXX:536 ("void" to "altogether void"); *Marbury v. Madison*, 5 U.S. 137 (1803), 177 ("an act of the legislature"); Harrison, "Reconstruction Amendments," 375 at 435 (asserting, with citation to *Marbury*, that "a first principle of the Constitution" is that an act by a federal institution "in excess of constitutional power is a legal nullity").

26. Thomas Jefferson, *Notes on the State of Virginia* (William Peden, ed., 1954), 129 ("bind up").

27. Jefferson's Fair Copy, First Annual Message, [by November 27, 1801], *JP*, XXXV:648 ("a nullity"); Draft of Message to the Senate, [before November 12, 1801], *JP*, XXXV:656 ("void"); Steele, *Jefferson*, 252 ("use of the word"); Thomas Jefferson to Abigail Adams, July 22, 1804, Lester J. Cappon, ed., *The Adams–Jefferson Letters: The Complete Correspondence between Thomas Jefferson and Abigail and John Adams* (1959, reprinted 1987), 275 (describing the Sedition law as "a nullity"); William Duane to Thomas Jefferson, June 10, 1801, *JP*, XXXIV:297; John Taylor, *Construction Construed, and Constitutions Vindicated* (1820), 168; James Madison to Edward Everett, August 1830, *ML*, IV:105 (asserting that the words "not law, but utterly null, void, and of no force or effect" were "synonymous with 'unconstitutional'").

28. *Stewart Kentucky Herald* [Lexington, Ky.], December 4, 1798 ("protest against"); *Albany Centinel* [Albany, N.Y.], January 29, 1799 ("evasion");

Timothy Pickering to Rufus King, December 14, 1798, quoted in Miller, *Crisis in Freedom*, 176 ("inflammatory").

29. Wilson Cary Nicholas to Thomas Jefferson, October 4, 1798, *JP*, XXX:556; Resolutions Adopted by the Kentucky General Assembly, November 10, 1798, *JP*, XXX:553 ("unconstitutional and obnoxious"), 554 ("an expression"), 555 ("concur in declaring"); Thomas Jefferson to Wilson Cary Nicholas, October 5, 1798, *JP*, XXX:557; Thomas Jefferson to James Madison, November 17, 1798, *JP*, XXX:579–580.

30. *The Palladium* [Frankfort, Ky.], November 13 and 20, 1798, cited and quoted in Ethelbert Dudley Warfield, *The Kentucky Resolutions of 1798: An Historical Study* (2d. ed., 1894), 88 ("to repeal"), 89 ("the people at large").

31. Warfield, *Kentucky Resolutions*, 94 ("the right and duty").

32. Warfield, *Kentucky Resolutions*, 93 (censure" and "the co-States"), 94 ("a party" and "agents").

33. Warfield, *Kentucky Resolutions*, 94 ("the right and duty"), 95 ("opinions"), 96, 99; Resolutions Adopted by the Kentucky General Assembly, *JP*, XXX:555; *The Centinel of Freedom* [Newark, N.J.], December 18, 1798.

34. Thomas Jefferson to James Madison, November 17, 1798, *JP*, XXX:580 ("the Kentucky resolves"); Thomas Jefferson to John Taylor, November 26, 1798, *JP*, XXX:588–590.

35. James Madison to N.P. Trist, May, 1832, *ML*, IV:218 ("habit"); Peterson, *Jefferson Image*, 64; McCoy, *Last of the Fathers*, 9–37 (contrasting Madison's and Jefferson's temperament); Mary Sarah Bilder, "James Madison, Law Student and Demi-Lawyer," 28 *Law and History Review* (2010), 389 at 439; Gienapp, *Second Creation*, 49–50, 69, 110–112, 208.

36. Peterson, *Thomas Jefferson*, 615 (asserting the impossibility of stating precisely Jefferson's theory in his resolutions); Freehling, *Prelude*, 207 (describing both the Virginia and Kentucky Resolutions as "enigmatic").

37. Virginia Resolutions, December 21, 1798, *MP*, XVII:189 ("warranted" and "duty, to watch").

38. Virginia Resolutions, December 21, 1798, *MP*, XVII:189 ("the compact" and "the plain sense"); Powell, "Principles of '98," 689 at 718 ("This seemingly"), 717 ("For Madison, the Constitution was the creature of collective action by the states as a body").

39. Virginia Resolutions, December 21, 1798, *MP*, XVII:189 ("in case of a deliberate"). The editors of the Madison *Papers* reprint the Resolutions as they were passed by Virginia's legislature which deleted the word "alone" that Madison had originally inserted after "the states." For Madison's original language for the Third resolution, see *Aurora General Advertiser* [Philadelphia, Pa.], December 22, 1798.

40. Virginia Resolutions, December 21, 1798, *MP*, XVII:189 ("forced constructions" and "palpable"), 190 ("necessary and proper").
41. Thomas Jefferson to Wilson Cary Nicholas, November 29, 1798, *JP*, XXX:590 ("invitation"); *MP*, XVII:187.
42. Thomas Jefferson to John Taylor, November 26, 1798, *JP*, XXX:589 ("declarations").
43. Virginia Resolutions, December 21, 1798, *MP*, XVII:191n2; James Madison to James Robertson, March 27, 1831, *ML*, IV:166 ("emphasis"), James Madison to Edward Everett, August 1830, *ML*, IV:105 ("synonymous").
44. *Debates in the House of Delegates of Virginia, Upon Certain Resolutions Before the House, Upon the Important Subject of the Acts of Congress Passed at their Last Session, Commonly Called, The Alien and Sedition Laws* [Richmond, Va., 1798], 4 ("overleaped"); [John Taylor], *An Enquiry into the Principles and Tendency of Certain Public Measures* (1794), 54 ("must watch over"), 55 ("the people themselves"); John Taylor to Thomas Jefferson, June 25, 1798, *JP*, XXX:434 ("right of the State governments").

    For attributions to Taylor, see Malone, *Jefferson*, III:404; Sharp, *American Politics*, 192; Mayer, *Constitutional Thought of Jefferson*, 202; Whittington, "Political Constitution," 1 at 4–5; Cornell, *Other Founders*, 239; Garry Wills, *A Necessary Evil: A History of American Distrust of Government* (1999), 127; Gutzman, "Virginia and Kentucky Resolutions," 473 at 480–482; Wilentz, *American Democracy*, 78; Bradley D. Hays, "A Place for Interposition? What John Taylor of Caroline and the Embargo Crisis Have to Offer Regarding Resistance to the Bush Constitution," 67 *Maryland Law Review* (2007), 200 at 202.
45. Virginia House of Delegates, *Debates*, 123 ("a clashing"), 164 ("speak their opinions"), 169 ("they were bound").
46. Virginia House of Delegates, *Debates*, 67, 116 ("proper arbiter" and "source of correction"), 12 ("different language"), 78 ("dangerous"). On the substitute resolution, see Virginia House of Delegates, *Debates*, 80–81, 182.
47. Virginia House of Delegates, *Debates*, 159 ("as an *opinion*" to "Virginia could").
48. Virginia House of Delegates, *Debates*, 46, 102, 120 ("style" and "For, if they were").
49. *Aurora General Advertiser*, December 22, 1798 ("the states *alone*").
50. Virginia House of Delegates, *Debates*, 73, 111 ("the existing"), 136 ("unfounded" and "as particular sovereignties").
51. Virginia House of Delegates, *Debates*, 85 ("a deputation"), 118 ("the people of America" and "the words").
52. Virginia House of Delegates, *Debates*, 46 ("the people and the states" and "the immediate"), 132 ("the people alone" to "parties to the contract");

Journal of the House of Delegates of the Commonwealth of Virginia, Begun and Held at the Capitol in the City of Richmond, on Monday, the Third Day of December, in the Year of our Lord, One Thousand Seven Hundred and Ninety-Eight, and of the Commonwealth the Twenty-Third (Richmond, 1798), 31.

53. Virginia House of Delegates, *Debates*, 26 ("the respective powers"), 28 ("to produce" and "a declaration").

54. Virginia House of Delegates, *Debates*, 29–30, 126, 160, 185. The Resolutions passed the House by a vote of 100 to 63 and in the Senate by a vote of 14 to 3. Virginia House of Delegates, *Journal*, 32–33.

55. James Madison to Thomas Jefferson, December 29, 1798, *MP*, XVII:191 ("zeal" to "clearly the ultimate"), 192 ("protesting").

56. "Address of the General Assembly to the People of the Commonwealth of Virginia," Virginia House of Delegates, *Journal*, 88 ("representative responsibility" to "a revolution"), 96 (approved by a vote of 80 to 58). Some have assumed that Madison was the author, but the editors of Madison's *Papers* cannot confirm that attribution. See Beeman, *Old Dominion*, 195; Risjord, *Chesapeake Politics*, 540; Editorial Note, *MP*, XVII:199–206.

57. "An Address of the Fifty-Eight Federal Members of the Virginia Legislature to their Fellow-Citizens, in January, 1799" (1799), 7 ("deviation"), 33; Virginia House of Delegates, *Journal*, 96 (rejected by a vote of 92 to 42). The authorship of the *Minority Report* is disputed, with some attributing it to John Marshall. See Kurt T. Lash and Alicia Harrison , "Minority Report: John Marshall and the Defense of the Alien and Sedition Acts," 68 *Ohio State Law Journal* (2007), 435–516.

58. George Washington to Bushrod Washington, December 31, 1798, John C. Fitzpatrick, ed., *The Writings of George Washington* (39 vols., 1931– 1944), XXXVII:81; George Washington to Patrick Henry, January 15, 1799, Washington *Writings*, XXXVII:89 ("dissolve"); Theodore Sedgwick to Rufus King, March 20, 1799, Charles R. King, ed., *The Life and Correspondence of Rufus King* (6 vols., 1894–1900), II:581 ("a declaration of war"); Timothy Pickering to Rufus King, December 14, 1798, King *Correspondence*, II:493 ("a right to disobey"); Alexander Addison, *Analysis of the Report of the Committee of the Virginia Assembly, on the Proceedings of Sundry of the other States in Answer to their Resolutions* (1800), 3.

59. Quoted in Bird, "Reassessing Responses," 519 at 530 ("opposed to the constitution"), 535.

60. *The Communications of Several States, on the Resolutions of the Legislature of Virginia, Respecting the Alien and Sedition Laws* (1799), 3 ("unjustifiable"), 5 ("private opinions").

61. *Communications of Several States*, 7 ("exclusively" and "judges"), 8.

62. *Independent Chronicle* [Boston], February 14–18, 1799 (*"to decide"*); quoted in Miller, *Crisis in Freedom*, 122 ("a traitorous enterprise").

63. *Independent Chronicle*, April 25–29, 1799 (*"political Telegraphs"* to "If the federal compact"); Smith, *Freedom's Fetters*, 247–257.

64. *Communications of Several States*, 15 ("inflammatory"), 16 ("their incompetency"), 18 ("highly expedient"), 19–20.

65. Frank Maloy Anderson, "Contemporary Opinion of the Virginia and Kentucky Resolutions, Part One," 5 *American Historical Review* (1899), 45 at 46–47, 53, 57; Bird, "Reassessing Responses," 519 at 546.

66. *Journal of the House of Commons, State of North Carolina, Begun and Held in the City of Raleigh, on Monday the Nineteenth Day of November, in the Year of our Lord One Thousand Seven Hundred and Ninety-Eight, and of the Independence of the United States of America the Twenty-Third* (Wilmington, 1799), 78 ("the principles"); Editorial Note, *JP*, XXX:557 (the vote in the House was 58 to 21 while in the Senate the vote was 31 to 9); Bird, "Reassessing Responses," 519 at 539–540; Theodore Sedgwick to Rufus King, March 30, 1799, King *Correspondence*, II:581. For Republicans who explicitly challenged the Federalist position that constitutional interpretation was "exclusively confined" to the federal courts, see Anderson, "Contemporary Opinion, Part One," 45 at 57; Frank Maloy Anderson, "Contemporary Opinion of the Virginia and Kentucky Resolutions, Part Two," 5 *American Historical Review* (1899), 225 at 231, 252.

67. "Political Reflections," [February 23, 1799], *MP*, XVII:242 ("Our state governments").

68. James Morton Smith, "The Grass Roots Origins of the Kentucky Resolutions," 27 *WMQ* (1970), 221–245; Elkins and McKitrick, *Federalism*, 615; Bradburn, "Public Mind," 565–600; Thomas Jefferson to James Madison, January 30, 1799, *JP*, XXX:665; John Dawson to James Madison, February 5, 1799, *MP*, XVII:225; Thomas Jefferson to Archibald Stuart, February 13, 1799, *JP*, XXXI:35.

69. *Reports of Committees in Congress to Whom were Referred Certain Memorials and Petitions Complaining of the Acts of Congress Concerning the Alien and Sedition Laws* ... (1799), 3 ("unconstitutional"), 10 ("innocent misconceptions").

70. Thomas Jefferson to James Madison, February 26, 1799, *JP*, XXXI:64 ("scandalous" and "that not a word"). The vote was 52 to 48.

71. Walter Jones and others to James Madison, February 7, 1799, *MP*, XVII:228 (*"wise* and *firm"*); John Taylor to James Madison, March 4, 1799, *MP*, XVII:245, 249n1.

72. Thomas Jefferson to James Madison, August 23, 1799, *JP*, XXXI:174 ("rally") (Jefferson calling secession "scission"); Thomas Jefferson to

Wilson Cary Nicholas, September 5, 1799, *JP*, XXXI:179 ("in deference").

73. Wilson Cary Nicholas to Thomas Jefferson, August 20, 1799, *JP*, XXXI:172; Thomas Jefferson to Wilson Cary Nicholas, September 5, 1799, *JP*, XXXI:179 ("to avoid"); John Breckinridge to Thomas Jefferson, December 13, 1799, *JP*, XXXI:266 ("improper").

74. Warfield, *Kentucky Resolutions*, 125 ("transgress" to "the unquestionable right"), 125–126 ("a nullification"); John Breckinridge to Thomas Jefferson, December 13, 1799, *JP*, XXXI:266.

75. Warfield, *Kentucky Resolutions*, 125 ("the several states"), 126 ("sovereignties" to "bow to the laws"); Thomas Jefferson to John Breckinridge, January 29, 1800, *JP*, XXXI:344 ("the subject").

76. James Monroe to James Madison, November 22, 1799, *MP*, XVII:278 ("present public engagement"); Thomas Jefferson to James Madison, November 26, 1799, *JP*, XXXI:243 ("violations" and "be said or done").

77. James Madison to Thomas Jefferson, January 12, 1800, *JP*, XXXI:299 ("the justifying Report"); Editorial Note, Report of 1800, *MP*, XVII:304; *Richmond Examiner*, December 3, 1799 quoted in Joseph McGraw, "'To Secure These Rights': Virginia Republicans on the Strategies of Political Opposition, 1788–1800," 91 *VMHB* (1983), 54 at 59 ("would prove").

78. Virginia House of Delegates, *Journal*, 38; *Alexandria Times* [Alexandria, Va.], January 2, 1800; James Madison to Thomas Jefferson, December 29, 1799, *MP*, XVII:297, 305; *The Virginia Report of 1799–1800* (1850), 237.

79. *MP*, XVII:298n2; Virginia House of Delegates, *Journal*, 77–79; Report of 1800, *MP*, XVII:307 ("watching over" and "infraction"), 308 ("faithful observance" and "secure its existence").

80. Report of 1800, *MP*, XVII:308 ("[I]n case of a deliberate").

81. Report of 1800, *MP*, XVII:308 ("the states are parties"), 309 ("in their highest sovereign" and "parties to the compact"). For confusion over Madison's resolutions, see Beeman, *Old Dominion*, 214–215; Ellis, *Union at Risk*, 4–5; McCoy, *Last of the Fathers*, 68; Ketcham, *Madison*, 396–397; Elkins and McKitrick, *Federalism*, 721; Miller, *Juries and Judges*, 54–56; Churchill, "Popular Nullification," 105 at 114; Watkins, *Reclaiming*, 78; Sheehan, *Madison and the Spirit of Republican Self-Government*, 132; Steele, *Jefferson*, 255; Halperin, *Alien and Sedition Acts*, 106–107; Jonathan Gienapp, "How to Maintain a Constitution: The Virginia and Kentucky Resolutions and James Madison's Struggle with the Problem of Constitutional Maintenance," in Levinson, *Nullification and Secession*, 53 at 90; Noah Feldman, *The Three Lives of James Madison: Genius, Partisan, President* (2017), 420, 430; Hays, *States in American Constitutionalism*, 26, 33.

82. Report of 1800, *MP*, XVII:308 ("a deliberate"), 309 ("a plain principle" and "the last resort"), 311 ("theoretically true").

83. Report of 1800, *MP*, XVII:309–310 ("The states then"), 309 ("in their highest").
84. Report of 1800, *MP*, XVII:310 ("evident" to "the interposition of the parties").
85. Report of 1800, *MP*, XVII: 311 ("the sole expositor" to "the forms of the constitution").
86. Report of 1800, *MP*, XVII:311 ("in relation"); James Madison to Edward Everett, August 1830, *ML*, IV:101(referring to the people and not the Court exercising "the final resort within the purview of the Constitution" in monitoring federalism through the amendment process).
87. Report of 1800, *MP*, XVII:312 ("fundamental principles" and "The authority of constitutions").
88. Report of 1800, *MP*, XVII:349 ("strictly within" to "among the farther measures"); 336–337 (reiterating that in the United States, "The people, not the government, possess the absolute sovereignty").
89. Report of 1800, *MP*, XVII:350 ("the first symptoms" to "only by maintaining").
90. Rakove, *Madison and the Creation of the American Republic*, 130 ("Madison's effort").
91. James Madison to Thomas Jefferson, January 4, 1800, *JP*, XXXI:288 ("the right of the Legislature"); James Madison to Thomas Jefferson, January 9, 1800, *JP*, XXXI:295.
92. Report of 1800, *MP*, XVII:309–310 ("states" and "the people ... in their highest sovereign capacity"); Memorandum from an Unidentified Correspondent, [*c.* 2 January 1800], *MP*, XVII:300 ("to announce" to "subterfuge"), 301n4 ("go to the foundation").
93. James Madison to Thomas Jefferson, October 17, 1788, *MP*, XI:298–299 ("fundamental maxims"); Gienapp, "Maintain a Constitution," 53 at 74.
94. Virginia House of Delegates, *Journal* (January 7, 1800), 71 ("irregular" to "the General Assembly"), 72 ("interpose for the purpose" and "against particular acts").
95. For another Federalist critique that failed to distinguish the Third from the Seventh resolution see Addison, *Analysis of Virginia Report*, 6.
96. Report of 1800, *MP*, XVII:350 ("palpable and alarming").
97. Buel, *Securing the Revolution*, 224 ("clearly drew"); Broadwater, *Jefferson, Madison*, 204; Thomas Jefferson to James Madison, November 26, 1799, *JP*, XXXI:243 ("violations"); Thomas Jefferson to Joseph Priestley, March 21, 1801, *JP*, XXXIII:394 ("mighty wave"); James Madison to Spencer Roane, May 6, 1821, *ML*, III:219 ("usurping experiment"); James Madison, "On Nullification," 1835/1836, *ML*, IV:415 ("a triumph"); Amar, "Of Sovereignty," 1425 at 1502; Edward J. Larson, *A Magnificent Catastrophe: The Tumultuous Election of 1800, America's First Presidential Campaign* (2007), 35–36, 73–78, 96–97, 104, 177, 186.

98. Gienapp, *Second Creation*, 53 ("America's most incisive"); Gienapp, "Maintain a Constitution," 53 at 89; Greg Weiner, *Madison's Metronome: The Constitution, Majority Rule, and the Tempo of American Politics* (2012), 105.

5 State Interposition during the Jefferson and Madison Presidencies

1. Leonard and Cornell, *Partisan Republic*, 134 ("defenses of states' rights").
2. Reginald C. Stuart, "James Madison and the Militants: Republican Disunity and Replacing the Embargo," 6 *Diplomatic History* (1982), 145 at 147; Samuel Eliot Morison, *Harrison Gray Otis, 1765–1848: The Urbane Federalist* (1969), 298; Raymond Walters, Jr., *Albert Gallatin: Jeffersonian Financier and Diplomat* (1957), 209; Leonard W. Levy, *Jefferson and Civil Liberties: The Darker Side* (1963), 140; Louis Martin Sears, *Jefferson and the Embargo* (1927); Burton Spivak, *Jefferson's English Crisis: Commerce, Embargo, and the Republican Revolution* (1979). For Madison's support of the embargo, see Malone, *Jefferson*, V:475–490; J.C.A. Stagg, *Mr. Madison's War: Politics, Diplomacy, and Warfare in the Early American Republic, 1783–1830* (1983), 19–22. Although state legislative resistance was directed at the totality of embargo laws and policies, the term "embargo" rather than "embargoes" is used.
3. Speech of the Governor, *Resolves of the General Court of Massachusetts, passed at the Session Began and Held, at Boston, on Wednesday, the Sixth Day of January, 1808* [Boston, 1808], 64 ("sedition"), 89–90; Answer of the House of Representatives, Massachusetts, *Resolves* (January 1808), 67; Answer of the Senate, Massachusetts, *Resolves* (January 1808), 70; *Independent Chronicle* [Boston], January 18, 1808; *A Letter from the Honorable Timothy Pickering, a Senator of the United States from the State of Massachusetts Exhibiting to his Constituents a View of the Imminent Danger of an Unnecessary and Ruinous War. Addressed to his Excellency, James Sullivan, Governor of said State* (1808), 3, 11.
   On Pickering, see Gerard H. Clarfield, *Timothy Pickering and the American Republic* (1980); Hervey Putnam Prentiss, *Timothy Pickering as the Leader of New England Federalism, 1800–1815* (1934; reprinted 1972); Kevin M. Gannon, "Escaping 'Mr. Jefferson's Plan of Destruction': New England Federalists and the Idea of a Northern Confederacy, 1803–1804," 21 *JER* (2001), 413–443.
4. Governor Sullivan to Col. Pickering, March 18, 1808, [Timothy Pickering], *Interesting Correspondence between his Excellency Governor Sullivan and Col. Pickering; in which the latter Vindicates Himself Against the Groundless Charges Made Against Him by the Governor and Others* (1808), 4 ("a constitutional act"), 5 ("first

principle"); Col. Pickering to Governor Sullivan, April 22, 1808, *Sullivan and Pickering Correspondence*, 8.

5. *New England Palladium* [Boston], June 10, 1808 ("which a majority" and "the LEGISLATIVE"); *The Democrat* [Boston], May 28, 1808. For studies overlooking this interposition, see Prentiss, *Pickering*, 59; Helen R. Pinkney, *Christopher Gore: Federalist of Massachusetts, 1758–1827* (1969), 107; James M. Banner, Jr., *To the Hartford Convention: The Federalists and the Origins of Party Politics in Massachusetts, 1789–1815* (1970), 298–299; Wilentz, *American Democracy*, 133; Richard Buel, Jr., *America on the Brink: How the Political Struggle over the War of 1812 Almost Destroyed the Young Republic* (2005), 44–48.

6. Speech of the Governor, *Resolves of the General Court of Massachusetts, passed at the Session Began and Held, at Boston, on the Twenty-Fifth Day of May, 1808* [Boston, 1808], 160 ("expediency"); Answer of the House of Representatives, Massachusetts, *Resolves* (May 1808), 165, 168; Answer of the Senate, Massachusetts, *Resolves* (May 1808), 171–172.

7. Douglas Lamar Jones, "'The Caprice of Juries': The Enforcement of the Jeffersonian Embargo in Massachusetts," 24 *AJLH* (1980), 307 at 319–320, 325; *United States v. The William*, 28 Fed. Cas. 614 (1808).

8. *The Democrat*, November 12, 1808; *New England Palladium*, November 18, 1808; *Massachusetts Spy* [Worcester, Mass.], November 23, 1808; *New York Post*, November 15, 1808; Virginia D. Harrington, "New York and the Embargo of 1807," 8 *Quarterly Journal of the New York State Historical Association* (1927), 143–151.

9. Harrison Gray Otis to Josiah Quincy, December 15, 1808, Henry Adams, ed., *Documents Relating to New-England Federalism, 1800–1815* (1877), 374 ("for the purpose").

10. Christopher Gore to Timothy Pickering, December 20, 1808, Adams, *Documents*, 376 ("what measures"); Timothy Pickering to Christopher Gore, January 8, 1809, Adams, *Documents*, 377 ("whatever great" and "obviously proper"), 378 (*"judging for themselves"*).

11. Clarfield, *Pickering*, 240–241.

12. *New England Palladium*, January 13, 1809 (*"The CONSTITUTION"*); *Salem Gazette* [Salem, Mass.], January 17, 1809 ("the DEATH WARRANT"); *Newburyport Resolutions and Memorial* (Newburyport, Mass.), [1809]), 4 ("powers unknown"), 5 ("immediate guardians"), 8 ("to interpose"), 14 ("an interposition"); Banner, *Hartford Convention*, 299; Spivak, *Jefferson's English Crisis*, 157; Wilentz, *American Democracy*, 131; Levy, *Jefferson and Civil Liberties*, 139.

13. *Boston Gazette*, January 26, 1809 ("Boston Constitutional Meeting"); *Columbian Centinel* [Boston], January 25, 1809 ("true intent" and "unprecedented"); Benjamin W. Labaree, *Patriots and Partisans: The*

Merchants of Newburyport, 1764–1815 (1962), 163, 166 (asserting the Memorial invoked "a doctrine of nullification"); Prentiss, *Pickering*, 66; Sears, *Jefferson and the Embargo*, 185; McDonald, *States' Rights*, 64; Banner, *Hartford Convention*, 118; Morison, *Harrison Gray Otis*, 311. Bradley Hays describes the anti-embargo resolutions "as efforts at Madisonian maintenance" in which the New England states "played the role of sentinel, sounding alarm at a national policy" they deemed unconstitutional." See Hays, *States in American Constitutionalism*, 41.

14. *The Patriotic Proceedings of the Legislature of Massachusetts, During their Session from January 26, to March 4, 1809* (1809), 16 ("citizens in the streets").

15. *Patriotic Proceedings*, 24 ("the capacity"), 32 ("a free country"), 33 ("stamped").

16. Report of the Joint Committee on Petitions, February 1, 1809, *Patriotic Proceedings*, 44 ("adequate"), 41 ("within the power"); 52 ("unjust" to "co-operate").

17. Sanford W. Higginbotham, *The Keystone in the Democratic Arch: Pennsylvania Politics, 1800–1816* (1952), 183 (describing the resolutions as threats of "disunion" and "forcible resistance"); *The Repertory* [Boston], February 24, 1809 ("inconsistent" and "we merely express"); The Memorial and Remonstrance of the Legislature of Massachusetts, *Patriotic Proceedings*, 105 ("spirit and intention"); Address of the Legislature to the People of the Commonwealth of Massachusetts, *Patriotic Proceedings*, 113.

18. *Boston Patriot*, March 3, 1809 ("within the constitutional" and "legally binding"); *Boston Patriot*, March 10, 1809 ("*their judgments*"); [Hezekiah Niles], *Things as they are; or, Federalism Turned Inside Out!!* (1809).

19. *Richmond Enquirer*, January 24, 1809 ("utterly inconsistent" to "a *judicial court*"); *Richmond Enquirer*, March 24, 1809.

20. *Richmond Enquirer*, January 24, 1809 ("dissolution" and "*necessary and proper*").

21. Delaware House of Representatives, January 30, 1809, in Ames, *State Documents on Federal Relations*, 37 ("the constitutional sovereignty"); Banner, *Hartford Convention*, 306n3 ("tepid responses"); Sears, *Jefferson and the Embargo*, 185 (describing Connecticut's response as an echo of the Virginia and Kentucky Resolutions, "the chief previous land-marks of the secession movement in the United States").

22. *Connecticut Herald* [New Haven, Conn.], February 28, 1809 ("cast a watchful" and "overleap").

23. *Boston Gazette*, March 6, 1809 ("encroachments"); *American Mercury* [Hartford, Conn.], March 2, 1809 ("no right").

24. *At a Special Session of the General Assembly of the State of Connecticut, held at Hartford, on the twenty-third day of February, A.D. 1809* (Hartford, 1809), 5 ("guardians"), 7 ("to maintain").

25. *At the General Assembly of the State of Rhode-Island and Providence Plantations, begun and holden by adjournment at East-Greenwich, within and for the State aforesaid, on the fourth Monday of February, 1809* ([Providence,], 1809), 32 ("unjust" and "rights of the general government"); *The American* [Providence, R.I.], March 10, 1809.

26. Thomas Jefferson to Henry Dearborn, July 16, 1810, J. Jefferson Looney et al., eds., *The Papers of Thomas Jefferson, Retirement Series* (16 vols., 2005–2019), II:537 ("us from"); Thomas Jefferson to Joseph C. Cabell, February 2, 1816, *Founders Online*, National Archives ("the government shaken"); Pinkney, *Christopher Gore*, 115 ("protested"); Bradford Perkins, *Prologue to War: England and the United States, 1805–1812* (1961), 181–182; Walter W. Jennings, "The Agitation for the Repeal of the Embargo Act," 13 *Social Science* (1928), 217–246.

27. Higginbotham, *Pennsylvania Politics*, 183–193; George Lee Haskins and Herbert A. Johnson, *Foundations of Power: John Marshall, 1801–1815* (1981), 322–331; Mary E. Cunningham, "The Case of the *Active*," 12 *Pennsylvania History: A Journal of Mid-Atlantic Studies* (1946), 229–247; Gary D. Rowe, "Constitutionalism in the Streets," 78 *Southern California Law Review* (2005), 401–456; *Olmstead v. The Active*, 18 F. Cas. 680 (1803). Although his surname was occasionally rendered as "Olmsted," most often it was spelled "Olmstead," therefore the latter spelling will be used.

28. *Penhallow v. Doane's Administrators*, 3 U.S. 54 (1795); *United States v. Peters*, 9 U.S. 115 (1809), 140 ("full authority"); Editorial Note, *DHSC*, VI:387 ("an early step"); *DHSC*, VI:387–515.

29. *Journal of the Senate of the Commonwealth of Pennsylvania, Which Commenced at Lancaster, the Seventh Day of December, in the Year of our Lord, One Thousand Eight Hundred and Two, and of the Independence of the United States of America the Twenty-Seventh* (Lancaster, 1802), 189 ("strained construction"); *The Statutes at Large of Pennsylvania* 479 ("supported or obeyed"), 479–480 ("any further means") Chapter 2340 (1803).

30. *Debates in the Legislature of Pennsylvania, on the Case of Gideon Olmstead* (Lancaster, Pa., 1810), 50 ("call out"); *Pennsylvania Debates on Olmstead*, 51; 9 U.S. 115, 117.

31. 9 U.S. 115, 140–141.

32. 9 U.S. 115, 136 ("at will").

33. 9 U.S. 115, 136 ("right of the state"); Rowe, "Constitutionalism," 401 at 437.

34. 9 U.S. 115, 136 ("the ultimate" and "that power").

35. *The Whole Proceedings in the Case of Olmsted and Others versus Rittenhouse's Executrices, as Contained in Documents on Record in the Courts of the United States and Pennsylvania* (1809), 93 ("serious difficulties"); *Connecticut Herald*, March 7, 1809 ("cries of Treason");

Salem Gazette, March 10, 1809 ("CIVIL WAR!"); Higginbotham, *Pennsylvania Politics*, 183, 194–195; Warren, *Supreme Court*, I:377–378.

36. *Acts of the General Assembly of the Commonwealth of Pennsylvania, Passed at a Session Which was Begun and Held at the Borough of Lancaster, on December 6, 1808* (1809), 200("balance between").

37. Rowe, "Constitutionalism," 401 at 424–426; *Gazette of the United States* [Philadelphia], March 27, 1809; *Pennsylvania Archives*, 4th Series, Vol. IV:691–701; Thomas Lloyd, *A Report, of the Whole Trial of Gen. Michael Bright, and Others; Before Washington & Peters, in the Circuit Court of the United States, in and for the District of Pennsylvania ...* (1809), 35–38. I thank John D. Gordan, III for bringing this last source to my attention.

For accounts that overlook the role of interposition in the *Olmstead* controversy, see Warren, *Supreme Court*, I: 382, 388; Higginbotham, *Pennsylvania Politics*, 198; Haskins and Johnson, *Foundations*, 322, 331; McDonald, *States' Rights*, 64–65; Powell, *History and Politics*, 124; Rowe, "Constitutionalism," 401 at 436; Hunter, "Sound and Fury," 659 at 671.

38. Pennsylvania, *Acts* (1808), 209 ("the authority" to "an impartial tribunal"); Higginbotham, *Pennsylvania Politics*, 197n46.

39. Warren, *Supreme Court*, I:378 ("the duty"), citing *American Citizen*, March 24, 1809, I:381 ("precipitating"), citing *New York Evening Post*, April 14, 1809; Ames, *State Documents on Federal Relations*, 49 ("eminently qualified").

40. Simon Snyder to James Madison, April 6, 1809, Robert A. Rutland et al., eds., *The Papers of James Madison, Presidential Series* (5 vols. to date, 1984–2018), I:105 ("unhappy collision"); Report of 1800, *MP*, XVII:311 ("beyond the grant").

41. James Madison to Simon Snyder, April 13, 1809, Madison *Papers, Presidential Series*, I:114 ("unnecessary" and "unauthorized"); *Report of 1800, MP*, XVII:311.

42. Caesar A. Rodney to James Madison, April 17, 1809, Madison *Papers, Presidential Series*, I:120 ("the principal offenders"); Executive Pardon, [May 6, 1809], Madison *Papers, Presidential Series*, I:174 ("a mistaken"); *Trial of General Bright*, 6–8, 201–207; James Madison to Caesar A. Rodney, April 22, 1809, Madison *Papers, Presidential Series*, I:131; Rowe, "Constitutionalism," 401 at 442–443.

43. *Annals of Congress*, House of Rep., 11th Cong., 1st Sess., (June 9, 1809), 258, 259 (William Milnor) ("a power"), 260 (the motion was tabled by a vote of 63 to 50).

44. M. St. Clair Clarke and D.A. Hall, comps., *Legislative and Documentary History of the Bank of the United States* (1832), 44("condemned").

45. Hammond, *Banks*, 114–119.

46. *McCulloch v. Maryland*, 17 U.S. 316 (1819); Hammond, *Banks*, 214; Clarke and Hall, *Legislative History*, 274 and 446. Interposition in the campaign to oppose the bank has largely been overlooked. See for example, Walters, *Gallatin*, 239; Hammond, *Banks*, 213.

47. Walters, *Gallatin*, 239–40; Hammond, *Banks*, 211–222, 233 ("insincere"); Lomazoff, *Bank Controversy*, 3 ("dynamic"), 11 ("ordinary politics").

48. *Journal of the Twenty-First House of Representatives of the Commonwealth of Pennsylvania, Commenced at Lancaster, on Tuesday, the fourth of December, in the Year of our Lord, One Thousand Eight Hundred and Ten, and of the Commonwealth the Thirty-Fifth* (Lancaster, 1810), 70.

49. Resolutions Adopted by the Kentucky General Assembly, November 10, 1798, *JP*, XXX:550 ("infractions" and "redress"); Pennsylvania House, *Journal*, 66 ("at all times" and "Should the general government").

50. *Journal of the Senate of the Commonwealth of Pennsylvania, Which Commenced at Lancaster, the Fourth of December, in the Year of our Lord One Thousand Eight Hundred and Ten, and of the Independence of the United States of America the Thirty-Fifth* (Lancaster, 1810), 104 ("the people of the United States"), 105 ("United States" and "Should the general government").

The first resolution was passed by a vote of 68 to 20 and the second by a vote of 68 to 21. See Pennsylvania House, *Journal*, 172, 183–184.

51. *Acts of the General Assembly of the Commonwealth of Pennsylvania, Passed at a Session Which was Begun and Held at the Borough of Lancaster, on Tuesday, the Second Day of December, in the Year of our Lord One Thousand Eight Hundred and Ten and of the Independence of the United States of America the Thirty-Fifth* (Philadelphia, 1811), 268 ("true spirit"); Pennsylvania House, *Journal*, 211–213, 217–218.

52. "Communication from Virginia Legislature to House of Representatives on the Bank of the United States," *ASP, Finance*, II:470 ("not only unconstitutional"); *Democratic Press* [Philadelphia], February 1, 1811; *The Spirit of Seventy-Six* [Washington, D.C.], February 5, 1811; *National Aegis* [Worcester, Mass.], January 30, 1811.

53. *Journal of the Senate of the Commonwealth of Kentucky, Begun and Held at the Capitol in the Town of Frankfort, On Monday the Third Day of December, 1810, and of the Commonwealth the Nineteenth* (Frankfort, 1810), 155–156; *Journal of the House of Representatives of the Commonwealth of Kentucky Begun and Held at the Capitol in the Town of Frankfort, On Monday the Third Day of December, 1810, and of the Commonwealth the Nineteenth* (Frankfort, 1810), 207–208.

54. *Votes and Proceedings of the Thirty-Fifth General Assembly, of the State of New Jersey. At a Session Begun at Trenton, on the Fifteenth Day of*

January, One Thousand Eight Hundred and Eleven, and Continued by Adjournment (Trenton, 1811), 411, 482–483; Lomazoff, *Bank Controversy*, 69.

55. *Ostego Herald* [Cooperstown, N.Y.], December 12, 1810 ("Mr. Bland's Protest"); *Votes and Proceedings of the House of Delegates of the State of Maryland, November Session 1810* (Annapolis, [1811]), 7, 9.

56. *Maryland House Proceedings, November 1810 Session* (Annapolis, 1810), 68 ("highly impolitic" and "an interposition"), 69–70; *Carolina Gazette* [Charleston, S.C.], December 28, 1810; Clarke and Hall, *Legislative History*, 410.

57. "Preamble and Resolutions, February 20, 1812," *Acts Passed at a General Assembly of the Commonwealth of Virginia. Begun ... on December 2, 1811* (Richmond, 1812), 143–152. While the question of instruction had already been discussed, the phrase the "right of instruction" only surfaces in newspaper accounts in 1811.

58. Virginia Assembly, *Acts*, 148 ("the people composing" and "how the *people*"), 149 ("to interpose" and "the Letters of *Publius*"); *Federalist* 26, p.169 ("guardians" and "sound the alarm") (Hamilton), December 22, 1787; *Federalist* 28, p.180 (Hamilton), December 26, 1787; Virginia Assembly, *Acts*, 149 ("state legislatures").

59. Virginia Assembly, *Acts*, 150 ("the state right"); *MP*, XVII:309–310.

60. Massachusetts interposition resolutions of 1813 declaring Louisiana's statehood as "not authorized by the letter, or the spirit, of the federal constitution" were yet another example of states sounding the alarm. *Niles' National Register*, (Baltimore, 1812), IV:287 (July 3, 1813); "Obligation of Instruction," *The Enquirer* [Richmond, Va.], April 19, 1811.

61. Stagg, *Madison's War*; [John Lowell], *Mr. Madison's War: A Dispassionate Inquiry into the Reasons Alleged by Mr. Madison For Declaring an Offensive and Ruinous War Against Great Britain* (1812); ASP, *Military Affairs*, I:322; J.C.A. Stagg, *The War of 1812: Conflict for a Continent* (2012).

62. *Annual Message to Congress*, November 4, 1812, Madison *Papers, Presidential Series*, V:429 ("novel"); [Gallatin], "Answers Relating to the Power of the President of the U.S. over Militia," June 1812, in Stagg, *Madison's War*, 259n145; *Albany Gazette* [Albany, N.Y.], September 21, 1812; David Thompson, *History of the Late War, Between Great Britain and the United States of America* (1832), 294–295; *Martin v. Mott*, 25 U.S. 19 (1827).

For scholars who agree with Madison, see Marshall Smelser, *The Democratic Republic, 1801–1815* (1968), 291; Morison, *Harrison Gray Otis*, 333; Robert L. Kerby, "The Militia System and the State Militias in the War of 1812," 73 *Indiana Magazine of History* (1977), 102 at 119; Stagg, *Madison's War*, 260; Donald R. Hickey, *The War of 1812:*

A Forgotten Conflict (1989), 260; McDonald, *States' Rights*, 66–67; Buel, *America on the Brink*, 164–166.

63. Roger Griswold to Connecticut Executive Council, June 29, 1812, reprinted in Theodore Dwight, *History of the Hartford Convention: With a Review of the Policy of the United States Government, Which Led to the War of 1812* (1833), 244 ("whether the militia"), 246 ("that the militia"); John Cotton Smith to William Eustis, July 2, 1812, ASP, *Military Affairs*, I:325–326; Roger Griswold to William Eustis, August 13, 1812, ASP, *Military Affairs*, I:326.

64. Governor Griswold to Connecticut Assembly, August 4, 1812, Dwight, *Hartford Convention*, 263, 266; *Report of the Committee of the [Connecticut] General Assembly, at their Special Session, August 25, 1812* (New Haven, 1812), 6 (offering the reminder that Connecticut was "a FREE, SOVEREIGN and INDEPENDENT State").

65. Caleb Strong to William Eustis, August 5, 1812, ASP, *Military Affairs*, I:323.

66. Advisory Opinion of Theophilus Parsons, Samuel Sewall, and Isaac Parker to the Governor and Council of Massachusetts, *ASP, Military Affairs*, I:324.

67. Advisory Opinion of Parsons and others, ASP, *Military Affairs*, I:324; Caleb Strong to William Eustis, August 21, 1812, ASP, *Military Affairs*, I:323.

68. *Resolves of the General Court of the Commonwealth of Massachusetts, Passed at the Session, in October 1812, and January 1813* (Boston, 1813), 75 ("at any time"), 76 ("a consolidation").

69. House's Answer, Massachusetts, *Resolves* (October 1812), 82 ("unconstitutional"); Senate's Answer, Massachusetts, *Resolves* (October 1812), 86 ("jealousy" and "hour of danger"); Annual Message to Congress, November 4, 1812, Madison *Papers, Presidential Series*, V:429 ("not one nation").

70. Message of Governor William M. Jones to the General Assembly of Rhode Island, October 6, 1812, *Niles' National Register*, III:180; Speech of Governor Martin Chittenden to the Vermont Legislature, October 23, 1813, E.P. Walton, ed., *Records of the Governor and Council of the State of Vermont* (8 vols., 1873–1880), VI: 419–421; *Journals of the General Assembly of the State of Vermont, at their Session Begun and Holden at Montpelier, in the County of Jefferson, on Thursday the Fourteenth of October, A.D. 1813* (Rutland, [1813]), 137–140, 198–208.

71. Morison, *Harrison Gray Otis*, 334 ("infringement"); Pennsylvania Resolution of March 10, 1814, ASP, *Miscellaneous*, II:238–239 ("astonishment"); Proclamation of Governor Martin Chittenden, November 10, 1813, *Records of Vermont*, VI:492; Ames, *State Documents on Federal Relations*, 64; Hickey, *War of 1812*, p.266–267; *The Repertory*,

January 15, 1814; Resolutions of New Jersey, February 12, 1814 in *Niles'
Weekly Register*, VI:11 (March 5, 1814).

72. Sears, *Jefferson and the Embargo*, 247–248.

73. *Resolves of the General Court of the Commonwealth of Massachusetts,
passed at their Session, Which Commenced on January 12 and ended
February 28, 1814* (Boston, 1814), 346 ("investigating"), 346–347
("unjust or unnecessary"), 353 ("the people"), 360 ("demand"); *Boston
Gazette*, January 24, 1814; *The Repertory*, January 29, 1814.

74. *The Repertory*, February 19, 1814.

75. [Lloyd's Report], *Report of the Committee of Both Houses to Whom
Were Referred the Memorials From Deerfield and Several Other Towns*
[Boston, 1814], 6 ("a gross and palpable"), 7 ("interpose"), 8 ("been
explained").

76. Lloyd's Report, 9 ("true spirit"), 10; Report of 1800, *MP*, XVII:349
(defending the right of a legislature to communicate with other states
and cooperate "in maintaining the rights reserved to the states, or to the
people").

77. Lloyd's Report, 12 ("unconstitutional and void"); Resolutions Adopted
by the Kentucky General Assembly, November 10, 1798, *JP*, XXX:551.

78. *Boston Gazette*, June 2, 1814 and June 6, 1814 ("interposition").

79. *Resolves of the General Court of the Commonwealth of Massachusetts,
passed at their Session which convened the 5th Day of October 1814 and
also at their Session which convened on Wednesday the 18th of
January 1815* ([Boston], 1814–1815), 558; *Boston Daily Advertiser*,
October 6, 1814 ("Officers").

80. Massachusetts, *Resolves* (October 1814), 568 ("a radical reform").

81. Massachusetts, *Resolves* (October 1814), 568 ("liable"), 569 ("fair
representation"); *Boston Commercial Gazette*, October 13 and 17, 1814.

82. Circular Letter, Massachusetts, *Resolves* (October 1814), 571 ("an
experiment"); Samuel Eliot Morison, *The Life and Letters of Harrison
Gray Otis: Federalist, 1765–1848* (2 vols., 1913), II:148; Hickey, *War of
1812*, p.277. Massachusetts elected twelve delegates, Rhode Island four,
Connecticut seven and two counties in New Hampshire and one in
Vermont each sent a single delegate.

83. *Public Documents, Containing Proceedings of the Hartford Convention
of Delegates; Report of the Commissioners while at Washington; Letters
from Massachusetts Members in Congress.* (1815), 3–4, 8, 10 ("a total
disregard"), 11 ("decided opposition").

84. *Proceedings of Hartford Convention*, 11 ("absolutely void" to "in cases
of deliberate"), 25.

85. *Boston Daily Advertiser*, "To the President of the United States, on the
subject of the New England-Convention," No. II. "The Nature of Our
Government," November 15, 1814 ("axioms"), No. III. "The Meaning of
the Federal Compact," November 16, 1814, No. IV. "Mr. Madison's

Opinion on State Sovereignty," November 17, 1814 ("a State Legislature"); *Federalist* 46, p.320 ("the authority"), (Madison), January 29, 1788; *Boston Daily Advertiser*, "To the President of the United States on the subject of the New England Convention," No. IV. "Mr. Madison's Opinion on State Sovereignty," November 17, 1814 (*"then* and *now"*).

86. *Proceedings of Hartford Convention*, 25–27 (the proposed amendments were to be submitted to all the state legislatures for their adoption or if deemed "expedient" submitted for adoption "by a convention chosen by the people of each state"); Daniel Webster to [William F. Rowland?], January 11, 1815, Charles M. Wiltse, ed., *The Papers of Daniel Webster, Correspondence* (7 vols., 1974–1986), I:181; Timothy Pickering to John Lowell, January 23, 1815, in Henry Cabot Lodge, *Life and Letters of George Cabot* (1877, reprinted 1974), 562.

87. James Madison to Wilson Cary Nicholas, November 25, 1814, James Madison Papers, Library of Congress ("the source" and "revolt and separation"); Thomas Jefferson to Lafayette, February 14, 1815, Thomas Jefferson Papers, Library of Congress ("venal traitors"); Thomas Jefferson to Henry Dearborn, March 17, 1815, Thomas Jefferson Papers, Library of Congress ("degradation"); Jack Alden Clarke, "Thomas Sydney Jesup: Military Observer at the Hartford Convention," 29 *New England Quarterly* (1956), 393–399; Ketcham, *Madison*, 595.

88. Winfield Scott to James Monroe, February 15, 1815, James Monroe Papers, Manuscript and Archives Division, The New York Public Library; Hector Benevolus, *The Hartford Convention in an Uproar! and the Wise Men of the East Confounded!* (1815).

89. *Proceedings of Hartford Convention*, 6 ("destined"); Harrison Gray Otis to Noah Webster, May 6, 1840 ("constitutional & peaceable"), Noah Webster Papers, Manuscript and Archives Division, The New York Public Library; *Otis' Letters in Defence of the Hartford Convention* (1824), 52, 66 ("question of *constitutional law*"). When Otis first conceived of a multi-state convention in 1808, he considered the convention a means of relief not *"inconsistent with the union of these States."* Harrison Gray Otis to Josiah Quincy, December 15, 1808, reprinted in Morison, *Life and Letters of Otis*, II:5.

On New England secessionism, see David H. Fischer, "The Myth of the Essex Junto," 21 *WMQ* (1964), 191–235; Banner, *Hartford Convention*, 307; Clarfield, *Pickering*; Gannon, "Northern Confederacy," 413–443; Morison, *Harrison Gray Otis*, 307; Daniel R. Dzibinski, "The Politics of Power: The Partisan Struggle Surrounding the War of 1812 and the Hartford Convention" (MA thesis, Florida State University, 1999), 86–118.

90. Harrison Gray Otis to Noah Webster, May 6, 1840 (*"nullification"*), Noah Webster Papers, Manuscript and Archives Division, The New York Public Library.

91. *Web(SFW)*, I: xiii; The Conscription Bill, December 9, 1814, *Web(SFW)*, I:30 ("unconstitutional and illegal" and "It will be").

6 State Challenges to the Supreme Court's Control over Constitutional Interpretation

1. *Hunter v. Fairfax's Devisee*, 1 Munford 218 (1809); *Fairfax's Devisee v. Hunter's Lessee*, 11 U.S. 603 (1813); *Hunter v. Martin, Devisee of Fairfax*, 4 Munford 1 (1814); F. Thornton Miller, "John Marshall versus Spencer Roane: A Reevaluation of *Martin v. Hunter's Lessee*," 96 *VMHB* (1988), 297–314; Charles F. Hobson, "John Marshall and the Fairfax Litigation: The Background of *Martin v. Hunter's Lessee*," 1996 *Journal of Supreme Court History* (1996), 36–50; Editorial Note, *DHSC*, VII: 778–785; "Marshall and the Fairfax Litigation: From the Compromise of 1796 to *Martin v. Hunter's Lessee*," Herbert A. Johnson et al., eds., *The Papers of John Marshall* (12 vols. to date, 1974–2006), VIII:108–121.

2. For exceptions to the tendency of emphasizing two options, see Ellis, *Union at Risk*, 11; Benedict, "Lincoln and Federalism," 1 at 4–19; Andrew C. Lenner, "John Taylor and the Origins of American Federalism," 17 *JER* (1997), 399 at 422; John Radabaugh, "Spencer Roane and the Genesis of Virginia Judicial Review," 6 *AJLH* (1962), 63 at 68–70; Timothy S. Huebner, *The Southern Judicial Tradition: State Judges and Sectional Distinctiveness, 1790–1890* (1999), 32–33.

3. 4 Munford 1, 8 ("its portion"), 9 ("The constitution"); *Federalist* 39, p.257 (Madison), January 16, 1788.

4. 4 Munford 1, 18 ("state authorities"), 19 ("respective spheres"), 24 ("power to enforce"); John Taylor, *Construction Construed, and Constitutions Vindicated* (1820), 146 (asserting that Article VI implied a "mutuality of the right of construction" of the Constitution).

5. *Hunter v. Martin, Devisee of Fairfax*, 4 Munford 1, 27 ("a mere newspaper"), 29 ("celebrated report"), 30 ("a perpetual"), 52 ("the compact" to "authorized to interfere"), 54; Rex Beach, "Spencer Roane and the Richmond Junto," 22 *WMQ* (1942), 1–17; Margaret E. Horsnell, *Spencer Roane: Judicial Advocate of Jeffersonian Principles* (1986); Huebner, *Southern Judicial Tradition*, 10–39.

6. Joseph Story to George Ticknor, January 22, 1831, *Life and Letters of Joseph Story* (William W. Story, ed., 2 vols., 1851), II:49 ("concurred"); *Martin v. Hunter's Lessee*, 14 U.S. 304, 333 ("compact between"), 325 ("by 'the people"), 346 ("the absolute right"); R. Kent Newmyer, *Supreme Court Justice Joseph Story: Statesman of the Old Republic* (1985), 112 (Story probably consulted Marshall, and "some of the words" in the opinion might have been

Marshall's); Marshall *Papers*, VIII:119 (Marshall "was in complete agreement" with Story's opinion).

7. 14 U.S. 304, 362; Gunther, *Marshall's Defense*, 9, 19 (coming close to identifying the sounding the alarm function by observing that, "Political restraints, not constitutional principles in the Court's keeping, impose what federalism limits remain on congressional authority"); Miller, "John Marshall versus Spencer Roane," 297–314; Samuel R. Olken, "John Marshall and Spencer Roane: An Historical Analysis of Their Conflict over U.S. Supreme Court Appellate Jurisdiction," 1990 *Journal of Supreme Court History* (1990), 125–141; G. Edward White, *The Marshall Court and Cultural Change, 1815–1835* (abridged ed.) (1991), 485–567; Cornell, *Other Founders*, 278–288; Mark R. Killenbeck, *M'Culloch v. Maryland: Securing a Nation* (2006).

8. Quoted in Killenbeck, *M'Culloch*, 57 ("settled"); James Madison, *Veto Message*, January 30, 1815, MPP, I:555; Dewey, "Madison Helps Clio," 38 at 52–55.

9. *American and Commercial Daily Advertiser* [Baltimore, Md.], January 23, 1818; *Baltimore Patriot*, February 18, 1818; *Votes and Proceedings of the House of Delegates of the State of Maryland. December Session, 1817* (Annapolis, 1818), Maryland State Archives, 13, 22, 24, 37; *Baltimore Patriot*, February 20, 1818; Patricia L. Franz, "Ohio v. The Bank: An Historical Examination of *Osborn v. The Bank of the United States*," 1999 *Journal of Supreme Court History* (1999), 112 at 115.

10. *Journal of the House of Representatives, at the First Session of the Twelfth General Assembly of the State of Tennessee, Begun and Held at Knoxville, on Monday, the Fifteenth Day of September, 1817* (Knoxville, 1817), 137, 161, 162 ("all lawful means"), 254, 290; Protest of William Young, November 22, 1817, Tennessee House, *Journal*, 291–292 ("a bold and dangerous"); "U.S. Branch Bank," dateline Nashville, January 31, 1818, reprinted in *Baltimore Patriot*, February 20, 1818 ("inoperative"); *Connecticut Herald* [New Haven, Conn.], January 6, 1818 ("ignorance").

11. Warren, *Supreme Court*, I:505; Hammond, *Banks*, 263; White, *Marshall Court*, 543; Killenbeck, *M'Culloch*, 68–69.

12. *Journal of the House of Representatives of the Commonwealth of Kentucky, Begun and Held in the Town of Frankfort, on Monday the Second Day of December, 1816, and of the Commonwealth the Twenty-Fifth* (Frankfort, 1816), 235 ("would promote"); *Journal of the House of Representatives of the Commonwealth of Kentucky House Journal, Begun and Held in the Town of Frankfort, on Monday the First Day of December, 1817 and of the Commonwealth the Twenty-Sixth* (Frankfort, 1817), 239, 245; *Argus of Western America* [Frankfort, Ky.], January 22, 1819; Sandra F. VanBurkleo, "'The Paws of Banks:' The Origins and Significance of Kentucky's Decision to Tax Federal Bankers, 1818–1820," 9 JER (1989), 457–487.

13. *Journal of the House of Representatives of the Commonwealth of Kentucky, Begun and Held in the Town of Frankfort, on Monday the Seventh Day of December 1818, and of the Commonwealth the Twenty-Seventh* (Frankfort, 1818), 16 ("Whether congress").

14. *Weekly Messenger* [Russellville, Ky.], January 26, 1819 ("to drive"); Kentucky House, *Journal*, 85, 234; *Argus of Western America*, January 8, 1819 (reporting on the debate in the House over the bill to tax branches of the bank "for the purpose of expelling them from this state"); *Argus of Western America*, January 29, 1819.

15. Killenbeck, *M'Culloch*.

16. Gunther, *Marshall's Defense*, 2 ("the most important"), 11; Cornell, *Other Founders*, 283 ("the most intense").

17. Marshall *Papers*, VIII:260 ("powers" and "devolved"), 277 ("entitled to great respect").

18. Marshall *Papers*, VIII:272 ("objects not entrusted").

19. *Niles' Weekly Register*, March 3, 1819 ("deadly blow"); *Richmond Enquirer*, March 23, 1819 ("firm Republicans"), quoted in Marshall *Papers*, VIII:282; quoted in Killenbeck, *M'Culloch*, 142 ("right to infringe"); John Marshall to Joseph Story, March 24, 1819, Marshall *Papers*, VIII:280 ("roused" and "*damnably heretical*"); John Marshall to Bushrod Washington, March 27, 1819, Marshall *Papers*, VIII:281 ("condemned").

20. Gunther, *Marshall's Defense*.

21. *Amphictyon*, Gunther, *Marshall's Defense*, 55 ("in a liberal"), 57 ("parties to the compact"), 58 ("would not").

22. *Amphictyon*, Gunther, *Marshall's Defense*, 58 ("the right").

23. *A Friend of the Union*, Gunther, *Marshall's Defense*, 88 ("concurs exactly").

24. John Marshall to Bushrod Washington, May 6, 1819, Marshall *Papers*, VIII:311 ("very serious" and "great man"); John Marshall to Joseph Story, May 27, 1819, Marshall *Papers*, VIII:314 ("unlike those").

25. *Hampden*, Gunther, *John Marshall's Defense*, 128, 146, 153 ("between two" and "jurisdiction").

26. *Hampden*, Gunther, *Marshall's Defense*, 146 ("impartial tribunal"), 147 ("the ultimate redress" to "to erect"), 147–148 (citing constitutional commentator St. George Tucker for the remedy of sounding the alarm interposition), 150–151 (quoting Pennsylvania's legislative interposition resolution of 1811).

27. *Hampden*, Gunther, *Marshall's Defense*, 154 ("the *exclusive* judge" to "force of public opinion").

28. John Marshall to Bushrod Washington, [*c.* June 28, 1819], Marshall *Papers*, VIII:317 ("considerable influence"); John Marshall to Bushrod Washington, August 3, 1819, Marshall *Papers*, VIII:373 ("should an attempt").

29. A Friend of the Constitution, Gunther, Marshall's Defense, 160 ("The equipoise" to "a new mode").

30. A Friend of the Constitution, Gunther, Marshall's Defense, 201 ("a mere league"), 202 ("independent sovereigns").

31. A Friend of the Constitution, Gunther, Marshall's Defense, 205 ("independent courts"). The Southern experience with no single Supreme Court during the Civil War revealed less dysfunctionality than Hamilton's description predicted. See J.G. de Roulhac Hamilton, "The State Courts and the Confederate Constitution," 4 *JSH* (1938), 425–448; Geoffrey D. Cunningham, "To Begin Anew: Federalism and Power in the Confederate States of America" (Ph.D. diss., Louisiana State University, 2015), 127–160.

32. James Madison to Spencer Roane, September 2, 1819, *ML*, III:143 ("combated"); Thomas Jefferson to Spencer Roane, September 6, 1819, Paul Leicester Ford, ed., *The Works of Thomas Jefferson* (12 vols., 1904–1905), XII:136 ("the true principles"); James Madison to Spencer Roane, September 2, 1819, *ML*, III:143 ("general and abstract"), 145 ("broad and pliant"), 143 ("landmarks"), 145 ("rule of construction"), 144 ("guardianship of the Constitution"), 145 ("a constructive assumption"), 143 ("expounding").

33. Thomas Jefferson to Spencer Roane, September 6, 1819, Jefferson *Works*, XII:136 ("[W]e find"), 137 ("wax"), 136–137 ("exclusively explaining" to "truly independent").

34. Thomas Jefferson to Spencer Roane, September 6, 1819, Jefferson *Works*, XII:136–137.

35. *Journal of the House of Delegates of the Commonwealth of Virginia, Begun and Held at the Capitol, in the City of Richmond, on Monday the Sixth Day of December, One Thousand Eight Hundred and Nineteen* (Richmond, 1819), 15, 26.

36. Virginia House of Delegates, *Journal*, 59 ("resist"), 57 ("change the whole character" to "the parties"); Gunther, *Marshall's Defense*, 17; Olken, "John Marshall and Spencer Roane," 125 at 136; Miller, *Juries and Judges*, 90.

37. Virginia House of Delegates, *Journal*, 58 ("re-trace"), 169, 178–179; *The Genius of Liberty* [Leesburg, Va.], March 14, 1820; Warren, *Supreme Court*, I:525; *Niles' Weekly Register*, XXI:296 (January 5, 1822); Herman V. Ames, *The Proposed Amendments to the Constitution of the United States during the First Century of its History* (1897), 256 (eight states passing resolutions disapproving of the suggested amendment).

38. A.G. Claypoole to William A. Crawford, September 17, 1819, *ASP*, Finance, IV:903.

39. *Journal of the House of Representatives of the State of Ohio, Being the First Session of the Eighteenth General Assembly, Begun and Held in the*

Town of Columbus, in the County of Franklin, Monday, December 6, 1819 (Columbus, [1819–1821]), 14 ("monied corporations").

40. *Journal of the House of Representatives of the State of Ohio, Being the First Session of the Nineteenth General Assembly, Begun and Held in the Town of Columbus, in the County of Franklin, Monday, December 4, 1820* (Columbus, [1819–1821]), 83–84.

41. *Report of the Joint Committee of both Houses of the General Assembly of the State of Ohio on the Communication of the Auditor of the State upon the Subject of the Proceedings of the Bank of the United States against the Officers of State in the United States Circuit Court,* 16th Cong., 2nd Sess., Miscellaneous Documents, No. 500 (1821), 645 ("the doctrine"); White, *Marshall Court,* 526.

42. *Joint Report,* Ohio Legislature, 646 ("the true text book"), 648 ("lightly"), 653 ("a mere private"), 649 ("rights, powers" and "progressively").

43. *Joint Report,* Ohio Legislature, 653; Salmon P. Chase, *The Statutes of Ohio and of the Northwest Territory, Adopted or Enacted from 1788 to 1833 ...* (1834) II:1185–1186, 1198–1199.

44. Ohio House, *Journal,* 393 ("gross injustice"); *Niles' Weekly Register,* XVII:65 ("not for any") (October 2, 1819); Kevin M. Gannon, "The Political Economy of Nullification: Ohio and the Bank of the United States, 1818–1824," 114 *Ohio History* (2007), 79–104 (describing Ohio's response to *McCulloch* as resting on a theory of nullification).

45. Warren, *Supreme Court,* I: 538; New Hampshire House of Representatives, June 28, 1821, *Niles' Weekly Register,* XX:313 ("its full support") (July 14, 1821); *Boston Weekly Messenger,* February 14, 1822 ("so long as").

46. *Osborn v. Bank of the United States,* 22 U.S. 738 (1824); White, *Marshall Court,* 524–535; Franz, "Ohio v. The Bank," 112–137.

47. Andrew Jackson, *First Annual Message,* December 8, 1829 *MPP,* II:462 (noting that "a large portion of our citizens" questioned "the constitutionality" of the law creating the bank); Andrew Jackson, *Veto Message,* July 10, 1832, *MPP,* II: 581–582 ("Mere precedent"); Lomazoff, *Bank Controversy,* 153 ("the Court had"); John Tyler, *Veto Message,* August 16, 1841, *MPP,* IV:64 ("unsettled question"). The implied powers issue addressed in *McCulloch* would only be resolved in a series of post–Civil War cases collectively known as the Legal Tender Cases.

48. *Cohens v. Virginia,* 19 U.S. 264 (1821).

49. *Journal of the House of Delegates of the Commonwealth of Virginia, Begun and Held at the Capitol, in the City of Richmond, on Monday the Fourth Day of December, One Thousand Eight Hundred and Twenty* (Richmond, 1820), 108 ("to examine"), 105 ("two legislative bodies" to "absolute supremacy"), 106 ("to make the state"), 108 ("sleepless vigilance"); White, *Marshall Court,* 505; Marshall, *Papers,* IX:108.

50. *Cohens v. Virginia*, Marshall *Papers*, IX:114 ("capable").

51. *Cohens v. Virginia*, Marshall *Papers*, IX:135 ("great authority"), 119 ("the true construction"), 120 ("self-preservation").

52. James Madison to Spencer Roane, May 6, 1821, *ML*, III:217 ("comments and reasonings" to "experiment"), 218 ("a just equilibrium"), 217 ("the constitutional boundary").

53. James Madison to Spencer Roane, May 6, 1821, *ML*, III:218 ("the latitude" and "encroachments"), 218–219 ("expected advantages"), 219 ("the character" to "In the case of").

54. James Madison to Spencer Roane, May 6, 1821, *ML*, III:222 ("individuals only").

55. "On the Lottery Decision," No. 1, *Richmond Enquirer*, May 25, 1821 ("cease to be"); "On the Lottery Decision," No. 2, *Richmond Enquirer*, May 29, 1821 ("bind the other"); "On the Lottery Decision," No. 4, *Richmond Enquirer*, June 5, 1821 ("A compact").

56. "On the Lottery Decision," No. 2, *Richmond Enquirer*, May 29, 1821 ("contest for rights"); "On the Lottery Decision," No. 1, *Richmond Enquirer*, May 25, 1821 ("sovereign and independent" to "the equilibrium").

57. James Madison to Spencer Roane, June 29, 1821, *ML*, III: 223 ("between the States"), 222 ("problem of collision"), 223 ("possibility of disagreements" and "trust to be vested").

58. James Madison to Spencer Roane, September 2, 1819, *ML*, III:145 ("was foreseen"); James Madison to Spencer Roane, June 29, 1821, *ML*, III:223 ("jarring opinions"); James Madison to Spencer Roane, September 2, 1819, *ML*, III:145 ("a regular course"); James Madison to Spencer Roane, June 29, 1821, *ML*, III:224 ("mutually contribute").

59. *Federalist* 37, p.234 ("marking the proper line"), 236 ("obscure") (Madison), January 11, 1788; James Madison to Spencer Roane, June 29, 1821, *ML*, III:222 ("Gordian").

60. James Madison to Spencer Roane, May 6, 1821, *ML*, III:217 ("impartially maintained").

61. John Marshall to Joseph Story, June 15, 1821, Marshall *Papers*, IX:167 ("virulence"), 168 ("the champion"); Joseph Story to John Marshall, June 27, 1821, Marshall *Papers*, IX:176 ("the whole doctrine"); 177 ("to prostrate"); Thomas Jefferson to William Charles Jarvis, September 28, 1820, Jefferson *Works*, XII:162 ("co-equal").

62. John Marshall to Joseph Story, July 13, 1821, Marshall *Papers*, IX:179 ("very many"); John Marshall to Joseph Story, September 18, 1821 Marshall *Papers*, IX:184 ("deep design" and "attack").

63. Thomas Jefferson to William Johnson, June 12, 1823, Paul Leicester Ford, ed., *The Writings of Thomas Jefferson* (10 vols., 1892–1899), X:232 ("there must be" and "the people of the Union").

64. James Madison to Thomas Jefferson, June 27, 1823, *ML*, III:325 ("tracing" and "every new point").

65. James Madison to Thomas Jefferson, June 27, 1823, *ML*, III:326 ("whether the Judicial authority").

66. James Madison to Thomas Jefferson, June 27, 1823, *ML*, III:327 ("extra-judicial" and "abuse").

67. James Madison to Thomas Jefferson, June 27, 1823, *ML*, III:327 ("remedy"); James Madison to Spencer Roane, May 6, 1821, *ML*, III:219.

68. Carter Goodrich, *Government Promotion of American Canals and Railroads, 1800–1890* (1960); Maurice G. Baxter, *Henry Clay and the American System* (1995); John Lauritz Larson, *Internal Improvement: National Public Works and the Promise of Popular Government in the Early United States* (2001).

69. James Madison to Thomas Jefferson, February 17, 1825, *ML*, III:483 ("politicians").

70. *Charleston Courier* [Charleston, S.C.], November 27, 1824 ("an entering wedge" to "public sentinels"); *City Gazette* [Charleston, S.C.], December 1, 1824; Freehling, *Prelude*, 115–117.

71. *Charleston Courier*, December 17, 1824, "Extract of a Letter to the Editor" ("rights to Congress"). The Senate passed the resolutions by a vote of 30 to 13.

72. *National Intelligencer*, January 1, 1825 ("double allegiance" to "the People themselves"); *Acts and Resolutions of the General Assembly of the State of South-Carolina, Passed in December, 1825* (Columbia, 1826), 88("right of remonstrating").

73. *Richmond Enquirer*, December 6, 1825; Thomas Jefferson to James Madison, December 24, 1825, reprinted in *Niles' Weekly Register*, XXXVII:79 ("the most sacred") (September 26, 1829) ("*The solemn declaration and protest of the commonwealth, of Virginia, on the principles of the constitution of the United States of America, and on the violation of them*").

74. Thomas Jefferson to James Madison, December 24, 1825, reprinted in *Niles' Weekly Register*, XXXVII:80 ("the usurpation" to "watchfulness") (September 26, 1829).

75. James Madison to Thomas Jefferson, December 28, 1825, *ML*, III:513 ("a valuable resort").

76. James Madison to Thomas Jefferson, February 24, 1826, *ML*, III:517–518.

77. *Niles' Weekly Register*, XXX:38 ("a commentary" and "to watch over") (March 18, 1826).

78. "Report of Debate in Virginia House of Delegates," February 28, 1826, David Garland, in *Richmond Enquirer*, March 2, 1826 ("except in cases").

79. "Report of Debate in Virginia House of Delegates," February 28, 1826, George Drumgoole, in *Richmond Enquirer*, March 2, 1826

("the crisis"); *Richmond Enquirer*, March 7, 1826; *Richmond Whig* quoted in *Niles' Weekly Register*, XXX:39 ("a second '98") (March 18, 1826).

80. *Niles' Weekly Register*, XXX:38 ("dependent") (March 18, 1826); *Richmond Enquirer*, March 2, 1826 ("the true principles").

81. *Richmond Enquirer*, December 5, 1826 ("the letter" and "against the encroachment").

82. James Madison to N.P. Trist, February 7, 1827, *ML*, III:551 ("labyrinth" and "between the exercise"); James Madison to Joseph C. Cabell, March 22, 1827, *ML*, III:571.

83. *Niles' Weekly Register*, XXXII:139 ("the usurpations"), 168 ("such 'deliberate") (April 21, 1827).

7 The Transformation of Interposition: The Theory of Nullification Emerges

1. Rabun, "Interposition," 49 at 80; Brisbane, "Interposition," 12; Miller and Howell, "Interposition"; Ralph L. Ketcham, "Jefferson and Madison and the Doctrines of Interposition and Nullification: A Letter of John Quincy Adams," 66 *VMHB* (1958), 178; Maier, "Road Not Taken," 1 at 7; Lacy K. Ford, Jr., *Origins of Southern Radicalism: The South Carolina Upcountry, 1800–1860* (1988), 123–126; Zavodnyik, *Age of Strict Construction*, 76; Anderson, *Federalism*, 18; Wood, *Nullification*, lxvii; John G. Grove, *John C. Calhoun's Theory of Republicanism* (2016), 92, 94. For some exceptions, see Tipton, *Nullification and Interposition*, 7; Hunter, "Sound and Fury," 659 at 662 (nullification and interposition "are often cited interchangeably, but are not, in fact, the same"); Rakove, "Hollow Hopes," 81 at 85 (identifying interposition as "a lesser version of state opposition" distinguishable from "outright nullification").

2. "Rough Draft of an Address to the People of South Carolina," [c. December 1, 1830], *CP*, XI:266 ("consolidated"); John C. Calhoun to [Frederick W.] Symmes, July 26, 1831, *CP*, XI:416 ("the sovereignty of the States"); "Speech of Daniel Webster," January 26–27, 1830 in *Webster-Hayne Debate*, 153 ("in the aggregate"); "The Constitution Not a Compact," February 16, 1833, *Web(SFW)*, I:571–619.

3. James Madison to Andrew Stevenson, November 27, 1830, *ML*, IV:131 ("a middle ground").

4. Brant, *Madison*, VI:483–484; McCoy, *Last of the Fathers*, 144; Grove, *Calhoun's Theory of Republicanism*, 111.

5. For depictions of a binary debate, see for example, Edward S. Corwin, "National Power and State Interposition, 1787–1861," 10 *Michigan Law*

Review (1911–1912), 535; Miller and Howell, "Interposition," 2 at 20; Stampp, "Perpetual Union," 5; Daniel Feller, *The Public Lands in Jacksonian Politics* (1984), 114; Massey, "State Sovereignty," 61 at 151; Zarefsky and Gallagher, "Public Discourse," 247 at 255; Timothy S. Huebner, *Liberty and Union: The Civil War Era and American Constitutionalism* (2016), 17; Bodenhamer, *U.S. Constitution*, 27.

For appreciation of a middle ground, see for example Major L. Wilson, "'Liberty and Union': An Analysis of Three Concepts Involved in the Nullification Controversy,'" 33 *JSH* (1967), 331–355; Ellis, *Union at Risk*, 11; David F. Ericson, "The Nullification Crisis, American Republicanism, and the Force Bill Debate," 61 *JSH* (1995), 249 at 252; Whittington, "Political Constitution," 1 at 14–17.

6. F.W. Taussig, *The Tariff History of the United States* (1892, 5th ed. rev., 1910); Freehling, *Prelude*, 25–86, 138–140; Bolt, *Tariff Wars*, 91–120.

7. *Niles' Weekly Register*, XXXIII:222 ("to bring back") (December 1, 1827), 283 (December 29, 1827); Bolt, *Tariff Wars*, 67–75.

8. *Columbia Gazette* [Charleston, S.C.], December 5, 1827 ("mischievous" and "the general government").

9. *ASP, Finance*, V:725 ("purely the act"), 726 ("a power unknown" and "to interfere"), 727 ("impartial").

10. *ASP, Finance*, V:730 ("to be watchful").

11. *ASP, Finance*, V:852 ("a right to remonstrate"), 853 ("have the right").

12. *ASP, Finance*, V:856 ("the mode" and "the memorials").

13. *ASP, Finance*, V:722, 849 ("beyond the fair demands").

14. *ASP, Finance*, V:873 (Indiana), 879, 885 (Ohio), 964 (New Jersey) ("successive decisions").

15. James Madison to General Lafayette, February 20, 1828, *ML*, III:619 ("electioneering zeal"); James Madison to Jonathan Roberts, February 29, 1828, *ML*, III:625 ("an undue weight" to "a permanent equilibrium"); James Madison to Mathew Carey, 1828, *ML*, III:636; Dewey, "Madison Helps Clio," 38 at 43–44, 50–52.

16. Taussig, *Tariff History*, 68–108; Bolt, *Tariff Wars*, 76–90.

17. *Niles' Weekly Register*, XXXV:223 (November 29, 1828) ("perish"); Brutus, *The Crisis: or, Essays on the Usurpations of the Federal Government* (1827).

18. John C. Calhoun to William C. Preston, November 6, 1828, *CP*, X:432 ("our wrongs"), 431 ("little aid"), November 21, 1828, 433.

19. "Rough Draft ... South Carolina Exposition," *CP*, X:444 ("unconstitutional").

20. "Rough Draft ... South Carolina Exposition," *CP*, X:494 ("the great difficulty" and "the line"), 496 ("The powers"), 498 ("this beautiful theory").

21. "Rough Draft ... South Carolina Exposition," *CP*, X:500 ("of nullifying" and "a strange misconception").

22. Calhoun attributed the essay (written by Madison) to Hamilton. "Rough Draft ... South Carolina Exposition," *CP*, X:506; *Federalist* 51, p. 351 ("The different governments") (Madison), February 6, 1788; "Rough Draft ... South Carolina Exposition," *CP*, X:508 ("clearly affirms").

23. "Rough Draft ... South Carolina Exposition," *CP*, X:508; "Report of 1800," *MP*, XVII:308 ("that in cases"), 309–310 ("States"). Calhoun misquoted Madison's phrase "the states, who are parties" by writing "the State, who are parties" – an error corrected with brackets by the editors of the Calhoun *Papers*.

24. "Rough Draft ... South Carolina Exposition," *CP*, X:510 ("the state can interpose" and "fully represents"), 512 ("and if so").

25. "Rough Draft ... South Carolina Exposition," *CP*, X:512 ("rests on").

26. "Rough Draft ... South Carolina Exposition," *CP*, X:520 ("modify" and "a disputed power").

27. "Rough Draft ... South Carolina Exposition," *CP*, X:528 and 530 ("interposition of the State").

28. *South Carolina State Gazette* [Columbia, S.C.], November 26, 1828 ("*a deliberate, palpable*" and "the sovereign power").

29. *Niles' Weekly Register*, XXXV:304 ("interposition"), 308 ("resistance") (January 3, 1829); James Madison to James Barbour, December 18, 1828, *ML*, III:662 ("its repeal"); "S.C. Protest," November 19, 1828, *CP*, X:535–539; *South Carolina State Gazette*, December 27, 1828.

30. *Acts and Resolutions of the General Assembly of the State of South Carolina, passed in December 1828* (Columbia, 1829), 17("to remonstrate"), 19 ("partial" and "ulterior measures").

31. *Resolutions of South Carolina General Assembly*, (1829), 86 ("restore Federal Legislation" and "Future measures") (Georgia Memorial, December 20, 1828); *Niles' Weekly Register*, XXXIX:340 (January 8, 1831).

32. James Madison to Joseph C. Cabell, September 7, 1829, *ML*, IV:46 ("the Tariff fever"); James Madison to Nicholas P. Trist, September 23, 1831 ("how little"), James Madison Papers, Library of Congress; James Madison to Richard Rush, December 4, 1820, *ML*, III:195; James Madison to Joseph C. Cabell, March 22, 1827, *ML*, III:571–574; Brant, *Madison*, VI:470–474.

33. James Madison to Joseph C. Cabell, February 2, 1829, *ML*, IV:11 ("to go into the newspapers"); "One of the People," "The Letters of Mr. Madison, No. 7," *Richmond Enquirer*, February 19, 1829 ("constitutional costume"); *Richmond Enquirer*, February 24, 1829.

34. *Resolutions of Virginia, On the Powers of the Federal Government. Report the Select Committee on the Resolutions of Georgia and South Carolina* (February 24, 1829), reprinted in *Resolutions of South Carolina General Assembly* (1829), 72("exposition"), 77 ("a majority" and "wholly void").

35. *Resolutions of Virginia*, 78 ("as the guardians" and "the right to construe").
36. *Richmond Enquirer*, March 6, 1829 ("forcible resistance").
37. *Richmond Enquirer*, February 26, 1829 ("any one state").
38. Ames, *State Documents on Federal Relations*, 180–183.
39. James Madison to Joseph C. Cabell, March 19, 1829, *ML*, IV:35 ("produce fresh torrents" and "silent appeal"); James Madison to Joseph C. Cabell, August 16, 1829, *ML*, IV:43 ("arbiter"); James Madison to Joseph C. Cabell, September 7, 1829, *ML*, IV: 47 ("the necessity").
40. James Madison to Joseph C. Cabell, September 7, 1829, *ML*, IV:46 ("Virginia doctrine").
41. James Madison to Joseph C. Cabell, September 7, 1829, *ML*, IV:46 ("extreme cases" and "the compact").
42. "Outline," September, 1829, *ML*, IV:18 ("fundamental error" and "in their sovereign character"); McCoy, *Last of the Fathers*, 134–135 ("might appear"). For Madison's continued insistence on the uniqueness of the Constitution, see James Madison to Daniel Webster, May 27, 1830, *ML*, IV:85; James Madison to W.C. Rives, March 12, 1833, *ML*, IV:289.
43. "Outline," September, 1829, *ML*, IV:19 ("by the people" and "by each within").
44. "Outline," September, 1829, *ML*, IV:19 ("usurpations" and "constitutional remedies").
45. James Madison to Joseph C. Cabell, August 16, 1829, *ML*, IV:42–44; "Outline," September, 1829, *ML*, IV:20 ("original rights").
46. *Journal of the House of Representatives in the Commonwealth of Kentucky, Begun and Held in the Town of Frankfort, on December 7, 1829* (Frankfort, 1829), 19 ("step further"), 20.
47. Kentucky House of Representatives, *Journal* (1829), 143, 149, 150 ("an appeal to arms").
48. Kentucky House of Representatives, *Journal* (1829), 152 ("the incontestable right"), 315, 329.
49. Speech of Robert Y. Hayne, of South Carolina, January 25, 1830, *Webster-Hayne Debate*, 73 ("The South Carolina doctrine" and "the good old"), 74 ("'Madison's Report'"), 79 ("first promulgated" and "when they believed").
50. Speech of Daniel Webster, of Massachusetts, January 26 and 27, 1830, *Webster-Hayne Debate*, 124 ("the States may interpose").
51. Speech of Daniel Webster, of Massachusetts, January 26 and 27, 1830, *Webster-Hayne Debate*, 125 ("a direct appeal" to "middle course").
52. Webster (January 26 and 27, 1830), *Webster-Hayne Debate*, 135 ("a little indefinite" to "unobjectionable").
53. Hayne (January 27, 1830), *Webster-Hayne Debate*, 165 ("a compact").

54. James Madison to Nicholas P. Trist, February 15, 1830, *ML*, IV:61 (*"individually"*), 63 ("the joint constituents"), 61 ("unprecedented"), 62 ("the partition line").

55. James Madison to Nicholas P. Trist, February 15, 1830, *ML*, IV:62 ("immediately"), 63 ("ulterior resorts" to "extra and ultra-constitutional").

56. James Madison to Nicholas P. Trist, February 15, 1830, *ML*, IV:66 ("be answered"); James Madison to Edward Everett, April 8, 1830, *ML*, IV:69–70; McCoy, *Last of the Fathers*.

57. Speech of Edward Livingston, of Louisiana, March 9, 1830, *Webster-Hayne Debate*, 463 ("full sovereignty" and "a compact"); James Madison to Edward Livingston, May 8, 1830, *ML*, IV:80; James Madison to Edward Livingston, January 24, 1833, *ML*, IV:268 (granting Livingston permission to publish his letter).

58. Livingston (March 9, 1830), *Webster-Hayne Debate*, 464 ("a constitutional right" and "shall finally decide"); James Madison to Edward Livingston, May 8, 1830, *ML*, IV:80 (congratulating him for avoiding errors made by other commentators).

59. Robert Y. Hayne to James Madison, March 5, 1830, James Madison Papers, Library of Congress ("the restoration" and "present views"); Robert Y. Hayne to James Madison, July 22, 1830, James Madison Papers, Library of Congress ("the true doctrines"); McCoy, *Last of the Fathers*, 140–141.

60. James Madison to Daniel Webster, May 27, 1830, *ML*, IV:84 ("unwilling"); James Madison to Edward Everett, August 1830, *ML*, IV:95–106; Mason, *Apostle of Union*, 75. Madison's letter, appended to Everett's article, was reprinted in 31 *North American Review* (October 1830), 537–546.

61. James Madison to Edward Everett, August 1830, *ML*, IV:95 ("viewing it" to "by the governments"), 95–96 ("by the States").

62. James Madison to Edward Everett, August 1830, *ML*, IV: 96 ("a compact").

63. James Madison to Edward Everett, August 1830, *ML*, IV: 100 ("the course"), 101 ("the final resort" and "the 'ultima ratio'").

64. James Madison to Nicholas P. Trist, February 15, 1830, *ML*, IV:63 (describing the right of revolution as "extra and ultra constitutional"); James Madison to Nicholas P. Trist, December, 1831, *ML*, IV:206 (explaining that when "the people, the parties to the Constitution" interposed per the Third Resolution they would be acting "in cases ultra-constitutional").

65. James Madison to Edward Everett, August 1830, *ML*, IV:105 ("to *concur*" to "the interposition"); Bradley D. Hays, "Nullification and the Political, Legal, and Quasi-Legal Constitutions," 43 *PJF* (2012), 205 at 217 ("were participants"); Hays, *States in American Constitutionalism*, 48 ("States were not"); Stampp, "Perpetual Union," 5 at 28 (by the 1820s

"state legislatures took for granted their right to 'instruct' their United States senators on how to vote on important legislation").

66. James Madison to Edward Everett, August 1830, *ML*, IV:104 ("several modes"); James Madison to "A Friend of Union and State Rights," 1833, *ML*, IV:335.

67. James Madison to Edward Everett, August 1830, *ML*, IV: 105 ("not law" and "synonymous"), 106 ("beyond the regular").

68. James Madison to Henry Clay, October 9, 1830, *ML*, IV:117 ("the nullifying doctrine"); James Madison to Joseph C. Cabell, May 31, 1830, *ML*, IV:86 ("or any equivalent word"); Jefferson's Draft, [before October 4, 1798], *JP*, XXX:539 ("a nullification"); James Madison to Edward Everett, September 10, 1830, *ML*, IV:110 ("the idea"); James Madison to Nicholas P. Trist, June 3, 1830, *ML*, IV:87; James Madison to Nicholas P. Trist, September 23, 1830, *ML*, IV:110–111.

69. James Madison to Nicholas P. Trist, December 23, 1832, *ML*, IV:228 ("the *plural* number" and "being less guarded").

70. *The American Annual Register; for the Year 1830–1831* (1832), 354–355 ("right and duty").

71. *Journal of the Convention of the People of South Carolina: Assembled at Columbia on the 19th November 1832 and again on the 11th March 1833* (Columbia, 1833), 59("by what name").

72. James Madison to James Robertson, March 27, 1831, *ML*, IV:166 ("collective"); James Madison to Nicholas P. Trist, December, 1831, *ML*, IV:204 ("the *ultimate* right"); James Madison to James Robertson, March 27, 1831, *ML*, IV:167 ("Who could").

73. Hays, "Nullification," 205 at 218, 219 ("offering alternative" and "turned the politics"); Daniel Walker Howe, *What Hath God Wrought: The Transformation of America, 1815–1848* (2007), 406–407.

74. Ellis, *Union at Risk*, 153; Cornell, *Other Founders*, 298–300.

75. Frederick W. Seward, *Autobiography of William H. Seward, From 1801 to 1834. With a Memoir of His Life, and Selections from His Letters From 1831 to 1846* (1877), 228 ("the text-book"); Peterson, *Jefferson Image*, 66; Bestor, "State Sovereignty," 117 at 118, 120; Rosenberg, "Personal Liberty Laws," 25 at 33; Leslie Friedman Goldstein, "State Resistance to Authority in Federal Unions: The Early United States (1790–1860) and the European Community (1958–1994)," 11 *Studies in American Political Development* (1997), 149–189; Peter Charles Hoffer, *Uncivil Warriors: The Lawyers' Civil War* (2018), 28, 191n15.

76. John C. Calhoun to Maximilian LaBorde and others, March 27, 1833, *CP*, XII:150 ("success"). For Virginia's response to South Carolina's nullification and the resolution of the crisis, see McCoy, *Last of the Fathers*, 154–155; James Madison to Andrew Stevenson, February 10, 1833, *ML*, IV:273; Peterson, *Olive Branch*; Ellis, *Union at Risk*, 158–177; Bolt, *Tariff Wars*, 128–140.

77. *Richmond Whig*, September 9, 1834 ("abstract"), reprinting editorial from the *Cincinnati Gazette*; Speech of W.O. Goode of Mecklenburg in Virginia House of Delegates on January 29, 1840, in *Richmond Enquirer*, February 13, 1840.

For the interchangeable use of the terms, see *Richmond Whig*, July 29, 1834; *Richmond Whig*, September 9, 1834, quoting editor of the *Cincinnati Gazette*; *Richmond Whig*, September 30, 1834; *Southern Patriot* [Charleston, S.C.], November 18, 1834; *Newark Daily Advertiser*, April 6, 1838; *Charleston Courier*, July 25, 1838; *Salem Gazette*, August 3, 1838; *The Cabinet* [Schenectady, N.Y.], March 23, 1841; *Charleston Courier*, July 28, 1841; *Macon Telegraph*, July 8, 1851; *Charleston Courier*, May 27, 1856.

78. James Madison to "A Friend of Union and State Rights," 1833, *ML*, IV:335 ("had no right" to "to establish").

79. James Madison to Edward Coles, August 29, 1834, *ML*, IV:357 ("powder under the Constitution"); James Madison to Edward Coles, October 15, 1834, *ML*, IV:367; "On Nullification," 1835–1836, *ML*, IV:395–425.

80. "On Nullification," 1835–1836, *ML*, IV:413 ("the States could interpose" to "plenary").

81. John Quincy Adams, *An Eulogy on James Madison ...* (1836), 54 ("calmer sensibility"); John Quincy Adams to Edward Everett, October 10, 1836, in Ketcham, "Letter of John Quincy Adams," 178 at 182 ("wide difference" and "the error").

82. James Madison to Nicholas P. Trist, January 18, 1833, *ML*, IV:268 ("twin"); James Madison to Joseph C. Cabell, September 16, 1831, *ML*, IV:196 ("from the same poisonous root"); James Madison to Matthew Carey, July 27, 1831, *ML*, IV:192 ("disastrous consequences").

83. Ellis, *Union at Risk*, 12 ("confused by"); Ericson, "Nullification Crisis," 249 at 269 ("unstable"); Ellis, *Union at Risk*, 183 ("resolved through").

8   State Interposition and Nullification on the Path to Secession

1. *Newburyport Herald* [Newburyport, Mass.], January 1, 1833 ("Counter-Proclamation"); Andrew Jackson, *Proclamation*, December 10, 1832, *MPP*, II:649 ("Secession").

2. Andrew Jackson, *Proclamation*, *MPP*, II:649 ("revolutionary act"), 644 ("the absurd"), 653 ("a peaceable remedy"); Virginia Resolutions, December 21, 1798, *MP*, XVII:189 ("a deliberate"); Andrew Jackson, *Proclamation*, *MPP*, II:642 ("discovery").

3. Andrew Jackson, *Proclamation*, *MPP*, II:643 ("the people"), 650 ("retained").

4. Childers, *Webster-Hayne Debate*, 138 ("sought"); Andrew Jackson, *Proclamation*, *MPP*, II:650 ("allegiance" and "obedience to laws"); Benedict, "Lincoln and Federalism," 1 at 4–19.

5. *Philadelphia Inquirer,* December 29, 1832 ("dangerous" to "annihilate").

6. *Philadelphia Inquirer,* December 29, 1832 ("the General Government"); *Charleston Courier,* November 29, 1833 ("State interposition"); *Philadelphia Inquirer,* December 29, 1832 ("a constitutional").

7. *Richmond Enquirer,* December 28, 1832 ("a peaceful").

8. *Richmond Enquirer,* December 28, 1832 ("merely *declare*"); *Richmond Enquirer,* May 3, 1833 ("conservative principle"); *Richmond Enquirer,* December 3, 1833; *Richmond Whig,* August 15, 1834 ("State Right principles"); *Richmond Enquirer,* January 5, 1833.

9. *Southern Patriot* [Charleston, S.C.], September 13, 1833 ("a Judicial Decision" and "a right reserved").

10. *Richmond Enquirer,* March 7, 1833 (reprinting speech delivered in Senate on February 14, 1833); *Richmond Enquirer,* March 9, 1833 ("*protested*").

11. *Georgia Telegraph* [Macon, Ga.], July 3, 1833 ("the great paramount"); reprinted in *Winyaw Intelligencer,* February 20, 1833 ("Jackson's doctrine"); *Charleston Courier,* November 29, 1833 ("middle ground").

12. *Richmond Enquirer,* May 3, 1833 ("the true doctrine"); *Richmond Enquirer,* August 16, 1833.

13. Peterson, *Jefferson Image,* 60 ("authorized exposition"); Remarks in the *Washington Globe* reprinted in *Albany Argus,* October 8, 1833 ("the offspring" to "the people of the several states"); *American Advocate* [Hallowell, Me.], October 16, 1833; James Madison to Edward Livingston, May 8, 1830, *ML,* IV:80. The *Globe's* claim of authorization is doubtful. See Peterson, *Olive Branch,* 93; Andrew Jackson to Martin Van Buren, September 19, 1833, John Spencer Bassett, ed., *Correspondence of Andrew Jackson* (7 vols., 1926–1935), V:212.

14. *Richmond Enquirer,* November 17, 1835 ("no remedies" and "every Southern Patriot").

15. "Liberty Platform of 1844," in Porter and Johnson, *Party Platforms,* 8 ("utterly null"); William M. Wiecek, *The Sources of Antislavery Constitutionalism in America, 1760–1848* (1977), 228 ("covenant with death"); Phillip S. Paludan, *A Covenant with Death: The Constitution, Law, and Equality in the Civil War Era* (1975).

16. "No person held to service or labor in one State, under the laws thereof, escaping into another, shall, in consequence of any law or regulation therein, be discharged from such service or labor, but shall be delivered up on claim of the party to whom such service or labor may be due." U.S. Const., Art. IV, Sec. 2, Clause 3.

17. Don E. Fehrenbacher, *The Slaveholding Republic: An Account of the United States Government's Relations to Slavery* (Ward N. McAfee, ed., 2001), 212.

18. Wiecek, *Antislavery Constitutionalism*, 156, 200–201("override traditional"); Thomas D. Morris, *Free Men All: The Personal Liberty Laws of the North, 1780–1861* (1974), 45, 53 and 56.

19. Levinson, "Nullification," 10 at 18 (observing that the personal liberty laws partook of "uncooperative federalism"); Bulman-Pozen and Gerken, "Uncooperative Federalism"; Marion Gleason McDougall, *Fugitive Slaves 1619–1865* (1891), 70; Bestor, "State Sovereignty," 117 at 137; Fehrenbacher, *Slaveholding Republic*, 216; Jeffrey Schmitt, "Rethinking *Ableman v. Booth* and States' Rights in Wisconsin," 93 *Virginia Law Review* (2007), 1315 at 1320; Andrew Delbanco, *The War before the War: Fugitive Slaves and the Struggle for America's Soul from the Revolution to the Civil War* (2018), 8.

20. H. Robert Baker, *Prigg v. Pennsylvania: Slavery, the Supreme Court, and the Ambivalent Constitution* (2012), 2–3("Slaveholders claimed"); *Prigg v. Pennsylvania*, 41 U.S. 539 (1842); Paul Finkelman, "*Prigg v. Pennsylvania* and Northern State Courts: Anti-Slavery Use of a Pro-Slavery Decision," 25 *Civil War History* (1979), 5–35; Paul Finkelman, "Sorting out *Prigg v. Pennsylvania*," 24 *Rutgers Law Journal* (1993), 605–665; Eric W. Plaag, "'Let the Constitution Perish': *Prigg v. Pennsylvania*, Joseph Story, and the Flawed Doctrine of Historical Necessity," 25 *Slavery and Abolition* (2004), 76–101; Leslie Friedman Goldstein, "A 'Triumph of Freedom' after All? *Prigg v. Pennsylvania* Re-examined," 29 *Law and History Review* (2011), 763–796.

21. 41 U.S. 539, 540 ("fundamental article" and "unqualified right"), 543 ("act of seizing"), 542 ("clearly constitutional").

22. 41 U.S. 539, 542 ("leading provisions" and "state magistrates"); *Milwaukee Sentinel*, March 24, 1859; Bestor, "State Sovereignty," 117–180; Rosenberg, "Personal Liberty Laws," 25 at 43; Michael E. Woods, "'Tell Us Something about State Rights': Northern Republicans, States' Rights, and the Coming of the Civil War," 7 *Journal of the Civil War Era* (2017), 242–268.

23. *The Liberator* [Boston], March 11, 1842 ("to be spit upon"); 41 U.S. 539, 630 ("scarcely deserves"); Joseph Story to John M. Berrien, April 29, 1842, reprinted in James McClellan, *Joseph Story and the American Constitution, a Study in Political and Legal Thought, with Selected Writings* (1971), 262–263n94 ("any State judge").

24. *Report of the Joint Special Committee of the Massachusetts General Court on the George Latimer Petition* (House Doc. 41) (Boston, 1843), 25 ("clue"), 25–26 ("leaves the States"); Delbanco, *Fugitive Slaves*, 183 ("walked through the door"); Morris, *Free Men All*, 114–115, 127; Finkelman, "*Prigg v. Pennsylvania* and Northern State Courts," 5 at 22; Rosenberg, "Personal Liberty Laws," 25 at 28. On the non-commandeering principle,

see *New York v. United States*, 505 U.S. 144 (1992); *Printz v. United States*, 521 U.S. 898 (1997).

25. William Ellery Channing, *The Works of William E. Channing*, D.D. (6 vols., 1847), VI:288 ("narrowest limits"); Charles James Faulkner to John C. Calhoun, July 15, 1847, *CP*, XXIV:444 ("the most deliberate"); Woods, "State Rights," 242 at 251; Bestor, "State Sovereignty," 117 at 137–139; Fehrenbacher, *Slaveholding Republic*, 222; R.J.M. Blackett, *The Captive's Quest for Freedom: Fugitive Slaves, the 1850 Fugitive Slave Law, and the Politics of Slavery* (2018), 36; *Niles' National Register* [Baltimore], March 20, 1847, p.35.

26. Rosenberg "Personal Liberty Laws," 25 at 29 ("Northern Nullification"); "The Address of Southern Delegates in Congress, to their Constituents," January 22, 1849, *CP*, XXVI:227 ("practically expunged"), 229 ("resistance"); Fehrenbacher, *Slaveholding Republic*, 225; Horace K. Houston, Jr., "Another Nullification Crisis: Vermont's 1850 Habeas Corpus Law," 77 *New England Quarterly* (2004), 252 at 266.

27. *Congressional Globe*, Senate, 31st Cong., 1st Sess., (February 6, 1850), appendix, 123 (Henry Clay) ("obstructions"); Robert C. Grier to James Buchanan, April 2, 1850, quoted in Rosenberg, "Personal Liberty Laws," 25 at 28 ("entirely unconstitutional"); Morris, *Free Men All*, 146; Fehrenbacher, *Slaveholding Republic*, 232; Paul Finkelman, "States' Rights, Southern Hypocrisy, and the Crisis of the Union," in Cogan, *Union & States' Rights*, 51 at 57; James Oakes, *Freedom National: The Destruction of Slavery in the United States, 1861–1865* (2013), 354–355.

28. Act of September 18, 1850, ch. 60, 9 *Stat.* 463 ("to aid and assist"); Fehrenbacher, *Slaveholding Republic*, 231–232.

29. "The Constitution and the Union," March 7, 1850, *Web(SFW)*, II:540 ("right" and "excuses"); Larry Gara, "The Fugitive Slave Law: A Double Paradox," 10 *Civil War History* (1964), 229 ("quiet the explosive"); Blackett, *Captive's Quest*, 29–32, 86 ("stirred passionate opposition").

30. "No. 78 – Resolutions on So Much of the Governor's Message as Relates to Slavery" (November 13, 1850), in *The Acts and Resolves Passed by the Legislature of Vermont, at the October Session, 1850* (1850), 53("the great principles"); *New York Tribune*, April 5, 1851, quoted in Stanley W. Campbell, *The Slave Catchers: Enforcement of the Fugitive Slave Law, 1850–1860* (1970), 52("burden its execution"); *Daily National Intelligencer* [Washington D.C.], December 19, 1850; Justice Samuel Nelson's grand jury charge to the U.S. Circuit Court in New York in April 1851, 10 *American Law Journal* (1851), 561 (considering Vermont's "hostile legislation" an encouragement to Southern secession).

31. *Mr. Webster's Speeches at Buffalo, Syracuse, and Albany, May 1851* (1851), 37("If men get together"); Daniel Webster to Millard Fillmore, April 13, 1851, Millard Fillmore to Daniel Webster, April 16, 1851,

Charles M. Wiltse, ed., *The Papers of Daniel Webster, Correspondence* (7 vols., 1974–1986), VII:232–233, 237 ("the stain").

32. *The Liberator*, April 25, 1851; Angela F. Murphy, *The Jerry Rescue: The Fugitive Slave Law, Northern Rights, and the American Sectional Crisis* (2016), 161.

33. Quoted in Morris, *Free Men All*, 151 ("first full-scale"); *Speech of Mr. Sutliff of Trumbull, on the Resolutions Introduced by Him Relative to the Constitutional Powers of Congress, and the Fugitive Slave Bill* (1851), 4 ("utterly unconstitutional"); "Free Democratic Platform of 1852," in Porter and Johnson, *Party Platforms*, 18 ("binding force").

34. Quoted in Morris, *Free Men All*, 165 ("important indications"); Rosenberg, "Personal Liberty Laws," 25 at 32 ("Most advocates").

35. Rosenberg, "Personal Liberty Laws," 25 at 31 ("forbearance"); Theodore Parker, *The New Crime against Humanity. A Sermon Preached at the Music Hall, in Boston, on Sunday, June 4, 1854* (1854), 72 ("not rash" and "our soil"); Morris, *Free Men All*, 168; Woods, "State Rights," 242 at 251; Jane H. Pease and William H. Pease, *The Fugitive Slave Law and Anthony Burns: A Problem in Law Enforcement* (1975); Albert J. Von Frank, *The Trials of Anthony Burns: Freedom and Slavery in Emerson's Boston* (1998); Earl M. Maltz, *Fugitive Slave on Trial: The Anthony Burns Case and Abolitionist Outrage* (2010).

36. Carl Schurz, *The Reminiscences of Carl Schurz* (2 vols., 1907), II:110 ("seek refuge"), 111 ("the 'nullifying' section").

37. *Richmond Enquirer*, November 12, 1850 ("the mad schemes"); *Daily Constitutionalist* [Augusta, Ga.], December 27, 1860 ("State interposition").

38. *Daily National Intelligencer*, February 1, 1851 ("the infection" and "to the Federal laws"); *New York Daily Tribune*, May 26, 1856; *New York Tribune*, January 10, 1862; Eric Foner, *Free Soil, Free Labor, Free Men: The Ideology of the Republican Party before the Civil War* (1970), 38–39, 90–92, 191–192.

39. *In Re Booth*, 3 Wis. 1 (1854); *Daily Globe* [Washington D.C.], August 28, 1850.

40. Baker, *Glover*.

41. *Unconstitutionality of the Fugitive Act. Argument of Byron Paine, Esq. and Opinion of Hon. A.D. Smith, Associate Justice of the Supreme Court of the State of Wisconsin* [1854], 1, 15 ("independent sovereignties").

42. *Unconstitutionality of the Fugitive Act*, 26 ("clearly, substantially" and "the sworn duty"), 26–27 ("to interpose").

43. *Unconstitutionality of the Fugitive Act*, 29, 31 ("authoritative" and "fruitful subjects").

44. *In Re Booth*, 3 Wis. 1, 30 ("repugnant").

45. *In Re Booth*, 3 Wis. 1, 21, 35, 36 ("neither becoming").

46. *In Re Booth*, 3 Wis. 1, 47 ("zeal"); Baker, *Glover*, 138 ("practical nullification"), citing John R. Sharpstein to William Streeter, February 6, 1855; *Unconstitutionality of the Fugitive Act*, 3 ("medium ground"); *In Re Booth*, 3 Wis. 1, 67 (note a1).

47. *In Re Booth*, 3 Wis. 1, 43 ("without thought"), 44 ("sharpen investigation"), 67; James Madison to Spencer Roane, June 29, 1821, *ML*, III:223–224 (anticipating that collective decisions by federal and state judges would eventually produce agreement about state and federal boundaries).

48. Von Frank, *Trials of Anthony Burns*, 203–219.

49. Morris, *Free Men All*, chapter 10 is entitled "Interposition, 1854–1858"; Fehrenbacher, *Slaveholding Republic*, 238.

50. *Congressional Globe*, Senate, 33rd Cong., 2nd Sess., (February 23, 1855), appendix, 213 (Benjamin Wade) ("an attempt"), 214 ("State rights").

51. *Congressional Globe*, Senate, 33rd Cong., 2nd Sess., (February 23, 1855), appendix, 220 (Judah Benjamin) ("maintaining the right"), 219 ("that State tribunals").

52. *Congressional Globe*, Senate, 33rd Cong., 2nd Sess., (February 23, 1855), appendix, 214 (Benjamin Wade) ("The General Government"), 215 ("a State must"), 222 ("the true interpretation").

53. *Congressional Globe*, Senate, 33rd Cong., 2nd Sess., (February 23, 1855), appendix, 235 (John Pettit) ("absolute" and "sovereign only"), 241 (William Seward) ("Federal Union"), 215 (Stephen Douglas) ("our complex system").

54. *Congressional Globe*, Senate, 33rd Cong., 2nd Sess., (February 23, 1855), appendix, 246.

55. *Ableman v. Booth*, 62 U.S. 506 (1859), 511–513. For depictions of *Booth* as an example of failed judicial nullification, see Warren, *Supreme Court*, II:533; Campbell, *Slave Catchers*, 47; Fehrenbacher, *Slaveholding Republic*, 237; David M. Potter, *The Impending Crisis, 1848–1861*, completed and ed. by Don E. Fehrenbacher (1976), 295; Michael J.C. Taylor, "'A More Perfect Union': *Ableman v. Booth* and the Culmination of Federal Sovereignty," 2003 *Journal of Supreme Court History* (2003), 101–115; Hunter, "Sound and Fury," 659 at 682–683. But see Baker, *Glover*, 174, 221n37 (disagreeing with the tendency to equate Wisconsin's actions with South Carolina–style nullification).

56. 62 U.S. 506, 514 ("determined that").

57. Karen Orren, "'A War Between Officers': The Enforcement of Slavery in the Northern United States, and of the Republic for Which It Stands, before the Civil War," 12 *Studies in American Political Development* (1998), 343 at 360 ("a major step"); 62 U.S. 506, 516 ("the line of division"), 517 ("sphere of action"); Rollin C. Hurd, *A Treatise on the Right of Personal Liberty, and on the Writ of Habeas Corpus and the Practice Connected With It: With a View of the Law of Extradition of*

Fugitives (1858), 164–202 (analyzing case law that established the long practice of concurrent jurisdiction by federal and state courts over the issuance of writs of habeas corpus).

58. 62 U.S. 506, 519 ("by force of arms").

59. 62 U.S. 506, 524 ("to guard against").

60. 62 U.S. 506, 525 ("subvert" and "foundations").

61. Wisconsin State Legislature, "Joint Resolution Relative to the Decision of the United States Supreme Court, Reversing Decision of the Supreme Court of Wisconsin," No. IV, Approved March 19, 1859, p.247 ("the great writ"), 248 ("the unquestionable right" and *"positive defiance"*); Michael J. McManus, *Political Abolitionism in Wisconsin, 1840–1861* (1998), 175 ("Resolves of '59").

62. "To the People of the State of Wisconsin," *Milwaukee Sentinel*, March 17, 1859; McManus, *Abolitionism in Wisconsin*, 175–176; Baker, *Glover*, 153–161.

63. *Milwaukee Sentinel*, March 24, 1859 ("State Rights and Byron Paine" and "to decide what powers").

64. *Milwaukee Sentinel*, March 24, 1859 ("co-ordinate powers" and "the tribunal of public opinion"); Schurz, *Reminiscences*, II:113 ("more matured judgment").

65. George Hoadley to Salmon P. Chase, April 9, 1859, quoted in Eric Foner, *The Fiery Trial: Abraham Lincoln and American Slavery* (2010), 134 ("we have got to come"); Rosenberg, "Personal Liberty Laws," 25 at 39; Speech of John R. French, April 26, 1859, in *History of the Oberlin-Wellington Rescue*, comp. Jacob R. Shipherd (1859), 242–244.

66. Timothy O. Howe to George Rublee, April 3, 1859, quoted in Foner, *Fiery Trial*, 134 ("Almost the whole country"); *Daily National Intelligencer*, April 1, 1859 ("the traditional heirloom" and "Virginia precedents"); *Daily National Intelligencer*, June 1, 1859 ("State rights meeting"); "The Resolutions of '98," *Daily National Intelligencer*, June 15, 1859.

67. "Republican Platform of 1860," in Porter and Johnson, *Party Platforms*, 32 ("new dogma").

68. "Democrat Platform of 1860," in Porter and Johnson, *Party Platforms*, 31 ("subversive"); "Democrat (Breckinridge Faction) Platform of 1860," in Porter and Johnson, *Party Platforms*, 31 ("with their property").

69. "Constitutional Union Platform of 1860," in Porter and Johnson, *Party Platforms*, 30 ("to *recognize*"). On the Constitutional Union campaign and Bell's vice presidential running mate, Edward Everett, see Mason, *Apostle of Union*, 243–268.

70. See Michael F. Holt, *The Election of 1860: "A Campaign Fraught with Consequences"* (2017), 194–199. Holt challenges the assumption that the election was primarily a referendum on slavery.

71. James Buchanan, *Fourth Annual Message*, December 3, 1860, in MPP, V:627 ("sovereign states" to "the people of the North"), 630 ("a

constitutional remedy"), 632 ("perpetual"), 626 ("incessant and violent"), 629 ("palpable violations"), 630 ("revolutionary resistance").

72. Abraham Lincoln to John A. Gilmer, December 15, 1860, *WL*, IV:152 ("very little" and "could hardly be justified"); Fehrenbacher, *Slaveholding Republic*, 248 ("incompatible"); "Resolutions Drawn up for Republican Members of Senate Committee of Thirteen," December 20, 1860, *WL*, IV:157 ("punishing all" and "safeguards to liberty").

73. First Inaugural Address, March 4, 1861, *WL*, IV:263 ("no purpose"); *Congressional Globe*, Senate, 35th Cong., 2nd Sess., (February 23, 1859), 1267 (James R. Doolittle) ("putting down slavery"); Bestor, "State Sovereignty," 117 at 127 ("there was no difference"); James Oakes, *The Scorpion's Sting: Antislavery and the Coming of the Civil War* (2014).

74. *Congressional Globe*, Senate, 36th Cong., 1st Sess., (January 24, 1860), appendix, 88 (Robert Toombs) ("been truer"); "Report of the Joint Committee on the Harper's Ferry Outrages," January 26, 1860 [Virginia Legislature, Doc. 57], p.21 ("the Legislatures"), 24 ("enactments conceived"); Robert Toombs to Robert Collins and others, May 10, 1860, *CTSC*, II:476 ("enemies in the North"); Robert Toombs to E.B. Pullin and others, December 13, 1860, *CTSC*, II:520 ("open and avowed"); Campbell, *Slave Catchers*, 170n1.

75. James M. McPherson, *Battle Cry of Freedom: The Civil War Era* (1988), 252–254; Fehrenbacher, *Slaveholding Republic*, 247; Pitcaithley, *Anthology*, 94–113.

76. "Speech Delivered on the 21st March, 1861, in Savannah, known as 'The Corner Stone Speech'," in Henry Cleveland, *Alexander H. Stephens, in Public and Private. With Letters and Speeches, Before, During, and Since the War* (1866), 721 ("the immediate cause"); Alexander H. Stephens, *A Constitutional View of the Late War Between the States; Its Causes, Character, Conduct and Results* (2 vols., 1868–1870), II:85–86, 521–524, I:542 ("whole subject of Slavery"), I:29 ("Federal authorities"); "A Sketch of the Remarks of G.W. Crawford, Made at the City Hall of Augusta on the 14th [December 14, 1860]," *Daily Constitutionalist*, December 27, 1860 (slavery was "planted in the Federal Constitution").

77. David W. Blight, *Race and Reunion: The Civil War in American Memory* (2001); Drew Gilpin Faust, *The Creation of Confederate Nationalism: Ideology and Identity in the Civil War South* (1988), 59–60; Charles B. Dew, *Apostles of Disunion: Southern Secession Commissioners and the Causes of the Civil War* (2001); Finkelman, "States' Rights," 51–79; Michael E. Woods, "What Twenty-First-Century Historians Have Said about the Causes of Disunion: A Civil War Sesquicentennial Review of the Recent Literature," 99 *Journal of American History* (2012), 415 at 439; Pitcaithley, *Anthology*.

9 State Interposition during and after the Civil War

1. J.M. Hofer, "Development of the Peace Movement in Illinois during the Civil War," 24 *Journal of the Illinois State Historical Society* (1931), 110–128; Frank L. Klement, *Lincoln's Critics: The Copperheads of the North* (1999); Jennifer L. Weber, *Copperheads: The Rise and Fall of Lincoln's Opponents in the North* (2006); Richard E. Yates, "Governor Vance and the Peace Movement, Part I," 17 *North Carolina Historical Review* (1940), 1–25; Richard E. Yates, "Governor Vance and the Peace Movement, Part II," 17 *North Carolina Historical Review* (1940), 89–113; John E. Talmadge, "Peace-Movement Activities in Civil War Georgia," 7 *Georgia Review* (1953), 190–203; Horace W. Raper, "William W. Holden and the Peace Movement in North Carolina," 31 *North Carolina Historical Review* (1954), 493–516; Wilfred B. Yearns, "The Peace Movement in the Confederate Congress," 41 *Georgia Historical Quarterly* (1957), 1–18; Alan Conway, *The Reconstruction of Georgia* (1966), 7; Emory M. Thomas, "Rebel Nationalism: E.H. Cushing and the Confederate Experience," 73 *Southwestern Historical Quarterly* (1970), 343 at 352; Marc W. Kruman, "Dissent in the Confederacy: The North Carolina Experience," 27 *Civil War History* (1981), 293–313.

2. Leon F. Litwack, *North of Slavery: The Negro in the Free States, 1790–1860* (1961); John Gerring, "A Chapter in the History of American Party Ideology: The Nineteenth-Century Democratic Party, 1828–1892," 26 *Polity* (1994), 729 at 735; Jean H. Baker, *Affairs of Party: The Political Culture of Northern Democrats in the Mid-Nineteenth Century* (1998).

3. Eric Foner, *The Second Founding: How the Civil War and Reconstruction Remade the Constitution* (2019); Laura F. Edwards, *A Legal History of the Civil War and Reconstruction: A Nation of Rights* (2015), 90–176.

4. Democratic Platform of 1852, Porter and Johnson, *Party Platforms*, 17 ("main foundations"), 25, 30; *Weekly Houston Telegraph*, August 21, 1860.

5. *Boston Post*, May 7, 1860 ("pronounce against"); *Daily National Intelligencer* [Washington, D.C.], January 19, 1860; *The Constitution* [Washington, D.C.], "Speech of Hon. J.L.M. Curry," March 16, 1860; *Weekly Houston Telegraph*, June 12, 1860; *Newark Daily Advertiser*, March 21, 1861; *New York Tribune*, January 10, 1862; *Boston Post*, July 7, 1862; *The Patriot* [Harrisburg, Pa.], September 17, 1863.

6. Marshall L. DeRosa, *The Confederate Constitution of 1861: An Inquiry into American Constitutionalism* (1991), 135 ("each State"); Kenneth C. Martis, *The Historical Atlas of the Congresses of the Confederate States of America: 1861–1865* (1994), 8; G. Edward White,

"Recovering the Legal History of the Confederacy," 68 *Washington and Lee Law Review* (2011), 467 at 498–509.

7. Robert Gray Gunderson, *Old Gentlemen's Convention: The Washington Peace Conference of 1861* (1961), 95.

8. *The Constitution* [Washington D.C.], July 10, 1860; Jefferson Davis to the Confederate Congress, April 29, 1861, Dunbar Rowland, ed., *Jefferson Davis: Constitutionalist, His Letters, Papers, and Speeches* (10 vols., 1923), V:69 ("a *compact*"), 73 ("the right of each State").

9. *Daily National Intelligencer*, September 13, 1860 ("a *Government*" and "a *constitutional redress*").

10. James Buchanan, *Fourth Annual Message*, MPP, V:631 ("the people in each"), 632 ("intended to be"). For treatments of Buchanan's message that overlook his reliance on Madison's concept of the foundation of the Constitution, see Philip Shriver Klein, *President James Buchanan: A Biography* (1962), 360–363; John T. Hubbell, "Jeremiah Sullivan Black and the Great Secession Winter," 57 *Western Pennsylvania Historical Magazine* (1974), 255 at 259–262; Elbert B. Smith, *The Presidency of James Buchanan* (1975), 148–152; Jean H. Baker, *James Buchanan* (2004), 124–125.

11. "Jefferson," *Daily True Delta* [New Orleans, La.], December 2, 1860 ("bound itself"); "Virginia Dethrones her own Gods," *Philadelphia Inquirer*, May 8, 1861 ("the *whole* family"); *New York Herald*, June 18, 1861.

12. Joel Parker, *The Right of Secession. A Review of the Message of Jefferson Davis to the Congress of the Confederate States* (1861), 31 ("as a State remedy" and "in accordance").

13. *Boston Daily Advertiser*, July 4, 1861 ("Is Secession" and "imaginary right").

14. *Boston Daily Advertiser*, July 4, 1861 ("sort of interposition" to "a little plain truth").

15. James Buchanan, *Fourth Annual Message*, MPP, V:635 ("to coerce"), 636 ("cemented" and "the sword"); *Daily Constitutionalist* [Augusta, Ga.], February 28, 1861 ("by violence"); Jeremiah S. Black to James Buchanan, November 20, 1860, J. Hubley Ashton, ed., *Official Opinions of the Attorneys General of the United States* ... (12 vols., 1852–1870), IX:517–526.

16. Pitcaithley, *Anthology*, 338–339.

17. Jessica Ann Cannon, "Lincoln's Backyard: Maryland in the Civil War Era" (Ph.D. diss., Rice University, 2010), 93; Charles Branch Clark, "Politics in Maryland during the Civil War, Part One," 36 *Maryland Historical Magazine* (1941), 239–262; Charles Branch Clark, "Politics in Maryland during the Civil War, Part Two," 37 *Maryland Historical Magazine* (1942), 171–192; Baker, *Affairs of Party*, 19–45.

18. George L. P. Radcliffe, *Governor Thomas H. Hicks of Maryland and the Civil War* (1901); Baker, Affairs of Party, 47–55; Stephen D. Engle, *Gathering to Save a Nation: Lincoln and the Union's War Governors* (2016), 18–20, 45–47, 60–61; Cannon, "Maryland in the Civil War Era," 99–103.

19. Abraham Lincoln to Winfield Scott, April 25, 1861, WL, IV:344 ("to watch" and "the bombardment"); Abraham Lincoln to Winfield Scott, April 27, 1861 (Lincoln's explicit authorization for Scott to suspend the writ of habeas corpus), WL, IV:347.

20. *The Civilian* [Cumberland, Md.], May 2, 1861, "Message to the Legislature," April 26, 1861 ("a neutral position" and "to take sides").

21. *Journal of the Proceedings of the [Maryland] House of Delegates. In Extra Session* (Frederick, 1861), 15, 21, 107 ("unconstitutional"), 108 ("slaughter"), 222; *The Sun* [Baltimore, Md.], April 30, June 12 and 13, 1861; Baker, *Affairs of Party*, 43, 58.

22. *Ex parte Merryman*, 17 F. Cas. 144 (1861), 153 ("determine what measures"); Brian McGinty, *The Body of John Merryman: Abraham Lincoln and the Suspension of Habeas Corpus* (2011); Jonathan W. White, *Abraham Lincoln and Treason in the Civil War: The Trials of John Merryman* (2011); George Clarke Sellery, *Lincoln's Suspension of Habeas Corpus As Viewed by Congress* (1907); Mark E. Neely, Jr., *The Fate of Liberty: Abraham Lincoln and Civil Liberties* (1991), 185–209.

23. Maryland House of Delegates, *Journal*, 224 ("solemn protest" to "the great safe-guard").

24. Maryland House of Delegates, *Journal*, 293 ("the unconstitutional"), 301; *The Sun*, June 22, 1861, Report of the Proceedings of the House, June 21, 1861; *Congressional Globe*, 37th Cong., 1st Sess., (August 3, 1861), 417 (Wilkinson) ("an insult"), 418 (Hale), 419 (Trumbull) 420 (Bayard) and (Fessenden).

25. Kentucky 1850 Constitution, Article XIII, Sec. 3 ("inviolable"); Beriah Magoffin to Simon Cameron, April 15, 1861, *The War of the Rebellion: A Compilation of the Official Records of the Union and Confederate Armies* (128 vols., 1880–1901), Ser. 3, Vol. I:70 ("Kentucky will furnish"); Edward Conrad Smith, *The Borderland in the Civil War* (1927), 64–65; Martis, *Historical Atlas*, 26; Lowell H. Harrison and James Klotter, *A New History of Kentucky* (1997), 185–194; William W. Freehling, *The South vs. the South: How Anti-Confederate Southerners Shaped the Course of the Civil War* (2001), 53–54; Harold D. Tallant, *Evil Necessity: Slavery and Political Culture in Antebellum Kentucky* (2003); Anne E. Marshall, *Creating a Confederate Kentucky: The Lost Cause and Civil War Memory in a Border State* (2010), 20; William C. Harris, *Lincoln and the Border States: Preserving the Union* (2011), 83–100; Patrick A. Lewis, *For Slavery and Union: Benjamin Buckner and Kentucky Loyalties in the Civil War* (2015).

26. Marshall, *Confederate Kentucky*, 21 ("police state"); Preliminary Emancipation Proclamation, September 22, 1862, WL, V:434 ("shall be"); John Harrington to Jennie Swift, January 19, 1863, quoted in Marshall, *Confederate Kentucky*, 25 ("I enlisted").

27. *Journal of the House of Representatives of the Commonwealth of Kentucky, September 2, 1861 – March 3, 1863, Vol. II* (Frankfort, [1863]), 1122 ("a theory" and "new doctrine"), 1124. Members of Congress and Lincoln himself were uncertain if the seizure and permanent forfeiture of property was constitutional either by acts of Congress or presidential proclamation. See LaWanda Cox, *Lincoln and Black Freedom: A Study in Presidential Leadership* (1981), 15; Louis P. Masur, *Lincoln's Hundred Days: The Emancipation Proclamation and the War for the Union* (2012); Harold Holzer, *Emancipating Lincoln: The Proclamation in Text, Context, and Memory* (2012).

28. Kentucky House of Representatives, *Journal*, 1347 ("anti-slavery"), 1348 ("war measures" to "wait with the Democrats"), 1349 ("all lawless").

29. *Acts of the General Assembly of the Commonwealth of Kentucky, passed ... at the Adjourned Session, which Commenced January 8, 1863* (1863), "Resolutions Concerning National Affairs," 391 ("unconstitutional acts"); E. Merton Coulter, *The Civil War and Readjustment in Kentucky* (1926, reprinted, 1966), 162.

30. James M. McPherson, *Battle Cry of Freedom: The Civil War Era* (1988), 298 ("restored government" and "de jure government"); Engle, *Gathering to Save a Nation*, 86–87, 129, 261–262.

31. Proclamation Suspending the Writ of Habeas Corpus, September 24, 1862, WL, V:437 ("all Rebels"); Message to Congress in Special Session, July 4, 1861, WL, IV:430; J.G. Randall, *Constitutional Problems under Lincoln* (1951); Daniel Farber, *Lincoln's Constitution* (2003).

32. Trial of Clement L. Vallandigham, Arraignment and Charge, May 6, 1863, *Official Records*, Ser. II, Vol. V:634 ("sympathy"); Abraham Lincoln to Erastus Corning and others, June 12, 1863, WL, VI:266 ("words addressed" to "Must I shoot"); McPherson, *Battle Cry of Freedom*, 598 ("the whole country").

33. *Journal of the House of Representatives, of the State of Indiana, During the Forty-Third Session of the General Assembly, Commencing Thursday, January 8, 1863* (Indianapolis, 1863), 20 ("infamous"), 57 ("under the tyrants' plea"); *Macon Daily Telegraph* [Macon, Ga.], March 26, 1863; Kenneth M. Stampp, *Indiana Politics during the Civil War* (1949), 158–178; Frank L. Klement, *The Copperheads in the Middle West* (1960), 52–58; Emma Lou Thornbrough, *Indiana in the Civil War Era, 1850–1880* (1965), 183–190.

34. Indiana House of Representatives, *Journal*, 82 ("as it originally existed").

35. Indiana House of Representatives, *Journal*, 223 ("lost all regard"), 724 ("millions"), 720 ("the free communities"); Mary Frances Berry, *Military Necessity and Civil Rights Policy: Black Citizenship and the Constitution, 1861–1868* (1977), 75, 92.

36. Indiana House of Representatives, *Journal*, 704–705 ("unconstitutional"), 727 ("not in rebellion"); *Philadelphia Inquirer*, March 17, 1863.

37. D.S. Phillips to Lyman Trumbull, December 24, 1862, quoted in Klement, *Copperheads in the Middle West*, 58 ("rash or vicious"); *Journal of the House of Representatives of the Twenty-Third General Assembly of the State of Illinois, at their Regular Session, Begun and Held at Springfield, January 5, 1863* (Springfield, 1865), 7 ("a disastrous"); *Journal of the Senate of the Twenty-Third General Assembly of the State of Illinois, at their Regular Session, Begun and Held at Springfield, January 5, 1863* (Springfield, 1865), 46 ("vigorous prosecution"); Arthur Charles Cole, *The Era of the Civil War, 1848–1870* (1919), 295–297; Bruce S. Allardice, "'Illinois is Rotten with Traitors!' The Republican Defeat in the 1862 State Election," 104 *Journal of the Illinois State Historical Society* (2011), 97–114.

38. Illinois Senate, *Journal*, 298; Klement, *Copperheads in the Middle West*, 59–60; Engle, *Gathering to Save a Nation*, 269–270; Hofer, "Development of the Peace Movement," 110–128.

39. Illinois Senate, *Journal*, 296 ("arbitrary"), 297 ("to warn" and "monstrous usurpations").

40. Illinois Senate, *Journal*, 232 ("unconstitutional"), 233; *Boston Evening Transcript*, February 18, 1863.

41. *Journal of the Assembly of the State of Wisconsin. Annual Session, A.D. 1863* (Madison, 1863), 620 ("unwise"); Frank L. Klement, *Wisconsin in the Civil War: The Home Front and the Battle Front, 1861–1865* (1997), 75–77; Richard N. Current, *The History of Wisconsin. Volume II. The Civil War Era, 1848–1873* (1976), 403–406; *Wisconsin Patriot* [Madison, Wis.], March 28, 1863.

42. Abraham Lincoln to Andrew G. Curtin, December 21, 1860, *WL*, IV:158 ("to maintain"); A.G. Curtin, "Inaugural Address to the Assembly," *Pennsylvania Archives*, Ser. 4 (1902), Vol VIII:336 ("can voluntarily"); Erwin Stanley Bradley, *The Triumph of Militant Republicanism: A Study of Pennsylvania and Presidential Politics, 1860–1872* (1964); Jack Furniss, "Andrew Curtin and the Politics of the Union," 141 *Pennsylvania Magazine of History and Biography* (2017), 145–176.

43. Stanton Ling Davis, *Pennsylvania Politics, 1860–1863* (1935), 207; Bradley, *Militant Republicanism*, 157–158; *Philadelphia Inquirer*, January 6, 7, and 14, 1863.

44. *The Legislative Record: Containing the Debates and Proceedings of the Pennsylvania Legislature for the Session of 1863* (Harrisburg, 1863), 886 ("startling usurpations" and "right to differ"); Davis, *Pennsylvania*

Politics, 207; Bradley, *Militant Republicanism*, 157–158, 282; *Philadelphia Inquirer*, January 6, 7, and 14, 1863.

45. William Gillette, *Jersey Blue: Civil War Politics in New Jersey, 1854–1865* (1995), 222 ("an empty"), 206–234; Charles Merriam Knapp, *New Jersey Politics during the Period of the Civil War and Reconstruction* (1924), 78–95.

46. *Journal of the Nineteenth Senate of the State of New Jersey, Being the Eighty-Seventh Session of the Legislature* (Morristown, 1863), 10, 11 ("gross violations").

47. New Jersey Senate, *Journal*, 113 ("aid and comfort"), 120 ("in all measures").

48. Governor Parker's Inaugural Address," *State Gazette and Republican* [Trenton, N.J.], January 21, 1863 ("by the exercise"); *State Gazette*, January 21, 1863 ("We should take care" to "power is prone"); Knapp, *New Jersey Politics*, 83; Gillette, *Jersey Blue*, 214.

49. *State Gazette*, January 21, 1863 ("virtually suspends" and "true principles").

50. *Acts of the Eighty-Seventh Legislature of the State of New Jersey, and Nineteenth Under the New Constitution* (1863), 510 ("for conquest"), 512 ("clearly given"); New Jersey Senate, *Journal*, 318 (receiving copies of Kentucky's interposition resolutions of February 1863).

51. William M. Robinson, Jr., *Justice in Grey: A History of the Judicial System of the Confederate States of America* (1941), 411 ("[d]isgruntled politicians"); Alexander C. Niven, "Joseph E. Brown, Confederate Obstructionist," 42 *Georgia Historical Quarterly* (1958), 233 at 241; Carleton Beals, *War within a War: The Confederacy against Itself* (1965), 127; John B. Robbins, "The Confederacy and the Writ of Habeas Corpus," 55 *Georgia Historical Quarterly* (1971), 83 at 95; Joseph H. Parks, *Joseph E. Brown of Georgia* (1977), 273; Paul D. Escott, *After Secession: Jefferson Davis and the Failure of Confederate Nationalism* (1978), 205.

52. Frank Lawrence Owsley, *State Rights in the Confederacy* (1925), 1 ("Died of State Rights"); Donald E. Wilkes, Jr., "From Oglethorpe to the Overthrow of the Confederacy: Habeas Corpus in Georgia, 1733–1865," 45 *Georgia Law Review* (2011), 1015 at 1054–1057n150 (summarizing the scholarship exploring why the South lost the Civil War); Michael Albert Powell, "Confederate Federalism: A View from the Governors" (Ph.D. diss., University of Maryland, 2004), 25–31; David D. Scarboro, "North Carolina and the Confederacy: The Weakness of States' Rights during the Civil War," 56 *North Carolina Historical Review* (1979), 133–149; May Spencer Ringold, "The Role of the State Legislatures in the Confederacy," 48 *Georgia Historical Quarterly* (1964), 255 at 256; Paul Quigley, *Shifting Grounds: Nationalism and the American South, 1848–1865* (2012), 188 ("State-

centered criticisms of national government policies showed that federalism was a problem for Confederate nationalism just as it had been in the prewar United States").

53. Curtis Arthur Amlund, *Federalism in the Southern Confederacy* (1966), 97 ("the issue of states' rights"); White, "Legal History of the Confederacy," 467 at 498–499 ("a possible reading"); DeRosa, *Confederate Constitution*, 41 ("the collective interests").

54. Joseph E. Brown to Jefferson Davis, May 8, 1862, *Official Records*, Ser. 4, Vol. 1, Sec. 2, p.1119–1120 ("expressly"), 1116 ("State rights"); Governor Letcher to Governor Pickens, April 28, 1862, quoted in Powell, "Confederate Federalism," 129n20 ("palpable violation"); *House of Delegates of the State of Virginia, for the Extra Session, 1862*, appendix, Doc. No. 1, "Message of the Governor of Virginia, May 5, 1862 (Richmond, 1862), iii (*"unconstitutional"* to "we can mark"); Governor's Message, November 6, 1862, *Journal of the State of Georgia, at the Annual Session of the General Assembly, Begun and Held in Milledgeville, the seat of Government, in 1862* (Milledgeville, 1862), 33 ("not only a palpable"); "An Act to Further Provide for the Public Defense," April 16, 1862, *Official Records*, Ser. 4, Vol. 1, Sec. 2, p.1095–1097; William L. Shaw, "The Confederate Conscription and Exemption Acts," 6 *AJLH* (1962), 368 at 405.

55. Joseph H. Brown to Alexander H. Stephens, September 1, 1862, CTSC, II:605 ("military despotism"); Zebulon B. Vance to Jefferson Davis, November 11, 1862, *Official Records*, Ser. 1, Vol. 51, Part 2, p.645 ("duty"); Message of Zebulon B. Vance to the North Carolina Legislature, November 17, 1862, *Official Records*, Ser. 4, Vol. 2, p.188 ("at pleasure seize" and "the rights of our people"); Yates, "Peace Movement, Part I," 1 at 10–11; Marc W. Kruman, *Parties and Politics in North Carolina, 1836–1865* (1983), 246–248; Barton A. Myers, *Rebels against the Confederacy: North Carolina's Unionists* (2014), 68–69.

56. Zebulon B. Vance to Jefferson Davis, February 9, 1864, *Official Records*, Ser. 1, Vol. 51, Part 2, p.818 ("resisted"); Zebulon B. Vance to Jefferson Davis, March 9, 1864, *Official Records*, Ser. 1, Vol. 51, Part 2, p.831 ("studied exclusion"), 832 ("outrages"); Jefferson Davis to Zebulon B. Vance, March 31, 1864, *Official Records*, Ser. 1, Vol. 51, Part 2, p.846 ("official action").

57. Quoted in David Williams, Teresa Crisp Williams, and David Carlson, *Plain Folk in a Rich Man's War: Class and Dissent in Confederate Georgia* (2002), 116 ("When this war"); Joseph H. Brown to Alexander H. Stephens, February 20, 1864, CTSC, II:633 ("denounce"); *Message of His Excellency Joseph E. Brown to the Extra Session of the Legislature, Convened March 10, 1864* ... (1864), 15, 20 ("the guardians"), 19 ("to make *illegal*"), 20 ("sound the alarm"). For how Georgia's interposition

has been overlooked, see, for example, James Horace Bass, "The Attack upon the Confederate Administration in Georgia in the Spring of 1864," 18 *Georgia Historical Quarterly* (1934), 228; Robinson, *Justice in Grey*, 413; Robbins, "Writ of Habeas Corpus," 83 at 93; Parks, *Joseph E. Brown*, 266; Paul D. Escott, "Georgia," in W. Buck Yearns, ed., *The Confederate Governors* (1985), 74; Wilkes, "Habeas Corpus in Georgia," 1015 at 1048–1056; James M. McPherson, *Embattled Rebel: Jefferson Davis as Commander in Chief* (2014), 72–73.

58. "Speech on the State of the Confederacy, Delivered Before the Georgia Legislature, at Milledgeville, Georgia, March 16, 1864," in Henry Cleveland, *Alexander H. Stephens, in Public and Private, With Letters and Speeches, Before, During, and Since the War* (1866), 761 ("a strong"), 767 ("unwise"), 782 ("to order the arrest").

59. Cleveland, *Stephens Letters*, 783 ("deliberate judgment" to "the question of constitutionality"), 786 ("faithful sentinels"). Some scholars have described Stephens' remarks as bordering on "sedition" and tantamount to "treason." See Shaw, "Confederate Conscription," 368 at 393; Parks, *Joseph E. Brown*, 277.

60. "Resolutions on the Suspension of the Habeas Corpus," [Georgia], March 19, 1864, *Official Records*, Ser. 4, Vol. 3, p.234–235 ("a dangerous assault"); I.W. Avery, *The History of the State of Georgia from 1850–1881…* (1881), 273; Parks, *Joseph E. Brown*, 282–283.

61. *Daily Constitutionalist*, May 20, 1864 ("[W]ho are to keep watch" and "the State Legislatures"), citing *History of Congress*, Vol. I, p. 439.

62. *Resolutions of the Legislature of the State of Mississippi in Relation to the Recent Act of Congress of the Confederate States Suspending the Privilege of the Writ of Habeas Corpus*, (April 5, 1864), 2 ("dangerous"); Timothy B. Smith, *Mississippi in the Civil War: The Home Front* (2010), 32, 44–45, 94; John K. Bettersworth, *Confederate Mississippi: The People and Policies of a Cotton State in Wartime* (1943), 80; Robert W. Dubay, "Mississippi," in Yearns, ed., *The Confederate Governors* (1985), 128.

63. Mississippi Legislature, *Resolutions*, 2 ("impute to the President" and "in the *legitimate exercise*"); *Journal of the Congress of the Confederate States of America, 1861–1865* (7 vols., Washington, D.C., 1904–1905), May 12, 1864, VII:55.

64. *Journal of the House of Commons of the General Assembly of the State of North Carolina at its Adjourned Session, 1864* (Raleigh, 1864), 44 ("solemn guarantees"), 45 ("destructive" and "a consolidated"); *Hillsborough Recorder* [Hillsborough, N.C.], May 25, 1864; Kruman, *Politics in North Carolina*, 261.

65. Confederate Senate Report, March 16, 1865, *Official Records*, Ser. 4, Vol. 3, p.1150 ("laid aside" and "great repugnance"); *Richmond Whig*, May 24, 1864 ("unconstitutional").

66. Laura F. Edwards, *Gendered Strife and Confusion: The Political Culture of Reconstruction* (1997), 22("of poor white"); J.G. Randall and David Donald, *The Civil War and Reconstruction* (2d. ed., 1961); David Donald, *The Politics of Reconstruction, 1863–1867* (1965); Charles Fairman, *Reconstruction and Reunion, 1864–1888, Part One* (1971); Harold M. Hyman, *A More Perfect Union: The Impact of the Civil War and Reconstruction on the Constitution* (1973); Michael Les Benedict, *A Compromise of Principle: Congressional Republicans and Reconstruction, 1863–1869* (1974); Eric Foner, *Reconstruction: America's Unfinished Revolution, 1863–1877* (1988); Hugh Davis, *"We Will Be Satisfied With Nothing Less": The African American Struggle for Equal Rights in the North during Reconstruction* (2011).

67. David Quigley, *Second Founding: New York City, Reconstruction, and the Making of American Democracy* (2004), 63 ("must be condemnation"); Alan Singer, "Reconstruction Era New York State Democrats: Deserving the 'Execration of History'" 99 *New York History* (2018), 196–208; Michael Les Benedict, *The Blessings of Liberty: A Concise History of the Constitution of the United States* (1996), 208; Harrison, "Reconstruction Amendments," 375 at 434; Mark A. Graber, "The Second Freedmen's Bureau Bill's Constitution," 94 *Texas Law Review* (2016), 1361 at 1362; Foner, *Second Founding*, 33–34, 107, 120.

68. *Daily Albany Argus*, January 15, 1868 ("scheme of usurpation"); *Albany Evening Journal*, January 15, 1868 ("lunatic resolutions"); *Daily Albany Argus*, January 15, 1868 ("the Radical cabal"); *Daily National Intelligencer*, January 17, 1868; *New York Tribune*, January 15, 1868.

69. Quoted in George Henry Porter, *Ohio Politics during the Civil War Period* (1911), 247 ("wagons filled"); David A. Gerber, *Black Ohio and the Color Line, 1860–1915* (1976), 38; Michael Les Benedict, "The Rout of Radicalism: Republicans and the Elections of 1867," 18 *Civil War History* (1972), 334–344.

70. William H. Seward to Rutherford B. Hayes, February 5, 1868, *The Journal of the Senate of the State of Ohio, For the Regular Session of the Fifty-Eighth General Assembly, Commencing on Monday, January 6, 1868, Being the Ninth Legislature Under the New Constitution* (Columbus, 1868), 144 ("the safe-keeping"); *The Journal of the Senate, of the State of Ohio, For the Adjourned Session of the Fifty-Eighth General Assembly, Commencing on Monday November 23, 1868, Being the Ninth Legislature Under the New Constitution* (Columbus, 1869), 166 ("centralizes").

71. *Cincinnati Daily Gazette*, February 10, 1868 ("in direct conflict"); Ohio Senate, *Journal*, 152 ("to overthrow"), 154.

For examples of overlooking Ohio's interposition, see Porter, *Ohio Politics,* 248–254; Robert D. Sawrey, *Dubious Victory: The Reconstruction Debate in Ohio* (1992), 136–137; David M. Gold, *Democracy in Session: A History of the Ohio General Assembly* (2009), 202–203.

72. *Daily State Register* [Des Moines, Iowa], February 26, 1868 ("disregard existing laws"); *Journal of the House of Representatives of the Twelfth General Assembly of the State of Iowa, Which Convened at the Capitol, In Des Moines, Iowa, January 13, 1868* (Des Moines, 1868), 124–125, 195, 201–202, 247–248, 253, 310; Michael Les Benedict, *The Impeachment and Trial of Andrew Johnson* (1973).

73. Foner, *Reconstruction,* 550 ("rampant violence" and "openly dedicated"); Erik Mathisen, *The Loyal Republic: Traitors, Slaves, and the Remaking of Citizenship in Civil War America* (2018), 172–173 ("one of the most fraudulent"); George Rable, "Republican Albatross: The Louisiana Question, National Politics, and the Failure of Reconstruction," 23 *Louisiana History* (1982), 109–130; Ella Lonn, *Reconstruction in Louisiana after 1868* (1918), 292–307; Charles Vincent, *Black Legislators in Louisiana during Reconstruction* (1976), 183–188; William Gillette, *Retreat from Reconstruction, 1869–1879* (1979), 121–133.

74. Foner, *Reconstruction,* 554 ("aroused"); Gillette, *Retreat from Reconstruction,* 124 ("states' rights resolutions"); *Journal of the House of Delegates of the State of Virginia, for the Session of 1874–1875* (Richmond, [1875]), 133 ("gross and wanton" and "sacred right"); *Pomeroy's Democratic* [Chicago, Ill.], January 16, 1875; Lonn, *Reconstruction,* 304.

75. *Journal of the House of Delegates of the State of West Virginia, for the Twelfth Session, 1875* (Charleston, 1875), 30 ("if admitted"), 58 ("the overthrow"), 91 ("a gross violation"), 120–121.

76. *Augusta Chronicle and Sentinel,* January 17, 1875 ("Committee on the State of the Republic"); *Macon Weekly Telegraph,* January 19, 1875 ("Centralism" and "For the first time"); *Macon Weekly Telegraph,* January 26, 1875 ("a palpable" and "to resort").

77. *Journal of the Senate of the State of Ohio, For the Regular Session of the Fifty Seventh General Assembly, commencing on Monday, January 1, 1866* (Columbus, 1866), 24 ("infractions of the organic law"); *Journal of the House of Representatives of the State of Ohio, For the Regular Session of the Fifty-Ninth General Assembly, Commencing on Monday, January 3, 1870* (Columbus, 1870), 282 ("is unauthorized"); *St. Louis Republic* [St. Louis, Mo.], January 20, 1891; Bolt, *Tariff Wars,* 6 (noting that "every congressional tariff debate" after 1824 "included constitutional arguments" raising the constitutionality of a protective tariff).

78. *Laws of the General Assembly of the State of Pennsylvania, Passed at the Session of 1873, in the Ninety-Seventh Year of Independence, With an Appendix* (1873), Joint Resolution, (March 28, 1873), 895; *The Patriot*, March 21, 1873; *Jamestown Journal* [Jamestown, N.Y.], January 28, 1870; *New York Herald*, May 3, 1870; *Houston Daily Union*, November 26, 1871.

79. *Washington Reporter* [Washington, Pa.], February 19, 1873 ("meddling" to "a strong consolidated government").

80. *Washington* Reporter, February 19, 1873 ("to preserve" and "was compelled").

81. *Acts of the General Assembly of Alabama, passed at the Session of 1878–1879, Held in the City of Montgomery, Commencing 2d Tuesday in November, 1878* (1879), 493 ("the exclusive jurisdiction" and "the spirit"), 494 ("for such action").

82. Baker, *Glover*, 165 ("Secession tainted"). For the association of interposition with nullification and the stigmatization of the 'Principles of '98,' see *Boston Journal*, January 23, 1866; *Times Picayune*, October 25, 1866; *New York Tribune*, July 19, 1867; *The Patriot*, March 28, 1870, March 28, 1874, April 17, 1880; *Richmond Whig*, December 15, 1871; *Albany Evening Journal*, January 23, 1872; *Topeka Weekly Capital*, March 8, 1894; *Times Picayune*, May 18, 1903; *Macon Daily Telegraph*, January 5, 1908.

83. All three Amendments contained a final section asserting that "Congress shall have power to enforce" each Amendment "by appropriate legislation." See Foner, *Second Founding*, xix–xx ("[T]he Reconstruction amendments greatly enhanced the power of the federal government, transferring much of the authority to define citizens' rights from the states to the nation").

10   Modern Interposition by States and "Nullification"

1. Woodrow Wilson, *Constitutional Government in the United States* (1908), 173 ("the relation of the States"), 188 ("confidence"); Sidney M. Milkis, *Theodore Roosevelt, the Progressive Party, and the Transformation of American Democracy* (2009), 16 ("prospect of expanding").

2. Austin Raynor, "The New State Sovereignty Movement," 90 *Indiana Law Journal* (2015), 613 at 618.

3. *Lochner v. New York*, 198 U.S. 45 (1905); Sean Beinburg, "Progressivism and States' Rights: Constitutional Dialogue between the States and Federal Courts on Minimum Wages and Liberty of Contract," 8 *American Political Thought* (2019), 25 at 28 and 37.

4. William G. Ross, *World War I and the American Constitution* (2017), 1 ("profoundly"), quoted in Ross, *World War I*, 17 ("marks the

beginning"), 35–36; "The Conscription Bill, December 9, 1814," *Web(SFW)*, I:30 ("the solemn duty"); Edward S. Corwin, "War, the Constitution Moulder," *New Republic* (June 9, 1917), 154 ("the principle" and "that the national government").

5. Jeanette Keith, "The Politics of Southern Draft Resistance, 1917–1918: Class, Race and Conscription in the Rural South," 87 *Journal of American History* (2001), 1335 at 1354 ("known nationally"), 1335 at 1355 ("state convention"); Ross, *World War I*, 22; Zachary Smith, "Tom Watson and Resistance to Federal War Policies in Georgia during World War I," 78 *JSH* (2012), 293–326.

6. Ross, *World War I*, 186 ("The need to conserve"); Sean Beinburg, "Neither Nullification nor Nationalism: The Battle for States' Rights Middle Ground during Prohibition," 7 *American Political Thought: A Journal of Ideas, Institutions, and Culture* (2018), 271 at 272 ("one of the major").

7. Quoted in Ross, *World War I*, 198 ("that the States"); Beinburg, "Neither Nullification nor Nationalism," 271 at 278 ("threatened"); I.A. Newby, "States' Rights and Southern Congressmen during World War I," 24 *Phylon* (1963), 34 at 47.

8. Beinburg, "Neither Nullification nor Nationalism," 271 at 298 ("between federal and state"); David E. Kyvig, *Explicit and Authentic Acts: Amending the U.S. Constitution, 1776–1995* (1996), 226 ("gave the national government").

9. Michael E. Parrish, "The Great Depression, the New Deal, and the American Legal Order," 59 *Washington Law Review* (1984), 723 at 739 ("New Deal reforms"); *New York Times*, December 16, 1937, p.4 ("paramount principles"); Franklin D. Roosevelt, Second Inaugural Address, January 20, 1937 ("ill-housed"); John Robert Moore, "Senator Josiah W. Bailey and the 'Conservative Manifesto' of 1937," 31 *JSH* (1965), 21 at 36, 38; William E. Leuchtenburg, *The Supreme Court Reborn: The Constitutional Revolution in the Age of Roosevelt* (1995), 218 (noting that opponents of the New Deal protested that the Wagner Act "trenched upon the reserved power of the states").

10. William R. Childs, "Texas, the Interstate Oil Compact Commission, and State Control of Oil Production: Regionalism, States' Rights, and Federalism during World War II," 64 *Pacific Historical Review* (1995), 567 at 573 ("believed they did not" and "states' officials"), 580 ("to forestall"), 595 ("the states, not PAW"), 596 ("State officials took seriously").

11. Edward S. Corwin, "Congress's Power to Prohibit Commerce: A Crucial Constitutional Issue," 18 *Cornell Law Quarterly* (1933), 477 at 504 ("whatever validity"); Edward S. Corwin, "The Passing of Dual Federalism," 36 *Virginia Law Review* (1950), 1 at 4 ("superseded"), 23 ("whether the constituent States"); Leuchtenburg, *Supreme Court*, 213–236;

Barry Cushman, *Rethinking the New Deal Court: The Structure of a Constitutional Revolution* (1998).

12. Porter and Johnson, *Party Platforms*, 435 ("eradicate"), 466–467 ("cornerstone" and "Congress has no power"); Kari Frederickson, *The Dixiecrat Revolt and the End of the Solid South, 1932–1968* (2001); Robert G. Parkinson, "First from the Right: Massive Resistance and the Image of Thomas Jefferson in the 1950s," 112 *VMHB* (2004), 3 at 7; Glenn Feldman, "Southern Disillusionment with the Democratic Party: Cultural Conformity and 'the Great Melding' of Race and Economic Conservatism in Alabama during World War II," 43 *Journal of American Studies* (2009), 199–230.

13. U.S. Const. Amendment XV, Sec. 1 ("of race, color"); U.S. Const. Amendment XIV, Sec. 1 ("persons"); *Journal of House of Representatives, of the State of Mississippi, at a Regular Session Thereof, Convened in the City of Jackson, January 7, 1890* (Jackson, 1890), 86 ("theory and practice"); Bradley G. Bond, *Political Culture in the Nineteenth-Century South: Mississippi, 1830–1900* (1995), 245–251; Michael Perman, *Struggle for Mastery: Disfranchisement in the South, 1888–1908* (2001), 70.

14. *Brown v. Board of Education of Topeka*, 347 U.S. 483 (1954) (*Brown* I); *Brown v. Board of Education of Topeka*, 349 U.S. 294 (1955) (*Brown* II), 300 ("prompt and reasonable start"), 301 ("with all deliberate speed").

15. Numan V. Bartley, *The Rise of Massive Resistance: Race and Politics in the South during the 1950s* (1969), 128–129; Nadine Cohodas, *Strom Thurmond and the Politics of Southern Change* (1993), 281; George Lewis, *Massive Resistance: The White Response to the Civil Rights Movement* (2006), 62; John A. Kirk, *Beyond Little Rock: The Origins and Legacies of the Central High Crisis* (2007), 100; William P. Hustwit, *James J. Kilpatrick: Salesman for Segregation* (2013).

16. *Richmond News Leader, Interposition: Editorials and Editorial Page Presentations* (1956), (November 28, 1955), 16 ("right of interposition" to "a coequal party"); Parkinson, "Massive Resistance."

17. *Richmond News Leader ... Editorials*, (November 28, 1955), 18 ("flagrant"), (December 30, 1955), 40 ("the basic right" and "may take many forms"), 41 ("may range from" and "to excite reflection"); James Jackson Kilpatrick, *The Sovereign States: Notes of a Citizen of Virginia* (1957), 97.

18. *Richmond News Leader ... Editorials*, (November 29, 1955), 19 ("the regional field"); Joseph E. Lowndes, *From the New Deal to the New Right: Race and the Southern Origins of Modern Conservatism* (2008), 41 ("claiming to defend"); James J. Kilpatrick to Harry F. Byrd, January 18, 1960, quoted in Lewis, *Massive Resistance*, 64 ("a rallying cry"); Parkinson, "Massive Resistance," 3 at 8.

19. Bartley, *Massive Resistance*, 126 ("the theory"); Lewis, *Massive Resistance*, 65 ("to unite"); Lowndes, *Modern Conservatism*, 41

("Whites across the South"); Hustwit, *Kilpatrick*, 52. Senator Harry F. Byrd of Virginia introduced the phrase "massive resistance" into the debate over *Brown*. See Bartley, *Massive Resistance*, 146; John Kyle Day, *The Southern Manifesto: Massive Resistance and the Fight to Preserve Segregation* (2014), 82; Lewis, *Massive Resistance*, 1, 3; Sarah H. Brown, "The Role of Elite Leadership in the Southern Defense of Segregation, 1954–1964," 77 *JSH* (2011), 827–864; Parkinson, "Massive Resistance."

20. Quoted in Bartley, *Massive Resistance*, 126 ("to nullify"); Lewis, *Massive Resistance*, 64 ("the legal position").

21. Quoted in Lowndes, *Modern Conservatism*, 42 ("a bunch of hogwash"); quoted in Bartley, *Massive Resistance*, 136 ("foolish"); quoted in Lowndes, *Modern Conservatism*, 42 ("hysterical bravado").

22. Bartley, *Massive Resistance*, 128 ("interposing the 'sovereignty' of the state"). For how the history of interposition was overlooked in the 1950s, see Day, *Southern Manifesto*, 14; James W. Ely, Jr., *The Crisis of Conservative Virginia: The Byrd Organization and the Politics of Massive Resistance* (1976), 41; "Interposition vs. Judicial Power: A Study of Ultimate Authority in Constitutional Questions," 1 *RRLR* (1956), 465 at 466; Brisbane, "Interposition," 12; Herbert O. Reid, "The Supreme Court Decision and Interposition," 25 *Journal of Negro Education* (1956), 109 at 115; Miller and Howell, "Interposition," 2–48; Robert J. Harris, (Review of James Jackson Kilpatrick, *The Sovereign States: Notes of a Citizen of Virginia*), 20 *Journal of Politics* (1958), 229 at 230.

23. February 1, 1956, 1 *RRLR* (1956), 445, 447 ("settle the issue" and "to take all appropriate measures"); *Richmond News Leader … Editorials*, (February 2, 1956), 51 ("bring us back").

24. Opinion of J. Lindsay Almond, Jr., February 14, 1956, 1 *RRLR* (1956), 464 ("legally nullify"), 462 ("when it nullified"), 464 ("stern protest" to "an appeal of last resort").

25. February 2, 1956, 1 *RRLR* (1956), 437 ("a question of contested power" to "constitutionally available").

26. Georgia, February 9, 1956, 1 *RRLR* (1956), 438–440; Mississippi, February 29, 1956, 1 *RRLR* (1956), 440–443; Florida, May 2, 1957, 2 *RRLR* (1957), 707–710; South Carolina, May 2, 1956, 1 *RRLR* (1956), 443–445; Louisiana, May 29, 1956, 1 *RRLR* (1956), 755 ("to void"); Arkansas, November, 1956, 1 *RRLR* (1956), 1117 ("interposing").

27. Tennessee, January 22, 1957, 2 *RRLR* (1957), 481 ("condemnation"), 482 ("its solemn duty"), 483 ("all States and the Congress").

28. Tony A. Freyer, "The Past as Future: The Little Rock Crisis and the Constitution," in Elizabeth Jacoway and C. Fred Williams, eds., *Understanding the Little Rock Crisis: An Exercise in Remembrance and Reconciliation* (1999), 150 ("state 'interposition' laws"); Lewis, *Massive Resistance*, 62 ("designed to counteract"); Michael Perman, *Pursuit of Unity: A Political History of the American South* (2009), 280 ("450

laws"); Walter F. Murphy, "Desegregation in Public Education – A Generation of Future Litigation," 15 *Maryland Law Review* (1955), 221–243; Hays, *States in American Constitutionalism*.

29. Day, *Southern Manifesto*, 126, 160 ("a clear abuse"), 162 ("encroachments"), 216–217.

30. Quoted in Day, *Southern Manifesto*, 91 ("a solid front" and "a solemn protest"), 110 ("the doctrines of nullification"), 112–121.

31. Quoted in Day, *Southern Manifesto*, 162 ("intention to resist") (emphasis added), 136 ("are illegal").

32. *Congressional Record*, Senate, 84th Cong., 2nd Sess., (March 12, 1956), 4462 (Wayne Morse) ("the doctrine of interposition" to "Calhoun was walking"), 4463 (Hubert Humphrey) ("leaves no room").

33. Day, *Southern Manifesto*, 134 ("quickly issued").

34. Raymond T. Diamond, "Confrontation as Rejoinder to Compromise: Reflections on the Little Rock Desegregation Crisis," 11 *National Black Law Journal* (1988), 151–176; Tony A. Freyer, "The Little Rock Crisis Reconsidered," 56 *Arkansas Historical Quarterly* (1997), 361–370; Jacoway and Williams, *Little Rock Crisis*; Tony A. Freyer, "Politics and Law in the Little Rock Crisis, 1954–1957," 66 *Arkansas Historical Quarterly* (2007), 145–166; Kirk, *Beyond Little Rock*; Bartley, *Massive Resistance*, 146; Michal R. Belknap, *Federal Law and Southern Order: Racial Violence and Constitutional Conflict in the Post-Brown South* (1987), 29–30.

35. Parkinson, "Massive Resistance," 3 at 15 ("a fatal blow"); *Cooper v. Aaron* 358 U.S. 1 (1958), 17 ("neither be nullified"); Numan V. Bartley, *The New South, 1945–1980* (1995), 223–260; Tony Freyer, *The Little Rock Crisis: A Constitutional Interpretation* (1984), 139–163.

36. 358 U.S. 1, 18 ("declared the basic principle" and "It follows that") (emphasis added); David Landau, "Political Institutions and Judicial Role in Comparative Constitutional Law," 51 *Harvard International Law Journal* (2010), 319 at 325–326.

37. *Bush v. Orleans Parish School Board*, 188 F. Supp. 916 at 922 ("amorphous concept"), 926 ("not a *constitutional* doctrine") (E.D. La. 1960), affirmed *per curiam*, 365 U.S. 569 (1961).

38. Paul D. Moreno, "'So Long as Our System Shall Exist': Myth, History, and the New Federalism," 14 *William and Mary Bill of Rights Journal* (2005), 711 ("new federalism"); Robert A. Schapiro, "Not Old or Borrowed: The Truly New Blue Federalism," 3 *Harvard Law and Policy Review* (2009), 33 at 38 ("passed irrevocably"), 38–39 ("The Court has insisted"); *National League of Cities v. Usery* 426 U.S. 833 (1976).

39. Schapiro, "New Blue Federalism," 33 at 35 ("conceptualize federalism"); Heather K. Gerken, "Federalism 3.0," 105 *California Law Review* (2017), 1695 at 1696 ("operating system"), 1700 ("neither the state"

and "they govern"); Ann E. Carlson, "Iterative Federalism and Climate Change," 103 *Northwestern University Law Review* (2009), 1097 at 1099 (describing state responses to climate change as the result of "repeated, sustained, and dynamic lawmaking efforts involving both levels of government").

40. Levinson, "Nullification," 10 ("a nullificationist"); Thomas E. Woods Jr., *Nullification: How to Resist Federal Tyranny in the 21st Century* (2010), 8; Keely N. Kight, "Back to the Future: The Revival of the Theory of Nullification," 65 *Mercer Law Review* (2014), 521 at 534; Ernest A. Young, "Marijuana, Nullification, and the Checks and Balances Model of Federalism," in Levinson, *Nullification and Secession*, 125 at 127; Adam Olson, Timothy Callaghan and Andrew Karch, "Return of the 'Rightful Remedy': Partisan Federalism, Resource Availability, and Nullification Legislation in the American States," 48 *PJF* (2018), 495–522.

    Missouri's House Bill 85 was signed into law on June 14, 2021, Mo. Rev. Stat. § 1.420 (2021).

41. Woods, *Federal Tyranny*; Clyde N. Wilson, *Nullification: Reclaiming Consent of the Governed* (2016); Wood, *Nullification*, xli ("originally meant"); Mark A. Graber, "Almost Legal: Disobedience and Partial Nullification in American Constitutional Politics and Law," in Levinson, *Nullification and Secession*, 146 at 148 ("consigned"); Ryan Card, "Can States 'Just Say No' to Federal Health Care Reform? The Constitutional and Political Implications of State Attempts to Nullify Federal Law," *Brigham Young University Law Review* (2010), 1795 at 1798; John Dinan, "Contemporary Assertions of State Sovereignty and the Safeguards of American Federalism," 74 *Albany Law Review* (2010), 1637 at 1639; Hunter, "Sound and Fury," 659 at 718; Levinson, "Nullification," 10 at 22.

42. Dinan, "Contemporary Assertions," 1637 at 1641, 1667 ("fall short"); Olson et al., "Nullification Legislation," 495 ("the states have the ability"), 495 at 505 ("pure"); Raynor, "New State Sovereignty," 613–658 ("State Opposition Laws"); Read and Allen, "Nullification," 91 at 93n9.

43. Uniting and Strengthening America by Providing Appropriate Tools Required to Intercept and Obstruct Terrorism (USA PATRIOT) Act, Public Law No. 107–156, 115 Stat. 272 (2001); REAL ID Act, Public Law No. 109–113, 119 Stat. 302 (2005); Patient Protection and Affordable Care Act, Public Law No.111–148, 124 Stat. 119 (2010).

44. Bulman-Pozen and Gerken, "Uncooperative Federalism," 1256 at 1280n85 ("A primary criticism").

45. Dinan, "Contemporary Assertions," 1637 at 1644 ("highlighted"), 1660; Priscilla M. Regan and Christopher J. Deering, "State Opposition to REAL ID," 39 *PJF* (2009), 476–505.

46. Robert S. Claiborne, Jr., "Why Virginia's Challenges to the Patient Protection and Affordable Care Act Did Not Invoke Nullification," 46 *University of Richmond Law Review* (2012) 917 at 919 ("intruded upon"); *California v. Texas*, 593 U.S. ___ (2021).

47. Peter S. Holmes, Seattle City Attorney to U.S. Attorney Brian Moran, Acting Secretary of Homeland Security Chad F. Wolf, Attorney General William Barr, and Chief Counsel Scott K. Falk (July 24, 2020), 2 ("a federal law enforcement role"), 4 ("federal intervention"); Executive Order 13933 of June 26, 2020, "Protecting American Monuments, Memorials, and Statues and Combating Recent Criminal Violence," 85 *Federal Register*, No. 128 (July 2, 2020); Lorraine Marie A. Simonis, "Sanctuary Cities: A Study in Modern Nullification?," 8 *British Journal of American Legal Studies* (2019), 37–81.

48. Ellen Rosenblum, Oregon Attorney General v. John Does 1–10, the United States Department of Homeland Security, United States Customs and Border Protection, the United States Marshals Service, and the Federal Protective Service, Complaint, U.S. District Court for the District of Oregon, July 17, 2020, Case No. 3:20-cv-01161-HZ, p.5 ("violate the state's sovereign interests"); John Dinan, "The Institutionalization of State Resistance to Federal Directives in the 21st Century," 18 *The Forum* (2020), 3–23.

49. Dinan, "Contemporary Assertions," 1637 at 1640 ("vow non-acquiescence"), 1651 ("the legitimacy"); John D. Nugent, *Safeguarding Federalism: How States Protect Their Interests in National Policymaking* (2009), 57 ("a great many options").

50. Bulman-Pozen and Gerken, "Uncooperative Federalism," 1256 at 1259 ("states use regulatory power"), 1272 ("strongest form"); Dinan, "Contemporary Assertions," 1637 at 1667 ("states can 'talk back'").

51. Dinan, "Contemporary Assertions," 1637 at 1666; Hunter, "Sound and Fury," 659 at 662 and 667; Claiborne, "Virginia's Challenges," 917 at 931; Kight, "Theory of Nullification," 521 at 527; Read and Allen, "Nullification," 91 at 96; Simonis, "Sanctuary Cities," 37 at 68; Zavodnyik, *Age of Strict Construction*, 76.

52. Levinson, "Nullification," 28 ("Interposition" and "a certain Paul Revere function"); Michael Stokes Paulsen, "The Civil War as Constitutional Interpretation," 71 *University of Chicago Law Review* (2004), 691 at 711; Michael Stokes Paulsen, "Captain James T. Kirk and the Enterprise of Constitutional Interpretation: Some Modest Proposals from the Twenty-Third Century," 59 *Albany Law Review* (1996), 671 at 686; Mark R. Killenbeck, "Political Facts, Legal Fictions," in Levinson, *Nullification and Secession*, 223 at 225–226.

53. In *McCulloch v. Maryland*, Chief Justice Marshall, in upholding the congressional charter of a national bank, found that such a power was not precluded by the Tenth Amendment, noting: "Even the 10th

amendment ... omits the word 'expressly,' ... [and those] who drew and adopted this amendment had experienced the embarrassments resulting from the insertion of this word in the articles of confederation, and probably omitted it to avoid those embarrassments." *McCulloch v. Maryland,* 17 U.S. 316 (1819), 406–407.

The *Hammer v. Dagenhart* Court, in striking down the federal child labor law as beyond Congress' commerce power, made clear that "[t]he grant of power to Congress over the subject of interstate commerce was to enable it to regulate such commerce, and not to give it authority to control the States in their exercise of the police power over local trade and manufacture." *Hammer v. Dagenhart,* 247 U.S. 251 (1918), 273–274; *United States v. Darby,* 312 U.S. 100 (1941).

54. *Printz v. United States,* 521 U.S. 898 (1997), 935 ("The Federal Government"); Erwin Chemerinsky, "The Values of Federalism," 47 *Florida Law Review* (1995), 499 at 515–516 (commenting on Justice O'Connor's conclusion, writing for the Court in *New York v. United States,* 505 U.S. 144 (1992), that the Court improperly conflated "what was once separate Article I and Tenth Amendment analyses" thereby establishing "state sovereignty [as] a limit on congressional powers"); Evan H. Caminker, "*Printz,* State Sovereignty, and the Limits of Formalism," *Supreme Court Review* (1997), 199–248.

55. Graber, "Partial Nullification," 146 at 149 ("partial nullification"); Sanford Levinson, "Zombie (or Dinosaur) Constitutionalism? The Revival of Nullification and Secession," in Levinson, *Nullification and Secession,* 1 at 3 ("neonullification").

Selected Short Titles

The following short titles are used in the notes when a source has been cited in two or more chapters.

Amar, "Of Sovereignty"
Akhil Reed Amar, "Of Sovereignty and Federalism," 96 *Yale Law Journal* (1987), 1425–1520.

Ames, *State Documents on Federal Relations*
Herman V. Ames, ed., *State Documents on Federal Relations: The States and the United States* (1906, reprinted 1970).

Anderson, "Right of State Legislatures to Instruct"
Clinton Lee Anderson, "Right of State Legislatures to Instruct United States Senators" (MA thesis, University of North Carolina, 1962).

Anderson, *Federalism*
Lawrence M. Anderson, *Federalism, Secession, and the American State: Divided, We Secede* (2013).

Baker, "Fugitive Slave Clause"
H. Robert Baker, "The Fugitive Slave Clause and the Antebellum Constitution," 30 *Law and History Review* (2012), 1133–1174.

Baker, *Glover*
H. Robert Baker, *The Rescue of Joshua Glover: A Fugitive Slave, the Constitution, and the Coming of the Civil War* (2006).

Banning, "Hamiltonian Madison"
Lance Banning, "The Hamiltonian Madison: A Reconsideration," 92 *Virginia Magazine of History and Biography* (1984), 3–28.

Banning, "Republican Ideology"
Lance Banning, "Republican Ideology and the Triumph of the Constitution, 1789 to 1793," 31 *William and Mary Quarterly* (1974), 167–188.

Banning, *Sacred Fire*
Lance Banning, *The Sacred Fire of Liberty: James Madison and the Founding of the Federal Republic* (1995).

Beeman, *Old Dominion*
Richard R. Beeman, *The Old Dominion and the New Nation, 1788–1801* (1972).

Benedict, "Lincoln and Federalism"
Michael Les Benedict, "Abraham Lincoln and Federalism," 10 *Journal of the Abraham Lincoln Association* (1988), 1–45.

Bestor, "State Sovereignty"
Arthur Bestor, "State Sovereignty and Slavery: A Reinterpretation of Proslavery Constitutional Doctrine, 1846–1860," 54 *Journal of the Illinois State Historical Society* (1961), 117–180.

Beveridge, *Marshall*
Albert J. Beveridge, *The Life of John Marshall* (4 vols., 1916–1919).

Bilder, *Madison's Hand*
Mary Sarah Bilder, *Madison's Hand: Revising the Constitutional Convention* (2015).

Bodenhamer, *U.S. Constitution*
David J. Bodenhamer, *The U.S. Constitution: A Very Short Introduction* (2018).

Bolt, *Tariff Wars*
William K. Bolt, *Tariff Wars and the Politics of Jacksonian America* (2017).

Bradburn, "Public Mind"
Douglas Bradburn, "A Clamor in the Public Mind: Opposition to the Alien and Sedition Acts," 65 *William and Mary Quarterly* (2008), 565–600.

Brant, *Madison*
Irving Brant, *James Madison* (6 vols., 1941–1961).

Brisbane, "Interposition"
Robert Brisbane, "Interposition: Theory and Fact," 17 *Phylon* (1956), 12–16.

Broadwater, *Jefferson, Madison*
Jeff Broadwater, *Jefferson, Madison, and the Making of the Constitution* (2019).

Bulman-Pozen and Gerken, "Uncooperative Federalism"
Jessica Bulman-Pozen and Heather K. Gerken, "Uncooperative Federalism," 118 *Yale Law Journal* (2009), 1256–1311.

Caldwell, *Findley*
John Caldwell, *William Findley from West of the Mountains: A Politician in Pennsylvania, 1783–1791* (2000).

Chernow, *Hamilton*
Ron Chernow, *Alexander Hamilton* (2004).

Childers, *Webster-Hayne Debate*
Christopher Childers, *The Webster-Hayne Debate: Defining Nationhood in the Early American Republic* (2018).

Cogan, *Union & States' Rights*
Neil H. Cogan, ed., *Union & States' Rights: A History and Interpretation of Interposition, Nullification, and Secession 150 Years after Sumter* (2014).

Cornell, *Other Founders*
Saul Cornell, *The Other Founders: Anti-Federalism and the Dissenting Tradition in America, 1788–1828* (1999).

Dewey, "Madison Helps Clio"
Donald O. Dewey, "James Madison Helps Clio Interpret the Constitution," 15 *American Journal of Legal History* (1971), 38–55.

Edling, *Hercules*
Max M. Edling, *A Hercules in the Cradle: War, Money, and the American State, 1783–1867* (2014).

Elkins and McKitrick, *Federalism*
Stanley Elkins and Eric McKitrick, *The Age of Federalism: The Early American Republic, 1788–1800* (1993).

Ellis, *Union at Risk*
Richard E. Ellis, *The Union at Risk: Jacksonian Democracy, States' Rights, and the Nullification Crisis* (1987).

Federalist
Jacob E. Cooke, ed., *The Federalist* (1961).

Freehling, *Prelude*
William W. Freehling, *Prelude to Civil War: The Nullification Controversy in South Carolina, 1816–1836* (1965).

Gienapp, *Second Creation*
Jonathan Gienapp, *The Second Creation: Fixing the American Constitution in the Founding Era* (2018).

Goebel, *Supreme Court*
Julius Goebel, Jr., *History of the Supreme Court of the United States: Antecedents and Beginnings to 1801* (1971).

Gunther, *Marshall's Defense*
Gerald Gunther, *John Marshall's Defense of McCulloch v. Maryland* (1969).

Gutzman, "Virginia and Kentucky Resolutions"
K.R. Constantine Gutzman, "The Virginia and Kentucky Resolutions Reconsidered: 'An Appeal to the *Real Laws* of Our Country'," 66 *Journal of Southern History* (2000), 473–496.

Halperin, "Special Relationship"
Terri D. Halperin, "The Special Relationship: The Senate and the States, 1789–1801," in Kenneth R. Bowling and Donald R. Kennon, eds., *The House and Senate in the 1790s: Petitioning, Lobbying, and Institutional Development* (2002), 267–291.

Hammond, *Banks*
Bray Hammond, *Banks and Politics in America from the Revolution to the Civil War* (1957).

Harrison, "Reconstruction Amendments"
John Harrison, "The Lawfulness of the Reconstruction Amendments," 68 *University of Chicago Law Review* (2001), 375–462.

Hays, *States in American Constitutionalism*
Bradley D. Hays, *States in American Constitutionalism: Interpretation, Authority, and Politics* (2019).

Hunter, "Sound and Fury"
Ryan S. Hunter, "Sound and Fury, Signifying Nothing: Nullification and the Question of Gubernatorial Executive Power in Idaho," 49 *Idaho Law Review* (2013), 659–724.

Ketcham, *Madison*
Ralph Ketcham, *James Madison: A Biography* (1990).

Lahav and Newmyer, "Law Wars"
Alexandra D. Lahav and R. Kent Newmyer, "The Law Wars in Massachusetts, 1830–1860: How a Band of Upstart Radical Lawyers Defeated the Forces of Law and Order, and Struck a Blow for Freedom and Equality under Law," 58 *American Journal of Legal History* (2018), 326–359.

Leonard and Cornell, *Partisan Republic*
Gerald Leonard and Saul Cornell, *The Partisan Republic: Democracy, Exclusion, and the Fall of the Founders' Constitution, 1780s–1830s* (2019).

Levinson, "Nullification"
Sanford Levinson, "The 21st Century Rediscovery of Nullification and
Secession in American Political Rhetoric: Frivolousness Incarnate, or
Serious Arguments to Be Wrestled With?" in Levinson, *Nullification and
Secession*, 10–52.

Levinson, *Nullification and Secession*
Sanford Levinson, ed., *Nullification and Secession in Modern Constitutional
Thought* (2016).

Lomazoff, *Bank Controversy*
Eric Lomazoff, *Reconstructing the National Bank Controversy: Politics and
Law in the Early American Republic* (2018).

Maier, "Road Not Taken"
Pauline Maier, "The Road Not Taken: Nullification, John C. Calhoun, and the
Revolutionary Tradition in South Carolina," 82 *South Carolina Historical
Magazine* (1981), 1–19.

Maier, *Ratification*
Pauline Maier, *Ratification: The People Debate the Constitution, 1787–1788*
(2010).

Malone, *Jefferson*
Dumas Malone, *Jefferson and His Time* (6 vols., 1948–1970).

Mason, *Apostle of Union*
Matthew Mason, *Apostle of Union: A Political Biography of Edward Everett*
(2016).

Massey, "State Sovereignty"
Calvin R. Massey, "State Sovereignty and the Tenth and Eleventh
Amendments," 56 *University of Chicago Law Review* (1989), 61–151.

McCoy, *Last of the Fathers*
Drew R. McCoy, *The Last of the Fathers: James Madison and the Republican
Legacy* (1989).

McDonald, *States' Rights*
Forrest McDonald, *States' Rights and the Union: Imperium in Imperio, 1776–
1876* (2000).

Miller and Howell, "Interposition"
Arthur S. Miller and Ronald F. Howell, "Interposition, Nullification and the
Delicate Division of Power in a Federal System," 5 *Journal of Public Law*
(1956), 2–48.

Miller, *Juries and Judges*
F. Thornton Miller, *Juries and Judges versus the Law: Virginia's Provincial Legal Perspective, 1783–1828* (1994).

Pasley, *"Tyranny of Printers"*
Jeffrey L. Pasley, *"The Tyranny of Printers": Newspaper Politics in the Early American Republic* (2001).

Peterson, *Jefferson Image*
Merrill D. Peterson, *The Jefferson Image in the American Mind* (1960).

Peterson, *Olive Branch*
Merrill D. Peterson, *Olive Branch and Sword – The Compromise of 1833* (1982).

Pitcaithley, *Anthology*
Dwight T. Pitcaithley, ed., *The U.S. Constitution and Secession: A Documentary Anthology of Slavery and White Supremacy* (2018).

Porter and Johnson, *Party Platforms*
Kirk H. Porter and Donald Bruce Johnson, comps., *National Party Platforms, 1840–1964* (1966).

Powell, *History and Politics*
H. Jefferson Powell, *A Community Built on Words: The Constitution in History and Politics* (2002).

Powell, "Principles of '98"
H. Jefferson Powell, "The Principles of '98: An Essay in Historical Retrieval," 80 *Virginia Law Review* (1994), 689–744.

Rabun, "Interposition"
James Rabun, "Documents Illustrating the Development of the Doctrine of Interposition: 1790–1832," 5 *Journal of Public Law* (1956), 49–89.

Rakove, "Hollow Hopes"
Jack N. Rakove, "Some Hollow Hopes of States'-Rights Advocates," 67 *Arkansas Law Review* (2014), 81–90.

Rakove, *Original Meanings*
Jack N. Rakove, *Original Meanings: Politics and Ideas in the Making of the Constitution* (1996).

Read and Allen, "Nullification"
James H. Read and Neal Allen, "Living, Dead, and Undead: Nullification Past and Present," in Levinson, *Nullification and Secession*, 91–124.

Risjord, *Chesapeake Politics*
Norman K. Risjord, *Chesapeake Politics, 1781–1800* (1978).

Rosenberg, "Personal Liberty Laws"
Norman L. Rosenberg, "Personal Liberty Laws and Sectional Crisis: 1850–1861," 17 *Civil War History* (1971), 25–44.

Sharp, *American Politics*
James Rogers Sharp, *American Politics in the Early Republic: The New Nation in Crisis* (1993).

Stampp, "Perpetual Union"
Kenneth M. Stampp, "The Concept of a Perpetual Union," 65 *Journal of American History* (1978), 5–33.

Tipton, *Nullification and Interposition*
Diane Tipton, *Nullification and Interposition in American Political Thought* (1969).

Tulis and Mellow, *Legacies of Losing*
Jeffrey K. Tulis and Nicole Mellow, *Legacies of Losing in American Politics* (2018).

Warren, *Supreme Court*
Charles Warren, *The Supreme Court in United States History* (3 vols., 1922).

Webster-Hayne Debate
Herman Belz, ed., *The Webster-Hayne Debate on the Nature of the Union, Selected Documents* (2000).

Whittington, "Political Constitution"
Keith E. Whittington, "The Political Constitution of Federalism in Antebellum America: The Nullification Debate as an Illustration of Informal Mechanisms of Constitutional Change," 26 *Publius: The Journal of Federalism* (1996), 1–24.

Wilentz, *American Democracy*
Sean Wilentz, *The Rise of American Democracy: Jefferson to Lincoln* (2005).

Wood, *Empire of Liberty*
Gordon S. Wood, *Empire of Liberty: A History of the Early Republic, 1789–1815* (2009).

Wood, *Nullification*
W. Kirk Wood, *Nullification, a Constitutional History, 1776–1833. Volume 2: James Madison and the Constitutionality of Nullification, 1787–1828* (2009).

Yazawa, *Contested Conventions*
Melvin Yazawa, *Contested Conventions: The Struggle to Establish the Constitution and Save the Union, 1787–1789* (2016).

Zarefsky and Gallagher, "Public Discourse"
David Zarefsky and Victoria J. Gallagher, "From 'Conflict' to 'Constitutional Question': Transformations in Early American Public Discourse," 76 *Quarterly Journal of Speech* (1990), 247–261.

Zavodnyik, *Age of Strict Construction*
Peter Zavodnyik, *The Age of Strict Construction: A History of the Growth of Federal Power, 1789–1861* (2007).

Index